UNDERSTANDING
PHOTOGRAPHY

Marshall Cavendish

Editor John Farndon
Art Editor Chris Walker

Published by Marshall Cavendish Books Limited
58 Old Compton Street
London W1V 5PA

ISBN 0 86307 441 3

Printed and bound in Hong Kong by Dai Nippon Printing Company

INTRODUCTION

Some old diehards will tell you that equipment is irrelevant to a *real* photographer, that Cartier-Bresson would be Cartier-Bresson even if he was shooting on a battered old box camera. This is probably true, but there is no doubt that having the right equipment certainly helps. And if you specialize in certain types of photography — such as underwater photography — the right equipment is actually essential.

Recent years have seen not only an enormous increase in the sheer number of different items on the market, but also in their complexity and sophistication, as the 'computer revolution' has taken off. The equipment market is now a nightmare of alternatives and technical specifications, and making a rational choice can seem almost impossible. There is usually plenty of advice available for the beginner buying a first camera — though even this is often conflicting. But the more experienced photographer, seeking to add to an outfit in the best possible way, is usually left to fend for him or herself. It is our intention in this book to put that right, as well as clarifying the choice for the beginner.

The pace of technological innovation in the camera industry is such that by the time this book goes to press some of the information will inevitably be out of date. Nevertheless, the general principles remain true, and should help you make the right choice if you're buying. If some of the items described in the book seem too expensive and specialized for you ever to buy, bear in mind that you can always *hire* them — this after all, is what many professionals do. There are photographic equipment hire shops in most major cities. Even if you never intend to buy another piece of equipment, have a look through this book; you may find something that you can hire and add an entirely new dimension to your photography.

CONTENTS

Chapter 1
CAMERAS
THE 35mm SLR

First of all, it shows the scene exactly as it will appear on film. This means that the picture can be composed very accurately It also ensures accurate composition even when different lenses are fitted to the camera. Consequently, there is a vast range of alternative lenses for every SLR which can be fitted in place of the standard lens to give a desired effect. This is what makes the SLR so versatile.

Secondly, it makes the camera very suitable for a through-the-lens (TTL) exposure metering system. This measures the amount of light actually coming through the picture taking lens and so helps give precise exposure.

Every modern SLR has TTL exposure metering, but there are a number of different systems for controlling exposure. In each camera, the meter reading must be translated into exposure settings (aperture and shutter speed) to give correctly exposed pictures. On some cameras, the exposure settings are set completely automatically (*auto exposure* systems). On others, the photographer sets either aperture or shutter and the camera sets the other control automatically (*aperture* or *shutter priority*). On others the photographer has to set both controls *manually*. On the fourth type, there is a choice of exposure systems (*multi-mode*). Each exposure system has something different to offer the photographer.

There are many different types of camera, but for the serious amateur photographer, the choice is usually between three basic types of camera: 35mm SLRs, 35mm 'compacts' and roll film cameras. Both 35mm SLRs and 'compacts' use cassettes of 35mm film which gives negatives or slides 36 x 24mm—the film, including sprocket holes, is 35mm wide. Roll film cameras, however, use film that comes in rolls almost twice as wide, which means that each film frame can be 60mm wide—the length varies with the camera. Because the roll film frame is much bigger, roll film cameras give better quality pictures than 35mm cameras using 35mm film and are preferred by many professionals. Unfortunately, they are generally more expensive to buy and load with film, and tend to be very bulky.

Of the three types of camera, the 35mm SLR has long been the most popular with serious amateur photographers—although the increasingly sophisticated compacts are gradually gaining ground. The 35mm SLR owes its tradition of high quality optics. The camera gets its name from its viewing system (SLR stands for Single Lens Reflex). The viewfinder shows the scene directly through the picture-taking lens—the light is reflected via a mirror (angled at 45° behind the lens) and a specially-shaped prism called a *pentaprism*. This system has two advantages.

Camera choice *The range of cameras that are available is very large. The most important differences between them is in the way the meters work*

Aperture priority-Nikon FE

1 Meter on *The exposure meter is switched on. The switch for the meter on the Nikon FE is in the film wind lever, which is pulled out to switch it on*

2 Set aperture *On aperture priority cameras, the aperture ring on the lens is then set to the f-number that the photographer has chosen*

Foreground flowers *Aperture priority automatics work well when depth of field is important. A small aperture was chosen here to keep everything in focus*

When the shutter release is pressed right down, the aperture is closed down to the value chosen by the camera, and the shutter fires.

Because this type of camera allows the user to set the shutter speed that is needed, it tends to find favour with camera users for whom the shutter speed is the most important factor. Sports photographers, for example, need to know exactly what shutter speed is set on the camera at the time of exposure, because it is usually important that the subject of the picture will be 'frozen' in motion rather than blurred. The user of a shutter priority automatic gives up control of the aperture that is used, but for many purposes control over the aperture is less important than selection of the best shutter speed.

With aperture priority automatics, the situation is reversed. Instead of setting the shutter speed, the user picks the aperture, and the camera selects an appropriate shutter speed. The Nikon FE is a camera of this type. The sequence of operations for this camera begins with the user setting an aperture on the scale around the lens. The choice of aperture is usually dictated by the depth of field (the distance that is sharp) required in the photograph. Having set the aperture, the photographer looks through the viewfinder and pulls the lever wind backwards. This switches on the meter and moves a small needle in

Speedy skateboard *If the subject of the picture must be frozen in motion, a shutter priority automatic will be easiest to use*

3 Viewfinder *Looking through the viewfinder, a scale is visible on the left hand side of the focusing screen, on which shutter speeds are marked. A needle swings over the scale, and comes to rest at the shutter speed that will be set by the camera's automatic meter*

4 Releasing shutter *At the moment of exposure, the aperture closes to the f-number chosen by the photographer, and the shutter speed is set by the camera to give the correct exposure*

7

Manual metering-Olympus OM1

1 Meter on *The Olympus OM1 has a separate meter switch. This must be operated before a light meter reading can be taken with the camera*

2 Set aperture *In this instance, the photographer first sets the aperture to a value that will give sufficient depth of field for the subject*

3 Viewfinder *A needle on the left hand side of the focusing screen moves over a pair of marks. Exposure is correct when it is centred*

4 Shutter speed *In this case, the photographer adjusts the shutter speed to balance the meter needle. The shutter speed dial is around the lens mount*

5 Release shutter *After focusing and composing the picture, the shutter release is pressed. Both aperture and shutter have been manually set*

the viewfinder to indicate the speed at which the shutter is going to operate. When pressure is applied to the shutter button the shutter will be released at the speed indicated in the viewfinder.

This system of operation is no better or worse than the shutter priority method, but is suited to a different type of photography, in which the aperture is considered by the photographer to be more important than the shutter speed. If a portrait is the subject of the picture, for example, the photographer must be sure that the whole of the model's face is in focus, so the aperture that is set is of great importance. Since the subject is unlikely to move very much, the shutter speed is less crucial.

Aperture priority automation is favoured by a lot of camera manufacturers, because the system requires fewer connections between the camera lens and body. To build a shutter priority automatic, on the other hand, some kind of mechanical linkage is needed between body and lens, to ensure that the correct aperture is set at the moment of exposure.

Manual cameras

Although shutter priority and aperture priority automatic cameras are the most common types, some other cameras fit into neither of these two categories. These are fully automatic cameras, and those which set the exposure without any intervention by the photographer—so-called 'programmed' cameras.

Manual cameras, such as the Olympus OM-1, have a meter needle visible through the viewfinder, but leave the photographer to do the work of changing the shutter speed and the aperture. To set the correct exposure on the OM-1, for example, the photographer first switches on the meter—on some manual cameras this is incorporated into the shutter release—and sets either the aperture or the shutter speed to the chosen value. Looking through the viewfinder, a meter needle is visible, and a pair of pincer-like claws. By adjusting either the aperture or the shutter speed, the photographer can bring the needle to rest between the claws—a position which indicates that the film will receive correct exposure. Over and under-exposure are indicated by the needle being too high or too low.

There are a number of variations on this method of exposure metering, which are similar in their method of operation, but which differ in the way that the meter reading is indicated. In the match-needle type of camera, there are two needles. Instead of lining up one needle between claws in the viewfinder, the photographer aligns the two needles to set the correct exposure. Over- and under-traffic light displays, where an LED of a particular colour or a certain combination of LEDs lights up when the exposure is correct. Over and under-exposure is indicated in this case by an LED of a different colour, or in a different position in the finder, lighting up.

This manual system of exposure sett-

Manual metering-Olympus OM1

1 Meter on *Manual cameras can be used in two different ways. The procedure in this second example again begins by turning on the exposure meter*

2 Set shutter *Here the photographer is especially concerned that the right shutter speed is set, so he adjusts this control first*

3 Viewfinder *To centre the needle this time the photographer adjusts not the shutter speed control, but the aperture ring*

Exposure compensation *Backlit subjects require extra exposure, and some auto cameras have an exposure compensation dial to provide this facility*

ing, while more time consuming than an automatic system, does allow the photographer full control of the aperture and shutter speeds that are being set, and for this reason is often preferred by professional photographers. It is also marginally cheaper to build into a camera, so is often found on the more inexpensive models in a camera range.

'Programmed' automation

This system, which is used in some of the more modern cameras, has a pre-programmed sequence of apertures and shutter speeds which will be set according to the lighting conditions. In the

4 Adjusting aperture *Since the photographer considers the f-number to be of secondary importance, he can adjust it freely to balance the meter*

5 Release shutter *If the meter needle is between the claws, the film will receive the correct exposure when the shutter release is pressed*

Shutter priority–Canon AE1

1 Set shutter *On shutter priority automatics such as this Canon AE-1, the first stage is to set the shutter speed to the chosen value*

2 Half press release *Gentle pressure on the shutter release switches on the camera and activates the through the lens exposure meter*

3 Viewfinder *A needle indicates the aperture which the camera has chosen. If this is off the scale, chose another shutter speed*

4 Release shutter *When the shutter button is pressed all the way down, the aperture is closed to the value selected by the exposure meter*

brightest light, a fast shutter speed and small aperture will be set by the camera and as more exposure is required, the camera will automatically change the shutter speed to a progressively slower setting, and open the iris diaphragm to a wider aperture. The photographer has no control over the speeds and apertures that are used.

A trend that seems likely to be adopted by more and more cameras is the multi-program system used in the Canon T70 and T80. Instead of just one exposure program, these cameras have three alternatives (the T80 has also alternative applications of two of the programs). What this means is that the photographer can select a particular program to achieve a particular technique.

On the T70, the programs are set to suit the lens—telephoto, wide-angle, standard. The idea is that on the telephoto program, for instance, the shutter speed is kept high to reduce the chances of camera shake. The wide angle program keeps the aperture small to maximize depth of field. On the T80, however—which also incorporates autofocus (see page 29)—the trend towards 'user-friendly' cameras is taken still further, and the programs are presented in terms of subjects and techniques. The photographer is shown pictograms for each of the four program modes—deep focus, stop action, shallow focus and 'flowing'—as well as the standard program, in a display on top of the camera. Any one of these can be set to suit the subject. This gives the photographer a quite remarkable degree of control over the appearance of the picture with none of the bother of complex exposure setting.

The big advantage of automatic cameras is that you never miss a shot through fiddling with the exposure controls and you can concentrate on creating pictures, not technique. Nevertheless, there are occasions on which it is useful to have some direct manual control over exposure. Many automatic cameras do have manual override facilities, but if you buy an automatic because it has manual mode, it is worth checking just how versatile the manual mode is—on many automatics, the range of manual shutter or aperture settings is severely restricted.

Some cameras have a backlight switch which gives a one stop overexposure increase when pushed, and others have an exposure compensation dial, which allows the photographer to dial in a preset amount of exposure compensation. On cameras that lack either of these facilities, exposure compensation can still be made by changing the film speed set on the dial of the camera.

A few cameras have what is described as a 'memory lock'. This is a switch or button, which locks the meter when pressed. If a backlit portrait is the subject of the picture, the photographer will move in close to the subject, take a meter reading from the model's face, depress the memory lock and then move back to recompose the picture before pressing the shutter release.

SLR FEATURES

Once you have decided which type of exposure system best suits your needs, you can start to look at individual SLRs. There is an enormous range on the market, some makers offering ten or more models, and it can be difficult to make a choice. Fortunately, very few modern SLRs are bad value for money—the price is nearly always a genuine reflection of the quality.

It usually makes sense to buy the best you can afford, but it is worth thinking about how you expect your interest in photography to develop. If you never buy any more equipment, then the best you can afford may indeed be the wisest choice. But if you plan to improve your outfit gradually, it may be better to pay slightly less and buy an economy model from the range of one of the big SLR systems manufacturers. That way, you can uprate piece by piece without making all your accessories redundant.

Specifications are important—a high-flash synchronization speed or off-the-film metering may prove invaluable. But do not go on specifications alone. Remember, to achieve impressive specifications at a low price, the maker may have had to skimp in other areas. This section gives an idea of the most important qualities to look for.

Camera choice *There are so many cameras on the market that choosing an SLR is no longer an easy matter*

Weight and size
Most 35 mm SLRs have a basic body weight in the range 500 to 600 g, approximately the weight of three average size paperback novels. This does vary from model to model but most SLR cameras are now quite a lot lighter than the models of a few years ago.

Clearly a very light camera is the most suitable for a photographer who intends to use it hand-held for long periods, as in the coverage of sporting events. Photographers who pursue energetic hobbies—like walking or climbing—will also find that small cameras take a load off their shoulders. With photographic work where the stable support of a tripod is likely, such as a bird photography, the weight of the camera is a much less important consideration.

Since Olympus introduced their OM-1 model, the first of a new generation of smaller SLRs, most manufacturers have tried to make cameras small as well as light. Given the fixed size of the film, lenses and reflex viewing system used by SLRs, however, a further significant miniaturization of overall size seems unlikely—which is why photographers often turn to the pocket-sized compacts. And as more cameras incorporate autofocus and automatic wind-on, the size of the average SLR may actually increase.

It is an easy matter to measure the dimensions of a camera or to weigh it, but judging the robustness of a camera is a different matter. Just because a camera is heavy and looks solid does not mean that it will stand up to rough treatment. A poorly engineered bracket or hinge will fail whatever its dimensions. The only practical way of judging robustness is by reputation, and the fact that professionals who do demand a lot of their equipment have tended to buy Nikon or Canon is something of a guide.

Lightness is often achieved by the increased use of plastics and thinner castings—in most cases this reduces the strength and resilience of a camera.

Few amateurs, however, need equipment that will withstand a great deal of wear and tear. Only if you enjoy exotic locations or go in for a strenuous hobby, such as free-fall parachuting, will you really need such a rugged SLR.

The lens
Cameras are often sold complete with a standard lens. In the case of 35 mm SLRs this means one of either a 50 mm or 55 mm focal length. Such a lens gives an image that closely resembles the way the human eye views the scene.

There is usually a choice of several standard lenses, which normally have maximum apertures of $f/1.4$, $f/1.8$ or $f/2$. The first of these has the largest maximum aperture, and will be the most expensive. However, choosing a good standard lens purely on the basis of price will not necessarily result in the model that produces the best pictures. An $f/1.4$ lens may well cost twice as much as an $f/2$ lens, but when used at full aperture, the $f/2$ lens will probably produce better pictures. It may seem surprising then, that people are prepared to pay more for wide-aperture lenses.

The reasons are simple—if a lens has a wide maximum aperture, it gathers a lot of light. This means the focusing screen is brighter, and focusing more accurate. Also, in dimly lit conditions, more light will get to the film and it will be possible to use a faster shutter speed with a lens that has a wide maximum aperture. These advantages make such lenses attractive to photographers who need fast shutter speeds, and who often shoot pictures in bad light—candid photographers, for example, frequently need lenses with

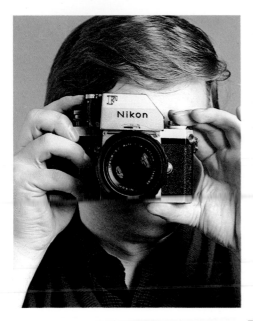

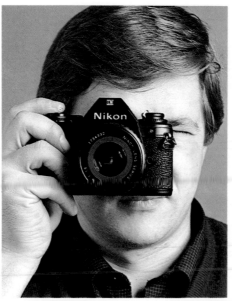

Old and new *Most modern cameras are much lighter and less bulky than their predecessors. The larger one shown here was made in 1973*

distant detail. Many of these lenses are not only expensive but of limited use and their availability is only relevant if you have a specialist application in mind. For example, if you are interested in wildlife photography, a comprehensive range of telephoto lenses could be most useful.

The shutter

All 35 mm SLRs use simple, focal fla plane shutters. These shutters are placed right in front of the film and controlled either mechanically or electronically. Mechanical systems usually have twelve speed steps from 'B' (which means that the shutter stays

wide maximum apertures.

Unless you are convinced that you need the extra light-gathering power of a lens with a wide maximum aperture, it is a better idea to buy one with a more modest specification, and save your money to buy film.

In the quest for more compact cameras, lens design has now followed the lead of camera bodies. Fortunately, mass-production has ensured that these lighter lenses are not significantly more expensive than older, more bulky, types.

Some manufacturers offer two ranges of lenses. The smaller lenses are mechanically less rugged, and optically different from their heavier counterparts, but the results that are produced with a compact lens from a reputable manufacturer should be every bit as good as those from a bulkier lens.

The lenses for most SLR cameras are fitted with a bayonet mount—a simple twist and lock action mounts the lens on the camera body. In the past, many cameras used a screw thread to mount the lens on the camera, and this at one time was almost universal. Though there are many secondhand cameras and lenses of this type available, only one or two manufacturers now use the screw thread method of lens fitting on their current models.

The disadvantage of the bayonet system is that it is far from universal. Although a few manufacturers share the same mount, it is generally impossible to use the lenses from one maker on the body of another. Independent manufacturers make lenses with a variety of mounts, so choice is not limited to lenses made by the manufacturer of your camera (see box).

One thing that has improved enormously with the development of the modern SLR is the range of interchangeable lenses. All the major manufacturers offer a comprehensive selection ranging from 6 mm fisheyes —that gather everything in front of the camera into one circular image—to 2000 mm mirror lenses that act like telescopes, magnifying the smallest

Interchangeable lens mounts

The manufacturers of SLR cameras usually take a very independent approach to the development of their new models. Nowhere is this more obvious than in the design of lens mounts. Most camera manufacturers have adopted a unique way of fitting lens to camera, that is used by no other company. In recent years, though, there has been some degree of co-operation between companies, and a few cameras share the same mount.

On the other hand, some manufacturers have developed their own bayonet mount, and then found that it limited the further development of their cameras, so they introduced a second type of bayonet mount. A range of models from one manufacturer has used no less than three different systems of coupling lens to camera!

When buying an SLR, remember that independent lens makers—those who do not also make cameras—also supply lenses in a number of fittings. Make sure that the camera you want has lenses available from sources other than the camera manufacturer, or you may find that your choice is very restricted.

Pentax, Cosina, Chinon, Ricoh and Topcon all use the Pentax 'K' bayonet mount that is quickly becoming a standard fitting. A lens from any one of these manufacturers will fit the body of any other, and the camera will work perfectly. Topcon, however, also use a different unique bayonet on their Super DM model.

Contax and Yashica use the same lens mount. Lenses are freely interchangeable.

Rollei and Voigtlander also use the same mount as each other—so both brands can share the same lenses.

Zenith, Praktica and Alpa all use the 42 mm 'universal' screw thread, not a bayonet, on their cameras. Alpa use a unique bayonet on one of their models, and Praktica, similarly, employ a unique bayonet fitting. To complicate matters still further, Praktica also have another system —electrical coupling. This feeds information from lens to camera, so some of their lenses, and one of their cameras, have electrical contacts fitted to the screw thread fittings.

Mamiya use two separate, non-interchangeable bayonet lens mounts and all other manufacturers, including Canon, Nikon, Olympus and Minolta, use exclusive bayonet lens mounts.

Wide aperture *Standard lenses with wide aperture are not always better. This picture was taken with an f/1.2 50 mm lens at full aperture. Definition is poor—look at the digital clock*

Better quality *An f/1.7 standard lens produced much better results, but a longer shutter speed was necessary. The lens was only half the weight of the f/1.2 equivalent, and a third of the price*

open as long as the button is depressed) through one second, ½ second and so on up to 1/1000 second. The mechanism is controlled by either a dial on the top plate or a ring on the lens. The dial is marked not with fractions, but with numbers—½ second is marked as 2, ¼ second as 4 and so on to 1000. This series of steps is also used in those electronic exposure systems that give shutter speed priority. A few aperture-priority automatic cameras have no shutter speed dial. Since these cameras are designed to be used automatically at all times, the lack of a manual shutter speed control is not a great problem. If you require control over the shutter speed, however, it is highly unlikely that you will have much use for a camera of this type.

Viewfinder and focusing screens
The incorporation of more and more electronics into the camera and the use of the viewfinder to display information has concentrated attention on this part of the camera. Some manufacturers produce cameras that have easily interchangeable viewfinders. The normal eye level pentaprism can be exchanged for a finder that can be used at waist level, or one that gives a greatly magnified image which is useful for copying work. As such viewfinders are intended for special purposes it is easy to decide whether or not their possible applications will interest you.

Although a standard focusing screen is suitable for most applications, many cameras accept interchangeable focusing screens, even if the viewfinder itself is fixed. While this used to be a feature found only on the most expensive cameras, it is now available even on quite cheap ones. The screen fitted as standard to many cameras may have several focusing aids—usually both microprisms and a split image rangefinder—and the screens that are available as alternatives differ from one manufacturer to another.

Some cameras accept screens that have no focusing aids at all, while others have microprisms all over, If you have very special interests, and want to take photographs through microscopes, for example, you may need a special screen.

Since the range of screens available varies so much from one company to another it is a good idea to check details of the more unusual screens with a camera salesman, who should be able to explain what is available to fit the camera that you are considering buying. For most applications, though, a standard screen is quite satisfactory.

Viewfinder information
Most cameras have some information in the viewfinder about the shutter speed or aperture that has been set. Some have a great deal more information, such as the number of frames of film that have been used, or whether the camera is set on manual.

This information is passed on to the photographer in a number of ways. There may be a scale of apertures down one side of the screen. A small LED lights up alongside one of these to indicate the aperture in use. An alternative is a needle which swings across a scale and comes to rest alongside the

aperture or shutter speed that has been set by the photographer.

A more direct method of indicating the aperture is a device which is sometimes called a Judas' window. This looks like a tiny window at the top of the viewfinder image, through which the photographer can see the aperture setting ring. Though this works well with lenses made by the same firm that made the camera, lenses made by other companies may not have the aperture ring in the same place, and no indication of aperture will be visible.

Viewfinder information systems work well in average conditions, but when buying a camera it is a good idea to see whether the settings are visible both in very bright light (point the lens at a bright shop spotlight) and in very dim light, or when the subject is very dark in colour.

Some photographers prefer an uncluttered viewfinder, and like to have the bare minimum of information visible.

Hot shoes and flashguns
On top of the viewfinder most manufacturers provide a slide-on connection, a *hot shoe* or *accessory shoe,* for one of the small electronic flashguns currently available. The built-in contacts link the gun to the camera and fire the flash at the moment when the shutter is open. Because of the way the shutter works, it is not advisable to set a faster shutter speed than 1/60 or 1/125 while using a flashgun with an SLR. On the more sophisticated electronic cameras the use of the hot shoe automatically programs the shutter to fire at one of these speeds.

Some electronic cameras that have so-called dedicated flash capability can provide even more sophisticated couplings between camera and flash. For example, some cameras will operate at the correct synchronization speed for flash only when the flashgun is ready to make an exposure. If it is not, the camera will revert to the normal automatic mode of working, and will make an exposure

using available light. Such cameras often have a 'flash ready' indication visible in the viewfinder, and some also have a 'confidence light' that comes on if the subject is within the range of the flashgun.

It is probably clear from this description that a few dedicated flash systems are extremely sophisticated. When buying an SLR, it is as well to think carefully about whether you are likely to need this degree of complexity. Sophisticated dedicated flashguns are more expensive than the more ordinary types, and the extra expense may not be justified unless you have special requirements.

Motor drives and winders

The first time that you use a camera fitted with a motor winder or autowind, the feeling is very seductive. There is no need to do anything but press the shutter release—all the winding on is done for you. In fact such units can create a different approach to camera handling, because you never have to move your eye from the viewfinder. This is particularly true if the motor is coupled with fully automatic exposure control. The disadvantage is that it is easy to take frame after frame indiscriminately without concentrating hard enough on getting the 'decisive moment'.

Motor winders are easy to attach they are usually screwed into place on the camera base plate. They are powered by a set of batteries fitted into a compartment in the winder. The speed of winding on is usually about 2 frames a second. Not all cameras can be used

with an autowinder, and if they can, only a unit made for a particular camera will fit. Autowinders are not interchangeable between different makes of camera.

A few cameras have two different types of motor available—a simple, inexpensive motor winder, and a more sophisticated unit called a motor drive. Since the two motors often look very similar, it is difficult to see why the drive is twice or three times the price of the winder. The reason is twofold—speed and robustness. Motor winders usually operate quite slowly in comparison to drives, some of which can run a roll of 36 exposures through a camera in three and a half seconds. Such high speed operation demands more heavily built components and more complex and sturdy mechanisms.

Since motor drives are made to professional standards, and should run many thousands of rolls of film without

trouble, they are clearly going to be expensive. Unless you need really fast operation, then you are unlikely to need the sophistication offered by a motor drive, and an autowinder would be adequate.

Other features

A few cameras have a mirror lock—the mirror that reflects the image on to the focusing screen can be locked in the 'up' position. In practice, this feature is of little use for everyday photography, but some photographers like to lock up the mirror to reduce vibration. This procedure blacks out the viewfinder screen. The facility is of greatest value when using very long focus lenses or photographing through telescopes, where any vibration is undesirable.

A self timer, or delayed action, gives about a ten second delay before the shutter is released, and this allows the photographer to get into the picture. It is

Motor drives *Professionals often use costly motor drives (attached to camera) to catch action like this, but an autowinder (alongside) is adequate for most purposes*

also useful for damping down vibration, as the photographer's finger is not on the shutter release at the moment of exposure. In this respect it is useful if you are using the camera on a tripod, and you do not have a cable release with you.

Exotic extras

Those cameras designed for professional use are the basic units of entire systems intended for use in special situations. Underwater housings and radio-controlled shutter releases can look very glamorous to those unacquainted with them but you should remember that they are all intended to do specific jobs. The purchase of such equipment, which is often very expensive, should only be contemplated if you are absolutely sure that you are going to use it for quite a while. If you want to try something out, then the nearest big city will usually have a company specializing in photographic equipment hire. The availability of such items, which you may rarely or never use, should never be allowed to colour your judgement as to the camera that you buy.

Making a selection

When trying to decide which camera to buy, first sort out those areas of photography that interest you most. If you are not sure, you may have to purchase equipment that is flexible enough for use in a variety of situations. But if you are only interested in taking portraits of friends, or landscapes, you will only need simple equipment.

Once you have narrowed the area of choice a little, get some brochures on the cameras in which you are interested. Try to ignore the sales talk as much as possible and concentrate on the facts. Publicity leaflets have technical data pages where the hard information is collected. If one particular aspect is emphasized by the manufacturer and seems impressive, ask yourself whether it is of any advantage to you. A shutter that works at 1/2000 of a second is of little use if your interest is architecture. However, a good motor-drive facility and a well matched range of zoom lenses may be just what a budding sports photographer is looking for.

Once you have narrowed the choice, go into a shop and try out the cameras on your short list. Do not let the shop staff try to hurry you into an inappropriate selection. Whatever your choice, you will have to use the results of that decision for quite a while. A few hours consideration may save frustration in the years to come.

BUILDING AN SLR SYSTEM

With such a bewildering array of 35 mm SLR lenses and accessories on the market it can be hard to decide what to buy next and, for many people, building up an outfit is a rather haphazard process. Often they find themselves with an expensive accessory that they hardly ever use while lacking an essential item. To avoid these problems and build up a well-balanced system suitable for all situations, you must plan your purchases carefully.

SLR systems are designed to cater for many different needs and a 'complete' outfit need not include every available accessory. A complete outfit is simply one that suits your needs exactly and no more—it is clearly wasteful to have a complete set of macro lenses if you never do any close-up work.

It is important, therefore, to try and get a clear idea of just what kind of photography you intend to do in the future. If you want to specialize in architectural photography, for instance, the balance of your system should be tipped towards this, and an early purchase should be a 28 or 35 mm shift lens (see page 86). If your main interest is close-up photography, it is probably worth buying a 50 mm macro as your first lens instead of the standard. Although expensive, the macro can give very sharp, punchy results with close-ups and can also be used for normal photography.

If, on the other hand, your interest in photography is more general, or if you have no clear idea of where you want to go, you should try to build up a versatile, balanced system that can give good results in a wide variety of situations.

Camera and lens

Planning should begin at the outset, when you buy your first camera body. Rather than simply buying the best camera you can afford, think carefully about how you expect your interest in photography to develop. If you never buy any more equipment, then the best you can afford may indeed be the wisest choice. But if you plan to improve your outfit gradually it is important to buy a camera that you can uprate without making all your lenses and accessories redundant. In particular, the lens mount should be compatible with the camera you want.

Essentially, this means buying a camera from one of the SLR systems manufacturers. Although cameras from these manufacturers are generally more expensive, most have an economy model—the Nikon EM or the Olympus OM10, for example—which is often very

Standard filters *These filters are all you need for most situations. They are 81A, 82A, red, yellow and polarizing. Having lenses with the same filter mounts greatly reduces costs. The lenses here all have 49 mm threads*

good value for money. Many lenses and accessories within these systems will suit both the cheapest and most expensive cameras in the range. So when you

Complete outfit *As well as cameras and lenses this outfit contains many other useful items such as tape, filters, spare batteries, reflecting material,*

eventually want to buy a more expensive camera you can simply buy a new body and continue to use the rest of your outfit.

People tend to automatically buy the standard 50/55 mm lens with their first SLR. But with many cameras, you can buy just the body and then choose the lens separately—the best lens need not be the standard lens. Although often of very high quality, the standard lens is very much a compromise between the coverage of a wide angle and the selectivity of a telephoto. If you never buy another lens, it is perhaps a good compromise, but as soon as you start to acquire additional lenses, you will probably find that you use the standard lens less and less.

A suitable first lens, therefore, might be a medium wide angle such as a 35 mm. This is generally the cheapest wide angle lens in the manufacturer's range and is not so wide as to cause constant problems with perspective. If you anticipate buying a medium telephoto in he near future, though, it would be worth getting a 28 mm or even 24 mm.

Nevertheless, there are two significant drawbacks to the wide angle as a first lens. First, if you have no darkroom or shoot mostly on slide film, it is far harder to take advantage of the facility for composing the picture after processing. Indeed it may be positively annoying—and expensive—if all but a few of your pictures are not perfectly framed at the time of shooting. For experienced photographers, this does not present a serious problem: they can adapt their style to the lens and compose well even with a wide angle lens. But for those only just beginning to develop their eye, it can be far harder composing with a wide angle. Indeed for the newcomer to photography, it is probably better to go the other way altogether and settle on a medium telephoto such as an 85 mm as a first lens. With the telephoto, it is far easier to be selective and fill the frame without moving unnervingly close to the subject.

The second drawback of the wide angle lens is the problem of unflattering perspective for portraits. While this can be overcome simply by moving back and cropping the picture later, it is again better to buy the 'portrait' lens, a medium telephoto, if you intend to take a lot of portraits.

Another alternative is to buy a zoom. A typical wide-to-tele zoom has a range from 35 to 70 mm and may seem to provide a focal length for most situations, giving sufficient coverage for landscapes and, at the other extreme, good perspective for portraits—apparently the ideal compromise. Unfortunately, zoom lenses tend to be bulky, slow—maximum aperture for a zoom may be about f/3.5 compared with f/1.4 for a typical standard—and, most importantly, can cost twice as much as fixed focal length lenses. Furthermore, most photo-

Outfit alternatives *A large outfit is cumbersome and for portability the minimum of equipment is best*

graphers find that they tend to use a zoom only at the two extremes of the zoom range, and rarely use intermediate focal lengths. If you have enough money for a zoom, therefore, it might be better to spend it on a pair of fixed focal length lenses instead, since these will give better quality results.

However, there is a great deal to be said for having just one lens to carry around and, as a single lens, a zoom is very versatile. The zoom can be kept permanently on the camera body and, if you have no other major accessories, your outfit is therefore just a single unit. A single unit is much easier to carry around all the time—you do not even need a gadget bag. And again, for the beginner, using a zoom is one of the best ways of learning to compose in the viewfinder.

So, if you are still developing your eye for a picture and do not intend to

acquire a second lens for some time, a zoom might be a good choice after all. But instead of a wide-to-tele zoom, which will become partially redundant as soon as you buy another lens, think about a medium telephoto zoom, say 75–150 mm. This is ideal for portraits and a range of other subjects. When you do want a second lens, it will be nicely complemented by a wide angle. Remember, though, to look for one of the new generation of lightweight zooms, or the advantage of mobility will be lost—go for speed and lightness rather than a big zoom range.

First accessories

Once you have made your decision and bought your first camera and lens, you may not make another major purchase for some time. But there are a number of small items you can buy that will improve your outfit in the meantime—indeed it

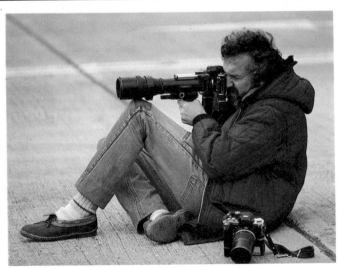

Professional's choice As a general editorial and nature photographer, Peter Kaplan carries a large range of lenses in his outfit. These include a 15 mm super-wide angle, 16 mm full frame fisheye, 24, 35, 85, 180, 200 macro, 300 (f/2.8) and 400 mm Novoflex. The lenses are colour coded so that he can tell at a glance which is which

The all rounder Colin Molyneux uses a car full of equipment when on assignment. But as a basic outfit he takes at least two camera bodies with motors, 20, 55 macro, 80-200 zoom and 300 mm lenses, a perspective control lens, a tripod and an exposure meter. As most of his work is in colour he usually carries polarizing and graduated filters

The basic outfit *A body and three lenses, 24, 35 and 100 mm, are perfectly adequate for most situations*

may even be worth delaying your next big purchase until you have these items. If your eyesight is poor, a correction lens viewfinder (costing little more than a few rolls of film) is a must.

Towards the top of the list are filters. You do not need a full range of filters—special effects filters in particular are largely unnecessary—but two or three can be invaluable.

Get a skylight filter when you buy your first lens and keep it in place on the lens permanently. Its most important function is to protect the lens from dirt and damage and it does this very well, and there are a few occasions in which it positively improves pictures by filtering out UV light.

If you use mainly black and white film, a medium yellow or orange filter is also useful for darkening blue skies so that clouds show up better. If you shoot most on colour slide film you will find an 81A/B or similar filter (see page 122) can extend the range of photography more than you might appreciate. Without this filter, the excessive blueness of photographs taken in cloudy overcast weather may put you off shooting in these conditions. The warming filter reduces this blueness considerably. It may also help to add a pleasant light tan effect to skin in sunny conditions.

If you add to these filters a polarizing filter and a lens hood (see page 118), you should be equipped to shoot in a wide range of conditions yet still remain mobile. There is no need to buy a large gadget bag at this stage: it simply encourages you to fill it up with unnecessary bits and pieces. A few filters and rolls of film slot into pockets far more conveniently. If your camera and lens need protection, either get the

proper carrying case or a suitable small lightweight bag.

An inexpensive, but good quality table-top tripod (plus cable shutter release) might also be worth buying at this stage if your first lens is a telephoto zoom or even just a telephoto. If you have a fairly fast lens, a tripod is not really necessary; concentrate on improving your technique to obviate the need.

Prime choice *Fixed focal length lenses on two bodies are fast and easy to use*

Zoom choice *A body and a zoom gives an outfit which is versatile yet compact*

Using a lens as slow as the zoom, however, you will often find you need to shoot at very slow shutter speeds in poor light—and with a telephoto the problems of camera shake at slow shutter speeds are that much more pronounced. A tripod will also allow you to use the minimum aperture when you need it for good depth of field. Remember, though, that lightweight tripods are by no means completely stable and must be used very carefully.

First major purchase
Many photographers tend to assume that the next major purchases after the camera should be extra lenses. A good flashgun, though, can sometimes be far more useful, greatly extending the versatility and usefulness of a camera, particularly at night or indoors. Try to avoid the temptation to buy a cheap unit—a good, powerful flash gives noticeably better results.

A large powerful unit such as the Braun F910 will enable you to take the kind of pictures you could hardly contemplate before, but it is far from portable. At this stage, a small compact but still fairly powerful gun—Guide Number 32 metres 100 ASA—is useful. This can easily be carried around at all times yet should provide plenty of illumination for fill-in and snap-shots.

Some photographers buy a full-size tripod after the flashgun but this accessory is rarely as useful as it seems. Carrying even a light tripod around soon becomes very tiring and it is a great temptation to leave it at home when you go out on a photo expedition. Unless you have very specific reasons for using a tripod, then—such as still life work, architectural shots, close-ups or low light photography—you are usually better off with the cheaper and much more convenient alternatives, fast film and push processing.

Ornithologist's choice For his pictures, Gordon Langsbury has a basic outfit with two bodies (one with Kodachrome 64, one with Ektachrome 200), 28, 55 macro and 300 mm prime lenses, an 80-200 mm zoom and a 500 mm mirror lens. He also uses a teleconverter to extend the range even further and has a monopod which is portable and so useful for holding the long lenses steady when stalking birds

Action equipment Motor sports usually require long lenses and so David Winter's most used lens is a 300 mm f/2.8 which, because of its fast maximum aperture is easy to focus and allows fast shutter speeds. He also carries 24, 105 and 600 mm lenses and uses two camera bodies

Extra lenses

Once you have your range of minor accessories and a flashgun, you can begin to think about a second lens. But the choice is very difficult. Including those made by independent manufacturers, there may be several hundred lenses on the market that fit your camera.

The first decision to make concerns focal length. This depends partly on what lens you already have and partly on any special interests you have. If you have a 28 or 35 mm lens already, it makes sense to buy a medium telephoto—a 28 and a 85 mm make a good pair, as do a 35 and a 105 mm. Similarly, if your standard is a telephoto, a medium wide angle would make a good second lens.

If your first lens is the traditional 50 or 55, though, you have to choose which way to go, wide angle or telephoto. This decision is largely personal preference but, as it is always possible to selectively enlarge a photograph that contains unwanted detail, a wide angle is probably more useful. A 35 mm is too close to 50 mm to be very valuable so go for 28 or 24 mm.

Those who decide a medium telephoto is the answer may be tempted to buy one of the popular 135 mm lens. Surprisingly, perhaps, this is the least satisfactory solution if you are building up a comprehensive outfit. It falls awkwardly between two points—too long for portraits but too short to bring in distant detail. If you subsequently buy either the 105 mm lens for portraits or a 200 mm for sports shots, the 135 becomes redundant.

Again the solution to the dilemma might seem to be a zoom. Yet as a second lens, you have already lost the advantage of mobility—once you start to carry extra lenses around one more makes little difference. Also, by the time you come to buy your second lens your eye for composition should have developed enough for you to be able to work happily with fixed focus lenses. Finally, for the photographer who never enlarges pictures above postcard size, the quality of a medium-priced zoom may be good enough.

Really, then, the basis of a balanced outfit is a medium telephoto and a medium wide angle. This combination should be good for a wide variety of shots and you can supplement them at a later date with a 17 mm and a 200 or 300 mm lens. With this range of lenses you should be equipped to deal with most general photographic situations.

If in doubt about whether to buy lenses from your camera manufacturer's range or from an independent maker, bear in mind the following points. Independently made lenses are generally cheaper than their 'system' counterparts and often perform quite well—particularly those at the popular focal lengths. Nevertheless, it might be better to wait until you can afford a system lens. For the higher price you usually get very high quality optics and if all your lenses are from the same manufacturer you should find them much easier to use. Your outfit may also be more saleable—should you ever want to sell it—with a uniform set of high quality lenses rather than a hotchpotch. If you do decide to buy a lens from an independent maker, remember to check that focusing and aperture rings turn in the same direction as your other lenses. If your lenses focus in different direction you may have problems focusing on moving subjects.

Completing the outfit

In many ways, once you have a balanced collection of four or five lenses, a suitably powerful flashgun, and a few essential small accessories such as filters, your outfit is already fairly complete and there is no need to spend money on any other major items, except for specific purposes. From this stage on, then, you could begin to uprate your system.

Nevertheless, there are a few other items worth mentioning. Close-up equipment can greatly extend your range of subject matter at quite a low cost. Supplementary lenses are undoubtedly the most convenient and economic route to close-ups but they do not give such high quality as extension tubes. Extension tubes, however, are considerably more expensive and are usually sold only as sets. This is a shame since a single 7 mm extension tube in combination with a basic lens is really all you need for most close-ups. Longer tubes tend to languish unused in a drawer. If you do see a 7 mm tube available separately, therefore, it is worth getting.

Surprisingly many amateur photographers spend vast sums of money on a motordrive or winder, but they rarely justify the expense. If you use your left eye for viewing, a motor winder might make the camera more comfortable to use and overcomes the problem of the lever wind poking you in the eye. But a motor drive adds considerable weight to a camera that might otherwise be compact and convenient. More significantly, they can consume film at a prodigious rate—and this is perhaps the crux point in building up any system.

Never spend so much on equipment that you cannot buy film. The equipment is of course useless unless you take pictures with it. It is an old but valid truth that you can take a string of masterpieces on the simplest of cameras. So rather than buy the next expensive lens, consider spending the money on film instead—the practice could widen the scope and quality of your photography far more than the lens ever could. And this is, after all what 'building up a system' is all about.

COMPACT CAMERAS

As the popularity of the 35 mm SLR has soared, the serious photographer has tended to ignore some of the alternatives. Among the neglected breeds is the compact 35 mm camera. Yet the 35 mm compact is less than half the size of the average SLR and the performance of some of the better compacts can be extremely good. If you already own an SLR or a larger camera, a compact camera may be a valuable addition to your range of equipment—ideal for slipping into the pocket on those days when you do not want to carry a bulky SLR around. If you have no camera, a 35 mm compact may be a worthy first choice.

Most compact 35s weigh between 200 and 400 grams. This compares with 600 to 800 grams for the average SLR. So the compact is very light, but it is also small. The typical compact is about 110 mm wide, 70 mm high and 55 mm deep. An SLR, on the other hand, typically measures 145 by 100 by 100 mm. There are even smaller cameras on the market—the popular 110s and the 16 mm 'spy' cameras—some of which are no bigger than a matchbox. Unfortunately,

Size and weight *The smallest compact cameras are the size of a cigarette packet, and even the biggest is lighter than an average SLR*

these miniature cameras take smaller film sizes which yield poor results when enlarged to any considerable extent. It can also be difficult to obtain transparency film for 110s and smaller. So, for the serious photographer, a compact that takes 35 mm film is a much better choice of camera.

Although there are some very sophisticated cameras towards the top end of the range, the majority of 35 mm compacts are fairly basic, designed for lightness and simplicity of construction and operation. Any refinements introduced are usually devices to make the camera easier to operate over a wide range of conditions. In fact, there are some compacts that not only have automatic exposure but also automatic focusing—all you have to do to take perfectly exposed, sharp pictures is to press the shutter release.

Nevertheless, there is considerable variation between the compacts on the

Compact choice *The simplest of these cameras has scale focusing and no meter, but the most sophisticated is fully automatic, and even focuses itself*

Collapsible lens *The lens adds considerable bulk to a camera, and in an effort to save space, some manufacturers fit sliding lens barrels to their cameras*

Built-in flash *On this compact a flash tube pops up at the touch of a button. Although a separate gun gives better results, this feature is undoubtedly convenient*

market. Some have only one shutter speed and one aperture setting, others have a full range. Some have automatic exposure, others have a built in light meter. The cheapest have no exposure guidance at all. But there are two important features which the majority of 35 mm compacts have in common: a fixed lens and a separate viewfinder.

The lens
Unlike the interchangeable lenses for SLRs, the fixed lens on most compacts cannot be changed to give different focal lengths. This simplifies construction and helps keep the camera small, but it considerably restricts its versatility. Nevertheless, this should not put you off buying a compact, as the standard lens should prove to be more than adequate for most situations.

More important is lens quality. This varies immensely from camera to camera. Pictures taken on the cheapest compacts are rarely good enough for very large prints. The better compacts can produce pictures as good as most SLRs. The only way to establish how well the lens performs is to test it yourself in the shop (see page 81).

On the compacts, the lens has a focal length of 30 to 40 mm, shorter than the standard SLR lens, and physically much smaller. A short focal length also gives a relatively large depth of field and a wide angle of view. The large depth of field means that focusing is less critical than on an SLR with a standard lens, but it can be harder to throw unwanted background detail out of focus even on cameras with variable aperture. The wide angle of view allows the camera to be used in fairly confined spaces but may

lead to unpleasant distortion in close-up portraits. Essentially, the compact is easier to use than an SLR, but is usable over a narrower range of situations.

Framing the subject
Most compacts have a very simple viewing system. The viewfinder is just a tunnel through the camera body fitted with lens elements to adjust the viewing angle to match the camera lens. Most viewfinders of this type have frame markings to show the scene that will actually appear on the film.

Like the fixed lens, the separate viewfinder has a number of drawbacks, but it is this feature more than anything that makes the 35 mm compact so much smaller, lighter and cheaper than the average SLR. Unfortunately, because the viewfinder is separate, you do not see quite the same area of the scene that is recorded on film. The difference is negligible when the subject is at some distance, but when you move in closer than two metres, parallax error (caused by the distance between the lens and the viewfinder) can be a problem. Although the subject appears to be perfectly framed in the viewfinder, the top of the head can easily be cut off in a close portrait.

To combat this, most compact cameras have small parallax compensation marks in the viewfinder. The subject must be kept within these marks to ensure perfect framing of close-ups. On the more expensive models, marks on the viewfinder are moved automatically to correct parallax error. As the lens is focused on nearby objects, the frame markings move across the viewfinder and down. This is a valuable feature but it adds much to the cost of a camera.

Focusing
Although with a relatively wide angle lens focusing is not so critical, most 35 mm compacts still need focusing. Since you do not see the view through the lens, you cannot focus by eye.

With the most basic cameras, the photographer estimates the distance to the subject and sets this on a scale around the lens. Sometimes the scale is calibrated with symbols showing typical subjects. A mountain represents infinity, and a head and shoulders indicates the minimum focusing distance of about two metres from the camera.

Although this sounds rather imprecise, it works quite well most of the time. Compact cameras are most often used in bright light at moderately small apertures, so depth of field is great, and focusing errors are less important. More care must be taken at wide apertures as there is less depth of field.

The better compact cameras are fitted with rangefinders that give very precise focusing, and a small but growing number of compact 35 mm cameras have automatic focusing combined with automatic exposure. This makes them exceptionally easy to use.

Two different automatic focus systems are available: one uses the contrast of the subject to focus the picture: the other uses an infra-red beam. Neither system is completely foolproof—the infra-red system cannot 'understand' windows, for example—but with most cameras it is possible to focus manually in situations where errors can occur. If there is no manual override however, there is little you can do to compensate, so it is worth looking for a camera with this facility if you buy an automatic.

Compact colour *You do not need the versatility of an SLR for snapshots, and many compacts are capable of excellent results if used with care. All these pictures were taken with a simple 35 mm pocket camera*

Exposure

Just as automatic focusing is becoming more and more common, so is automatic exposure control. This is a logical move because the compact is an ideal 'snapshot' camera, particularly appropriate for candid photography, where ease of operation is essential. Nevertheless, manual exposure override is valuable to the serious photographer. Before you buy, examine the camera to see how much control over aperture and shutter speed settings it offers.

The simplest cameras have no adjustments to make, and these cameras only produce good pictures on a sunny day out of doors. Slightly more sophisticated ones have a fixed shutter speed but change the aperture automatically according to the lighting conditions. Even when there is no manual override,

Tiny controls *With smaller compacts it can be difficult to make shutter and aperture adjustments quickly*

you can deliberately 'fool' the camera by setting the 'wrong' film speed on the ASA dial and under- or overexpose for creative effect.

An alternative system adopted on a few compacts is a fixed aperture, and a shutter speed that changes to suit the prevailing light. These cameras can be fooled in the same way. In addition, they usually have a 'low speed' warning which indicates that a tripod or a flash should be used. This takes the form of a flashing or glowing light in the viewfinder which appears when the shutter speed is too slow to use the camera safely hand-held. Some cameras lock the shutter release in low light, thus effectively preventing wrong exposure.

The most sophisticated automatic cameras work in a number of different ways. Some have programmed automation, which gives a wide aperture and long shutter speed in low light. The settings are progressively changed as the light becomes brighter, until in bright sunlight a small aperture and fast speed is set. Other compacts set the exposure by shutter or aperture priority (see pages 7-10) in much the same way as automatic SLRs.

The light meter on both automatic and manual 35 mm compacts rarely works through the lens, and is usually located near the viewfinder or close to the lens. Frequently, the light meter cell is mounted on the front of the lens barrel so that a filter screwed onto the lens will cover the meter as well, and exposure is automatically adjusted for the filter. If the meter is positioned so that it is not covered when a filter is used, however, you have to calculate the exposure change necessary and make manual adjustments to the controls if possible.

The shutter

Because they have fixed lenses, the shutters on compacts are usually the leaf or blade type, set between the elements of the lens (see page 208). Leaf shutters are simpler, cheaper and lighter than the

Easy control *Slightly larger cameras often have bigger controls which you may find easier to operate*

focal plane shutter of the SLR and they are much quieter in operation. This can be a considerable advantage in candid or wildlife photography when you do not want to attract attention.

The range of shutter speeds available on 35 mm compact cameras varies, some having only a single shutter speed and others a range as good as an SLR. Few, however, have shutter speeds of 1/500 second or more, and this limits their ability to freeze rapid movement. It can also be a disadvantage in very bright sunshine, particularly as few compact lenses will stop down beyond f/16.

At the other end of the range, he compact camera is similarly limited as few have slow shutter speeds and many do not have a B setting. This means that the compact camera cannot be used in very low light conditions. Nevertheless, in practice, the range of shutter speeds is adequate for most situations.

Film speeds

With very few exceptions, compact cameras cannot be set to as wide a range of film speeds as SLRs. The fastest film speed setting is often 400 or 500 ASA. As with the limitations imposed by the shutter speeds, this limits the versatility of the compact but is rarely a serious practical problem. Some of the cheapest compacts, however, are not designed for films slower than 100 ASA and this means that slow, fine grain colour slide films cannot be used. It is important to ensure that the camera you choose can take these films.

Not many 35 mm compact cameras are as versatile as an SLR, but they are exceptionally easy to use. Light and simple to operate, and frequently totally automatic, they leave the photographer completely free to concentrate on taking good pictures. Compacts can perform as well as most SLRs, but they vary tremendously in both specification and performance, you should be careful to ensure that the camera suits your pocket and your particular needs.

RANGEFINDER CAMERAS

The modern 35 mm SLR is one of the most versatile cameras ever developed and there are probably few photographic tasks it cannot accomplish. Before the mid 1960s when the SLR began to dominate the photographic scene, a different type of camera held sway—the 35 mm rangefinder. And even today, there are still many photographers who prefer to use rangefinder cameras.

Strictly speaking, the term 'rangefinder' could be applied to some of the modern fixed lens cameras that use a rangefinder focusing aid, but these are more usually called compacts (see pages 20 to 23). The basic principles of the distinctive rangefinder focusing system are also covered on pages 202 to 203. This article covers rangefinders both old and new with interchangeable lenses.

Because rangefinder cameras have fewer moving parts than most SLRs, they are often quieter, smaller and lighter. They are therefore less conspicuous than SLRs and this makes them popular with certain types of photographic journalists and people interested in recording everyday life without distracting the attention of their subjects.

Some photographers find that the direct viewing system of a rangefinder helps them to achieve greater contact and intimacy with their subjects than SLRs. This can affect the style of their photography and the results can be seen in their pictures. For work in low light levels, the clear, direct viewfinders of rangefinder cameras cannot be excelled, since they are unaffected by the maximum aperture of the lens being used. They focus wide angle lenses with greater accuracy than an SLR, and do not suffer from annoying black out at the moment of exposure—something that can be particularly useful when taking pictures with flash. With an SLR it is possible to take a picture and remain uncertain as to whether the flash has fired because your eye is pressed up against the viewfinder at the moment it blacks out.

Some older rangefinder cameras are so sturdily built as to be nearly indestructible and are classics of camera design. Many people collect old models as an investment as early models are rare and quite valuable and their value increases as time goes by. Even so, old rangefinder cameras need not be bought just as ornaments—there are many camera repairers capable of putting even

Rangefinder systems *Although the range of lenses available for use with rangefinder cameras is more limited than that for SLRs, it is still adequate for most purposes, and more compact than any 35 mm reflex system*

the oldest rangefinder into good working order. Very old rangefinders may be comparatively rare, but they are likely to be around for many years.

The choice available

Though there are fewer rangefinders available now than there were in the past, you can still buy an interchangeable lens model, either new or used, at a reasonable price. The basic principle of operation is too good for the type to die out completely, and some sophisticated models are still being made.

The most prestigious rangefinders in the world are Leicas. Leica was the first company to make 35 mm still photography popular, and many features of today's cameras originated with the Leicas of the 1920s. Both the cassette and the frame size of 35 mm cameras came from Leica. Their reputation is founded on high-quality, precision construction, and so their cameras have never been cheap. Though a Leica can cost two or three times as much as a good SLR, many professionals consider them good value for money. You can find some examples of the more common older Leicas for a reasonable secondhand price and you ould get a good used Leica for the same price as a new SLR.

In the 1930s, the main competitor of the Leica was another German-made camera, the Contax. Between them, Leicas and Contaxes have had an enormous influence on camera design. The Japanese camera industry which now dominates the world of photography achieved many of its early post-war successes simply by producing high-quality copies of Leicas and Contaxes. The best cameras produced in the early years of the Japanese camera industry were probably those made by Nikon and Canon. Both these types have developed

French cafe One of the most well known exponents of rangefinder cameras is Henri Cartier-Bresson, famous for his simple, true to life shots. It is in candid shots like this that the small, unobtrusive rangefinder camera comes into its own

Old and new Both cameras feature interchangeable lenses. The Minolta, shown top, has a bayonet mount, which allows lenses to be changed very quickly. The Canon, shown below, is an older, screw mount model

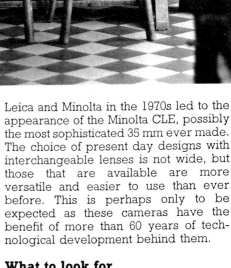

a following in the world of camera collectors, but it is still possible to find good examples of these cameras at reasonable prices. It was with these cameras that photojournalists in the 1930s such as Henri Cartier-Bresson and Alfred Eisenstaedt established an entirely new style of documentary photography, the unobtrusive style now popularized as 'candid'.

Many cheap rangefinder cameras come from the Soviet Union. After World War 2, Russia seized much camera technology from Germany as reparations. The most spectacular example of this was the shipment of virtually the entire Contax factory to the Soviet

Union. Ever since, the Russians have been making Contaxes and selling them at very low prices under the brand name 'Kiev'. An inexpensive Leica-type rangefinder, the Fed, is also made in the Soviet Union. Neither of these cameras has the same high degree of workmanship as their German originals, but they are sold at such low prices that this hardly matters.

Present day production of high-quality rangefinder cameras is now concentrated in two parts of the world, Canada and Japan. Modern Leica rangefinders are made in Canada, where a factory was set up after the war. A cooperative manufacturing deal between

Leica and Minolta in the 1970s led to the appearance of the Minolta CLE, possibly the most sophisticated 35 mm ever made. The choice of present day designs with interchangeable lenses is not wide, but those that are available are more versatile and easier to use than ever before. This is perhaps only to be expected as these cameras have the benefit of more than 60 years of technological development behind them.

What to look for

If you intend to buy a rangefinder camera, you are much more likely to contemplate buying a used camera than you would be if you wanted an SLR. Not only can rangefinders last longer than SLRs because they have fewer parts, but there may also be some features found on older cameras that are not available on current models.

Lens mounting is an example. Early Leicas had lenses that simply screwed into place. A cam-following roller in the camera body transferred distance information from the lens focusing mount to the rangefinder. The system was reliable and very sturdy, but meant that lens changing was rather slow. Leica discontinued their screw mount system and replaced it with a quicker bayonet in the 1950s, but in its time the Leica screw

blinds if the camera is left facing the sur without a lens cap. Most shutter blind are made of black rubberized fabric and, with careless use, it is possible to burn holes clean through the shutters Shutter blinds on Nikon SPs and some Canons were made of black titanium or stainless steel, and these are more resistant to heat. Nevertheless, scorch marks are a sign of careless handling and such cameras should be avoided.

Viewing and focusing

It is the viewing and focusing system of a rangefinder camera that is its most important single feature, and a variety of

mount was an international standard. The Leica thread survives today in Russian Fed cameras and it is also used for many enlarger lenses. Lenses to fit Leica screw mounts were made by many different manufacturers, and although those made by Leica were probably the best, some of those made by Canon and Nikon were also extremely good and can sometimes be found in camera shops. Although these lenses were older designs that were developed without the aid of modern computer technology, the problems of lens design for rangefinder cameras are somewhat simpler than those for SLRs, and as a result these lenses often give results that are as sharp as those from modern lenses. Canon rangefinders also take Leica screw lenses.

Contaxes are equipped with a much more convenient bayonet lens mount, but, unfortunately, old Contaxes are not as good a buy as old Leicas, Canons and Nikons because they were made with a very elaborate shutter mechanism which tends to become unreliable with time. Nikon rangefinders, however, combined the Contax bayonet mount with a Leica-type shutter, and these cameras are much more reliable. The Contax bayonet was in two parts. Standard lenses bayonetted directly into a rotating inner sleeve and connected to the rangefinder mechanism, while wide angle and tele-photo lenses fitted onto an outer bayonet and turned the focusing mechanism indirectly through a special coupling cam. Because of this you should be careful when buying lenses for Contax, Nikon and Kiev rangefinders. There are slight differences between the coupling action of Nikons and Contaxes so that, although the lenses made by each manufacturer fit the other's cameras perfectly, they will not necessarily couple to the rangefinder mechanism properly. Nikon lenses designed for use on Contaxes have a small red 'C' on the front lens rim, and need minor modi-

fication by a professional camera repairer to work on Nikon models.

The range of lenses available for rangefinder cameras is not as wide as that for SLRs. The efficiency of range-finders compared with SLR focusing systems declines with longer focal lengths, and it is impractical to use a rangefinder with lenses longer than 135 mm. No better illustration of this can be found than the fact that some manufacturers, including Leica and Canon, made special reflex housings for use with long lenses that effectively converted their rangefinders into SLRs. In general, rangefinder lenses can be found in focal lengths ranging from about 21 mm to 135 mm, though very fast older lenses are not common. An exception is the $f/0.95$ 50 mm lens made by Canon in the late 1950s, which was the fastest lens ever made for 35 mm cameras. Unfortunately, the image quality is not very good, and the lens is more useful for soft focus effects than for normal picture taking.

While you are examining the lens mount of a camera you are contemplating buying, be sure to have a look at the shutter blinds that can be seen at the back of the camera when the lens is removed. One weakness of rangefinders is that there is no SLR mirror system to prevent the sun's rays from acting as a burning glass and scorching the shutter

approaches to viewfinder design have been used by different manufacturers over the years. The early screw thread Leicas had a slightly inconvenient view-ing and focusing system. The subject is first focused through a rangefinder window, then the eye is moved to a separate viewfinder window to compose the picture. But most cameras have the rangefinder and viewfinder combined in a single window.

Bayonet mount Leicas, Canons, and the Minolta CLE all have viewfinder optics that make the scene through the finder look slightly smaller than life size. Although this shortens the effective base length of the rangefinder (see page 202) and reduces the accuracy of the focusing mechanism slightly, it makes it possible for the viewfinder to include a greater range of frame lines for different focal length lenses and for the rangefinder spot to have sharp edges so that split image focusing can be used on suitable subjects. By contrast, Nikons and Con-taxes used viewfinders that showed the subject lifesize, combined with a long rangefinder baseline. This means that photographers who preferred to view their subjects with their left eyes could simply hold the camera viewfinder in front of their right eye, and by leaving both eyes open see the viewfinder frame lines apparently superimposed on their field of view.

Some Canons had a special magnifying mechanism built into the viewfinder optical system that enabled the rangefinder spot to be seen very much enlarged. This increased the effective rangefinder baseline for greater accuracy.

A useful feature found on bayonet mount Leicas and the Minolta CLE is automatic frame lines in the viewfinder. The camera senses the focal length of the lens that is mounted with the help of a cam on the back of the lens, and shows appropriate frame lines in the viewfinder. Leicas also have a frame line selector lever to enable the effects of different focal length lenses to be previewed so that you can decide which lens to use.

The current Leicas, the M6 and M4-P, can be fitted with a very quiet winder that can transport film at two frames per second. Fitting a motor to older models can be more difficult. Although Nikon virtually originated the modern battery powered motor drive, their old rangefinder cameras need to be modified slightly if a motor is to be fitted, and the appropriate motor is in any case an exceptionally scarce collector's item. A spring-powered motor for early screw thread mount Leicas was made, though once again, this is now very much a collector's item. The special base mounted wind lever attachments that were made for Leicas and some other rangefinders are also rare items. These enabled the user to wind on the film with one hand and release the shutter with the other, thereby obtaining framing rates comparable with motorized winders. Some Canons and Leicas were made with base winders built in.

The Leica M4-P automatically displays frame lines for 28, 35, 50, 75, 90 and 135 mm lenses, while the Minolta CLE shows lines for 28, 40 and 90 mm lenses. In both cameras the frame lines are automatically displaced slightly in the viewfinder to compensate for parallax errors when focusing on objects at different distances. In both the Minolta and the Leica the frame lines are illuminated by a separate window on the front of the camera. This system, though more complicated and expensive, gives

Auxiliary finder *Cameras which do not show frame lines for different lenses require an extra finder as shown, when used with lenses other than standard*

Minolta system
This compact outfit can be bought as a set. The components are all of very high quality

Russian cameras
Though not made to the same high standards as some others, they are rugged and inexpensive

brighter frame lines in low-light conditions, but is not found on older or less expensive cameras.

One point about the rangefinder mechanisms of these cameras deserves special mention: although rangefinders are inherently sturdier than SLRs, they are not indestructible. And if a rangefinder camera is dropped or otherwise abused, the part that is most likely to be damaged is the finely adjusted, relatively delicate rangefinder mechanism itself. A rangefinder mechanism that is out of adjustment inevitably gives unsharp, out of focus pictures. But there is a simple check you can make to test for this. Set the focusing ring on the lens at infinity and then look through the viewfinder at a distant object, such as a television aerial or a tree. If you can see two images in the rangefinder spot, this means the rangefinder mechanism is out of alignment and needs servicing.

One feature found on only one interchangeable lens rangefinder is autofunction. The Minolta CLE achieves this by measuring the light reflected from a pattern on the shutter blind and from the film itself during exposure. This small, lightweight camera combines the best features of rangefinder technology with modern SLR electronics and is perhaps the ideal choice for someone who wants to take advantage of the portability, unobtrusiveness and speed of rangefinder cameras in poor or rapidly changing light conditions.

Do you want one ?
Rangefinder cameras are not for everyone—if they were, they would never have been displaced by SLRs. But for those photographers who need the special advantages offered by interchangeable lens rangefinders, they are a camera type worth considering seriously. Before spending a lot of money on an expensive rangefinder it would probably be a good idea to buy or borrow a much cheaper fixed lens compact camera with a rangefinder focusing system. If this way of using a camera appeals to you, and your favourite lens focal lengths are less than 135 mm, then a rangefinder could be a sensible choice for you.

AUTOFOCUS CAMERAS

Pressing the shutter at just the right time often means the difference between success and failure. Yet it is all too easy to miss the 'decisive moment' just because you are concentrating on getting the subject in focus. One increasingly popular solution to the problem is autofocus, either in the form of a genuine 'point and shoot' camera with automatic exposure and focusing, or a specially made self-focusing SLR lens that fits on a normal SLR.

Autofocus cameras and lenses are ideal for taking quick, candid shots, where speed is of the essence—many professional candid photographers and photojournalists are now beginning to use them as a back-up to a normal SLR. They are also useful in situations where you are unable to focus manually, such as when holding the camera above a crowd, or for remote control shots.

Autofocus systems may be fooled in a number of circumstances (see table on page 32) and may fail to give sharp pictures with some types of subject. Because autofocus takes a fraction of a second to operate, all the cameras actually fire the shutter after you press the release button and not at the precise moment of pressure. Rapid, sudden action shots can therefore be completely mistimed.

Flash shots are also complicated by the fact that a wrong distance setting on an autofocus camera will also throw the exposure setting out. The aperture **automatically selected depends on the film speed set and on the distance.** Nevertheless providing you avoid the obvious pitfalls, autofocus cameras and lenses can guarantee that most pictures taken in good light are perfectly sharp. For people with poor eyesight or for those unfamiliar with focusing techniques they can be invaluable.

Autofocus SLRs
Recently, a stir was caused in the SLR market by the introduction of two cameras with autofocus besides a host of other remarkable electronic features. These

Autofocus lens *The Canon FD 35-70 mm zoom lens is a bulky but convenient way of turning your 35 mm SLR into an autofocus camera. The zoom feature is manually operated*

ameras, the Canon T80 and the Minolta
000, seem likely to set the pattern for
LR development in years to come. The
Minolta is the more expensive of the two
nd boasts what is perhaps a more sophis-
cated system, but it is, inevitably that
uch harder to use. The Canon, on the
ther hand, is aimed squarely at the
hotographer who wants photography to
e as straightforward as possible. The
Canon, in many ways, is the complete
point and shoot' SLR.

These two cameras are not the only
utofocus SLRs on the market. Pentax
nce marketed one, the Pentax ME-F, and
many professionals use the Nikon F3AF
utofocus SLR, with its 'Opto Electronic
ocusing System'. This consists of a
pecial viewfinder, special body and a
choice of two autofocus lenses at 80mm
nd 200mm. The system is very effective
nd reliable and gives top quality
esults. Unfortunately, it is also very
expensive, the body alone costing four
or five times as much as a mid-range
SLR, and the lenses costing almost as
much. Both the Canon and the Minolta are
within the price range of many amateur
photographers.

Surprisingly, perhaps, both the Canon
and the Minolta use completely different
autofocus systems. First of all, they
use a different system to drive the
focusing ring to focus the lens. With
the Minolta, the focus drive motor is in
the camera body, and the drive is linked
to the lens via low-resistance gears.
With the Canon, however, the motor is in
the lens, and each lens has its own
motor.

At first glance, the advantage might
appear to be with the Minolta, because
only one motor is needed, however many
lenses are used, and lenses could
apparently be lighter, smaller and
cheaper because they do not each
incorporate their own motor. However,
the Minolta system means that the camera
cannot be used with ordinary, non-
autofocus lenses, because the lens mount
is unique—unlike the Canon. And, as
it happens, the Canon lenses are only a
little more expensive and heavier—
largely because they make extensive use
of plastic. The standard lens for the Canon
weights barely 15g more than the Minolta,
at 210g. While the bodies for each
camera weigh exactly the same. The use
of plastic may mean the Minolta lenses
are more durable under heavy use, but
few amateurs subject their equipment to
the kind of rigours that would bring out
this difference.

The Minolta and the Canon also use
completely different methods for detecting when the image is focused. Both are
passive (see below), but while the Canon
relies on image contrast to measure
sharpness, the Minolta uses a Honeywell
Visitronic TCL module which measures
sharpness using a split image.

The Canon system is actually a development of the earlier Canon system
for an autofocus SLR lens, the AL-1 (see
picture left and below in text). This
depended on three CCD sensors (Charge

Coupled Devices, like those in video
cameras), arranged to coincide with the
focal plane of lens. These sensors
measure the way brightness is distributed in the picture. If the image
is unsharp, shadows and highlights are
diluted by light spillage. Contrast is
at a maximum when the image is sharp. So
the motor winds the focus on the lens in
and out until it reaches the point where
contrast is at a maximum. The main
drawback of this system is that it is
less reliable when light levels are low,
and contrast is poor—just the conditions when autofocus is most valuable.

The Minolta 7000, by comparison, depends on the relative displacement of a
pair of split images. Working rather like
the split-image wedge in the focusing
wedge (see page 202), it recognizes
the focus by detecting when the images
coincide, simply winding the lens forward
until the images coincide. Unfortunately,
it too needs reasonably bright conditions
to work well.

Nevertheless, both the Canon and
Minolta systems are very effective in
most conditions. They are ideal for the
photographer who wants the scope of an
SLR but cannot be bothered with
technicalities. They are also ideal for the

Autofocus SLR *The Minolta 7000 is
one of the first autofocus SLRs,
designed to make SLR photography as
simple and reliable as with any
point-and-shoot camera—without
losing any of the quality and
versatility of the SLR*

photographer who prefers to devote
his attention to composition rather than
focusing. And they are ideal for the
inexperienced photographer who wants
to follow focus on rapidly moving subjects, such as sports—experienced
photographers will probably find manual
focusing quicker.

If you sometimes want the extra
control possible with manual focusing
and sometimes want the ease and
reliability of autofocus SLRs, one
possible alternative—apart from fitting
manual lenses to the Nikon AF or the
Canon—is to buy one of the increasing number of autofocus SLR lenses
(see page 32).

Autofocus cameras

Compact 35 mm cameras with autofocus
are largely intended for the amateur 'snap-
shots' and are generally not as versatile
as an SLR although some offer a host of

sophisticated facilities designed to make life easier for the photographer. The Canon, for instance, offers auto film load, motor wind and rewind, and a camera shake warning sign. The Yashica-2 has an LED display to indicate the focusing distance and another warning light that illuminates when flash is necessary.

There are a number of different types of system used to focus the cameras. The *passive* system—often called the Visitronic system after the original model developed by Honeywell—uses two rangefinder windows to match an image of the subject and project it on to light sensitive cells (see pages 200 to 201). The *active* system works by sending out a signal of infrared light or sound which bounces off the subject and returns to the camera. There is also a prototype system now being developed which uses two photoelectric cells to measure the intensity of the image coming through the lens.

All of them are operated in a similar way. To focus an autofocus camera, you press the shutter release—on the SLR lenses, you press a special focus button. The autofocus mechanism focuses the lens using a spring or electric motor to wind it out to the correct position.

With the older, spring driven mechanisms, you cannot refocus the lens until you have taken a picture. With electric motors you may be able to refocus simply by releasing the shutter and depressing it again. This facility is known as repeatable prefocus.

Most autofocus lenses have repeatable prefocus, but many autofocus cameras, particularly those using the passive system, do not. It is worth paying a little extra to ensure you have this facility—it

Ricoh 50 mm f/2 *This was an early autofocus lens to appear on the market and has the versatile K fitting*

can be very annoying to have to waste a shot if the subject moves before you press the shutter fully or if you decide not to take the picture.

It is also worth making sure that the camera has a focus lock. This is important because nearly all autofocus cameras focus on a small spot in the centre of the frame. They therefore focus incorrectly if the subject is not in the centre of the frame. If, in a shot of a couple of people, the gap between them is in the centre of the frame, the camera will focus not on the people but on the background. With a focus lock, you can aim the camera so that one of the people is at the centre of the frame, set the focus and then hold it while you swing the camera round to achieve the desired composition. All but the most basic cameras now have this facility.

Autofocus cameras also focus incorrectly if the subject is too close to the camera. With a subject nearer than the

Autofocus cameras *can be fooled by railings or cage bars, tending to focus on them rather than the subject behind*

amera's minimum focusing distance, ne mechanism usually focuses on infinity. Minimum focusing distance varies lightly from camera to camera—some only focus down to 120 cm, while others go down to 90 cm and if you intend to do a considerable amount of close work, it may be worth searching for a camera that will focus at shorter distances—the extra 30 cm may make all the difference.

Unfortunately, the lens on an autofocus camera is usually fixed—only a few of the more advanced cameras allow lenses to be changed. Like 35 mm compact cameras, the lens is normally in the order of 38 mm in focal length, giving a fairly wide angle of view and good depth of field even at maximum aperture. Few of the lenses are very fast—they usually have a maximum aperture of f/2.8—since the cameras are not intended for use in extreme conditions—only the sophisticated Canon AF35ML with its f/1.9 40 mm lens has any pretensions to speed.

Again, the range of shutter speeds available is rarely very wide. The Konica C35AF, for example, which was the first autofocus camera to be marketed internationally, has only a very simple

Wrong again *Autofocus cameras without a focus lock focus on the background through a centre of frame gap between subjects. Cameras with a focus lock like the Yashica, left, allow you to focus and then recompose*

exposure system with a maximum shutter speed of 1/250 second—this is not fast enough to freeze rapid action. Some of the more expensive cameras have a maximum speed of 1/500 second, but none have anything faster.

Choice of autofocus camera eventually boils down to the focusing system most appropriate to the type of conditions in which you are likely to use the camera—some photographers benefit more from a camera using the active system, others prefer the passive system. Neither system has been proved more or less accurate in focusing. The difference comes in their limitations.

Most passive systems need plenty of light to function properly and in low light, they will fail altogether. In situations where flash would be necessary, a passive autofocus camera cannot be used. These are often the situations where autofocus is most valuable—for candid shots or amusing pictures of parties. Several cameras that use the passive system have a low light warning which indicates when it is too dark for them to operate. A few passive autofocus cameras have their own light source which directs a beam of light at the subject and allows the focusing mechanism to work in complete darkness, but this type is much more expensive.

The active system, on the other hand, has no problem operating in low light and functions equally successfully in brilliant daylight or pitch darkness. Ultrasound, however, can be fooled by

Too close *Most autofocus cameras have a limited focusing range, usually between 90 and 120 cm. Shooting too close to a subject will yield unsatisfactory, blurred results (below) as the camera automatically focuses on infinity. The Canon autofocus zoom lens focuses automatically to 100 cm but this can be overridden by a manual setting down to 50 cm. The only way that you can obtain close-ups with your autofocus is to shoot within the permitted focusing distance and then enlarge the image later, if you have prints made*

glass which reflects the sound while infrared systems can be fooled by highly reflective, polished surfaces.

If you already own an SLR, and feel that an autofocus camera does not give you quite the flexibility you want, you may prefer to spend a little more and buy an autofocus lens.

Autofocus lenses

The autofocusing lenses produced by Ricoh, Canon and others have added another dimension of versaility to the 35 mm SLR. Although they cost about twice the price of a normal lens, they are completely self-focusing, using a separate optical-electronic rangefinder in a bulky housing around the lens which also contains the batteries and a motor to drive the lens.

It is, perhaps, inevitable that one of the first such lenses to be produced has the 'standard' focal length of 50 mm. It is a Ricoh lens with a maximum aperture of *f*/2 which uses the Honeywell Visitronic system. The lens is wound out continuously to focus on the subject, so it is possible to follow moving objects smoothly.

The Canon 35–70 mm *f*/4 zoom AF, on the other hand, does not focus continuously but moves instead to one of eight zones—1, 1.2, 1.5, 2, 3, 5, 10 metres, or infinity. Depth of field covers any slight focus discrepancies which may result. For more accurate focusing, this can be overridden by manual setting down to 50 cm. The focal length is set manually, but the autofocus works at all zoom settings.

The lens uses the same type of focusing system as Canon's AF35ML autofocus camera. To activate the system,

a button on the lens is pressed, and when focusing is completed, a bleep is emitted. No indication is given of the distance set, the only check being the view through the SLR finder.

Their bulk can make autofocus lenses rather unwieldy, but many professionals, particularly sports and action photographers, are adding the Canon lens to their range of equipment. For amateur use, the Ricoh has the advantage of a Pentax K-mount which means that it can be attached to any one of the large number of SLRs now using this fitting.

Indicative, perhaps, of the way independent lens manufacturers may approach autofocus in the future is Vivitar's remarkable 200 mm *f*/3.5 autofocus lens. Using the right mount it will fit on most makes of camera—Canon, Contax/Yashica, Minolta, Nikon AIS, Olympus and Pentax KA. It is little bigger than a normal manual focus 200 mm lens—the only difference is the lens's broad collar and battery compartment underneath. Like the Ricoh, it uses a Honeywell Visitronic unit to provide accurate autofocus in reasonably bright light.

Problem subjects:

Those without strong vertical lines—waves at sea or window blinds
Those with little or no contrast
Those with bars or railings between themselves and the camera (Visitronic system cameras)
Those with window glass between subject and camera (infrared systems)
Those with strong reflections or those strongly backlit
Two subjects with a gap in between them (cameras without prefocusing)

Rollerskaters *and other action subjects are ideally suited to autofocus cameras which can focus quickly and efficiently on centrally located subjects like this one—even if they are moving rapidly towards the camera*

Built-in flash *Most autofocus cameras include built-in flash. This is often a pop-up unit activated by pressing a switch in the rear of the camera. Some autofocus cameras have a warning light to indicate when the flash must be used*

Autofocus features

Most autofocus cameras are fitted with a 38 mm lens, and have built in flash and a minimum focusing distance of between 90 and 100 cm. But there are a few which offer a range of useful additional features

Camera	AF system	Special features
Cosina 35 AF	Visitronic	Manual focusing option, self timer
Fujinon Flash AF	Visitronic	Built-in light beam for low light photography, shutter lock
Minolta Hi-Matic AF2	Infrared	Repeatable prefocusing, self timer
Yashica Autofocus	Visitronic	LED focus set signal, prefocusing facility, low light warning signal
Ricoh AF-2	Visitronic	Built-in light beam, repeatable prefocusing, motorized film load, advance and rewind
Canon AF35ML	Infrared	Auto film load, motor wind and rewind, repeatable prefocusing, camera shake warning signal, self timer

ROLL FILM CAMERAS

With modern lenses and film, the quality possible with 35 mm film is good enough for most amateur photographers, yet many professionals still prefer to use a roll film camera whenever possible. Small enough to be hand held, roll film cameras take larger negatives that can give large high quality prints. Different cameras take different sized pictures, but even the smallest roll film negative is nearly three times the size of a 35 mm negative—the largest is over four times the size.

Roll film cameras are all larger than 35 mm. The extra size and weight makes roll film cameras slower to operate, and they lend themselves best to deliberate, considered styles of photography.

If you have been used to using a smaller camera, it may come as a shock to pick up a roll film camera. It might seem very bulky and awkward to use. If there is not a prism fitted, the image on the focusing screen is reversed, and panning the camera to the left makes the image move to the right. One or two roll film cameras do not have an instant return mirror, and when you press the shutter release the viewfinder blacks out until the winding crank is turned to advance the film. This can be very disconcerting if you are not used to it. On the other hand, the big focusing screen makes viewing very easy and quick, and helps in composing the picture.

Film formats

You might hear some roll film cameras referred to as 'six-by-six' or 'two-and-a-quarter-square' cameras — this is simply the size of negatives they produce, which are six centimetres (or two and a quarter inches) square. The 6 × 6 cm format is certainly the most common, but there are a number of others.

Some models take a picture that measures 6 × 7 cm, and a few take pictures that are 6 × 4.5 cm. The larger the picture, the fewer frames you can fit on a roll of standard (120) film; with a 6 × 4.5 format you can take 15 frames, with a 6 × 6 format 12 frames, and with the largest size, 6 × 7, only ten frames. Certain types of film are available in a double length roll—220 film—and this gives twice as many frames, but the choice of film speeds is very limited.

Since 6 × 6 cameras produce a square negative, they never have to be turned on one side. Vertical pictures are produced by cropping the sides, and horizontals, by cropping at top and bottom. 6 × 4.5 cameras normally produce a horizontal picture, and must be turned through 90° for a vertical composition. Consequently, they have to be used with a prism viewfinder. The same is true of the Pentax 6 × 7, but the Mimaya 6 × 7 SLR has a revolving back which makes a prism unnecessary.

Much is made of differences in film

area between 6 × 7, 6 × 6 and 6 × 4.5, but in reality, the useful area of each is fairly similar. The difference between 6 × 6 and 6 × 4.5 is largely that the square format can be cropped after exposure to a vertical or a horizontal. This choice is not available if you opt for the smaller format. 6 × 4.5 cameras are

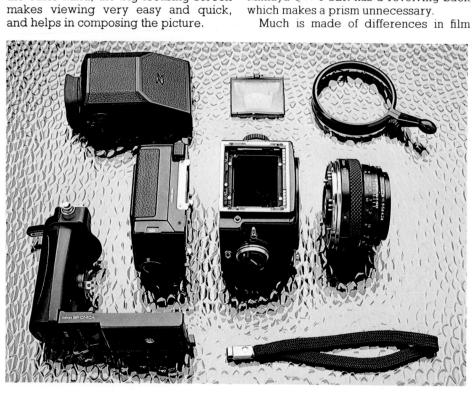

generally cheaper, though, and give you an extra three frames per roll of film.

The modular approach

The camera body of a roll film camera can be thought of as a basic shell on which to build. This is literally true in the case of a few models, where the body contains only the reflex mirror and a simple shutter. The other components—lens, film magazine, focusing screen and viewfinder—bolt onto this simple box.

This approach produces cameras which look very different from their 35 mm counterparts. They look very box-like, and this impression is reinforced by the folding direct vision focusing hood that is often supplied with the camera in its standard form. This hood can be replaced with a variety of prism view-finders, like those on 35 mm SLRs, which make viewing much easier. Some cam-

eras can be fitted with prisms that have a built in through-the-lens (TTL) meter, and this can sometimes be linked to the aperture and shutter speed to provide fully automatic exposure control. Normally, though, photographers use a separate hand held meter with roll film cameras, unless TTL metering is vital.

Magazines

Unlike 35 mm cameras, many roll film cameras accept interchangeable film magazines—backs that simply clip on and off the back, allowing you to change the film in an instant. With these magazines, you can change from colour film to black and white in a matter of seconds even in mid roll. Or you can make quick test shots—testing equipment and lighting—with Polaroid film and switch to your chosen film for the real session.

The most comprehensively equipped

cameras accept many different types of magazines. Hassleblad cameras, for example, can be fitted with magazines that take 120 and 220 film, Polaroid film, sheets of cut film, and long rolls of perforated 70 mm film allowing as many as 100 exposures without changing magazines. On 120 film alone, three different formats of negative are available— 6 cm square, 4 cm square, and 6 × 4.5 cm.

Not all roll film cameras can take interchangeable backs. An interchangeable back adds considerably to the cost of a camera, and some cameras are available in two models, one with, and one without interchangeable backs.

Certain cameras have a motor drive which can be attached as an accessory, but a couple of cameras have the motor built in. Whichever approach is adopted, motor drives for roll film cameras seem pedestrian compared to autowinders for 35 mm cameras. A framing rate of one picture per second is quite a respectable speed for a motor driven roll fim camera. The thin, sprocketed ribbon of 35 mm film can be driven through a camera at a speed that would quickly snap the broad strip of roll film.

Lenses and shutters

The standard lens on a roll film camera usually has a longer focal length than that of a 35 mm camera, but its maximum angle of view is about the same. 6 × 4.5 and 6 × 6 cameras are usually fitted with a 75 or 80 mm lens as standard, and 6 × 7 with a 100 or 105 mm.

The maximum aperture of these lenses is usually two stops smaller than a 35 mm camera lens, typically f/2.8 or even f/3.5. This is not really a handicap in practice because roll film cameras do not lend themselves to shooting pictures in low light conditions, and at any given

Boxy bodies
Roll film cameras are much more square than 35 mm cameras, but the Pentax 6 × 7 looks like a 35 mm SLR and can be used in the same way. (below).

Modular construction
(far left) To give maximum flexibility, all major parts on roll film SLRs are inter-changeable

aperture, the depth of field available is less than it would be on a smaller format camera. This means that roll film camera lenses are rarely used at full aperture, except for focusing.

Like the bodies, roll film camera lenses are larger and more expensive than their 35 mm equivalents, and there are fewer different focal lengths available. Unfortunately, each camera takes only lenses made by the camera manufacturer. It is not possible to buy cheap lenses from an independent company.

For a 6 × 6 camera, a typical wide angle lens is one with a focal length of 50 mm. Although direct comparisons are difficult because of the different negative shape, a 50 mm roll film camera lens gives an angle of view that corresponds to a lens for a 35 mm camera with its focal length of between 28 mm and 35 mm. A typical portrait lens for 6 × 6 camera is 150 mm—this roughly corresponds to an 85 mm lens for a 35 mm camera.

For roll film cameras that use leaf shutters—like Hasselblads—the shutter is inside the lens. So each lens for these cameras has to have a shutter and can be very expensive. Other roll film cameras have focal plane shutters similar to those in most 35 mm cameras. Focal plane shutters are in the camera body so the lenses are usually considerably cheaper.

There are advantages to both shutter types. Focal plane shutter cameras can be developed into a 'system' more cheaply, but flash synchronisation is only possible with a small number of shutter speeds. With leaf shutters, flash can be synchronized with all speeds. For many types of photography this is a considerable advantage. For instance, freezing action with flash or using flash as a fill-in with daylight often needs a fast shutter speed. This is only possible with a leaf shutter. Several roll film systems with focal plane shutters in the camera body have one or two lenses with leaf shutters for just this reason. The Hasselblad 2000FC, for example, has an integral focal plane shutter for use with the light F series lenses but will also take the leaf-shuttered C series lenses of the other Hasselblads.

Whether leaf or focal plane, however,

Polaroid Back *The great advantage of owning a camera with interchangeable backs is that you can switch film in mid roll. Here the photographer has changed from roll film to Polaroid to make a lighting test*

35 mm

6 × 4.5

The range of shutter speeds on a roll film camera is not usually as extensive as on a 35 mm camera because the shutter is bigger and heavier to open. A range from 1 second to 1/500 of a second is normal, with only a very few cameras offering 1/1000, and only one, the Hasselblad 2000FC, offering a speed of 1/2000. In general, cameras with leaf shutters have slightly slower top speeds than those fitted with focal plane shutters.

Mechanical control *The leaf shutter on the Hasselblad 500CM is purely mechanical, and a slotted rod cocks the shutter. The adjacent pin releases it*

Choosing and buying

Even the most basic roll film camera gives considerably better quality than most 35 mm cameras, and if you can find a secondhand TLR, it is well worth the effort. Features, such as interchangeable magazines and lenses are expensive, and a new roll film camera is a major investment.

It is, therefore, a good idea to be sure you have the right camera before laying out any money. If you live in a large city, it is usually possible to hire roll film equipment for a day or two to see how it handles. If this is not possible, a camera club, or a local adult education class may give you access to a roll film system.

Film format and price are perhaps the most important considerations but there are many other factors that can affect your choice of roll film camera. Some systems have lenses and accessories that are not available to fit competing cameras—Bronica, for example, have a unique perspective control lens that allows the photographer more versatility when dealing with architectural subjects. The Pentax 6 × 7 is particularly easy to use, and the Hasselblad system has by far the widest range of lenses and accessories. Any of these factors might influence your decision. In terms of quality, you cannot lose, and a print from a roll film camera, however much it costs, will be superior to one made from a smaller format.

Film packs
When a camera has a fixed back, film can often be preloaded to save time when changing rolls

Roll film formats *Any format gives a good deal more picture area than 35 mm. These examples show the exact size and proportions of the three common formats. 35 mm is shown at the top for comparison. Below it are 6 × 4.5, 6 × 6, and 6 × 7 cm*

2¼ sq

6 × 7

LARGE FORMAT CAMERAS

The term 'large format' is often used for any camera with a negative larger than 35 mm. Strictly speaking, though, it only applies to certain types of camera which give very large negatives, usually 5 × 4 inches but sometimes much larger. Though made primarily for professional use, they have some unique features which make them worth considering by any enthusiast.

Most large format cameras are bulky, heavy and slow to use. They do not have eye level reflex viewing or quick, easy focusing, and usually have to be supported on a tripod. They can also prove expensive to run, and a single transparency can cost as much as a whole roll of 35 mm film.

Nevertheless, their large negatives give far better image quality than smaller formats, and their construction gives great control over the image. If these are your primary considerations, then one of these cameras may suit you.

Large format cameras are very popular with photographers who believe in a carefully crafted style, with meticulous attention to composition. This style is particularly suited to landscape photography, but some photographers, such as Ken Griffiths, use a large format camera for reportage work because they make the photo-session a special occasion.

Advantages of large format

The more you enlarge a negative, the more quality you inevitably lose. The great advantage of large negatives is that they do not need to be enlarged so much —image quality is therefore superior to all other formats. It is easy, also, to print a small part of the negative and still retain good quality, so precise framing is less important—the image can be cropped at the printing stage.

Processing is less critical than with smaller negatives, and films can be 'pushed' without undue harm to image quality—even dirt and fingerprints are tolerable. Conversely, with correct processing quality is superb and results can be impressive. Retouching is also easier than with smaller formats.

As well as a large negative size, large format cameras offer great versatility. With the long bellows extension they provide, the subject can be reproduced life size on the film even with a standard lens. Perspective and depth of field can be controlled in ways impossible with any other type of camera, by moving the rear or the front standard of the system. As well as the to-and-fro movement of focusing, vertical, horizontal and angular displacements are possible, and even the shape of the final image can be controlled: subjects can be made to look longer, for instance, without the exaggerated perspective of a wide angle lens.

Large format cameras are also extremely reliable, because they do not have to be light and compact, and can therefore be very sturdily built. Very often, old models in perfect working order can be bought, and many photographers work regularly with one of these as their standard camera—particularly the beautifully-crafted wood and brass cameras such as the Gandolfi.

Modular concept *From lens panels and focusing screens to polaroid backs and extension rails, the basic monorail (top) accepts a range of components*

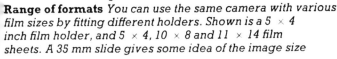

Range of formats *You can use the same camera with various film sizes by fitting different holders. Shown is a 5 × 4 inch film holder, and 5 × 4, 10 × 8 and 11 × 14 film sheets. A 35 mm slide gives some idea of the image size*

Negative sizes

The commonest negative size is 5 × 4 inches, and this is a fairly standard professional format. A metric version, 9 × 12 cm, is also available. The film holders for 5 × 4 inch and 9 × 12 cm often have the same external dimensions, so they may be used interchangeably. The same applies to some other film sizes.

Both roll film and cut film are available, in a fairly wide range. Other formats can be found too—the smallest is 2¼ × 3¼ inch, next comes 3¼ × 4¼ inch (quarter plate), then 4¾ × 6½ (half plate), 5 × 7, (equivalent to 13 × 18 cm) and 6½ × 8½ inch (whole plate). The really large formats are 10 × 8 inches (equivalent to 18 × 24 cm), 11 × 14 inches and 12 × 20 inches, known as 'banquet'.

Apart from 5 × 4 inch, most professional photographers use 5 × 7 or 10 × 8 inch formats. The choice of films for the 'plate' sizes is rather restricted and film manufacturers seem to be slowly phasing them out.

Types of camera

Large format cameras consist of a front standard and a rear standard, connected by a bellows. The front standard incorporates the lens and shutter, while the focusing screen and film plane are in the rear standard. The distance between the two can be varied to give different image sizes, and one or both standards

can be tilted to control perspective and depth of field.

Most of the cameras are of modular construction, which means that components are interchangeable with others in the same range—there is no camera 'body' as such. You could, for instance, make use of any of several film backs, bellows or lenses. On some cameras, especially the monorail type, almost any part can be changed, and even the negative size can be varied by fitting special adapters.

A wide variety of large format cameras have been made over the years, but modern ones fall into three categories. The first is the wooden *field camera*, such as those made by Gandolfi or Deardorff,—the latter has remained unchanged for the last 50 years or more.

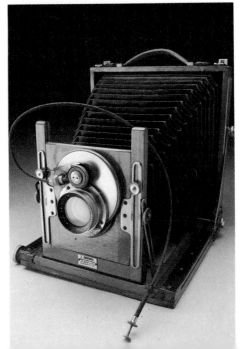

Antique *Large format cameras can make good secondhand buys, and you can find a collector's piece in working order. This fine camera dates from 1910*

Arca Swiss *This light, manageable monorail camera costs about the same as a good SLR. The wide range of components gives the system versatility*

Although more limited in range of movements and less strong than other types, it is popular with landscape photographers because it is light and folds up into a compact package. Models which give 5 × 4 inch, 5 × 7 and 8 × 10 inch negative sizes are available, though Deardorff also make 11 × 14 inch cameras to order.

A more versatile version of the field camera is the *technical camera*, such as the MPP. These are generally made of metal and are bulkier than field cameras, but also fold up quite small and are very sturdy. More movements are possible than with a field camera, and this type can also be hand-held—some even have rangefinders.

Folding technical cameras usually have a *baseboard*, which opens like a drawbridge when the camera is opened. The lens moves back and forth over the baseboard for focusing. The baseboard should drop below a horizontal position, otherwise it will appear in the picture in wide angle shots.

The commonest negative size on a technical camera is 5 × 4 inches, though there are miniature versions which give 2¼ × 3¼ inch negatives on roll film, and 5 × 7 inch types are also available.

The most versatile and sophisticated camera is the *monorail*. Front and rear standards are mounted on a rail, and can be moved independently in any direction. When wide angle lenses are used, the two standards are very close

$f/4.5$ is quite a fast lens, and a maximum aperture of $f/6.3$ is not unusual. These apertures are mainly used for focusing—the taking aperture is usually a couple of stops smaller, to improve image quality. On 5 × 4 inch, taking apertures tend to be between $f/11$ and $f/22$, while on 10 × 8 $f/64$ is not unusual. This is because the small enlargement factor reduces the effect of diffraction, and also because many large format lenses need small apertures if they are to give sharp results over a large area.

For the camera's movements to be exploited to the full, the lens must cover a wide field—otherwise even a small movement of either standard shifts the image off the film plane. The usual wide angle lens for 5 × 4 is 90 mm, though the Schneider 65 mm is also used, and is roughly equivalent to a 20 mm lens on a 35 mm camera. There are also a few long lenses, mostly 210 mm or 360 mm for 5 × 4 inch format.

Lenses are mounted in their own shutters, although a few technical cameras have focal plane shutters. 'Studio' shutters which can be attached separately are also available, and they can be used with any lens.

Film holders

Large format cameras are loaded by means of a film holder, which has to be pre-loaded in the dark before shooting. The standard film holder is the *double darkslide* or DDS, also called a *double cut film holder*. Manufactured in several of the standard sizes from 2¼ × 3¼ inch to 11 × 14 inch, it takes two sheets of cut film. Film holders have only been standardized over the last 30 years or so, so older cameras may have their own

unique holders, and unless you buy plenty of them with the camera you may have trouble finding more. Pre-WW2 single metal holders were often interchangeable, and can also be exchanged with Rada roll film holders. These accept adapters which allow the use of cut film, and which may still be available from some dealers. Another holder, known as the Grafmatic, holds six sheets of 5 × 4 inch film in a rapid change magazine, and fits almost all cameras which accept the DDS type.

Roll film holders are also available for large format, and are semi-standardized. Some fit almost any camera with a standard 5 × 4 inch spring back, while others fit any with a ground glass removable back. Others still are not interchangeable at all, and fit only one camera. It is essential that you check your camera before buying any kind of film holder.

Most of the major manufacturers make film in sheets and rolls in the majority of the large formats. Here, too, the commonest is 5 × 4 inch. The main restriction is that of speed—as a rule, only medium and medium-slow films are available. Neither Kodachrome nor the faster colour films are available in large format sizes. Ektachrome 64 and Agfa 50 are both available in 5 × 4 and 10 × 8, but Tri-X, Plus-X and some colour negative films are only made in 5 × 4 inch size.

Choosing a large format camera

As with other types of camera, your choice depends on your needs—the types available are quite different, and suit different sets of priorities. Price, too, can be a significant factor.

From the point of view of convenience and interchangeability, 5 × 4 inch is the best format for most purposes—a wider range of films and film holders is available, and roll film adaptors are easier to find than for the larger sizes.

together, so a special bag bellows is available for this purpose. Sinar are among the best known cameras of this type. Some of these cameras have a facility for *on-axis movements*, which means that the standards pivot on the lens axis rather than the base of the camera. This arrangement makes camera movements and focusing quicker and easier.

Monorails are capable of the best results of all large format cameras, but they demand the most skill on the part of the photographer. Furthermore, they are the slowest to use, and the most awkward to carry. The commonest size is 5 × 4 inches, with 5 × 7 inch and 10 × 8 inch sizes also available. Small 2¼ × 3¼ inch versions are sometimes found, as well as 11 × 14 inch models. A number of obsolescent half- and whole-plate sizes can be bought secondhand.

Lenses

Lenses are generally mounted in panels, which simply clip into the front standard of the camera, so you can fit any lens whose image covers the format you are using. Resolving power is not as important as with smaller formats, because the image is rarely enlarged much. Also, because the camera is used on a tripod, small apertures can be used, so performance is usually good anyway.

New lenses for large formats are expensive, but you can buy old ones in good condition quite cheaply—lenses such as the old Dagor or the Tessar can be found at bargain prices. Some of the lenses in use today date back to the turn of the century, and still perform satisfactorily.

Since the 'standard' lens for a given format is roughly equal in focal length to the diagonal of the negative, the standard for the 5 × 4 inch format is 150 mm, and 300 mm is standard for 10 × 8. In practice, though, slightly longer lenses are used—180 mm and 360 mm.

Maximum apertures are small in comparison to those for 35 mm format:

Darkslide *Most of the large format cameras are loaded with this type of film holder, which is fitted in the dark before use, holding two sheets of film. Many types of film can be used and even Polaroid film is available*

Sinar Handy *Most large format cameras are used on a tripod—this model has a grip which allows it to be hand-held. The camera can be detached from the grip and used as the rear standard of a monorail*

Roll film back *Some cameras can be used with roll film holders—this one gives 6 × 7 cm size negatives on 120 or 220 film*

to buy a new camera, and price is an important factor, then a wooden field camera is a good choice. However, some good secondhand buys can be found—a used technical camera can cost a tenth of the new price, and is more versatile than a wooden model. The best buys are usually recent but obsolete models from manufacturers still in existence—the pre-Mk VIII MPP Micro technical is an example. Such cameras can be found for about the price a medium zoom for a 35 mm SLR.

If you are buying a secondhand camera, you should inspect it carefully—rough treatment is often betrayed by a battered exterior. Check also that the bellows are not worn or perforated, and ensure that all controls and movements operate smoothly. The shutter release should work consistently on all speeds. If the camera has a flash synchronization facility, test its operation with a series of polaroid tests. With care, you can find good quality, reliable equipment—if you make the right choice, your experiments in large format photography should be rewarding.

Larger formats are also more expensive, especially when you consider the price of suitable enlargers. However, if faultless image quality is your first priority, then you might consider something larger than 5 × 4 inches.

If portability is very important, then a wooden camera has the advantage over the other types, as it is light and compact. Furthermore, you can buy a new model for little more than the price of a used technical camera. Remember, though, that camera movements are limited. If, on the other hand, compactness is not important, but you want the widest possible range of camera movements, then a monorail is your best bet, even though you will need some practice before you can use it to the full.

Some of the more sophisticated cameras are very expensive—a new 10 × 8 monorail with a couple of lenses can cost as much as a small car. If you want

Large format kit *With this diy kit you can build yourself a wooden monorail with the full range of movements*

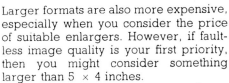

Chapter 2
SPECIAL CAMERAS
INSTANT CAMERAS

Press the button on an instant picture camera, and a minute later you have a fully developed print. Any mistakes you make can be put right straight away with a second shot, so instant photography is both enjoyable and easy. And you can show your subject the picture on the spot for an instant reaction.

A great advantage of instant picture cameras is that they are simple to operate. Even the more sophisticated models do not need exposure meters or a knowledge of normal camera controls. The majority are bought by amateurs who use them for snapshots, family pictures, shots of friends, parties, and so on—and so the cameras tend to be cheap and stylish, though more expensive and versatile models are available.

Simplicity and speed make instant photography very attractive to those people who do not want to bother with the technicalities of more expensive equipment. But it is also useful to serious amateurs and professionals for test shots and visual notebooks.

One disadvantage of instant photography is that, with a few unusual exceptions, you can have only one print per shot. You cannot instantly make identical prints unless the subject is completely static, allowing more than one shot. Should extra copies be required, print copying services are available. But these involve a similar wait to having prints made from nega-

tives, at a slightly higher cost, and lower quality.

Another disadvantage is that because the print is made in the camera, either the equipment is bulky compared with the average simple camera, or the print size is rather small.

There is not a wide range of different film types available for use with each camera, and the film types are not interchangeable between cameras. At most, you will have a choice of either black and white or colour film packs designed for use with your camera.

Instant film systems were pioneered by Polaroid in the US. The company had built its reputation on the manufacture of polarizing material, but the cameras make no use of this material. The inventor of the original system was Dr Edwin H. Land, so Polaroid cameras are sometimes called Land cameras. When Polaroid brought out their SX-70 dry film system, Kodak entered the market with a film and camera with similar properties.

Instant picture frames
As each camera is designed to use a specific type of film it is important to

Instant cameras *The range available includes (from left to right) a folding SLR, an autofocus camera, one with built-in flash, a simple Polaroid and a peel-apart-film type*

understand the differences between the two basic film systems. The older peel-apart film is produced by Polaroid alone, and the more modern dry or integral film packs are manufactured by both Polaroid and Kodak for their own systems.

The peel-apart type involves pulling a tab once the picture has been taken. This squeegees the two layers of the film together, with viscous chemicals between them. After a set time—usually a minute—at room temperature, the two layers are peeled apart to reveal the picture. One layer is in fact a negative, but in most film packs this is useless and must be thrown away. Some cameras take black and white films which yield a negative which can be used conventionally in an enlarger to make further prints.

Once the layers are peeled apart, the print is left to dry. For a permanent print, the surface must be lacquered. When handling this type of film you must be very careful, especially when children are present, for chemicals on the print and the disposable layer are not only sticky and unpleasant but contain a strong alkali which is poisonous and may burn your skin.

The newer type of film is a single dry film pack, in systems made by both Polaroid and Kodak. The chemicals are sealed within the print material, which is thicker than normal. All processing takes

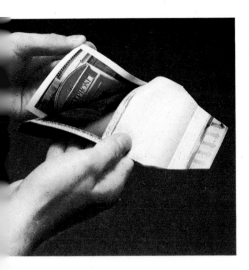

Peel-apart film *Polaroid backs for medium format cameras and some older instant picture cameras use rather messy film that must be peeled apart*

place within this enclosed space and the chemicals are neutralized after development. The image needs no lacquer and is permanent. The design of this kind of film is much more complex but more reliable than peel-apart film. You do not have to time the development, as you do with the older type, as processing stops automatically. Furthermore, the temperature does not matter as much. However, the cost of this type of film is much greater. In both the Polaroid and Kodak systems, as soon as the picture has been taken the print is ejected from the camera automatically. Within a few seconds the picture begins to appear, and in a matter of minutes the colour print is fully developed.

One advantage of Polaroid dry film over the Kodak equivalent is that the batteries which power the motorized film ejection system are contained within the film packs themselves. As they will handle far more than the ten shots in each pack, there is no chance of running out of power. The Kodak system uses separate batteries in the camera.

There are important differences between instant film (of either type) and

normal print film. Because the print is made directly, there is no way of adjusting for slight exposure errors as you can when developing and printing normal films. All that you can do is to make corrections on the camera's light-to-dark control for a second shot. To minimize errors, the makers ensure that the film is not too contrasty. This results in softer tones, weaker colours and less 'brilliance' than conventional prints.

Instant pictures have an appearance of their own, though some people do not like the colours in them compared with normal slides or prints. The manufacturers aim for good skin tones by flash, and often the colour under these conditions will be better than with normal film.

Exposing the film

Exposure, with most instant cameras, is automatic. Some models use a fixed aperture, some give a choice of two apertures (usually represented by weather symbols), and others use a range

of apertures, linked to the shutter speeds to form a programmed autoexposure system (see page 383). The shutter speeds are varied to give the correct exposure, and can be as long as 14 seconds on the more sophisticated cameras. The fastest shutter speeds, however, are often rather slow compared with those on conventional cameras. The popular dry film cameras have top speeds as slow as 1/125 and even 1/80, though the Kodak cameras are better than the Polaroid ones in this respect. Peel-apart film is more sensitive to light than dry film, and some cameras using it have top speeds of up to 1/500.

The light–dark control (which with Polaroid cameras can change the exposure by up to three stops) is the only way of manually modifying the expos-

Pop out film *Some cameras have little motors that push out the film after you take the picture. The image then develops itself automatically and there is no negative to peel back*

Holiday snaps
Instant pictures are ideal for give-away snaps or pre-testing composition

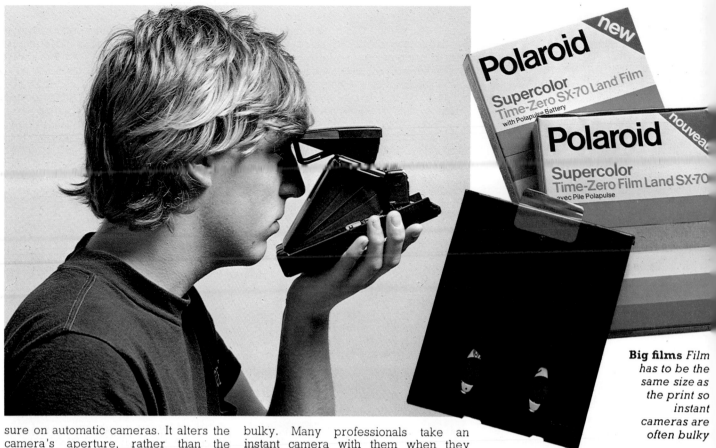

Big films *Film has to be the same size as the print so instant cameras are often bulky*

sure on automatic cameras. It alters the camera's aperture, rather than the shutter speed, so it can be used with the built-in or specially made flashguns and flashbars. The increasing availability of electronic flashguns to fit these cameras has greatly reduced the cost of instant photography.

Focusing and framing
Most of the cheaper cameras have a fixed lens set for around two to three metres, relying on depth of field to get subjects at other distances reasonably sharp. Some models, whose lenses are not fixed, feature rangefinders or zone focusing (using symbols). There are also some cameras, including the most sophisticated Polaroid models, which have automatic focusing.

Although there are no interchangeable lenses as such, some Polaroid cameras can be fitted with converter lenses and close-up attachments, which alter the flash as well as the focus.

Viewfinders are normally of the direct vision type, occasionally with the addition of a bright-line frame. A few more professional models have rangefinders, and the top Polaroids are big format single lens reflexes. However, even with the reflex cameras, the finders are not as clear or easy to use as normal 35 mm SLR finders. With the cheaper cameras, the finders may be little better than the sort found on the cheapest conventional 110 models.

Bulk and accessories
Some Polaroid models, mainly the SLRs, have the advantage of folding flat, making them more convenient to carry. The other instant picture cameras, notably the Kodak models, are very bulky. Many professionals take an instant camera with them when they search for locations, or on the actual shoot. They are used to keep a record of the site, to give prints to models, and so on. The camera must take up as little space as possible in the outfit case, and so the folding Polaroid models are ideal.

The availability of accessories is extremely variable and depends on the specific model. The only accessories available for most instant cameras are neckstraps and flash units. Some better models, however, also accept special cable releases, tripod adaptors, self timers, and cases.

Professional use
The ability to see a print almost immediately has resulted in professionals using instant picture film to test lighting setups and effects. However, most instant picture cameras are not suitable for this purpose because of their automatic exposure systems. Therefore, special Polaroid backs are available which are designed to fit such models as 10 × 8 and 4 × 5 inch studio cameras, and Bronica, Hasselblad, Mamiya, and Rollei SL66 and SLX models. Most instant picture backs use peel-apart films as they are closer to normal films in terms of colour, contrast and exposure than the dry types. Nevertheless, the result can only be used as a rough guide.

There are also a couple of Polaroid professional rangefinder press cameras (originally the Mamiya Press models) which feature interchangeable lenses. These cameras have manual shutter speed and aperture controls. One model, the 600, will take only Polaroid film, but the more expensive 600SE also accepts conventional rollfilm.

The choice
In many cases, the choice of camera will be determined by the type of film you want to use, which in turn will be determined by cost. The simpler cameras are often low price models designed to attract people to the system. The main cost of using instant pictures is in the film packs, and the most basic cameras in each range are effectively 'loss leaders' —units with little profitability but whose low price encourages many people to purchase one, with the likelihood of large sales of film. Such cameras are therefore ideal for casual use. If you want to take a lot of instant pictures,

however, the cost of the equipment will eventually be completely outweighed by the cost of materials, and so justify a greater outlay on the camera.

Instant pictures typically cost between twice and three times as much as conventional enprints, the peel-apart variety being the cheaper.

You must decide how sophisticated you need the camera to be—whether you want auto focus facility, reflex viewing, larger prints, and so on. To get anything like the versatility of the 35 mm SLR you must pay a lot for your camera, sometimes almost as much as the conventional model itself. The simple cameras are mainly intended to take pictures, in sunlight or with flash, at distances of two to three metres. If you want your camera to do any more than this, your choice will be more limited,

and more expensive. Many people choose cameras using dry film because it is more convenient, with no waste paper or messy chemicals. And the final factor is the size of the camera.

There are two main reasons for a serious photographer owning an instant camera—as an addition to a normal camera outfit, and for sheer enjoyment. Even considering the high cost per print it is not an expensive pleasure. Carrying an instant camera allows the photographer to give people prints to thank them for helping with normal shots

(which could be slides they will never see). The simple cameras work well and, unless you pay a great deal, there is little difference between the models. An instant camera is worth considering and fun to use when you get one. They are ideal for party snaps and quick pictures which record the occasion and can immediately be given away to friends. Instant picture cameras are also very useful if you want to check on the composition of a shot and need an immediate result before taking the 'proper' picture with a conventional camera.

Comparison
Instant pictures are smaller and have less subtle colours than enprints

Not compact
A 35 mm camera (left) looks tiny beside an instant camera

TOUGH CAMERAS

If you want a camera that is yet more versatile, you can buy an unfashionable secondhand SLR. Used Exas and Prakticas are cheap and give you access to a huge range of lenses; you should be able to buy a couple of bodies and three or four lenses for the price of a modest new SLR. Alternatively, you can buy a camera with a more unusual lens mount but with a wider specification. Mirandas, for example, are often absurdly cheap and minor faults, such as faulty self timers, can be used to help get the price reduced.

Cameras made in Russia can be bought new as cheaply as many other secondhand SLRs, and can give excellent results considering their low price. The Kiev, which is a copy of the Contax, has Leica-type interchangeable lenses and is cheap and quiet. But the

Waterproofing *Guard against water or spray with a waterproofed camera or a camera and housing. Minolta's Weathermatic (left) and the Ricoh A2 with housing (below) are robust, but, for rough work, cheap old cameras are better (right)*

Most people treasure their camera and would not dream of subjecting it to any form of rough use. But from time to time a camera may be required to either go with the photographer into a dangerous place, or even go where the photographer does not dare. One hazard that is commonly encountered is rain or sea spray, but flying grit, mud, or perhaps even stones are typical problems at car and motorcycle races. But risks can be minimized if you use the proper equipment.

Choosing the equipment

One way to avoid damage to equipment is not to use it. Instead, use cheap, expendable equipment. The cheapest—they can even be free—are old box cameras, 126 cameras or even 110s. The results may not be grand, and the range of conditions in which you can use them may be limited, but it is often possible to acquire a stock of such cameras at no cost, simply by asking friends and acquaintances.

For greater versatility, you can get worthwhile cameras for less than the price of a roll of process-paid colour film, if you know where to look. There are many excellent non-reflex cameras from the 1950s and 1960s, with high quality (but scale-focusing) lenses of reasonable speed, say $f/2.8$ or $f/3.5$, and shutters with a good range of speeds.

most famous Russian camera is the Zenith, also available under other names, such as Cambron in the USA.

The Zenith has its limitations, though none of them are serious. It has a limited range of shutter speeds—none faster than 1/500, none slower than 1/30, except for B. It is heavy, and takes obsolescent M42 screw thread lenses. Its tripod bush is annoyingly located to one side, rather than being central on the baseplate. This means that people tend to overtighten tripod screws, to hold the camera firmly when taking vertical shots, and this can damage the far end of the tripod bush. This, in turn, can prevent the shutter from operating properly.

Zeniths do tend to suffer from shutter defects, but apart from that they are rugged and very cheap. Their lens, while not good, is perfectly adequate for most purposes. Anyone who may have to use a camera under unfavourable conditions, yet requires SLR versatility, could consider a Zenith.

At similar cost, you should be able to find good twin-lens reflexes. These will give you the quality advantage of the

New but cheap *cameras, particularly those made in the USSR, are ideal substitutes for more expensive models*

larger format, and are virtually indestructible—old Yashicamats, Microcords and other Rollei copies seem to go on working forever. Rollfilm folding cameras are not such a good choice, because they are mechanically weaker.

For the utmost in versatility, you can buy a high-quality camera. Old Nikon Fs, for example, are about the same price as a modest, new SLR, but their strength is legendary. Rolleiflexes are another good choice.

Also worth considering is the tough little Robot camera. With its stainless-steel body and built-in spring-driven 'motor drive', it is ideal for relatively low-cost remote operation. Its strength is tank-like, and although alternative lenses are hard to find, it is easy to make an adapter for the simple screw mount. Its drawbacks (which account for its low secondhand price) are its relatively limited specification, its 24 × 24 mm picture format, and the need to use film

cassettes that are unique to the Robot.

If you intend to photograph extensively in difficult conditions, it may be worth buying a purpose-built camera. Usually these are of limited specification but they are built to withstand the most appalling conditions. In any event, simplicity is always the best policy when choosing equipment for specialized use. Mechanisms that are not incorporated cannot go wrong, so always use the simplest camera compatible with doing the job. Beware of electronics, especially if you work in rain or sea spray.

The best known, and probably the best, special-purpose camera is the Nikonos. This is not only waterproof down to about 50 m deep, it is also mechanically extremely strong. A scale-focusing 35 mm $f/2.5$ lens is not particularly extraordinary (there are others for underwater use); much more impressive is the fact that you can hose the camera down after a hard day's work.

Fujica's HD (Heavy Duty) cameras are not as rugged as the Nikonos but they are much cheaper. They can survive the occasional dousing, but are not designed for underwater use. The Minolta 110 amphibious camera is cheap, strong and simple, but it is essentially a box camera with the limiting 110 format.

There are only two accessories that really concern the hazardous-use photographer: the meter and the flash. The cheapest secondhand Weston meter you can find is the best choice. Use it inside a tough, clear plastic bag in rain or spray, allowing maybe ⅓ stop to account for the bag. For flash, use either a cheap electronic unit inside a plastic bag or a bulb flash. These are powerful, reliable and inexpensive secondhand.

Custom-built cameras

Some of the most extreme conditions are encountered by industrial photographers. But a camera protected for one particular type of hazard will, most likely, be unsuitable for use in other types of hazard. For this reason, camera housings are made to order; ready-made housings are usually available only for underwater use.

A camera that is well protected against blasts, for example, might be so bulky as to be unsuitable for photographing the interior of an oil or gas well—often necessary during exploration. In a pressurized well, a main consideration is the risk of starting an explosion. And the camera must be kept small and simple to minimize costs. So instead of an elaborate arrangement of controls, operated through multicore cables, a self-contained camera and housing are used, operated automatically by battery powered timers.

In the darkness of an underground well, the image path must be kept separate from the illumination path, and this adds to the complexity of the housing. Nevertheless, the design remains fairly conventional, using the usual industrial 'O' ring rubber seals, for example, to make the housing gas tight.

UNDERWATER CAMERAS

Anyone who has ever tried sub aqua diving knows that the underwater environment provides the photographer with some beautiful and fascinating subjects. As more and more people have become interested in diving as a hobby, so the demand for underwater cameras and other equipment has grown.

The main problem involved in using a camera underwater is, of course, that of keeping the film and working parts dry. There are a number of cameras made with a watertight case which enables them to be used either in wet weather on land, or underwater. Underwater housings are impermeable casings into which ordinary cameras can be fitted to protect them. A part in the front of the housing allows light to reach the camera lens, while there are windows in the top or rear of the housing for viewfinding.

But sub aqua cameras and housings have to be more than just waterproof. Working underwater presents the photographer with a number of special problems. The water itself acts as a combined variable colour and diffusion filter, visibility is rarely more than 30 metres and is often considerably less, while refraction (the deflection of the

path of light) underwater reduces the angle of the lens and can cause pincushion distortion and colour faults.

Limited visibility requires you to get very close to your subject in order to pick up detail. So, for photographing underwater landscapes, large creatures, or group shots of other divers, most underwater photographers prefer to use a wide angle lens. Occasionally, of course, you cannot get close enough to use a wide angle, so an underwater long focus lens must be used instead.

The problem of poor visibility is made worse by refraction. As light passes through the port in the housing, the change from water to air refracts or deflects it. A flat port can reduce the angle of view of the lens by up to one third, a 35 mm lens becoming equivalent to a 50 mm. Refraction can be partially 'corrected' by fitting a hemispherical or 'dome' port to the housing. With the lens properly positioned behind such a dome, the worst of the refraction effect is eliminated.

When it comes to choosing sub aqua equipment, your decision will depend upon how seriously your take your underwater photography, whether or not you already own an SLR suitable for housing and how much you can afford to spend. The cheapest camera capable of being used underwater is a 110 model and can be purchased for about half the price of a budget SLR. Expensive underwater housings can cost as much as 100 times more.

Your choice may also depend on the sort of diving you do.

For the driver—and the photographer—the sea can be thought of as three distinct layers. The first extends about five metres down from the surface, and in this region you can dive using only a face mask and snorkel. In this layer too, photography is comparatively simple because daylight penetrates the water, providing enough natural illumination for taking pictures, and pressure is not great so even the simplest underwater cameras can be used.

The next layer extends from five metres to about 50 metres down. Scuba

Sub aqua range *This group of cameras and housings includes (left to right) the 110 Weathermatic, Ikelite housing, Nikonos IVa, Ricohmarine AD-1 housing with camera and the Hanimex Amphibian*

gear is essential. And because much less sun penetrates this far, artificial light—ie flash—is needed for photography. The water pressure increases at greater depths, and you must take great care to ensure that water does not seep into your camera. Very sophisticated housings are needed when you dive to the limits of scuba apparatus.

The remainder of the oceans—deeper than 50 m—are strictly out of bounds for the amateur diver. Very elaborate equipment is needed both for photography and for survival. The water above filters out almost all light and generates enormous pressures that can force moisture into the housing.

Underwater cameras

Cameras suitable for use underwater are those that have a perfectly sealed, often plastic, case to keep out water. There are two types: the all-weather cameras which are designed for use in wet weather but which are capable of being used underwater and those that are specifically designed for the job

The most elementary all weather camera us the robust plastic 110 format Weathermatic made by Minolta. It can be used at depths down to 5 m, but the narrow angle of the lens means that it can only produce reasonable results in shallow clear waters

Hanimex, too, produce a 110 all weather camera, the MF Amphibian. Slightly more expensive than the Weathermatic it has a depth rating of 45 m, motor drive and a built-in flash unit. It can also be fitted with an underwater close-up attachment. A more sophisticated version of the same camera is marketed by Sea and Sea under the name of the Pocket Marine 110 It

Plastic bag *Though only suitable for use at moderate depths, this simple housing is inexpensive and robust*

Lens change *The Nikonos offers a range of interchangeable lenses, though some of them cannot be used out of the water*

includes all the features of the Amphibian but also has a separate flash facility.

A camera called the Aquamatic, which should not be confused with a company of the same name, takes the larger 126 instamatic cartridge It has an interesting freeflooding design. The front of the camera containing the aperture and shutter mechanism can be flooded with water while the lens and film remain dry. This feature gives the camera a depth capability of 70 m—deeper than the requirements of most sub aqua divers.

One of the most versatile purpose-built underwater cameras is the Nikonos IVa. This is a 35 mm with a direct vision viewfinder. It also has a large, optional clip-on frame finder for use when wearing a face mask when it is difficult to get your eye very close to the built-in finder. The camera can be fitted with a large range of accessories produced both by Nikon and by independent manufacturers. These include dedicated flash, extension tubes and framers for extreme close-up and macro work and lens converters with which you can change a standard lens into a wide angle or fisheye. The range of lenses which can be fitted to the Nikonos includes a 90 mm and a 35 mm which have plane ports and have focal lengths of 120 mm and 47 mm, respectively, underwater. The other two lenses produced by Nikon for use on the Nikonos are fully corrected for underwater use and cannot be used on land. They are the 28 mm and 15 mm UW Nikkor.

The Nikonos IVa has an automatic exposure system metering off the film plane. It has a depth capability of about 70 m. This is deeper than most sub aqua divers are likely to go to. Although primitive by land camera standards, the Nikonos is one of the most widely used underwater cameras and can give results of the highest quality. For those underwater photographers who want the full versatility offered by a land camera, however, there is no alternative to an underwater housing.

Underwater housings

An underwater housing is a watertight enclosure which can take an ordinary camera but which enables all the controls to be operated from the outside. There are a number of ready built housings designed to take 35 mm or other format cameras while, for the DIY enthusiast, materials and control assemblies can be purchased and housings built at home.

The cheapest and simplest watertight housing is a flexible plastic bag with a rigid porthole. The camera is held in position inside by a plastic strap. Designed for use in wet weather or underwater, the bag is sealed with a clip and the camera can be operated by inserting a hand into an integral glove. The bags called EWA bags, are available in a variety of sizes accepting all formats up to large roll SLRs. They are limited to a depth of 10 m and care should always be taken to avoid sharp edges which may puncture the bag.

Of a more rigid design is the Ricoh-marine AD. It is a clear, compact, polycarbonate case which accepts the Ricoh AD-1 or A-2 cameras. The cameras feature clockwork wind and programmed auto exposure systems and the 38 mm lens is coupled into the housing porthole for focusing underwater. Unfortunately, the rotating porthole mount which changes the focus becomes very stiff at great depths as a result of the increased water pressure. By the time that the maximum depth of 30 m is reached, the ring may be difficult to move at all.

Other rigid underwater housings are designed to take a larger range of cameras. But despite the growing popularity of underwater photography, the market is still very small and the equipment tends to be expensive especially if it has to be made to order.

Most 110, 35 mm compact and simple 35 mm SLRs can be fitted with housings of some kind, but those with interchangeable viewfinders are the most suitable. It is difficult to get close to the viewfinder when wearing a face mask so the action speed and system finders produced for the Nikon F range, the Canon F1 and the Pentax LX make focusing underwater much simpler due to the larger, brighter image.

Ikelite produce a comprehensive range of ready built transparent polycarbonate housings which can take cameras varying in size from 110 to medium format SLRs. Those designed to take 35 mm SLRs can accept most makes of camera. Costs are reduced by using the same outer moulding in all cases. The interior of the housing is custom built to suit the specific control positions of each type of SLR. Focusing, exposure and wind on are controlled externally through a series of gears and levers and all housings have interchangeable domed ports. The camera is fixed into the housing by its tripod thread in such a position as to allow viewfinding through the rear of the housing. Ilkelites can be used down to the limits of safe air diving and cost slightly less than the cameras they are designed to carry.

Slightly more expensive are the acrylic housings. These can either be bought ready made, or in component form for construction at home. Their acrylic construction makes subsequent modification or repair easy.

For the Canon F1 and the Nikon F series cameras, robust cast alloy housings are made. The cameras can be carried with or without a motor drive and acrylic windows in the rear and on top of the housing allow viewfinding and setting of controls. The housings feature interchangeable ports and fittings for flash arms and meters.

Another alloy housing with similar specifications that can accept a larger range of SLRs also has an optical reducer which allows for viewfinding using fixed finder cameras. With this attachment, the whole viewing screen can be seen but at a reduced size. This tends to make accurate focusing difficult, particularly with wide angle lenses. Alloy housings cost around half as much again as the cameras they hold.

At the top of the price range are the underwater housings for medium format cameras. Although their high cost places them out of reach of the average amateur photographer, they might be a suitable item for group purchase by specialist sub aqua clubs.

Hasselblad produce a housing for their non-reflex SWC camera. In common with most of the more expensive housings it features the Ivanoff corrector. This device corrects for refraction at the air water interface and allows a flat port

to be used with no reduction in the angle of the lens. The housing is made in robust alloy but with the corrector it is a bulky piece of equipment with a tendency to be front heavy.

For their EL cameras, Hasselblad make a stainless steel housing. It is tubular in shape, the camera being mounted with the lens located centrally. It has a depth capability of 300 m, but its size and construction make it heavy and unwieldy at all depths.

Just as large but easier to handle underwater is the alloy housing for the Mamiya RB 67. It features Ivanoff type correction allowing all but the 37 mm full frame fisheye lens to be used with a flat port.

Housings can also be bought custom made to fit your requirements whatever

In action *The separate flash facility on the Pocket Marine 110 makes this compact camera especially versatile*

equipment you own. Before buying any housing, however, it is always worth checking to make sure that your camera can be housed. It should be capable of taking a wide angle lens and ideally should feature a range of interchangeable viewfinders. Compromising with an unsuitable camera or an inadequate housing could be a costly mistake and if you have little money to spend, an all weather camera might be the best introduction to underwater photography. On the other hand, if you already own a good SLR, and want to use it to its fullest capacity, a rigid sub aqua housing may be the best choice.

Camera and case *Some housings, such as the Ricohmarine AD-1 here, are designed to fit specific cameras*

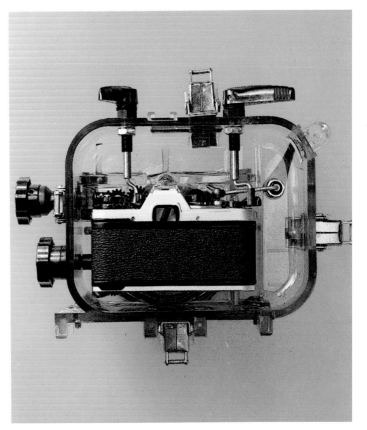

Ikelite housing *Despite its curious appearance, this housing is extremely robust and simple to operate*

CAMERAS FOR 3-D

One of the attractions of stereo photography is that quite effective results can be achieved with little or no special equipment. Nevertheless, using cameras and attachments specifically designed for this type of work can add greater sophistication and consistency to your work.

Unfortunately, with the exception of a few very expensive and specialized cameras, there are only a few items of new equipment on the market today. Unless you are prepared to make your own equipment, then, you are left with three main choices: you can use a slide mechanism with an ordinary camera; you can buy used equipment; or you can use a stereo *beamsplitter*.

Slides and beamsplitters

The stereo slide is the simplest and cheapest equipment. All you need is some sort of jig which allows your usual camera to be moved sideways between exposures. Some people make their own and some use macro focusing rails or similar appliances with the camera mounted sideways. You can use any camera of any format, and the distance you move the camera between exposures is readily variable. This is particularly useful as, although a movement of around 60 mm is fine for most subjects

Nikon adaptation *This custom built camera, made from two Nikon FMs, takes 16 stereo pairs on standard 35 mm format. Built by R I Harding, it retains most of the Nikon features as well as separate setting of shutter, aperture and focusing (right).*
A hand-held viewer, *for photographs or drawings, was once popular.*
Stereo projector *Many of these are now very scarce collectors' items*

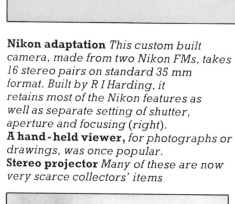

a smaller separation is desirable for close-ups, and a wider separation allows you to produce startling landscapes. The main drawback is that you are limited to static subjects.

Beamsplitters are another fairly simple option. These attach to the front of a normal lens and use mirrors or prisms to split the field of view. The taking windows are around 60 mm apart, and the two images are brought together so that they enter the camera's lens side by side.

There is at least one beamsplitter still available new. This is made by Pentax and, although intended for use

Stitz stereo adapter *This can be used on lenses with focal length varying from 50 to 300 mm*

with Pentax standard lenses it can be used with other models with focal lengths between 40 mm and 55 mm if they have the same or (via adapter rings) similar filter sizes. In the past a number of other manufacturers made them, and it is still possible to pick them up secondhand. Leitz and Nikon made them for their rangefinder cameras, Zeiss offered one for the Contaflex cameras, and there was another model known as the Stereax. The better beam-splitters are those using prisms as they are more robust, though older types are prone to fungus.

Beamsplitters are relatively cheap, convenient and easy to find so they are favoured by many stereo enthusiasts. Unfortunately, they have a fixed separation and so are not really suitable for close-ups, and there is inevitably a small loss of quality when compared with the unadorned prime lens.

Both of these limitations are overcome by the rare and expensive twin lens adapters made for Leicas and Contaxes. The standard lens was replaced by a matched pair of shorter focus lenses in a common focusing mount—33 mm for Leicas, 35 mm for Contax. The separation is tiny, but this is ideal for close-up work. For pictures taken at normal distances, a prism device similar to a beamsplitter could be used. These adapters have one main drawback though—the two images on the film are not the same way round. One of them is transposed, so the film has to be cut up and remounted for use in a viewer.

Stereo cameras

Beamsplitters and stereo slides are undoubtedly the easiest and cheapest ways of taking stereo pictures. But a stereo camera offers much better quality. Several formats are available from large plate models right down to sub-miniature 16 mm types. This type of photography was very popular in the last century and so many of the cameras date from this time. Others date from the 1950s when there was a resurgence of interest in this type of work.

A large number of the older cameras

are of use only as collectors' items as they used film sizes and types which are no longer available. It is sometimes possible to convert plate cameras to take cut film, but you have to cut the film yourself. The most usual sizes were 120 × 80 mm, 130 × 60 mm and 107 × 45 mm, though non-standard sizes also abound. Another major drawback with this type of equipment is that it is much sought after by collectors who do not use it, forcing prices to very high levels—at least as much as a new SLR and sometimes much higher.

With a few exceptions, roll film stereo cameras are even more enthusiastically collected. The forerunner of the twin lens Rolleiflex was a stereo camera and

The Nimslo 3-D camera *gave a full colour stereo print that can be viewed directly, without a viewing aid*

fetches a small fortune. Roll film stereo formats are also unstandardized, but at least it is slightly easier to construct transparency viewers for roll film pictures than it is for plates. Even so, most users of both roll film and plate cameras tend to use prints. Late roll film cameras, such as the Duplex, are highly priced simply because there is little else on the market. 35 mm cameras are not (as yet) widely collected but, once again, their prices are kept high by the laws of supply and demand. Although formats were never standardized only three are commonly encountered.

The first, and the nearest there is to a

Stitz stereo viewer *Loaded with a 35 mm standard pair, this is a fixed focus viewer of Japanese make*

standard, gives stereo pairs where each picture is 23 × 24 mm. For efficient film use, and to obtain a suitable separation between the pictures, they are arranged so that each pair is separated by two frames in between them. Cutting and mounting the pictures can be quite tricky, though Kodak mount Kodachrome in 101 × 45 mm standard card mounts for a small additional fee. This format is found in a moderate number of cameras dating mostly from the 1950s. The Stereo Realist is the best known, but the Iloca Stereo, the Revere, the TDC Colorist, and even Kodak's Stereo 35 may be encountered from time to time.

The second format, 24 × 30 mm, was essentially the preserve of the French

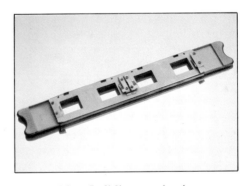

Slide holder *A sliding mechanism enables any of three formats to be selected for stereo projection.*
The Verascope F40 (*front and back views*) *is to be found mostly among prized collections*

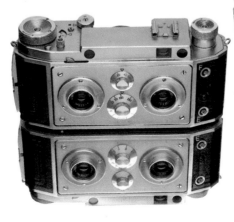

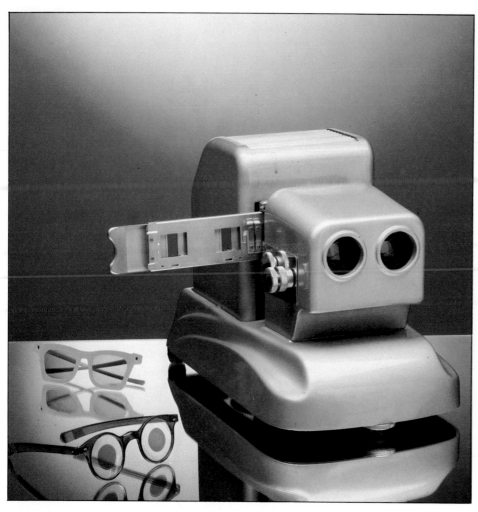

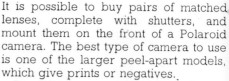

It is possible to buy pairs of matched lenses, complete with shutters, and mount them on the front of a Polaroid camera. The best type of camera to use is one of the larger peel-apart models, which give prints or negatives.

The other approach is to bolt two identical cameras together. This can be a complex and specialized job, and it is best done by experts. At least one company offers a camera body consisting of two Nikons joined together. However, this type of conversion is extremely expensive—as much as eight times the cost of a normal camera body—and lenses are extra. This presents another problem in that the two lenses must be of exactly the same focal length. Finding two lenses the same is not as easy as it may seem. Although a lens is stated to have a focal length of, say, 50 mm the actual length can be different by as much as five per cent. This means you need a certain amount of luck in your lens selection, although if you use lenses by one of the top manufacturers there are likely to be fewer problems.

firm, Richard. Their Homeos (1925) was the first 35 mm production still camera of all, and the F40 (1954) was arguably the finest stereo camera ever made. The Verascope F40, as it is more often known, was stunningly expensive (about 50 per cent more than a contemporary Hasselblad) and is correspondingly rare. The same viewing equipment may be used for this format as for the 23 × 24 mm, though you have to mount it yourself (if you can get the mounts).

The third format is the tiny Viewmaster Personal Stereo Camera format with an image size of about 14 × 12 mm. In these unusual and rather eccentric cameras the film path is diagonal across the camera back, and the exposures are staggered in pairs.

One disadvantage with stereo photography is that the print or slide has to be viewed under special conditions. This was overcome in the Nimslo 3-D camera, though it is not widely available. The images from not two but four identical lenses are superimposed during the film processing stage and overlaid with a transparent film. This is embossed to form a large number of cylindrical lenses. These give the 3-D effect by enabling the images to be viewed separately, depending on the view angle.

Specially made equipment

If you want to use a stereo camera but dislike or cannot find secondhand items, it is possible to make your own, or have a conversion made to standard cameras.

Projector and glasses *The best arrangement for viewing slides is to project them through differently polarized screens, and view them through polarized spectacles.*
The Zeiss Ikon beamsplitter (*right*) *is a high quality instrument which was popular during the 1950s and 1960s. If you can get one today you should expect to pay about the cost of a mid range SLR, complete with lens and case.*
The Iloca stereo camera *dates from about the mid 1950s, and is now rare*

Pentax beamsplitter *One of the few items of stereo equipment available new, is fitted with fixed mirrors*

Viewing the picture

Whatever system you use for taking the pictures, you are likely to need some equipment for viewing the results. Some people can fuse a stereo pair without any accessories, but most require some sort of viewer.

The traditional approach uses prints mounted on a (surprisingly standardized) card and looked at with a hand-held or table viewer which contains two lenses similar to magnifying glasses. This method is simple and very effective. And getting the viewer is no problem—virtually any of those made in the last 200 years may be used (stereo drawings preceded stereo photography). Making and mounting the prints is not particularly difficult if you do it yourself. With trade processing, however, there can be difficulties. Few processing houses will print the odd shaped formats, and if they do, the resulting prints are likely to be somewhat arbitrarily and differently cropped.

Stereo projection is even more awkward. As with the camera lenses, the projector lenses must be precisely matched. And the difficulties of aligning

Stereo viewer *Probably the greatest choice in 3-D equipment is in viewers. This one has variable focus*

twin projectors for one slide, let alone for a whole sequence, are so great that the only practical solution is to use a specially made stereo projector and stereo mounts—a strong argument for Kodachrome where the work of mounting the pictures is done for you.

Since the lefthand and righthand images are superimposed on the screen, you also need some way of distinguishing between them. The traditional method was to colour one green and the other red and to use spectacles with one lens of each colour. This system was used in cinemas showing stereo (3-D) movies.

Print viewer *The two stands are unfolded to support the twin lenses over the stereo print*

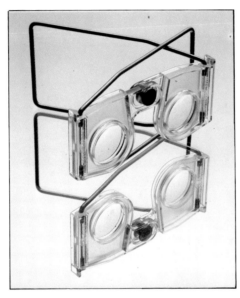

A more satisfactory approach, and the only practical one with colour pictures, is to use polarizers on the projector lenses and polarizing spectacles (like the filters). In order to maintain the polarization of the light it is essential that you have a metallic screen, and because quite a lot of light is lost in the polarizers, powerful lamps in the projectors and a good black-out are crucial requirements.

It was possible, during the 1950s, to obtain beamsplitters for use with movie cameras and projectors. You may still occasionally come across these and be tempted to use them. But they are not very successful with slide projection because of the registration and alignment problems involved.

Probably the most convenient and popular methods of viewing stereo pictures is to use individual viewers designed for slides. Although it is possible to buy viewers with built in light sources, simpler types using diffusers are perfectly adequate and have the advantage of being extremely portable. While it is possible to make these, or to adapt them from old stereoscopes, it is actually very easy to pick up new or secondhand models designed for 35 mm slides.

The Pentax beamsplitter is sold complete with a viewer, which although very

simple is capable of excellent results. But, alternatively, it is still fairly easy to pick up secondhand models. As with beamsplitters the best types use prisms rather than mirrors. Another very useful feature is the facility to vary the separation between the eyepieces. The best example is the one made by Leitz. But there are many cheaper, plastic viewers, and the better ones (such as the Zeiss model) are nearly as good as the Leitz model.

The main problem is, once again, one of non-standardization of equipment. But two types stand out as being most convenient. The first is the type designed to take a standard 5 × 5 cm slide mount with a split 35 mm frame, such as that given by a beamsplitter. GePe make a slide mount with a central division for this format. The second type is that which takes the standard Kodak stereo card mount.

Equipment sources

Apart from the Pentax outfit, you are unlikely to find any of this equipment in a normal camera shop. The best sources of stereo equipment are those shops catering for the collector, though this means that prices tend to be high. It is worth looking in junk shops and secondhand shops. Alternatively, most countries have groups of photographers who specialize in stereo work, and can direct you to the most likely sources of equipment.

There are very few shops specializing in stereo equipment. Probably the only dealer in new stereo cameras (adapted from standard models) is RI Harding & Co. Ltd, a repair specialist in London. And for stereo equipment generally, one of the best known dealers is Duval Studios Ltd, also in London. They stock used components, mounts, viewers and even projectors.

The Duplex 120 *is one of the more common stereo cameras. Its drawback is its very restricted lens separation*

WIDE-VIEW EQUIPMENT

Throughout the history of photography, the narrow angles of view of conventional cameras have frustrated camera users. We see the world through eyes that take in a wide panorama of the scene in front of us, yet cameras give what amounts to a small window on the world. A number of designs for giving wider views have been developed. The simplest is the wide angle converter, but there are also specialized lenses and cameras purpose-built for the job.

Converters

For the amateur photographer, one cheap and practical solution to the problem of getting very wide views is to use a wide angle converter—a device that fits on to the front of the prime camera lens to increase the view angle. The device is screwed into the filter thread, using a series VII adapter supplied with all converters. If you buy a converter, ensure that you get an adapter that fits the thread of your filter ring. You may need more than one adapter if you plan to use the converter with several lenses.

Converters are available in two basic types: wide angle and fisheye. Wide angle converters simply increase the angle of view of the prime lens, usually by about 30 per cent. They work best with lenses of 40 to 60 mm focal length.

Used with a 50 mm lens, for example, the combination produces an equivalent focal length of about 38 mm. These converters can be used with lenses of shorter focal length, but definition is poor, and vignetting occurs, particularly on lenses of 28 mm or shorter.

Fisheye converters give a more pronounced wide angle effect, and cause straight-line portions of the subject to be recorded curved on the film. They are similarly attached via an adapter ring to the lens. Fitted to a 50 mm lens, they fill the entire picture area—with no vignetting. With a 35 mm lens, some vignetting occurs, and with 28 mm, the image is circular. Used with a lens of even shorter focal length, the effect is simply a smaller circular image on film, and not a wider angle of view.

The main advantage of using converters (as opposed to panoramic cameras) is their low cost. Both types are inexpensive, but there are other points in their favour. They can be used with fixed lens cameras to increase the versatility of otherwise limited models. They can be used with a wide range of lenses, because adapter rings are interchangeable. And because converters reduce the focal length of the lens with which they are used, they can act as close-up supplementary lenses, producing a much closer minimum focusing distance than would be possible with the unaided lens.

Against these advantages must be weighed the fact that generally, pictures taken by converters are much poorer in quality than those of a conventional wide angle or fisheye lens. In some instances, performance at full aperture is barely acceptable, and to get good results, it is usually necessary to stop the prime lens down to $f/11$ or smaller. For fisheye pictures, however, which are primarily

Converters *are attached to the front of a prime camera lens via a series VII adapter, which screws into the filter ring. They perform best on lenses of focal lengths in the range 40 to 60 mm*

Super-wide angles *of view are achieved with fisheye lenses. But for general photography, the image produced by a full-frame fisheye (below left) is more practical than that of a circular image fisheye, which is more suitable for specialist or 'one-off' shots*

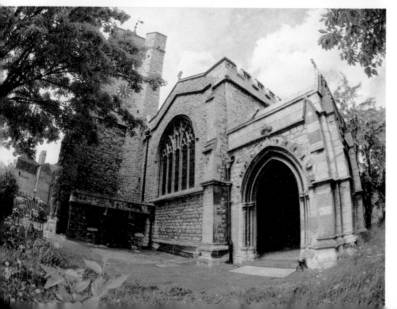

ovelties, poor definition might not be an important factor.

Some fisheye converters utilize the wide angle reflections of a highly reflective sphere. These are usually described as *bird-eye attachments*, and are of only limited use, even for casual photography. They record an image of the photographer and camera at the centre of each frame. For a few scientific applications, this imaging is desirable but generally, such devices can be regarded as little more than toys.

Wide angle lenses
The most common means of achieving a wide view is to fit a wide angle lens.

Large and fast
A 6 mm f/2.8 Nikkor fisheye lens towers monstrously above a compact 28 mm

A fisheye view
An astonishing 220° angle of view taken in by the 6 mm f/2.8 Nikkor fisheye. Standing well behind the camera, the photographer can even see his own outstretched hands

Ultrawide lenses—those with a focal length of 21 mm or shorter—are difficult to manufacture, particularly for SLR cameras. A major factor is that the retrofocus lens design that provides sufficient clearance for the camera's swinging reflex mirror requires great precision. As a result, these lenses are usually expensive, though it is possible to buy a 20 mm lens for about 25 per cent more than a comparable 24 mm.

Generally, ultrawides are much like ordinary wide angle lenses, except for the wider angle, but the shorter focal length lenses tend to be much heavier, bulkier and have enlarged front elements. Typically, maximum apertures in the 17 to 20 mm range are about f/4, but wider lenses are usually limited to f/5.6.

Perhaps the most distinguishing external feature of an ultrawide lens is the hood. This has a deeply scalloped appearance, because regions of the hood are cut away where the angle of view is widest so that they do not appear in the corners of the frame. When buying an ultrawide, check that a hood is supplied, or that a matched one is available as an extra, because at short focal lengths, a hood is essential for keeping stray light out of the lens.

Filters, too, are purpose-built. Usually, they are built-in, mounted in a rotating turret. This is not a luxury but rather an essential for good performance which would be impaired by unsuitable filters. In any event, the steeply convexed front element, which is a prominent feature of many of these lenses, makes the fitting of a conventional filter impossible. Although filter turrets offer only a limited range of colours, lens manufacturers can usually change one or more to a filter of the user's choice.

True ultrawide lenses show no distortion of straight lines in the picture area, and this is a requirement that becomes more difficult to fulfil as focal length is reduced. The practical limit, in terms of angle of view, is 120°. At 118°, the 13 mm Nikkor comes fairly close to this. True wide angles with an even wider angle of view are unlikely to be introduced in the future, because they are extremely expensive. Today, many are available only on special order. Even a large manufacturer is unlikely to sell more than 20 of any one model per year.

Fisheye lenses
Still wider views are achieved with fisheye lenses. These produce a characteristically distorted image, because straight lines on the subject bow outwards on the negative or slide. This uncorrected barrel distortion is unavoidable for such a wide angle of view.

Fisheye lenses were first made for practical applications, which stand out in marked contrast to the glamorous fashion pictures with which they are now associated. The original fisheye, the Hill sky lens, was used to make stereoscopic photographs of cloud cover. Other typical uses are for photographing the insides of boilers and pipes.

As with any lens, a fisheye forms a circular image. In some instances, the image fills the frame, but some fisheyes produce an image that is only 23 or 24 mm wide, at the centre of the film. Full-frame fisheyes are of more practical use to the creative photographer, but the circular type covers a wider angle of view—up to 220°—and is of more use in industrial and scientific applications. Invariably, both types have built-in filters, but focal length, maximum aperture, and other features differ widely between the various models.

A typical full-frame fisheye lens has an angle of view of 170°, a focal length of 16 mm, and a maximum aperture of f/3.5, but circular image fisheyes, because they are designed for specific applications, tend to be more exotic. A few have protruding rear elements, and must be used with the mirror locked up, but because they are often used on remote controlled, or unattended cameras, this hardly ever matters.

The standard *The type of view taken in by the 'standard' wide angle lens—the 28 mm*

Conversion *Used with a 28 mm lens, a wide angle converter (top) and fisheye converter (above) give very wide views*

Focal lengths of circular image fish-eyes range from 6 mm to about 10 mm, and maximum apertures are small—about f/5.6. Often, exceptionally short focal length models have no focusing helicoil, which is unnecessary because of the extreme depth of field. A 6 mm lens at full aperture, for example, records everything in focus from infinity to 11 cm from the lens surface.

Panoramic cameras

Designed exclusively to produce wide-angle pictures, panoramic cameras can be grouped into three types. The most elementary type is simply an ordinary camera with a lens that covers an exceptionally wide angle of view. Several different models are produced. Most of them are based on a Schneider Super-Angulon lens, which has a focal length of 65 mm. Other manufacturers make lenses of the same focal length, but the Schneider is by far the commonest. The lens gives wide angle results on the 5 × 4 inch format, and is fitted with a leaf shutter and a conventional iris dia-

phragm. These give shutter speeds ranging from 1 to 1/500 second and apertures in the range f/5.6 to f/22.

The various wide angle cameras that utilize this lens generally consist simply of a cone to support the optics, a sheet film holder, matt glass for focusing and an optional optical viewfinder. A helical screw built into the lens serves as a focusing mount. Cameras using lenses of this focal length include the Plaubel Wide Angle, the Sinar Handy, the Globus Super-Wide, and the Cambo Wide Angle 650. Some of these, such as the Cambo, have a limited amount of rising front but, generally, the lens is fixed.

A less common version of this fixed-lens–fixed-film system uses a 47 mm lens, but this covers only the 6 × 9 cm format, instead of the full 5 × 4 inch.

Although panoramic cameras utilize conventional formats, they produce pictures that are much wider than usual. The only camera to achieve such an outstanding performance with a fixed lens and film is the Linhof Technorama. This remarkable camera uses 120 rollfilm,

and takes pictures measuring 170 × 56 mm—nearly three times as wide as the standard 6 × 6 cm format, and covering a horizontal angle of view of about 90°.

The camera has a 90 mm f/5.6 lens and takes four exposures on each roll of film. Because the rays of light reaching the corners of the frame travel so much farther than those at the centre, the lens on this camera exhibits severe vignetting. To compensate for this problem, a filter is supplied with the camera. This has a neutral density spot at the centre, surrounded by clear glass. The filter serves to even out the exposure across the width of the frame. For its type, the Technorama is unique in its angular coverage, but its 90 mm lens can be used on any 25 × 20 cm (10 × 8 inch) format camera, and the resulting pictures cropped down to the same panoramic format.

Fixed-lens–fixed-film cameras are costly, mainly because of the exotic lenses they require, but they have considerable advantages over other types of panoramic cameras. They are virtually free from distortion, but

pherical objects in the corners of the frame appear oval, due to the extreme angle of view (see page 231). Where the correct rendering of buildings and other architectural features is important, then this type of camera is the best choice.

Another advantage is that the camera can be used in low-light conditions, because the shutter can be set for long exposures. This is not usually possible with other types of panoramic cameras, in which the lens or the entire camera moves during exposure.

A moving lens
The second way to produce a panoramic picture is to make the lens swivel quickly during the exposure. In this way, the lens need not have a very wide field of view, but the image is scanned across a wide area of film. Previously, many models utilized this principle though fewer have been made recently—the Widelux F7 and the Panon are examples. The Widelux F7 is fitted with a 26 mm f/2.8 fixed-focus lens, which revolves inside a narrow drum. The rear of the drum passes in front of the film, and incorporates a vertical slit which serves as a focal plane shutter.

The 35 mm film runs around half of the circumference of the drum along a curved path. The camera exposes film across only about two-thirds of this curved portion but, nevertheless, produces a picture that takes in an angle of view of 132° in the horizontal plane and 49° vertically. The pictures measure 24 × 39 mm, and on a 36 exposure roll, the camera makes only 21 exposures.

These 21 frames show some distortion (because of the movement of the lens) but this can be made less obvious by avoiding subjects with straight lines, or by directing the camera so that the optical axis is at an oblique angle to the sides of buildings.

The Widelux has an exceptionally wide angle of view, and is comparatively inexpensive—about the cost of a Nikon F3 and an extra lens. By comparison, the Linhof Technorama costs about four times as much.

The Panon camera corporation, which makes the Widelux in Japan, also manufactures the Panon camera. This works on a similar principle, but uses 120 roll-film, and is difficult to obtain.

Occasionally, other wide angle cameras that use the rotating lens principle become available second-

hand. The commonest of these is the Zenith Horizont, which was made in the USSR. This has a 28 mm lens and takes pictures measuring 24 × 58 mm on 35 mm film—an angle of view of about 120°. As with any secondhand camera, however, there might be problems of wear or accidental damage, so try the camera out before buying. A well cared for specimen could prove to be a bargain.

The main disadvantage of any rotating lens type of camera is limited exposure range. The Widelux has speeds of 1/15, 1/125, and 1/250, and a maximum lens aperture of f/2.8. Effectively, this means that with medium speed film the camera can be used only

Widest of the wide angles *The Globuscope panoramic camera revolves through a full 360° in a little over one second*

outdoors by day, or in brightly lit interiors. Fast film and uprated processing give an extra three stops, but in a dark church, for example, pictures would be impossible.

A moving camera
The other type of panoramic camera is that in which the entire camera revolves about a central axis. This design was once popular, and old models are sometimes used to take pictures of large groups of people. The subjects sit in a crescent formation around the camera, which revolves slowly on the tripod to make the exposure. The exposure is made through a narrow slit in the back of the camera. To compensate for the

movement of the camera body, the film is wound past the slit at a speed synchronized with the revolution.

Modern examples of this design revolve much faster. The main example is an American camera called the Globuscope, which spins through 360° in a little more than a second. The camera has a 25 mm f/3.5 lens and takes 35 mm film. Its horizontal angle of view is unlimited: as long as the shutter release is held down, the camera continues to revolve and expose film. Power is provided by a clockwork motor. A full 360° panorama occupies more than four conventional 35 mm frames, so the Globuscope takes only eight pictures per full-length roll.

Although the Globuscope takes in a full circle, it is limited in practice by a primitive exposure system. There is no shutter as such. Instead, the effective shutter speed is controlled by the width of a slit in the film plane. The plate that carries this slit is interchangeable, and the three different widths of slit supplied with the camera offer effective shutter speeds of 1/100, 1/200 and 1/400 sec. The maximum lens aperture is f/3.5 which limits the camera to outdoor daytime use. Furthermore, the shutter plates can be interchanged only when there is no film in the camera.

One other camera works on a similar rotation principle—the Arca-Swiss Roto which is much more sophisticated and expensive than the Globuscope. The Globuscope costs about half as much as the best 6 × 6 cm camera, whereas the Roto is four times this price. By way of compensation, it is a panoramic camera that does everything. It has an f/6.8 75 mm lens, producing pictures 56 × 475 mm in size. The slit at the back of the camera is adjustable in width, and further exposure control is possible by a TTL meter, which controls the speed of rotation of the camera.

The Roto has several other unusual features, including a shift lens. This is particularly valuble, because panoramic cameras cannot be tilted upwards—this would simply lead to half the panorama showing a higher part of the subject, and the other half showing the ground. By raising the lens instead, the camera can remain horizontal while taking a picture of a higher part of the subject.

One revolution *of the Globuscope is usually sufficient to take in almost everything in the horizontal 360° scene*

Chapter 3
LENSES
WIDE-ANGLE LENSES

Of all the additional lenses you can buy for your camera, perhaps few are more useful than a wide angle, and, increasingly nowadays, people are using a wide angle, not just as an accessory lens but as their main lens, in preference to the traditional 50 or 55 mm.

Giving that extra coverage to include all the subject and greater depth of field to ensure that it is all in focus, wide angles can be invaluable in many situations. An additional attraction is that you can shoot to include more than the main subject area and then crop at your leisure to achieve the desired framing. Many compact 35 mm cameras are fitted with a lens of around 35 mm focal length because it makes the camera easier to use, maximizing depth of field to ensure sharp pictures without focus adjustment and minimizing the chances of misframing —otherwise a real problem with direct vision viewfinders.

Surprisingly, perhaps, the traditional 50 or 55 mm lens is actually a little too long to give completely 'normal' looking results on a 35 mm format: a focal length of about 43 mm is actually correct—this distance corresponds to the diagonal of the 24 × 36 mm frame. Some camera manufacturers already offer 38 mm, 40 mm or 45 mm lenses as options for standard lenses. If one of these focal lengths is not available for your camera, but you want to use a short focal length

Wide angle choice *Picking a wide angle lens is not easy. There are 150 different lenses which have focal lengths in the 24 to 35 mm range*

Looking down *The classic use for a wide angle lens is in a confined space. Here a 24 mm lens has been used to emphasize the curving spiral lines of the Guggenheim Art Gallery in New York*

lens as standard, you could buy a 35 mm wide angle.

Wide angles of 35 mm are usually the cheapest wide angle in a manufacturer's range, and are often as small and light as a 50 mm. They usually take the same filtration attachment size, focus quite close, and even the cheapest usually give reasonably good results. Another point in the favour of 35 mm lenses is that they are easy for an inexperienced photographer to use—some of the more disturbing effects of wide angle lenses are not produced at this focal length.

The angle of view of a 35 mm lens just matches that of most flashguns at around 60°, so flash pictures will be

frame, perspective is very pronounced. Depth of field is also great enough to keep both foreground and background sharp, when properly focused.

This can be invaluable for news photographers who have to take pictures in fast moving, crowded situations where there is little time to focus the camera.

28 mm lenses are usually a little larger and heavier than standard 50 mm lenses, but are generally quite reasonably priced. This is because it is a popular focal length, and the lenses can be made in comparitively large numbers. Image quality is usually fairly good, but the optical performance of a cheap 28 mm lens is unlikely to be up to the standard of a similarly priced 35 mm.

24 mm lenses may seem only a little shorter in focal length than 28 mm, but the difference in angle of view is considerable. Pictures on a 24 mm lens seem to 'spread out' obviously at the edges and corners of the frame. Perspective also tends to be much more pronounced than with a 28 mm lens, because the photographer must move in closer to fill the frame with the subject.

The corners of the picture taken with a 24 mm lens are inevitably darker than the centre. This is not a sign of bad manufacture, but an inherent problem with wide angle lenses. All lenses suffer this loss of brightness towards the edge of the frame: it simply becomes more obvious at short focal lengths.

This combination of factors makes it easy to spot picture taken with a 24 mm lens—the photographs have a characteristic 24 mm 'look'. This 'look' can often

Feast *Wide-angle lenses are useful for unobtrusive candid shots—people can be included in the edge of the frame while the camera is apparently pointing elsewhere*

Fast or small *Wide angle lenses that have a large maximum aperture tend to be big and heavy. These three lenses have a focal length of 35 mm, but range from f/1.4 to f/2.8*

completely illuminated. With any wider angle of view, the edges of the picture may not be properly lit unless you use a diffuser to spread the light.

Because the angle of view is close to that of the standard lens, pictures taken on a 35 mm lens do not look like typical wide angle pictures—it is often hard to tell them from those taken with a standard lens. If you want to use the 35 mm as your standard lens, this is obviously an advantage. But if you wish your wide angle to supplement a 50 mm lens, the difference should be more marked and you may prefer a lens with a shorter focal length.

A 28 mm makes a useful combination when paired with a 50 mm standard lens, or one of the newer 40 or 45 mm standards. It covers almost twice the area of the 50 mm lens and gives the typical wide angle 'look'. Whenever any strong foreground objects are included in the

be difficult to use effectively and it is probably best to avoid 24 mm lenses as your first wide angle, unless you are confident of your ability to exploit its characteristics. If you own a 24 mm and a 50 mm, you may find the gap between them uncomfortably large, and that you need a more moderate wide angle—like a 35 mm—to fill it.

Maximum apertures

All three wide angle focal lengths are widely available, with a choice of different maximum apertures from most manufacturers. Although very fast 50 mm lenses—lenses with a wide maximum aperture—are available, it is much more difficult to make a wide angle lens that has a really large maximum aperture. There are some mass produced fast wide angles which are very good value for money, but they cannot match the slow lenses for quality. Unless you can afford the best, avoid fast wide angles.

50 mm lens

Down on the farm *By showing both the horizon and the ground at the feet of the photographer, a wide angle lens lends itself to dramatic images*

Church in the trees *A high wall in the churchyard prevented the photographer from backing away from the subject and, with a standard 50 mm lens, the tower top is lopped off. Using a 35 mm lens (right) cured this, and some photographers use this lens as standard. 28 mm and 24 mm lenses include even more of the surroundings*

The most common maximum aperture for a 35 mm lens is $f/2.8$, though there are many $f/2$ lenses. Like the $f/2.8$s, the $f/2$ lenses generally give good quality results, but they are physically much larger. There are a few lenses as fast as $f/1.4$ and even $f/1.2$ and this extra speed may be invaluable in low light conditions, but they do not give as good definition. At the other end of the range, there are a few $f/3.5$ lenses' available at 35 mm but these are usually at the cheaper end of the market, and have a rather conservative specification by today's standards.

The typical 28 mm lenses are, like 35 mms, usually $f/2.8$s, and there are many good quality $f/2.8$ lenses available at a reasonable price. There are several $f/2$ lenses in this focal length, but unless you pay extra for a good lens, performance may be disappointing. 28 mm lenses with a maximum aperture of $f/2.8$ also tend to be considerably more bulky and heavy.

Again, most 24 mm lenses have maximum apertures of $f/2.8$, though there are a few $f/2$ versions available. One manufacturer even makes an $f/1.4$, but this is both large and expensive.

As a general rule, then, any wide angle lens with a maximum aperture larger than $f/2.8$ tends to be more expensive, heavier, bulkier, and does not produce such good pictures as a lens with a more moderate specification. However, performance varies not only with the speed of a lens but also from manufacturer to manufacturer.

Lens faults

Although most wide angle lenses made by camera manufacturers are generally very good, some of the cheaper lenses made by independent manufacturers may have noticeable design faults. These

35 mm lens

28 mm lens

24 mm lens

faults fall into three main categories: 'barrel' distortion: uneven illumination: and focus fall-off.

Most wide angle lenses suffer 'barrel' distortion to some extent (see page 224) particularly with close-ups. With a few lenses, however, this can reach a level that you may not accept. Be careful not to mistake distortion produced by the lens with distortion that you see on some viewfinder systems, notably the Zenith E—viewfinder distortion will not appear on film. When checking for barrel distortion check the viewfinder first with a standard lens by focusing on a distant horizon. Then repeat the check with the wide angle in place. If the horizon bows up in the centre much more with the wide angle in place, it has barrel distortion.

Uneven illumination often occurs at full aperture and is partly cured by stopping down, but it cannot be totally eliminated. The poorer quality wide angles may suffer badly from this fault, but costly lenses are usually better.

Focus fall-off to the edges is another very frequent fault, as a wide-angle may tend to have curvature of field, an aberration which can mean a lens focused at one metre in the centre of the picture is focused at two metres at the corners. The best wide-angles have floating elements to correct this fault, which is normally worse at close focus distances and is absent, even in the cheapest lenses, at infinity. Floating elements make a lens very costly, and most lens-makers produce their lenses to give best results at around 3 metres. You cannot trust wide angle lenses to give a flat focus field for close-ups unless specially designed or corrected to do so—which most wide angles are not.

Making your choice

There are over 150 different lenses between 24 and 35 mm available, and it can be difficult to decide which to buy.

If you are buying a wide angle to use as a standard lens, then a 35 mm is most useful, but if you already have a 55 mm lens, a 28 mm is probably more suitable. A lens as short as 24 mm is only really necessary for very specific uses, or if you already have a more moderate wide angle, such as a 35 mm.

If you use colour negative film, and only produce enprints, then there is little to choose between different lenses. But if you enlarge or project your pictures, quality is an important factor. Remember that the lenses that have less ambitious specifications are likely to give better results than those that sound good to be true. For example, an $f/1.2$ compact 24 mm lens that weighs next to nothing should make you immediately suspicious. If you can afford to buy from a reputable manufacturer, then do so, because wide angle lenses are particularly difficult to design and manufacture. If you have a limited budget, avoid 24 mm lenses altogether and those with large maximum apertures—stick to an $f/2.8$ 35 mm or 28 mm.

TELEPHOTO LENSES

There is nothing more disappointing than developing a roll of film and then finding that the main subject occupies a tiny area in the middle of each picture. It is not therefore surprising to find that after buying an SLR and standard lens, many photographers buy a telephoto lens or a zoom, because a focal length longer than the standard 50 mm produces an enlarged image. This seems to bring the subject closer to the camera, and gives pictures of distant subjects more interest and impact.

Looking through a camera fitted with a telephoto lens is like looking through a telescope, and telephotos have many uses in the same kind of circumstances that demand a telescope or binoculars. For photographing sport or wildlife, or picking out faces in a crowd, telephoto lenses are essential.

There is, however, another use for a telephoto lens which is less obvious than the enlargement which it produces on the film. On some occasions, getting close enough to the subject is not really a problem—portraiture is an example—but there are advantages to be gained from moving back, and putting some space between the camera and subject.

Lens hoods *The contrast of many pictures can be improved by the use of a lens hood, but this is often not included in the basic price of a lens*

Long lens choice *All these lenses give an enlarged image on film. The smallest is little bigger than a standard lens*

In order to fill the frame with a head and shoulders portrait, it is necessary to stand within about 60 cm of your subject when using a standard lens. Fitting a 105 mm lens enables you to move back to double this distance, and still get an image that is just as big. With a 200 mm lens, there will be nearly two and a half metres between you and your subject for the same image size.

Moving back from a portrait sitter can improve your pictures in two ways. First, by changing the perspective of the portrait, the nose of your sitter does not look so large in comparison to the rest of the head. Secondly, the sitter will be more relaxed; it is not easy to wear a serene expression when there is a camera a short distance from your face.

For both these reasons, most tightly cropped portraits look a lot better when shot on a long focus lens, and if you expect to be doing a lot of portrait work, it is worth considering buying one, even if you will have little use for it in other types of photography.

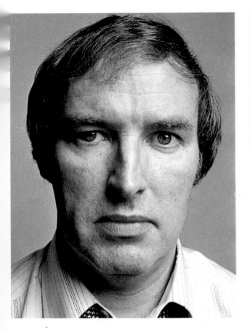

Portraits and telephotos *The picture on the left was taken with a standard lens, and looks distorted because the photographer was so close to his subject. Using a 85 mm lens enabled him to move back, so the perspective is more pleasant*

Telephoto or zoom ?

At first glance, it may seem that zoom lenses offer better value than fixed focal length telephotos. Zooms have a range of different focal lengths: some of them range from wide angle, through standard 50 mm, to telephoto. But fixed focal length telephotos have retained their popularity for a number of reasons. The most important of these is performance. For a photographer who demands top quality, zoom lenses are often inadequate. Few, if any, zooms are as good as the best lenses of fixed focal length.

Fixed focal length lenses are cheaper than zooms, too, because the optical construction of a fixed telephoto is much less complex and costly to assemble. This is especially noticeable at the cheaper end of the lens range—cheap telephoto lenses often produce acceptable results, whereas cheap zooms are frequently very poor indeed. If you do not have a lot of money to spend on a lens, a fixed telephoto will usually produce better results than a zoom lens of the same price.

Zoom lenses tend to be much heavier, and more bulky than fixed focal length telephotos and although a zoom might cover the range of several telephotos, many photographers find that they habitually use only part of the range of a zoom lens. If, for example, you own a 80-200 mm zoom lens and only use the lens at its 200 mm lens setting, it would be much less cumbersome to carry only a 200 mm fixed lens.

The final reason why many photographers prefer fixed telephoto lenses is the maximum aperture available—some telephoto lenses have one or two stops more than their zoom equivalent.

Steep steps *Telephoto lenses allow the photographer to move back, and this appears to compress depth and flatten out the subject*

Few 80 to 200 mm zooms have maximum apertures wider than *f*/3.5, but an *f*/2 135 mm lens is not unheard of. This means that photographs can be taken in dimmer light with the telephoto, or a faster shutter speed can be used.

Medium telephotos

The most popular focal lengths for telephotos range from about 85 mm to 200 mm. Anything shorter than 85 mm would not offer any significant advantage over a standard lens, and above 200 mm the weight and bulk of the lenses increases rapidly, and their maximum apertures are smaller. This means that, because of their bulk and weight, such lenses are hard to hold steady, and because their maximum aperture is smaller, a slower shutter speed is necessary. Consequently, lenses longer than 200 mm often need to be used on a tripod for best results. Such lenses are dealt with in a later article.

The most popular focal length in this range is the 135 mm lens. This is a useful all purpose telephoto which is usually

quite light and easy to hold, yet provides a convenient enlargement of about two and a half times compared to the image formed by a standard lens. It is perfectly suitable for portraits, and is not so long that you find yourself shouting instructions to your model, if you are taking portraits out of doors. For sport photography, or any picture where a larger image than normal is necessary, the 135 mm lens is a good compromise between lightness, compactness and high magnification.

Since there is so much demand for 135 mm lenses, economies of scale have brought prices down, and they are usually the cheapest telephoto in a manufacturer's range. The cheapest ones available cost no more than four rolls of process paid colour slide film.

Small telephotos

With the increasing popularity of compact 35 mm SLR cameras, there has been a swing towards smaller telephoto lenses, and this has frequently been achieved by simpler construction and so reduced size and weight. It has also meant that photographers have started buying shorter telephotos, such as the 85 mm and 105 mm focal lengths. These have long been popular among professional photographers, particularly photojournalists. They eliminate the unflattering perspective that close working with a standard lens can produce when taking portraits, and are often available in wide apertures—typical examples include an f/2 85 mm and an f/2.5 105 mm.

Some photographers consider these focal lengths too short to be useful, but they are compact, and produce an image which is double the size of that formed by a standard lens—quite ample under many circumstances.

200 mm lenses are at the upper end of the medium telephoto category. They produce a magnification of about four times compared to a standard lens, and are very popular for sporting events where the crowd is quite close to the competitors. They would be useful for tennis, but not so useful for soccer if the football players were at the other end of the pitch. Here, a much more powerful lens, such as a 400 or 600 mm, would be better for covering the distances involved.

A 200 mm lens forces the photographer to stand quite a way back from the subject compared to the camera-to-subject distance for a standard lens. This

has the effect of compressing apparent perspective. A line of cars, for instance, appears packed tightly together when photographed with a 200 mm lens.

This 'compression effect' is what a lot of photographers look for in a telephoto, but it can have drawbacks. It also compresses dust and haze in the atmosphere, and photographs of distant scenes with a 200 mm lens are often spoilt because of this. The atmosphere is only clear enough to get really crisp results over long distances on a few clear, frosty winter mornings. Over shorter distances, haze in the atmosphere is less of a problem, and will only intrude in very hot, dusty weather. A 200 mm lens should be useable over distances of up to 200 metres on most days of the year, without atmospheric mistiness becoming objectionable.

Camera shake

Just as a 200 mm lens magnifies the image four times compared to a standard lens, so also it emphasizes any camera shake by a factor of four. This means that faster shutter speeds are necessary if all camera movement is to be eliminated. A rough guide to the slowest shutter speed that can be used hand-held is that it is equal to the reciprocal of the focal length—a 50 mm lens can be hand-held at a 1/50 sec, (nearest common equivalent 1/60) a 135 mm at 1/135 sec (approximately 1/125) and a 200 mm lens at 1/200 (1/250). This can be very limiting, and may force the photographer to use a fairly wide aperture if a tripod is not available.

This may in turn lead to problems of depth of field—when a 200 mm lens is focused on a point ten metres away,

Standard 50 mm lens

85 mm telephoto lens

105 mm telephoto lens

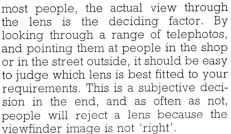

most people, the actual view through the lens is the deciding factor. By looking through a range of telephotos, and pointing them at people in the shop or in the street outside, it should be easy to judge which lens is best fitted to your requirements. This is a subjective decision in the end, and as often as not, people will reject a lens because the viewfinder image is not 'right'.

Choosing a lens

The choice of focal length is usually fairly easy, but the problems arise when it becomes necessary to choose between many similar brands. Many of the comments about choosing lenses in the section on zoom lenses (see pages 76 to 81) apply equally to telephotos, but there are a few other points to consider.

All long focus lenses should be used with a lens hood to give best results. The size of hood required will vary according to the focal length of the lens—a hood for a 200 mm lens will be unsuitable for a 105 mm lens. The better lenses of 135 mm and longer have built-in hoods, and those that do not often have hoods included in the price. A lens hood is an essential accessory and it may add a significant amount to the cost of a lens if purchased separately.

Similar comments apply to lens cases. Some people never use them, but other people consider them vital for keeping equipment clean. If you want one, make sure it will not add to the price, or at least take this into account when comparing prices of lenses.

Filters

If you use filters frequently, it is a good idea to take a close look at the size of filter needed for the lens you are buying. A number of manufacturers have standardized the filter size of their lenses as far as is practically possible, and all of the commonly used focal lengths from any one of these manufacturers take the same size.

Although adapter rings are available if filter sizes are not compatible, it is much simpler to buy a lens that will takes the same size filters as your standard lens.

A point which is often overlooked when buying a lens is the direction of movement of the focusing ring. Some lenses have a ring that must be turned clockwise to focus to infinity, others anticlockwise. It can be very dis-

A good case *If you do not have a camera bag, check that the lens price includes a case. This lens has a case and strap*

concerting to have to switch between the two systems, so check this, too, when you are looking at lenses.

Very cheap lenses often use a mechanism called a preset diaphragm to close the aperture from fully open to the working aperture. This eliminates all mechanical couplings between camera body and lens. Just before exposure, the photographer turns a ring, which looks identical to an automatic aperture setting ring. This closes the diaphragm, and comes to a halt at a point preset by the photographer. Although this system works perfectly well, it is very cumbersome and slow to use. Unless it is essential to buy the cheapest possible lens, it is worth spending the extra money and buying a lens with an automatic diaphragm.

The best lenses on the market are almost always expensive, and for most photographers it is necessary to strike a balance between cost and quality. Even if money is no object, compromise is sometimes necessary—the extra light gathering power of an *f*/2 lens may seem desirable, but has to be considered in the context of the extra weight of the lens when compared with an *f*/3.5 of the same focal length. Only the user of a lens can decide exactly what specification he or she requires, and how much such a lens is worth.

Roofs and houses *Because a long focus lens includes less of the subject, it is possible to crop really tightly for striking, dramatic compositions*

the depth of field is only 60 cm at an aperture of *f*/4.

This vicious circle—fast shutter speed needed to eliminate camera shake, so wider aperture selected, which in turn means inadequate depth of field—is shared by all telephoto lenses, not just the 200 mm. But the problems become more pronounced as focal length increases. The only real solution is to use either a tripod or a faster film.

The focal length of lens that will be most suitable for each individual photographer will largely be dictated by the type of photography for which he or she anticipates the lens will be used. For

135 mm telephoto lens

200 mm telephoto lens

Silver cowls *This series of pictures shows the field of view through the most popular telephoto lenses. All the pictures are printed from the whole of the 35 mm frame, so that it is possible to make a size comparison between them. Perhaps surprisingly, the 85 mm lens, which many photographers dismiss as being too short for most purposes, actually produces a very useful degree of magnification. The longest lens, the 200 mm, allowed the photographer to emphasize a small area of the subject*

SUPER-TELEPHOTOS

Long telephoto lenses, 200 mm and above, used to be thought of as exclusively specialist items, giving the professional an almost unfair advantage in wildlife and sports photography. But as the relative cost of photographic equipment comes down, more and more of these lenses are falling within reach of the amateur. While the really long lenses —over 600 mm—are still phenomenally expensive, some of the cheaper 300 to 400 mm lenses cost little more than a good standard lens.

Long telephotos in the 200 to 500 mm range are surprisingly useful for general photography. They are by no means restricted to the traditional telephoto roles of wildlife and sport. Their main value is in bringing subjects, both near and distant, closer, allowing you to isolate, say, small areas of the landscape or details on the side of a building. But they can be useful in other ways.

Most long telephotos, for instance, have extremely limited depth of field. This is ideal for isolating middle distance

Long lenses *Compared with a 350 mm mirror lens (right foreground) telephoto lenses are long and bulky*

subjects against an out of focus background—standard lenses can only do this for close subjects. This is one of the attractions for the sports photographer who wants to pick out a footballer against a crowd or the wildlife photographer shooting a bird against foliage. But it can be useful in many other types of photography. Another attraction is the way telephotos seem to compress distance, so that a city street appears full of cars, people and lampposts all jostling one another.

The very long focal lengths—1000 mm and longer—have more specialized uses: for photographing very shy wildlife, climbers on a distant rock face, or astronomical bodies, for example. Their use for general photography—mainly because of their extreme size and cost—is rather limited.

Long lenses are of two principle types: telephoto lenses and mirrors (the latter are covered in the next section). By far the majority are telephoto—few of the systems manufacturers market more than a couple of mirror lenses.

Although there are fewer long than medium telephotos on the market, there is still a wide range to choose from—Nikon alone make more than ten. The widest choice is at the 200 mm and 300 mm lengths. Further up the range—400 mm and above, the *super-telephoto* bracket—choice is restricted. There is quite a range of 1000 mm lenses but there are only a few as long as 2000 mm. Lenses longer than 2000 mm are very rare indeed, though 5200 mm lenses were made as recently as 1980 by Canon.

Your choice of telephoto depends upon the way you intend to use the lens and upon the price. Clearly, the main decision is what focal length to buy (see panel). But there are also a number of other factors to bear in mind.

Aperture
One of the main problems with long telephotos is the small subject area that they take in and this **severely** reduces the amount of light reaching the film. So long lenses inevitably have a slower effective speed than shorter lenses. As the focal length (and thus magnification) increases, so the speed of the lens decreases. Whereas a typical medium telephoto might have a maximum aperture of $f/3$, a 300 mm lens is as slow as $f/4$ and a 400 mm only $f/8$.

Since this slow speed considerably reduces the usability of long lenses in poor light, many manufacturers produce lenses designed to give a larger maximum aperture. Canon, for instance, make an $f/2.8$ 400 mm lens. The disadvantage is that in order to get the extra speed, these fast lenses incorporate extremely large front elements. This not only puts up the cost very considerably, but also the weight. While the $f/4$ 300 mm Canon weighs under one kilogram, the $f/2.8$ weighs 2.3 kg. Longer fast lenses are even more massive.

Even if you can afford the extra cost of a fast lens, the extra weight may also restrict the lens' usability more than the lack of speed on a slower lens. Up to 500 mm, a slowish telephoto is easy to carry around in a camera bag. Fast lenses tend to severely restrict your mobility.

At the other end of the aperture scale, minimum apertures on long telephotos tend to be smaller than on shorter lenses—at least $f/22$ or $f/32$. Some 1200 mm lenses stop down to $f/64$. Long lenses can be stopped down further than normal lenses because the effects of diffraction play a smaller part in their optical set-up. With the restricted depth of field of long lenses, this facility for stopping down (whch increases depth of field) is very useful so, faced with two lenses that are otherwise equal, choose the one with the smaller minimum aperture.

Aperture control mechanisms also vary from lens to lens. Although, most modern lenses, including telephotos, have automatic diaphragms that stop down to the set aperture as you press the shutter, a few long telephotos still have manual or *preset* aperture control. In these, you must close the iris **manually**.

Manual lenses have the disadvantages that either shots can be missed in the time it takes to close the iris, or they can be overexposed if you forget to stop down after focusing at full aperture. But these are offset by the cheapness of the system—you can add such a lens to your outfit for only a small outlay, even if you do not use it much. The optical quality of these cheap lenses can be surprisingly good, as they are comparatively easy to make. If you are mainly interested in landscape work, where speed is not essential, a preset lens is ideal. For sports or wildlife work, however, where the time taken to stop down a preset lens could mean a missed shot, an automatic diaphragm is essential.

Comparative dimensions *Two lenses, each of 400 mm f/5.6, can differ greatly in appearance, due to such factors as hood design, focusing mechanism and the arrangement of internal components*

Focusing
Focusing mechanisms are particularly important in telephoto lenses because of the narrow depth of field and the large movement. Focusing is usually carried out in the conventional way, by turning the focusing ring on the lens barrel. But there are two types of focusing mechanisms. In some lenses, the optical assembly is racked out and the front of the lens moves, just as with standard length lenses. Other lenses, however, at both ends of the range, are *internal focusing,* in which the overall length of the lens remains the same while

200 mm lens *Magnification increases with focal length, but image area is reduced*

300 mm lens *A smaller area of the object is framed, shot from the same distance*

400 mm lens *The extreme length of these lenses makes camera shake very likely*

1000 mm lens *The powerful magnification of a super-telephoto can clearly be seen*

elements within the lens are shifted.

Internal focusing lenses usually require less turning of the barrel for a given change of focus—this is important because standard telephotos have very long focusing movements and limited depth of field—and tend not to adjust their focus position when being carried around on the camera, as standard focus lenses do. This means that you can focus very quickly and even preset the focus so that you can simply point and shoot if necessary. Furthermore, the front ele-ment always stays in the same orientation, which means that you do not need to readjust polarizers or graduated filters after focusing. The simple barrel also makes the internal focusing lens easier to handle.

The disadvantage of internal focusing is that it is generally more difficult to make than standard focusing. Most of the lenses with internal focusing are therefore comparatively expensive. Although there are a number of comparatively cheap internal focusing telephotos, some may well have sacrificed optical quality. So it is probably safer to stick to standard focusing if you are buying a low priced lens. Some of the better lenses using standard focusing movements have a detachable focusing handle that fits on the focusing ring and makes focusing almost as easy as with internal focusing. Often this handle has two screw-in positions for rapid focusing. Nikon make a separate *focusing unit* of this type which will accept a range of super-telephoto heads.

A feature worth looking for, whether you buy a standard or internal focusing lens, is a *focus lock*. This is not a standard feature but, nevertheless, one which can prove very valuable. It allows you to preset a focus on the lens but still alter the focusing up to infinity, and simply snap back to the preset focus whenever you need it. This means that you could, for instance, preset the focus on a bend at a motor race, change focus for a few shots of the cars as they come into the bend and then snap to the preset when they reach the bend.

Alternatively, if rapid focusing is important, you could buy a Novoflex lens equipped with a Rapid Follow Focus (RFF) attachment. The RFF attachment is basically a pistol-grip carriage that fits the lens and allows you to focus simply by squeezing the spring-loaded grip. These lenses do not have helical focusing gear and so are very simple and relatively inexpensive. They can be adapted to fit most 35 mm SLRs and have proved popular with sports photographers.

Minimum focusing distances vary greatly. For example, most 300 mm lenses can focus down to about 3.5 m but some models can focus as close as 1.4 m, at which point the subject is only 3.3 times its image size on film.

This point is often overlooked when choosing a lens, but it can contribute greatly to the usefulness of a lens. A close-focusing telephoto lens is ideal for photographing, say, a butterfly that might be unwilling to settle on a flower if you are nearby. If you are keen on wildlife work, it is worth checking on the closest focus distance and what this will include in the frame, before committing yourself to a particular lens. You can estimate how wide its field of view will be at close distances by using a shorter lens at those distances. A 400 mm lens has one third of the field of a standard

lens, for instance, so you can estimate in the viewfinder roughly what the field of view of the 400 will be at the closest focusing distance. Bear in mind that you can use extension tubes to reduce the closest focusing distance but optical quality is often poor and you may run into problems with the very restricted depth of field.

Size and balance

Long telephotos are large and heavy, but there is a trend to making them smaller. However, in order to achieve compactness, some manufacturers have sacrificed optical quality in their cheaper models. In particular, cheap lenses suffer from *pincushion* distortion (see page 226) and, if you are buying a cheap compact telephoto, it is worth checking for this. With the lens on the camera, aim the camera at a straight vertical edge so that it is in the centre of the viewfinder. Then slowly pan the camera so that the edge moves across the viewfinder. If the lens suffers from pincushion distortion, the edge will bow in at the middle as it comes near the edge of the frame. Repeat this check with another lens to ensure the viewfinder is not at fault.

Although compactness is clearly desirable, a heavy lens need not be unmanageable if it is properly balanced. Remember, though, that it is not the lens itself that must be balanced but the lens–camera combination. Clearly, with very big lenses, the combination's point of balance is underneath the lens rather than the camera. so many lenses are fitted with tripod sockets.

Most of the more expensive lenses

ave the tripod bush attached to a collar
a the middle of the barrel. This collar
an be rotated so that you can shoot with
he camera at any angle between the
orizontal and vertical formats, without
emoving the camera from the tripod.
Iost tripod collars only rotate through
0° and this may prevent you from
etting the horizon square if you cannot
evel your tripod properly.

The cheaper lenses tend to have fixed
ripod sockets: one underneath and one
on the side. This means you must remove
the unit from the tripod to change the
format. It also means that you cannot
shoot at angles outside the 90° plane.

Threads and mounts

Many long telephotos have threads on
the front for screw-in filters, but filter
diameters tend to be large—72 mm is
common—and filters to match are fairly
expensive. So the larger lenses have a
slot towards the rear of the lens which
accepts smaller, less expensive un-
threaded Series VI filters. It is possible,
though, to use square filters on the front
of most long telephotos.

Lenses come in a diversity of mounts
and usually a lens will fit only one make
of camera. However, most of the
independent manufacturers' telephoto
lenses are geared to take the Tamron
Adaptall connectors which allow them to
be fitted into several different types of
SLR camera systems.

Image quality *Shots
taken out of doors on a
windy, hazy day by a
budget (left) and a mid
range (far left) 400 mm
lens show only subtle
differences in quality*

Typical telephotos
*are usually of the
external focusing type,
in which the physical
length of the lens varies
as the barrel is rotated.
A lens that employs
internal focusing
(below centre) has
several advantages,
including compactness,
a smooth action and a
constant length*

MIRROR LENSES

It you want a lens with a very long focal length, but are put off by the sheer size and cost of a telephoto, it may be worth considering a mirror lens. By 'folding' light with mirrors, these lenses give the same focal length as a telephoto in a much shorter barrel. And because they use mirrors rather than bulky, precision ground glass refracting elements, they tend to be lighter and cheaper.

There are a number of variations in design, but all modern mirror lenses are *catadioptric*—that is, they include a number of glass refracting elements as

Compactness and low cost are the main advantages of modern mirror lenses. The large lens, here, is a reflecting telescope—these work well as 'mirror' lenses. Long and short The difference in length of a 400 mm telephoto and a 400 mm mirror lens is very significant

ell as mirrors. And as a result they are often referred to as 'cats'. Japanese manufacturers have tended to concentrate on the Mangin mirror type, using rear silvered glass elements. This is ideal for very compact, close focusing lenses. European manufacturers such as Zeiss, on the other hand, concentrate more on lenses working on the Bouwers-Maksutov principle, using a large meniscus correcting element at the front. These cannot be made nearly as cheaply, but give better results (see page 222).

Although the range is now beginning to expand, particularly at the cheaper end of the market, the choice of mirror lenses remains limited compared with telephotos. At present, there are fewer than 50 different mirror lenses on the market, and these are restricted to a few focal lengths. Mirror lenses tend to be made only at focal lengths of 300, 500, 1000 and 2000 mm. There are exceptions (such as the Sunagor range), but if you want an intermediate focal length—400 mm, say,—you will probably have to buy a telephoto Indeed, only at 500 mm is there a wide range to choose from.

Nevertheless, the choice of alternative focal lengths is quite adequate for most people, and the compactness and low cost of mirror lenses may more than make up for the lack of choice.

Weight and cost savings
The savings in size and cost vary both with the focal length; and from manufacturer to manufacturer. Many of the independents have concentrated largely on the 300 and 500 mm lengths and aimed to produce extremely small, low cost lenses. A 300 mm mirror lens from one of the independents is only a little larger than a typical standard lens and is much the same price. The Ohnar 300 mm mirror, for instance, is just 67 mm long and 70 mm in diameter. Even a lightweight telephoto typically weighs twice as much and is two or three times as long.

The systems manufacturers have adopted a slightly different policy and none produce a 300 mm. Even their 500 mm lenses are not usually as small as the independents'. The Nikon 500 mm mirror, for instance, at one kilogram weighs almost twice as much as some of the cheaper mirrors. However, this extra

weight (and cost) is usually a reflection of better quality, and the savings in weight and cost over comparable telephotos is still considerable. Further up the range (1000 mm and longer), the savings can be even more significant. A 1000 mm mirror, for instance, is relatively easy to carry around, typically only 250 mm long and weighing under two kilograms: a 1000 mm telephoto may be three times as long and weigh twice as much. Again, such mirrors tend to cost half as much as a comparable telephoto.

Clearly then, if your only concern is compactness and cost, mirrors win out over telephotos at all focal lengths. However, mirror lenses have a number of other characteristics that may, ultimately, prove to be significant drawbacks.

Aperture
One of the most obvious differences between mirror lenses and telephotos in use is the mirror's lack of an aperture diaphragm. This means that the f-number is fixed by the diameter of the front element. Only one very expensive specialist mirror lens has an aperture diaphragm. The size of the fixed f-

number varies with the focal length. 300 mm mirrors are often *f*/5.6, while 500 mm mirrors are usually *f*/8 and 1000 mm mirrors *f*/11. Zeiss make a pair of faster lenses—a 500 mm *f*/4.5 and a 1000 mm *f*/5.6—but these are incredibly expensive, the 1000 mm costing more than a luxury sports car.

Because of the fixed aperture, exposure must be controlled largely by varying the shutter speed. While shutter priority cameras will still work automatically with a mirror lens fitted, aperture priority cameras must be operated manually. Normally, you have no choice over shutter speed: it is dictated by the lighting conditions. You can alter exposure by using neutral density filters to reduce the effective aperture. Most mirror lenses come with a pair of neutral density filters, but if they are not supplied, ND filters for a lens which only accepts giant front-mounted filters may almost cancel the saving.

The fixed aperture is a significant disadvantage in many respects. Most importantly, perhaps, mirrors are very slow lenses. Indeed, the central obstruction blocks out some of the light passing through the lens and means that the effective aperture is actually up to a full stop less than the nominal rating.

This reduces the usability of the lens significantly. With a nominal aperture of *f*/8 and an effective aperture of *f*/11, a 500 mm mirror must be used with a fairly slow shutter speed in all but the brightest conditions. This means that you will very rarely be able to hand hold a 500 mm mirror—even in bright sunshine you need fast 400 ASA (ISO) film to allow the 1/1000 second necessary for hand holding. The mirror's portability becomes less important when you have to carry a full-size tripod around all the time to support it properly.

The slow speed of the mirror also means that the focusing screen is very dim. Not only will you have difficulty seeing the subject clearly, particularly with the very long lenses, but you will not be able to use the microprism or split image for focusing, since most black out at apertures of less than *f*/5.6. So unless you can fit a ground glass focusing screen to your camera you may find it quite difficult to focus a long mirror lens.

Fixed aperture also means problems with depth of field. On long lenses, depth of field is restricted anyway, but with a mirror lens you cannot stop down to give the maximum possible depth. Indeed, even at the same *f*-stop, a mirror lens has less depth of field than a telephoto. This is because the central obstruction results in a disc of confusion (see page 208) which is actually a ring. Unfortunately, the eye can detect an out of focus ring easier than it can a disc.

A number of mirror lenses are now being marketed with special close focusing ability. Indeed most mirror lenses can focus closer than a comparable telephoto. The 400 mm Sigma, for instance, focuses down to as close as two metres to frame an area only 0.3 metres wide. But at this distance, the depth of field is extremely limited—probably little more than 3 mm—so you will only rarely be able to take advantage of this close focusing ability. The only advantage of the mirror's limited depth of field is that it compensates, to a small degree, for the darkness of the image when focusing. The image 'snaps' in and out of focus more noticeably.

Optics

Optically, the big advantage of mirror lenses is their freedom from chromatic and spherical aberration (see page 226). Long telephotos must incorporate bulky and expensive correcting elements. Unfortunately, this advantage is outweighed in other respects.

First of all, because of the ring-like disc of confusion, resolution is limited. Second, high flare level and low contrast problems in all long lenses, are particularly marked in mirror lenses. And third, mirror lens images suffer from a hot spot in the middle whereas with most telephotos illumination is even.

With good quality mirror lenses, the quality of results is usually acceptable though not as good as with a good telephoto.

Telescope mirrors

A number of mirror lenses on the market are made not by lens manufacturers but by telescope makers. The Schmidt Cassegrain mirror lens design was originally intended for astronomical use and the design is very popular as a comparatively portable telescope. The demand for such telescopes is quite high, so mass production has brought costs down.

An image which is to be viewed using an eyepiece at high power must be of very high quality, and a good telescope is more than adequate for photography. In addition, you can attach a wide range of purpose designed accessories to allow you to use the telescope by day or by night. The telescopes invariably use T2 mounts which allow virtually any make of camera to be used.

Conclusions

Mirror lenses of up to 500 mm focal length have applications in everyday photography, and are compact enough to be carried around when one might leave the equivalent refracting lens at home, though the mirror lens quality is noticeably worse.

Above 500 mm, mirror lenses come into their own, but the difficulty of using them tends to make them worthwhile only if you have a specific use in mind. However, as prices steadily drop many more amateurs may find a use for them.

Extra long focus *The 2000 mm Celestron 8 is a relatively inexpensive astronomical telescope through which details of the moon and planets or even distant nebulae can be viewed with outstanding clarity and at reasonable magnification. Fitted to a 35 mm SLR via a T-adapter and an inverter, to erect the image, such a set-up can be used for astrononomical as well as terrestrial subjects, such as wildlife, sports and architectural details*

Typical focal lengths *Mirror lenses are available most commonly in focal lengths of 300, 500, 1000 and 2000 mm. The greatest choice is offered in 500 mm, whereas there are remarkably few in intermediate focal lengths, such as 400 mm. The shots from left to right were taken from the same rooftop location on a hot, hazy day, using a 350 mm mirror lens and telescopes of 750, 1000, 1250 and 2000 mm focal length. For all these shots the use of a tripod was essential as even locating the subject is difficult when hand-holding the bigger models. The 2000 mm telescope gave fair results, despite unavoidable vibration*

ZOOM LENSES

The zoom is now the most popular additional lens for a 35 mm single lens reflex (SLR) camera. Until recently, people tended to buy a fixed telephoto lens—but now, zooms account for over half of lens sales.

The *idea* of zoom could hardly be more attractive. Buy just one lens, at possibly no more than the price of a single fixed lens, and you have at your command a whole range of lenses of widely varied focal lengths—that is, giving different image sizes.

What is more, the 200 mm lens's focal length is continuously variable. By a quick adjustment of the ring on the lens barrel, you can magnify the subject in the viewfinder to the exact size required —within the zoom's range.

And all this is possible without the inconvenience of carrying around

several lenses, or of changing lenses during picture-taking. A zoom can free you, in fact, to concentrate on more important things like the subject in front of your camera.

Clearly a zoom can expand your photographic horizons. But on close consideration, how often would you use the lens? Would your photography really be improved by the continuously variable focal length? Would you really exploit its advantages to the full? And how does one set about deciding what to buy from the many ranges of focal length available?

Categories of zoom

For the 35 mm camera user, the choice of a zoom lens used to be restricted to one with a focal length adjustable from about 80 to 150 or 200 mm—generally de-

scribed as a telephoto zoom. Today, this is no longer true.

Manufacturers are putting out increasing numbers of wide-angle zooms, with a typical range of 21 to 35 mm. And the medium-range, 'all-purpose' zoom, usually covering focal lengths from 35 to 80 mm, is also growing in popularity.

There is no set rule for the exact range of focal lengths offered in each category. Zooms of the telephoto type cover a particularly wide range. There are 50–135 mm, 90–200 mm, 70–230 mm, 75–150 mm, even 135–600 mm zooms—and one manufacturer offers a staggering 360–1200 mm model. But it is fair to say that

Rising to the occasion *Without a zoom this shot would have been missed: the fox disappeared too quickly for a change from a standard to long-focus lens*

he most popular telephoto zoom, usually considered the most versatile and manageable, remains the 80–200 mm. Indeed, this is now the most popular second lens for 35 mm SLR users.

Wide-angle zooms generally cover two zones of focal length: 24–35 mm and 28–50 mm. The medium range is more varied again, with combinations such as 35–70 mm, 40–80 mm, and 28–80 mm.

What the zoom can do

Most people would consider a zoom lens's greatest benefit to be that it allows you to fill the picture area over a considerable range of distances without having to change the camera position. At a football match, for example, you can

Wide-angle zoom
The two extremes of the 28-50 mm zoom show how different pictures of the same subject can be taken from the same viewpoint, This type of zoom comes into its own for pictures of buildings and in built-up places generally. The 50 mm setting gives, in effect, a standard lens

Zoom construction *The cutaway shows the considerable number of glass lens elements required. The central groups are usually the moving parts*

follow the play from a single position, ranging from shots showing the distribution of the players over the field to moderate close-ups of incidents.

Another way to use a zoom lens, which applies particularly to the medium range types, is to help you compose your shots in the viewfinder. Most pictures need a small amount of trimming along all or some of their edges, either for added impact or for balancing the composition. If you have your own darkroom, you can do this 'cropping' as a matter of course under the enlarger. With a zoom, you can perfect composition on-the-spot.

Another major feature of the zoom lens is its constant focus. This means that you can focus with the lens at its maximum telephoto setting, then zoom to a wider setting while the image remains sharp.

However, you should be aware that although the constant focus works perfectly on most good zoom lenses, there is sometimes a small change in focus that has to be corrected after zooming. Generally, the smaller the range of focal lengths offered by a zoom, the better it is likely to hold its focus. One type of zoom, known as the varifocus, needs to be refocused every time its focal length is adjusted.

Tennis *A classic use of the zoom: the camera position is fixed, but the image size can be adjusted to fill the frame*

The drawbacks

The greatest drawback is the zoom's poor light grasp for its size. A photographer accustomed to focusing on the bright image given by a standard lens working at, say, *f*/1.7, will be horrified at the low image brightness of a zoom whose maximum aperture is a mere *f*/3.5 or *f*/4. Not only is the image dimmer, but focusing is more difficult as the *f*-number increases. A few zooms, usually those with short focal lengths, do open up to *f*/2.8, but these are particularly bulky.

Added to this is the problem of increased light absorption. The amount of glass used in the complicated construction of a zoom absorbs and scatters light. It is a common experience for zoom users to find that when light is poor, the zoom makes picture taking impossible. Changing to a fixed lens, they find they can easily make a correct exposure at the same aperture; indeed, they may even be able to stop down.

Bulk is the second big snag. To achieve a successful zoom, the manufacturer has to use as many as 15, or even more, glass lens elements. This makes the zoom generally longer and heavier than an equivalent fixed focal length lens.

Most appreciate that in certain cases this is not a particular disadvantage because in any case the zoom is doing the job of two or possibly more lenses which would have to be carried about in its place. And it has to be said that some zooms have reached a remarkably compact standard of construction. But again the most useful zoom lenses, with a wide range of focal lengths and comparatively wide maximum apertures, are also the heaviest. They will probably unbalance the camera, making it impossible to carry comfortably on the neck strap, and will certainly rule out the use of your ever-ready camera case. The wide-angle, or medium-range zoom, will not, under any circumstances, be as compact as a standard or wide-angle fixed focal length lens.

You will hear conflicting reports about the image quality given by zoom lenses. But it is fair to say that zoom lens performance has not yet reached the level of other, fixed focal length lens types, and probably never will. On the other hand, it is improving all the time, and a zoom of reputable make will perform acceptably for all but the most demanding photographers—provided it is used within its limitations, that is, not at full aperture, and, when on a long focal length setting, with a fast enough shutter speed to 'freeze' the resulting exaggerated effects of camera shake.

Sharpness, however, is only part of the story when it comes to lens performance. Such things as image contrast, distortion, vignetting (fall-off of light towards the edges) and lens flare are also important. In each case, the complexity of a zoom counts against it.

Types of zoom

Zoom lenses can be divided into two basic types—the *one-touch* and the *two-touch*—according to how the movement of the lens elements is controlled. You will often see a third type—the *macro zoom*—advertised, which can also be used for close-up photography.

The two-touch or two-ring zoom has separate control rings around the lens barrel. Turning one adjusts the focus in the same way as on a normal lens. Turning the other ring zooms the focal length of the lens in and out.

With two-touch systems, operation is usually very smooth and you can easily make fine adjustments to the focal length to improve framing. But with two separate control rings your hand must switch from one to the other. This takes time and you could miss your picture.

With the one-touch system, however, one ring controls both zoom and focusing. Twisting the ring, in the normal way, controls the focus, while the lens is zoomed simply by sliding the ring up and down the barrel. Because the zoom action is like a trombone slide the one-touch zoom is often referred to as the *trombone* type.

Trombone type zooms can certainly be operated much more quickly than two-touch zooms and for any situation where rapid action is called for they are ideal. For sports photography, or even just tracking boisterous children around the garden, the speed with which the image can be framed and focused with a one-touch zoom is invaluable.

Unfortunately, it is difficult to make fine adjustments to focusing quickly, especially at maximum focal length. Although this is not a big disadvantage for most photographers, you will rarely find one-touch zooms on cine cameras for this reason. Another snag is that it may be difficult to keep the image in

One-touch zoom *The same ring is used for both zooming and focusing. Sliding it changes the focal length of the lens*

One-touch focus *Turning the ring on a one touch zoom brings the lens into sharp focus as on a conventional lens*

Two-touch zoom *The ring nearest to the camera changes the focal length of the lens*

Zoom effect *Changing a zoom's focal length during an exposure gives a dramatic impression*

conjunction with your standard lens, or a special supplementary lens.

If you wish to buy a macro zoom, a useful test is to see how close to an object you can focus. This will give you some idea of its macro capabilities. Some lenses will focus no closer than three metres and even with a long focal length the image on the negative is very small. Go for a lens which gives you the biggest image you are likely to want.

Lens faults with zooms

Very much more glass is used in the construction of a zoom lens than in a fixed focus lens and this literally magnifies the standard faults you find in any lens. The moving elements do, however,

Macro markings *Macro zooms are engraved with reproduction ratios (in orange here) as well as zoom, focusing and aperture scales*

create their own special problems which, in a quality zoom lens, should have been corrected by the lens designer.

A fairly common problem with some of the simpler and cheaper zoom lens constructions is a fault called vignetting —partial darkening of the image at the frame corners. Other zoom lens designs get round this by employing large lenses that seem unusually large for the maximum apertures that are offered. Few zoom lenses approach anywhere near the speed offered by comparable lenses of fixed focal length.

With a test, which should take in a range of apertures and the various focal lengths of the zoom lens, it may also be possible to detect signs of image distortion. You can do this by checking the trueness of horizontal and vertical lines at the very edges of the photograph. Lines at the edges bowing towards the centre of the picture indicate that the lens is suffering from *pincushion distortion.* If the lines bow outwards, this is described as *barrel distortion.* Evidence of distortion suggests a lens 'fault' only if the test camera faces the test subject absolutely square-on.

precise focus as you zoom, but for many people the advantages outweigh the disadvantages.

Some people suggest that one-touch zooms are so easy to use that photographers become lazy, and do not give enough thought to the choice of the correct focal length, but this is really only a matter of opinion. In the end, it may be the convenience and feel of the lens that tips the balance of whether you like it or not one way or the other.

Two-touch focus *The ring nearest to the front of the lens is used to bring it into focus in the usual way*

Macro zoom

If you wish to do a lot of close-up work, you may be tempted by the idea of a macro zoom.

The word 'macro' comes from the Greek 'makros', meaning 'long' and a macro lens is a lens designed to be used for extremely close-up work. Since at very close range, the image on the negative may be almost as large, if not larger, than life, the capabilities of macro lenses are often described in terms of the ratio between the actual size of the image on the negative and the size of the real thing.

The term 'macro' lens is fairly loosely applied, and although most macros produce an image on the negative about a quarter of life size (a ratio of 1 : 4), macros can give an image/life ratio of anything from 1 : 10 to 10 : 1. If the image is any bigger than ten times life size (a ratio of greater than 10 : 1), the lens ceases to be a macro and becomes a micro lens.

Only one or two macro zooms are designed specifically for close-up work ; most are standard zooms with an extra macro facility. Generally speaking, the overall image quality of a zoom lens fitted with macro is not as good as that of a plain zoom lens. If you intend to do a lot of close-up work, it is probably better to buy either extension tubes to work in

Distortion may vary from the pincushion pattern to the barrel shape during the course of the zoom range and it is not unusual for some of the older, and the newer but cheaper, designs to exhibit both. Unless either is particularly severe (a suggestion of worse lens faults too) there is no point worrying too much about it. With most modern zoom lens designs, you may not even notice the existence of distortion.

All lenses have their own image-forming characteristics and these are particularly significant if you do much colour work. A film test using your usual materials is essential if you want to match the fine nuances of colour reproduction which you get from your exist-ing lenses. Zoom lenses may be particularly difficult to match in this way, even if you do buy a lens from the same manufacturer.

Feel

A lens must feel 'right' if you are to use it comfortably and confidently. Before you buy, attach it to a camera and assess the feel. Some people prefer one-touch zooms, for instance, simply because they like the feel of the big focusing ring.

With some cheaper zoom lenses, the zooming and focusing action might feel uneven and gritty. Pay no attention to a salesman who might tell you that the lens 'has to wear in'—it will not, it will simply wear out.

Equally important are balance and weight. Few zooms can really be described as compact—some cine camera zooms are over 1 m long—but you must be sure that you can hold the lens still at relatively slow shutter speeds.

When you are in the shop, try the lens for length and weight and see how easy it is to handle. Attach the lens to your camera and try resting the barrel on your raised forearm while gripping the camera with your other hand. Then press the shutter with the index finger of the hand holding the camera. If the shutter is set at fairly slow speeds—1/60 and 1/30 second—you will soon discover how much the end of the lens barrel can wave up and down visibly.

Testing a lens before buying

The best way to buy a zoom, or any other kind of lens, is to take photographs with it. This means first narrowing down your choice to just a few lenses—preferably no more than three—and fitting them to your camera.

Most dealers will allow you to do this if the lenses are readily available, as long as you do not expect to take each one beyond the doorway of the shop in order to test it.

Choose a time when the shop isn't busy, and use a roll of slow colour transparency film like Ektachrome 64. Many cities have laboratories that will process these films in an hour or two (look in Yellow Pages) so you can see the pictures quickly. Unless you have plenty of time, do not use Kodachrome film which takes a rather long time for processing. Try to use a tripod, but if this is not practical, use a fast speed such as 1/250 second.

You will need to test a lens for four features: sharpness and contrast at normal distances, distortion (which is whether or not straight lines in the subject appear straight on the film), vignetting and close-up performance.

Lens testing *Take pictures of lettering from a distance to compare the performance of a number of lenses. The picture on the right shows the set-up that was used for these tests. The chart was photographed at the centre and edge of the picture, with a 135 mm lens and a 70-150 mm zoom at 70 mm and 150 mm*

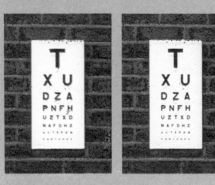

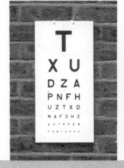
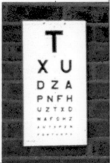

The 135 mm lens gave good quality results with the chart at the centre (left) and edge (right)

At 70 mm, the zoom lens gave quite a sharp image in the centre (left) but edge performance was much worse (right)

At 150 mm, the edge (right) was worse than the centre (left). Note vignetting and pincushion distortion (above)

On some zoom lenses, the maximum possible aperture is less at full focal length and on a dull day you may have to use a very slow shutter speed to compensate. If the lens is too heavy or too long to hold steady under these conditions, its usability will be restricted.

Mounts and features

The restrictions imposed by a particular camera mount on the choice of lenses available in that fitting can be great, and usually the popularity of that particular mount and the length of time it has been on the market are decisive factors. The popular ('universal') screw mount is exactly this and there is a great choice of zoom lenses for this.

The recent swing towards bayonet-type lens mounts has had the effect of restricting the choice of some of the newer and more sophisticated zoom lenses.

Start your selection by deciding what focal length range you would like your zoom lens to cover. Base this on your particular photographic requirements. Look then for the choice of lenses available in your camera fitting.

The list will probably contain lenses which have a fixed mount, and others which have an interchangeable mount or adapter. Fixed mounts are usually slightly cheaper, but you have to change the lens if you ever change the camera. With an interchangeable mount, how-

ever, you can choose to keep the lens when you buy a camera with a different mount, simply buying the appropriate adapter instead. Interchangeable mount lenses are now unfortunately not widely available.

Wide maximum apertures aid focusing and viewing considerably but, in comparison with lenses of fixed focal length, you pay heavily in terms of the additional size of the lens, its cost, and perhaps lowered standards of performance. By ordinary lens standards, however, there is no such thing as a wide-aperture zoom lens, as attractive as this would be for 'available light' photography. Normal maximum apertures start at $f/3.5$.

Sharpness and contrast

How 'good' a lens seems to be is a combination of these two qualities, and it is not really very helpful to separate them, except for very special purposes like document copying. The best object to photograph is probably fine lettering, such as a sign in a shop window, or a street poster. This first test should be carried out on a distant subject, which means, for most lenses, something at least ten metres away. In the test shown here, an optician's eye test chart was used because it is printed with a wide range of type sizes.

You will need to take photographs of the subject at the centre of the picture and at the edges, where the quality is generally poorer. It is also a good idea to test it both at the widest aperture (lowest f-number) and at some moderate aperture like $f/8$. When testing a zoom, you should ideally make tests at the shortest focal length, the longest focal length, and midway through the range. If you go through all the combinations of these three, you will have taken twelve pictures, so it is crucial to keep an

accurate record of what you do.

Distortion

This is much easier to test than sharpness, because it does not change when you stop the lens down, and is most pronounced at the edges of the picture. Turn the camera so that the long side of the frame is vertical, and line up the picture so that a vertical object, such as a lamp post is just within the frame. When testing a zoom lens, take pictures at the longest and shortest focal lengths and at one in between if possible. If you can arrange to include the vertical in your sharpness test, you will be able to save on film.

Vignetting

To test for vignetting, you will need a perfectly evenly illuminated subject. An overcast or uniformly blue sky is ideal. Point the camera at the sky, and make exposures at full aperture and at $f/8$. Do this at the three points in the zoom range: both extremes, and in the middle. Any vignetting will show up more if you underexpose slightly.

Close-up

Focus the lens on its closest distance, and take pictures of a sheet of newspaper, once again at full aperture and $f/8$. If you are testing a zoom lens, set it to the longest focal length, which will give the largest size. Macro-zooms usually set the longest focal length automatically when used in the macro mode.

Interpreting the results

Have the film processed, and examine the slides with a magnifier, or take the lens off your camera and use that. If you are making a comparative test between several lenses, it is a good idea to include an expensive lens among them. This way, you will have a yardstick with which to compare the other lenses.

Examine your target at the edges and centre of the frame, and compare the pictures taken by the yardstick lens with those at the same aperture and focal length, using the lenses under test. By carefully inspecting the fine detail in each picture, you should find it easy to

Close-up test *By photographing a newspaper, it is easy to weed out a second rate macro-zoom*

spot the differences between the lenses.

Your standards on the distortion test will depend on the kind of pictures for which you will be using the lens. For architectural photographs, straight lines on the subject must be rendered perfectly straight on the film, but this is much less important if a landscape is the subject.

Many lenses show vignetting at full aperture, with the centre of the frame perfectly exposed, but the corners slightly underexposed. The photographs of the overcast sky will show clearly if vignetting is present. Once again, how much vignetting you are prepared to tolerate will depend on the type of pictures you plan to take.

When you come to look at the close-up tests, do not forget that the only lens which will give really good results at short distances is a true macro lens, and while a macro zoom is fine for occasional close-up use, this is not what it is really best at doing.

If you have three zoom lenses to test, and economical use of film is important, these lens tests could be abbreviated by testing only at full aperture, and at the extremes of the zoom range. Though not quite as satisfactory, this would still provide the basis for a comparison.

Macro-zooms *Some zoom lenses can be used at close range to produce close-ups. They are usually not true macros, though*

FAST LENSES

When the light is low or when you have a slow film in the camera, you may find to your annoyance that you just cannot open the lens far enough to give correct exposure. With a long lens, when you may want a fast shutter speed to capture movement or reduce the effects of camera shake, this can happen even in fairly good light. The solution to this problem may be to buy a lens with a large maximum aperture.

It used to be difficult to combine a large maximum aperture with reasonable lens performance, but recent advances in lens production, such as computerized design, better optical glass and multi-coatings, have meant that even fast lenses—those with large maximum apertures—can give good quality at full aperture. Modern fast lenses range from lenses of normal design that give perhaps only a fraction of a stop extra to special aspheric lenses that can give up to two full stops.

The main obstacle to producing fast lenses is that as the aperture is opened further and further, many types of aberration become increasingly severe. The result is that image quality suffers—highlights in particular tend to flare. This sort of problem is normally overcome by stopping down. To give good results at wide apertures, fast lenses must include special correction elements.

Inevitably, the fast lenses are expensive and, in some cases, may cost ten times as much as their slow equivalent. The less expensive fast lenses, particularly telephotos, often achieve the necessary wide aperture correction by including more and larger elements, and for really large apertures must be very big and bulky indeed—the Canon FD 400 mm lens which has a maximum aperture of $f/2.8$, for instance, weighs 4500 grams and is 166 mm in diameter: the Canon is by no means unusual. Such lenses are difficult to use without a tripod and are very awkward to carry around. Smaller, lighter—though still large—fast lenses, on the other hand, achieve their speed by using specially shaped elements or special materials in the glass. This type of lens is the most expensive.

Genuinely fast lenses, therefore, tend to be specialist items and there is little point in paying out a great deal of extra money unless you are sure that you can use the low light facility. Similarly, you hardly need an expensive fast telephoto if you never take it out because it is so heavy. Neither is there much point in buying a superfast lens if you only use the maximum aperture once every few months—for those rare shots where the low light facility is essential, you could hire the lens.

Nevertheless, there are some semi-fast lenses that cost only a little more than their slower equivalents and these might provide a more practical alternative if you use the extra speed rarely. However, it is not worth paying much more for the difference between $f/2.5$ and $f/2.8$—such a small advantage is of little value.

Fast versions are available for lenses of most focal lengths, though there is no doubt that it is for telephotos that they have their main use.

Fast standard

A typical fast standard lens is the 50 mm $f/1.4$ lens which is available for most 35 mm cameras as an alternative to the traditional $f/2$ lens. The $f/1.4$ lens gives an additional stop, though the weight, cost and bulk are significantly greater too. As a compromise, and because lens speed is a selling point, many manufacturers offer standard lenses with maximum apertures of $f/1.9$, 1.8, 1.7, and even 1.6. But beyond $f/2$, every small gain in speed is at some expense—the diameters of the lens elements must be increased and the performance at small apertures deteriorates, giving a usable limit of $f/16$. A full extra element is needed to reach $f/1.4$.

Increasing the aperture beyond $f/1.4$ without severe loss of quality is very difficult and there are less than a dozen standard lenses available with apertures of $f/1.2$, which is only half a stop faster than $f/1.4$. At present, the fastest standard lens available is the 50 mm $f/1$ Noctilux-M, for the Leica M camera. Perhaps the fastest standard lens ever to have been on sale for general photography was a 50 mm $f/0.95$ Canon, designed for a rangefinder camera, but this has been discontinued. Lenses of this speed are used in closed circuit TV cameras, but are not adaptable to still cameras.

Nevertheless, a fast standard lens

remains something of a gimmick, since for most purposes an aperture of $f/2$ is quite large enough, and many professionals find that the sacrifice in quality necessary to achieve a wider aperture is too great. Surprisingly, however, fast lenses are valuable at short focal lengths.

Wide angles

Camera shake is not so severe a problem with wide angle lenses and it is not so important to have a wide maximum aperture to allow the use of fast shutter speeds. But lens corrections become more difficult as the angle of view increases and with lenses shorter than 28 mm a maximum aperture of $f/2$ is difficult to achieve without using large numbers of elements, making the lens bulky.

Nevertheless, considerable research and development has gone into producing lightweight fast wide angle lenses using special lens elements. It is in this range in particular that aspheric and floating elements are incorporated into the design.

An aspheric lens element has a surface which, while costly to produce, does not give many types of aberration associated with spherical elements, and so reduces the number of elements needed in the lens. This allows quality to be maintained even at wide apertures. Aspheric elements are sometimes used in standard lenses as well. But they can increase the cost of a lens by a factor of five to ten.

Ballet stage *A typical example of a situation in which a fast lens is a great asset. As flash photography is often forbidden in theatres, a fast lens is one solution to the problem*

Standard lenses *There is a great difference in size between the front elements of fast lenses and their slower counterparts. The larger lens has an aperture of $f/1.2$; the other, $f/1.8$*

Fast lenses (left) *You can buy fast lenses in many focal lengths. These range from 35 to 180 mm, and from $f/1.2$ to $f/2.8$. Not many photographers, however, could afford such a selection*

Fast telephoto *The faster the lens, the bulkier and heavier it becomes for a given focal length. This 180 mm f/2.8 lens weighs nearly one kilogram*

The floating element is coupled to the focusing control of the lens. It moves separately from the other elements to improve performance at closer distances. Like aspheric elements, the floating element allows wide apertures in wide angle lenses while avoiding undue deterioration in image quality.

Lenses of 35 mm focal length are available with apertures of f/2 and even f/1.4. Wider lenses, between 20 and 28 mm, can also have apertures of f/2, though such lenses are more difficult to make.

Fast wide angle lenses have particular advantages over normal speed lenses of similar focal lengths. The shallower depth of field possible with such lenses allows differential focusing techniques (see page 87). This is often not possible with slower wide angle lenses as their depth of field is so great, even at full aperture. This means that the fast lenses are more versatile even in normal light conditions. However, sometimes it may be necessary to use neutral density filters, which cut down the light travelling through the lens without affecting its colour, to allow correct exposure with a wide aperture.

However, it is in the telephoto range that fast lenses have the most practical value because camera shake is very much more likely. A fast lens helps you to avoid this by allowing faster shutter speeds to be used.

Fast telephotos

For telephoto lenses, a wide maximum aperture is particularly useful. Because of the method of construction, telephotos cannot have very wide maximum apertures—a 300 mm lens with a maximum aperture of f/2.8 is very fast. This means that even in fairly good light, you may not be able to give sufficient exposure for a slow film. An extra stop therefore considerably increases the versatility of the lens.

Fast lenses are also valuable in the telephoto range because they allow the use of higher shutter speeds to avoid the effects of camera shake. This means they can be used hand-held or for fast moving subjects in conditions where a slower lens could not. This again increases the versatility of that focal length.

Large aperture telephotos are particularly useful when a teleconverter is fitted. For example, when a ×2 teleconverter is used the focal length is doubled but the aperture is reduced by two stops. With a fast lens, the viewfinder image is still reasonably bright, and you can achieve correct exposure even in fairly low light.

Many long focus lenses, in the 85 to 200 mm range, have maximum apertures of f/2 or better. Typical examples are those from the Nikon range, such as the 85 mm f/1.4, and 105, 135 and 200 mm lenses all with maximum apertures of f/2. Other manufacturers such as Canon, Pentax and Leitz have comparable items. A few also produce 300 mm f/2.8 lenses, and Canon offer a 400 mm f/2.8 model.

For such lenses, the limits to large aperture performance are not set by spherical aberration, but rather by transverse chromatic—or lateral colour —aberration (see page 226). This aberration gives colour fringes to image detail, and gets worse with increases in focal length. Unlike spherical aberrations, no improvement is possible by stopping the lens down. But in the case of lenses designed to be used in low light, this would hardly be a convenient solution.

One cure is to use expensive and fragile calcium fluoride (fluorite) lenses in place of the usual glass elements. Many lenses still use this method. But now special ED (extra-low dispersion) or UD (ultra-low dispersion) glass is available. Light refracted through this type of glass is not spread (dispersed) as much as it is through normal optical glass and this reduces chromatic aberrations.

All fast, long focus lenses are large, heavy and expensive. They require very precise focusing as the depth of field, which reduces as focal length increases, is very small at full aperture. Reflex focusing is essential, and, in fact, can be more positive with these lenses. This is due to the brighter image, and because the reduced depth of field makes the point of focus more obvious.

However, with fast long focus lenses, the shallow depth of field can sometimes be a problem. There is little point in using a fast lens for low light exposures, if you then have to stop down to get the depth you want.

Very long focus lenses, in the 500 to 1000 mm focal length range, were once limited to very small maximum apertures. This was due not only to lateral colour, but also to the cost of large glass elements and the final size of the lens and focusing mount. Mirror lenses give compact alternatives in this class, though with the disadvantage of fixed apertures.

Now, however, ED glass is used in conventional designs to give apertures of f/4.5 for 500 mm lenses and f/5.6 for 800 mm models.

The IF-ED type of lens is also very useful. This has *internal focusing*, which means that a group of elements moves axially inside the lens barrel to focus the image so that as you focus, the lens stays a constant length rather than being racked in and out. Focusing is very light and swift, ideal for sports and wildlife photography. This type of design compensates, to some extent, for the bulkiness caused by large aperture designs.

Fast or slow ?

Choosing between a fast lens and the corresponding normal speed one is largely a matter of balancing the undoubted advantages against the bulk and cost. Remember, though, that a fast lens is not necessarily a better performer, aperture for aperture, than a slower one of the same focal length. Its maximum aperture performance may only be 'acceptable' and not even 'good' (aspheric lenses are the exception here).

The average user may never need to use an aperture larger than f/4. Few amateurs would actually need fast lenses, unless specializing in low light

photography. Even professionals tend to hire fast long telephotos, though they often own a fast standard or wide angle lens. Large aperture lenses also have their own special problems. For example, the accuracy of focusing needed at maximum aperture means that the view-finder must often be corrected for any deficiencies in the photographer's eye-sight by using dioptre adjustment lenses over the eyepiece—though this is not quite so important with the fast wide angle lenses.

The increase in speed offered by a fast lens may only be one stop, or even less. Considering the high cost of these lenses, this small gain has to be sorely needed to justify the extra expense.

When buying a lens, there is often a choice between a normal speed lens and a fast model made by the same manu-facturer. Before deciding, try using your standard lens at each of the apertures offered by the lenses. You may find that, with the sort of photography you do, the extra speed does not make a significant difference in ease of focusing. If you are also unlikely to use the maximum aperture offered by the fast lens very often, the normal lens is probably per-fectly acceptable—and the cost saving quite large. But if a bright viewfinder image or a high shutter speed is vital, and an extra stop would help signifi-cantly, then a fast lens may be essential.

It is for you to decide whether, given the type of photography you are most interested in, it is worth your while going to this extra expense.

Fast lens plus teleconverter *Medium speed lenses become very slow when used with a teleconverter, but fast lenses retain an acceptable maximum aperture*

Concert audience *Shooting a moving subject in low light presents special problems. Here, a fast lens allowed the photographer to freeze at least some of the movement by using a faster speed than a slow lens would have allowed*

SPECIAL LENSES

Shift lens *This Minolta 35 mm lens has a facility for controlling perspective both horizontally and vertically, as well as a control for changing the shape of the plane of sharp focus, from concave to convex, according to the subject.*
Perspective control *Converging verticals can be eliminated with perspective control. Compare the standard lens shot (left) with the PC lens version (right)*

There are frequent occasions when a photographer is faced with a situation which cannot be recorded with the conventional range of lenses. There are a great many subjects which, because of their shape, position or circumstances require special lenses to avoid problems, or otherwise improve the picture. For example, it can be difficult to avoid converging verticals when photographing tall buildings. Sometimes it is impossible to get a small enough aperture for sufficient depth of field when photographing still lifes, or a wide enough view when photographing landscape scenes. And in portrait work some softness in the image can be desirable even though lens manufacturers work hard to make their lenses sharp.

Special lenses are generally designed for specific purposes. They often employ highly complex construction with elements made from expensive types of glass and because of their limited appeal, are comparatively expensive. The most

Tilting lens *The Canon shift lens not only controls perspective but tilts to change the angle of the plane of sharp focus, controlling depth of field. If this is parallel to the film (above right) the background is unsharp. By tilting the lens to angle the plane of focus (above left) the background is made sharp*

useful of the special designs are shift lenses for perspective control; tilt/shift and variable field curvature (VFC) lenses for depth of field control; anamorphic lenses which give a wider than normal picture format; and soft focus lenses for control of image sharpness.

These lenses can greatly widen the scope of your photography. They make possible shots which would otherwise be impossible, or which would have to be done in a less satisfactory way. For example, shift lenses allow you to take large format pictures with your SLR which would otherwise require bulky and expensive large format equipment.

Perspective control lenses

To cope with the problems of photographing architecture and interiors, and to help generally when viewpoint is restricted, it is useful to be able to move the lens relative to the camera when framing. This is easy with large format technical cameras which allow a wide range of camera movements. But with medium and small format equipment the lenses are fixed rigidly to the camera bodies. To include the whole of a tall building, for example, it is necessary to tilt the camera upwards. But this results in converging verticals which make the building look as though it is about to fall over.

To overcome this problem, several manufacturers produce shift or perspective control (PC) lenses. These have special mechanisms which allow the front part of the lens to be moved parallel to the film. This movement is achieved by the use of a series of plates. The Olympus and Minolta lenses, for example, have one set which moves vertically and one which moves horizontally. Combining the two allows movement in any direction, though the amount of movement may be slightly restricted compared with using just one direction—vertical or horizontal. To allow full movement in any direction, the Nikon lens has just one set of plates but the whole of the lens can be rotated. With this lens fine adjustment is possible as the movement is controlled by a milled dial. With other lenses the movement is made simply by pushing the lens in the required direction, though some have the very useful feature of a locking device.

The lens diaphragm is included in the part of the lens that moves. This makes mechanical linkages between aperture and camera very difficult, so most of these lenses have manual diaphragms. In addition, the image from the lens tends to darken as it is moved off-axis so that through-the-lens (TTL) metering is almost essential, and with manual diaphragms this has to be done with the lens stopped down. This can make the lenses slow to use. The Minolta shift lens avoids this problem by having an automatic diaphragm, though this lens is quite bulky because of the complex linkages involved.

Most shift lenses have focal lengths of 35 mm as this is felt to be the most useful size. But for larger objects and more dramatic results, some manufacturers produce 28 mm versions. There are also lenses for medium format cameras—an example being the lens made for Bronica cameras which uses a bellows unit and lens mount similar to large format cameras and allows a similar range of movements.

Shift lenses made for 35 mm cameras are usually quite large—much larger than normal lenses of similar focal lengths. The Pentax lens has a very big front element, so to keep filter costs down it has the addition of a group of built-in filters.

Depth of field control

The Canon and Minolta shift lenses also have extra features which can be used to control depth of field. In the case of the Canon, the lens not only shifts but also tilts as well. This is achieved by setting the lens at an angle to the normal axis, and means that the plane of sharp focus in the subject is at an angle to the film plane rather than parallel to it so different subject distances are focused on different parts of the film. The lens rotates so that this tilting action can be made in any direction. This type of movement can be very useful for still lifes and other close-up work such as photographing scale models, which tend to be photographed partly at an angle rather than flat-on and so cause depth of field problems at close distances.

Another way of controlling the overall

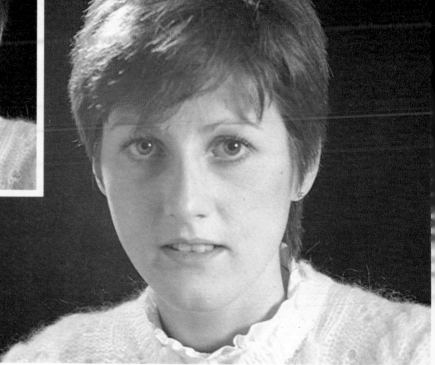

Varisoft telephoto *The Minolta 85 mm lens has a soft focus ring which can be set to give different degrees of sharpness*

sharpness of the picture is to alter the shape of the plane of sharp focus in the camera. Normally lenses are designed to give a flat field—that is, a flat image which coincides with the film. Field curvature is generally regarded as a lens fault (see page 232) as it usually results in the edges of the picture being unsharp. However, there are some lenses which allow some field curvature to be deliberately introduced. The Minolta 35 mm shift lens, for example, has this facility, called variable field curvature (VFC) making it one of the most versatile of its type.

The VFC control allows the curvature to be continuously varied from convex to concave with a flat field in between. If the lens is focused on the centre of the scene, an object at the edge which is at a different distance can be brought into focus, or put further out of focus, by employing the VFC control.

Once again, this facility is useful for still life work. With the main subject in the centre of the picture, other parts

further away—probably near the top of the frame—can be made sharp. However, those parts of the subject which are closer and near the edge of the frame will go even further out of focus, so the extent to which this device can be used is limited.

Soft focus lenses

Spherical aberration is really a lens 'fault' which is sometimes deliberately incorporated in a lens design. Early lenses which were insufficiently corrected for this aberration often produced 'soft' images, which some photographers find attractive. However modern lens designs and improved types of glass have largely eliminated this fault. In addition, faster film emulsions have resulted in the use of smaller working apertures which further reduce optical faults, so manufacturers have had to design soft focus lenses specially for the purpose.

A good example of this type of lens is the Minolta 85 mm Varisoft. This has a ring which can be turned to increase or decrease the soft focus effect, from sharp to very soft. This is a useful feature as without it the only control over the degree of softness is the aperture—the softness of the image is reduced as the aperture is stopped down. The softness control ring allows consistent results to be obtained at different apertures. Other lenses without this control often have 'honeycomb' attachments which can be used to increase the softness when the

lens is stopped down. These are glass filters which have surfaces formed in a honeycomb pattern to soften the image.

The effect given by a soft focus lens is different from that given by the normal type of soft focus filter. The latter simply diffuses the light to produce a general blurring. The effect of a soft focus lens is to produce a sharp image core which is covered and surrounded by a soft halo. This means that details can still be seen while retaining the soft effect. The lens gives you more control over the softness of the image than any other single piece of equipment. To achieve the same range of softness with filters, a wide selection would be needed. In common with the other lenses already mentioned, soft focus lenses use a fairly conventional optical arrangement. However there are other special purpose lenses which employ unconventional optics for their effect.

Widescreen lenses

Anamorphic (widescreen) lenses were originally developed for movie photography and contain prisms or cylindrical elements which 'see' the subject normally in one plane (the vertical) but take in a much greater proportion, by compressing it, in the other (the horizontal), so the image 'fits' on a 35 mm negative.

This optical set-up means that a much wider scene is recorded on the standard film format than would be possible with normal lenses and so a panoramic effect is achieved. However, the picture on the

Anamorphic attachment *When fitted to the front of the camera lens, this lens compresses a scene horizontally on film in order to take in a wide angle of view. When the transparency is projected, with the attachment mounted on the projector, the image is opened out to show its panoramic shape*

Compression *A normal shot (left) shows the scene as it appeared. The slide taken with an anamorphic lens (right) includes more horizontally*

negative or transparency is very distorted with everything 'squeezed' together on the horizontal axis. So to view or print the picture it is necessary to use the same or a similar lens to widen the image out again. The lenses used to take the picture fall into two groups—supplementary types which fit on to the front of a normal lens, and complete lenses which fit directly on to the camera body.

Supplementary lenses fit on to the front of most types of camera lenses by screwing into the filter mount and can be used, with an adapter, in front of a projector lens for showing slides. The ideal camera lens is the 50 mm or 55 mm standard. Shorter lenses tend to produce vignetting. When the anamorphic lens is added to the standard lens it gives a horizontal field of view equivalent to a lens of about 33 mm. The format produced by this lens is 2.25:1 as compared with the normal 1.5:1 of the 35 mm frame. More powerful anamorphic lenses are

available which give a format of 3:1, though these tend to be less popular as they are more difficult to use. The viewfinder image with all these lenses is distorted, which can make composition and focusing difficult, and the more squeezed the picture, the more difficult these things are. Some supplementary lenses also have their own focusing mechanisms which have to be used in conjunction with the focusing ring on the main lens, which makes them slow to use.

Complete anamorphic lenses are much simpler, though more expensive. Those which are designed for 35 mm stills cameras are often built using parts from the camera manufacturer's own lenses. The range of lens mounts available is limited, however, the most common being Nikon, Leica bayonet and Pentax

K (which can be mounted on a large range of budget SLR cameras).

Although these lenses are easy to fit and use they do have one major drawback—they limit you to using only one focal length, unlike the supplementary lenses which can be fitted to a range of lenses including zooms. Also, it is often necessary to buy a separate lens to fit your enlarger or projector.

Availability of special lenses

The availability of special lenses varies quite widely. Anamorphic lenses are available from a number of independent distributors who specialize in this field and who can supply other useful equipment such as adapters and wide projection screens. These distributors are based mainly in the UK, Australia and the USA but sell most of their equipment by mail order direct to the public. In some cases they actually make some of the equipment themselves and so can make adapters and screens to order.

In contrast, the shift, tilt/shift, VFC and soft focus lenses are largely made by camera manufacturers and are designed to fit their own equipment. This means that, with the exception of Pentax lenses which can be used on most K-mount cameras, if you want a particular lens you have to buy a camera of the same make. This can cause problems if you already own a camera of a different make. But if you feel that you really need one of these lenses, and are changing systems or are considering buying your first SLR, it is worth finding out which model most suits your needs and building your system around it. Most of the lenses of a particular type are very similar, with only minor variations, so choice is often a matter of personal preference.

The cost of most special lenses means that you have to use them often to justify the expense. Fortunately, with many of the lenses it is possible to hire them, and this may prove to be a more economical proposition for occasional pictures.

TELECONVERTERS

The cheapest teleconverters cost very little indeed. For little more than the cost of processing and printing a roll of colour film you can buy an accessory that doubles the focal length of any lens you own. At the other end of the scale, it is possible to pay nearly ten times as much, and still get a product that performs exactly the same function, and looks very similar, too.

A teleconverter, or *tele-extender* as it was originally known, is a small cylindrical accessory that fits between the camera body and the lens. Although it looks like a proper lens and contains a number of glass lens elements—usually between three and seven—it works only in conjunction with a proper or *prime* lens. The converter simply enlarges the image formed by the prime lens by spreading out the rays of light coming through the lens over a wider area. The degree of enlargement depends on the converter in use. Most converters enlarge the image two or three times, though some give a magnification of as little as 1.4 ×. A few converters have a two-position setting, and offer both 2 × and 3 ×. This is achieved by moving the optical components of the converter.

Since teleconverters have a male bayonet mount on one end, and a female on the other, they could theoretically be used with a lens of any focal length. In practice, though, they are used mostly with lenses of focal lengths in the 50 to 200 mm range. Outside these limits, the quality of the resulting pictures is very poor, unless the converter is specifically matched to the lens in use.

There is little point in using a teleconverter with a wide angle lens, because the combination of lens and converter gives a focal length little different from a standard lens.

Teleconverters are light in weight, and effectively double the potential of a photographer's outfit. This makes them a very attractive proposition. By using a standard lens, a teleconverter and a 135 mm telephoto, a range of four focal lengths from 50 mm to 270 mm is available. The weight and cost is probably little over half that of an outfit made up of prime lenses.

Because they simply enlarge the image formed by the main lens, the closest focusing distance does not change when a converter is attached. This means that teleconverters are very useful for close-up work because they form a large image while allowing the photographer to retain some distance between himself and the subject. With a short lens, the photographer would have to move very close to the subject to get a large image; with a telephoto lens, the minimum focusing distance is normally too great to get close enough to give a similar size image.

The drawbacks

In photographic optics, you very rarely get something for nothing, and teleconverters are no exception. In order to double or treble the focal length of a lens, image brightness has to be sacrificed. When the image is enlarged two times, its brightness falls to only a quarter of what it previously was. This is because the same amount of light is being spread over four times the area. To produce the same exposure on the film, the photographer must use an aperture two stops wider. Thus an $f/2$ standard lens is effectively converted to an $f/4$ 100 mm lens. When a 3 × converter is used, the light intensity is cut to one ninth, and a little over 3 stops extra exposure is needed. This can be a severe handicap, particularly in poor light. If your camera does not have a through-the-lens meter, this loss of light must be compensated for when setting the exposure. When light is read through the lens, the camera makes the compensation automatically, and no change in the exposure is needed.

Double up *The length and weight of a 200 mm lens linked to a teleconverter is much less than that of the 400 mm lens to which it is equivalent*

Converter types *Cheap converters (left) look similar to costly ones (right) but perform fairly well. Matched multipliers (far right) are available for some zoom lenses, and work best with the lens to which they are matched*

River boats *If a matched multiplier is available for a lens, it will give better results than an ordinary converter. The detail above is from a picture taken with a multiplier, the one below used a converter*

The other problem that is encountered with teleconverters is the actual quality of the image. Some converters are poor optically, and actually degrade the image formed by the main lens. Even the best converter is only as good as the prime lens with which it is used, and because the image formed by the main lens is enlarged, so are its aberrations.

In the best possible circumstances, teleconverters can turn in very good results, but not everyone can afford a top quality converter. This has led to converters being regarded as cheap but poor quality alternatives for those who cannot afford a proper telephoto lens.

These two drawbacks, light loss and poor quality, result from the nature of converters themselves, but there are other problems which are common to both lens/converter combinations and ordinary telephoto lenses.

Any long focal length lens amplifies the effect of camera shake, so a faster shutter speed must be used if the camera and lens is going to be hand-held. A tripod or other camera support allows you to use a slower shutter speed if you have to but many photographers find that they prefer to hand-hold the camera because this allows more flexibility.

The rule of thumb is that the minimum reliable shutter speed at which a camera

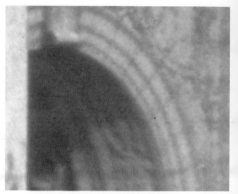

200 mm lens—enlarged 40 ×

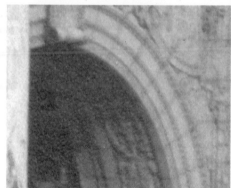

200 mm lens + Nikon converter 20 ×

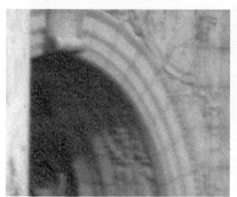

200 mm lens + cheap converter 20 ×

400 mm lens alone—enlarged 20 ×

Archway view *Great enlargement of the picture taken with a 200 mm lens gives poor results, and even a cheap converter can do better. A more costly converter gives slightly better quality, but not as good as a 400 mm lens*

and lens can be hand held is equal to the focal length of the lens in use. A 200 mm lens should not be hand held at speeds slower than about 1/250 sec, for example. If a 2 × converter is being used with the same lens, the combination has a focal length of 400 mm, and should only be hand held at speeds faster than about 1/500. Attempts to hand hold at slower speeds may lead to camera shake.

Long lenses limit the depth of field in a picture, and this is true of lenses used with converters too. The depth of field of a 200 mm lens is the same as that of a 100 mm lens used with a 2 × converter, provided that the aperture is the same, and the subject is equally distant. Although shallow depth of field is sometimes acceptable, and often quite desirable, there are some occasions when it is necessary to stop the lens down to increase the depth of field, and this can lead to exposure problems—slow shutter speeds and the risk of camera shake.

Buying a converter
Converters vary tremendously in price and quality. The cheapest converters can be expected only to produce mediocre results at best, whereas the most expensive ones made by the big camera manufacturers—Nikon, Canon, Pentax and Minolta—can produce pictures which are indistinguishable from those taken through a lens alone.

It may seem surprising that anyone buys a teleconverter which produces poor results, but the alternative—using only the same lens and greatly enlarging the resulting negative—is sometimes worse. Pictures taken with a cheap teleconverter may be slightly soft around the edges, but this is frequently acceptable. A greatly enlarged negative usually produces extremely grainy prints, and this is often less desirable than the slight loss of definition and contrast that a teleconverter would produce.

It may well be, then, that a very cheap teleconverter would be adequate for your purpose, particularly if your budget is tight, and you do not make big enlargements. If you can afford to, though, it is worth spending more money, because converters costing only slightly more produce pictures which are a lot better.

Very inexpensive converters use few elements, and frequently economize in other areas, too. Mechanically they may not be as well made as those with a slightly higher price tag, and the connections for automatic diaphragm operation may be slightly more 'sloppy'.

Dearer models use more elements—typically five to seven—and this shows up clearly in their superior performance. It is possible to get a good idea of what to expect from a converter by looking at the specification; more elements usually means better quality.

Branded converters

The large camera manufacturers sell teleconverters which are about as expensive as a top quality lens. Since most people think of converters as a cheap alternative to a longer lens, this seems unnecessary. Why buy a teleconverter to use with a 135 mm lens, when for the same money, you could buy quite a good 300 mm lens?

The answer is size and weight. A teleconverter adds very little to the weight of a camera bag, and for a professional who is already carrying three cameras, a motor drive and six lenses, an extra lens might be the last straw. A teleconverter adds only 40 mm or so to the length of a lens, but a separate lens of double the focal length is often double the size. This is a strong point in favour of converters.

The converters made by the big camera manufacturers are precision optical instruments, and are often designed to be used only with lenses of particular focal lengths. At least two manufacturers make one converter for lenses with focal lengths up to 200 mm, and another for longer focal lengths. This is necessary because, for best results, the rear elements of the lens must be close to the front elements of the converter. Long telephoto lenses have recessed rear elements, and converters to be used with them are fitted with protruding front elements which reach into the barrel of the main lens.

Some of the more expensive converters enlarge the image by a factor of 1.4. Though this may seem like an arbitrary figure, it is not. If an image is enlarged linearly by a factor of 1.4 (to be more precise, 1.412) it will be enlarged in area by a factor of exactly 2. The light loss will similarly be 2, and the exposure compensation required will be exactly one stop. This is more acceptable than the two stop loss that is produced by a 2 × converter.

Matched multipliers

A recent development in the field of teleconverters is that of *matched multipliers*. Although these superficially resemble ordinary teleconverters, they are designed at the same time as the lens with which they are to be used, and when attached to it they form an integrated optical unit.

Because they are matched to one lens, these multipliers will not produce good results when used with any other lens. When attached to the matching lens, though, multipliers can give pictures that are substantially sharper than those taken using the lens with an ordinary converter. Matched multipliers also work very well at short distances, which is where many lenses fall down. The extra elements provide added correction for close-up pictures.

It is impossible to overlook the drawbacks of teleconverters, and it would be misleading to pretend that they are unimportant. Whether the advantages conferred by teleconverters outweigh the disadvantages depends primarily on the type of photography you propose to tackle with them, and what sort of use the pictures will be put to. Teleconverters will never be a real substitute for a full range of lenses, but they double the versatility of an existing outfit at very little cost. Where sharpness is not absolutely critical, they can be a great asset and avoid the cost of a long lens which will only be used occasionally.

Misty portrait *The softness and lack of contrast of cheap converters can be used to advantage. A standard lens and converter are ideal for portraits*

EQUIPMENT FOR CLOSE-UPS

Most standard 50 mm lenses are designed to work at their best when focused on subjects at distances further than five metres. Acceptable images are possible down to about half a metre, and at this distance your standard lens will give an image on film that is about one ninth the size of its subject. The close-up equipment dealt with here can help your camera bridge the gap between this 1:9 image–subject ratio and the large magnifications (beyond about 17 times life size) that you need a microscope to obtain.

Close-up lenses

Close-up lenses are a fairly cheap and simple way of getting a large image. They are often called *supplementary* lenses because they cannot be attached directly to a camera body, but must be screwed into the front of another lens, usually the standard lens.

The power of a close-up lens is generally marked in *dioptres*. Dioptres are simply a measure of the power of a lens. They are equal to the reciprocal of the focal length. A +1 dioptre lens has a focal length of 1 metre, a +2 dioptre lens has a focal length of ½ metre, a +3 has a focal length of ⅓ metre, and so on. A standard lens fitted with a +1 dioptre supplementary lens would be able to focus on subjects between 40 cm away (with the focusing ring on the standard lens set at 60 cm) and 1 metre away (if the standard lens is set at infinity).

It is possible to use two or more close-up lenses together, but this can lead to some sacrifices in picture quality. Using a +4 with a +2 would, for example, give you a supplementary strength of +6 dioptres. If you do combine close-up lenses, the more powerful lens should be nearer to the camera.

For the price of about three close-up lenses, it is also possible to buy a zoom close-up attachment. This gives a continuously variable power, between, for example, +2 and +10 dioptres.

Though they are light to carry and easy to use, close-up lenses often tend to distort light passing through the edge of the prime lens. This can produce a noticeable fall-off in sharpness around the edge of the image. Some lens manufacturers make close-up lenses that have been specially designed to work with a particular lens. A matched pair gives better results than an unmatched combination although, unfortunately, few lenses are available with supplementary close-up lenses.

Peacock butterfly *Good quality like this can be achieved even with a simple supplementary close-up lens fitted to your camera*

Reversing ring *Many lenses give better extreme close-ups when fitted in reverse with a reversing ring adapter*

Extension tubes

One of the most popular ways of getting good, sharp, close-up pictures is to use extension tubes. These are a simple way of increasing the distance between the lens and the film plane, thereby allowing you to focus on subjects much closer than the normal limits of the lens. Extension tubes are usually sold in sets of three, four or five tubes of between about 5 mm and 30 mm. They can be used in any combination to provide a variety of magnifications. The longer the tube used the larger the magnification will be.

When you use a close-up lens, image quality can suffer because light is distorted by the close-up lens before it reaches the prime lens. With extension tubes, however, there is no extra glass and the prime lens can work as it was designed to, and provide a better quality image.

Unfortunately, the greatly increased distance between the lens and the film plane with extension tubes causes some light loss. It is relatively easy to compensate for this light loss by using a wider aperture or a slower shutter speed, and if you have a TTL meter compensation is made automatically. But the light loss does restrict the conditions under which extension tubes can be used. With a standard 50 mm lens at the end of 50 mm of extension tubes the image is life size and the lens aperture must be increased by 2 f-stops for correct exposure.

With extension tubes fitted, the link between the lens diaphragm and the camera body is interrupted. TTL metering systems will not work normally, therefore, and neither will lenses that do not stop down the aperture until the shutter is pressed. The problem is solved by 'automatic' extension tubes that have connections for the diaphragm operating mechanism and meter coupling devices. These save you the trouble of setting the aperture manually after focusing each shot, and also allow you to use the TTL meter on your camera in the normal way. Automatic tubes cannot be combined in twos and threes—they can only be used one at a time. Using automatic tubes in combination may even damage the camera.

Despite the drawbacks, a set of extension tubes is more versatile than close-up lenses since they can be used with any lens, regardless of the size of its filter thread. They are usually used in conjunction with the standard lens, but you can use a lens with a longer focal length. With a 90 mm or 135 mm lens, for instance, you can get a large image without having to move in as close to your subject. This extra distance is often very valuable since it permits better lighting, and you can avoid one problem sometimes met in close-up work—that of casting your own shadow on to your subjects.

Bellows

Most professional photographers involved in macro work would probably regard a set of extension bellows as essential equipment. Bellows work on the same principle as extension tubes—they take the lens away from the film plane to increase the magnification. With extension tubes the magnifications possible are limited by the fixed length of the tubes. With bellows, however, moving from one magnification to another is less time-consuming and the image size is continuously variable within the limits of the bellows. This makes it much easier to compose your pictures, filling the frame if necessary with the chosen image.

Most bellows stretch out between 100 mm and 200 mm and can therefore provide more powerful magnifications than a set of extension tubes. Nikon make a bellows extension clamp allowing you to join two sets of bellows together for a total extension of up to 438 mm. Using a 50 mm standard lens, this would fill the frame with a subject less than 5 mm across, but would need 6 stops extra exposure compared to the lens alone.

The lens in a bellows system fits into a metal plate that can move away from, or towards the camera on single or double metal tracks. On some cameras, the lens can be firmly locked in place once the correct focusing distance has been found by tightening a pair of knobs on the bellows.

Because of their size and because of the high magnifications they provide, bellows are almost always used with a tripod, or on their own bench stand to keep them steady. In macro work, where high magnifications inevitably mean a shallow depth of field, anything that makes it easier to hold accurate focus is of great value.

Bellows extensions suffer from the same drawbacks as extension tubes. There is inevitably a loss of light, because the light has further to travel, and with ordinary bellows, automatic diaphragm operation is lost. This can be avoided by using a special lens mounting plate on

Close-up lenses *Most close-up lenses are inexpensive, fitting to the front of the lens. The camera shown is fitted with a variable power zoom type*

Wing scales *To take photographs of extremely fine detail, such as these delicate wing scales, you will need to use a bellows extension unit*

Extension tube set *An extension tube fits between the camera and lens, and can be used with a standard lens to form life size images on film*

the front of the bellows and a double cable release, but this is an added expense. All bellows sets sacrifice automatic metering—unless the camera reads the exposure from the film surface—and metering will normally have to be done in the stopped-down mode or exposure will be incorrect.

One further problem that is encountered with bellows is that the lens cannot focus back to infinity. This is because even when the bellows are tightly compressed, the lens is still further from the film than it would be if it was attached directly to the camera. It is possible to get around this problem by using a special lens, called a *short mount macro lens*, in which the optical elements are mounted closer to the film. This lens has no independent focusing movement and it is focused simply by

moving the bellows in and out. In this way, it can focus on anything from infinity to a point almost touching the front element. Unfortunately, lenses like this are difficult to obtain.

With some bellows systems you can move the camera back and forth along the base track independently of the lens. This allows you to keep the lens at a constant distance from the subject so the image remains the same size while you move the camera body to bring it into focus. If you do not have this facility, the size of the image changes each time the lens is moved for focusing. This can be very irritating.

Another refinement on some expensive bellows is the facility to tilt the lens up and down and swing it from side to side. This is used to overcome problems caused by shallow depths of field with

awkward three-dimensional subjects.

Bellows vary in price depending upon whether they are a simple set for outdoor work or a sophisticated large system for studio use. Even the cheapest bellows will probably cost twice as much as a set of extension tubes.

Reversing rings

In normal use, the subject of a picture is much further from the lens than the film and most lenses are designed with this in mind. But when the lens-to-film distance is the same as or greater than the lens-to-subject distance, the performance of the lens is poor. You can get round this limitation by turning the lens round so that the front of the lens abuts the camera body. Of course, there are no suitable mounting points on the front of the lens and you need a special

Close up accessories-how close do they go?

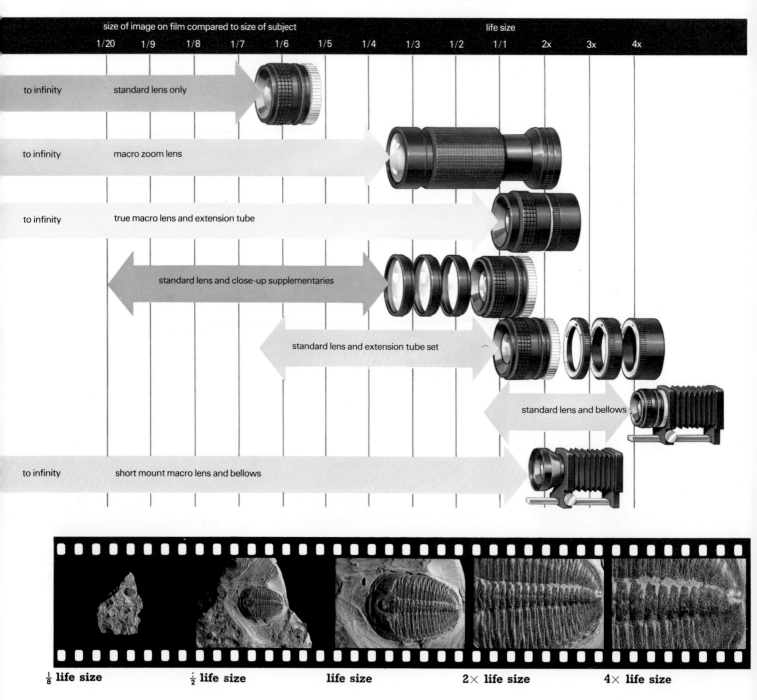

| $\frac{1}{8}$ life size | $\frac{1}{2}$ life size | life size | $2\times$ life size | $4\times$ life size |

reversing ring to make the attachment.

On one side, a reversing ring has a bayonet or screw mount to match the camera in use. The other side screws into the filter thread of the lens. On their own, reversing rings are of limited use and are usually combined with bellows or a set of extension tubes to give a much sharper image than a lens mounted in a conventional way.

Macro lenses

Macro lenses should not be confused with the close-up supplementary lenses mentioned earlier. A macro lens (sometimes called a 'micro' lens) is one that has been specially designed to work best at the short subject-to-lens distances needed to give high magnifications. It is a true camera lens in its own right, capable of focusing from infinity down to a few centimentres and can be used in conjunction with all kinds of close-up equipment. With a macro lens, however, you do not need extra close-up devices unless you want an image-subject ratio greater than 1 : 2.

Most macro lenses have a focal length of around 50 mm or 100 mm though at least one 200 mm macro lens is available. If you intend to do a great deal of close-up work, therefore, it might be better to buy a macro lens, rather than a standard lens or a normal short telephoto, since a macro of the appropriate focal length could substitute for either of these. A macro lens costs about 20 per cent over a general lens of the same focal length. Unfortunately, the maximum aperture of macro lenses is only about $f/3.5$ and, because they are designed for close-up work, the image quality suffers very marginally when the lens is focused on distant subjects.

Macro zooms

Macro zoom lenses arc not the same as macro (micro) lenses. Macro zooms very rarely focus down to the same short distances, and when large magnifications are used, sharpness is often much reduced. They are fine for occasional flower pictures, but where definition is important—copying for example—most of them are useless.

Macro zoom lenses work by moving certain lens elements within the body of the lens while holding other elements in a fixed position. They focus over the normal range using the standard focusing ring, but in the 'macro' mode, focus is achieved by turning the separate zoom ring.

Close-up chart *At short distances, the size of the image is more important than the distance from the camera to subject, so enlargement is expressed as a number—2× means that the actual image size on film is exactly half the size of the original subject. This chart shows the useful range of various combinations of equipment. Exact values depend on the specifications of the individual items, such as the maximum and minimum bellows extension available*

Garden spider *Careful lighting counts for as much as the right equipment. This garden cross spider would be difficult to spot in its natural habitat*

Bellows extension *Replacing extension tubes with a bellows set allows greater magnification, and a continuous, uninterrupted focusing range*

Lighting

The greatly reduced depths of field involved in macro work may make it necessary to stop down the lens to a small aperture to ensure the subject is properly in focus. You may find that there is insufficient light available for such a small aperture and if you do close-up work regularly it might be worth buying a small flash unit. A ring flash system is the most suitable but these can be expensive. A ring flash unit is a circular electronic flash that is attached around the front of the lens. It produces soft, shadowless illumination that is perfectly suited to macro work.

Macro choice

Before buying any macro equipment you should have a clear idea of the kind of pictures you want to take. If possible, take examples of likely subjects with you when visiting dealers. Then you can see just what the equipment can do.

Different devices suit different needs.

An inexpensive supplementary lens may be perfectly adequate for photographs of small flowers where the centre of the bloom is clear and the outer edges are attractively blurred. The same lens would not be suitable for someone wanting to record a stamp collection faithfully.

Think carefully about how often you are going to be taking close-up pictures that need really pin sharp images. If this is likely to be a frequent occurence, then it is worth buying a specially designed macro lens, or a bellows system. For most people, though, opportunities for ultra close-up pictures are rare, and one of the simpler accessories such as an extension tube set is quite adequate.

Chapter 4
CAMERA ACCESSORIES
FINDERS AND SCREENS

The pentaprism and standard focusing screen that are fitted to the average 35 mm SLR are ideal for everyday photography: when used with the standard lens, the image in the viewfinder is similar in scale to that seen by eye and is easy to see, while focusing aids make it easy to get a sharp picture. The viewfinder is bright, and the image snaps clearly in and out of focus.

Despite the ease with which this combination of screen and finder can be used, an increasing number of SLRs are built to accept interchangeable screens, and about half a dozen have interchangeable finders available. Those that do not usually accept a series of viewfinder magnifiers and accessories to increase their versatility. But if you only ever use a standard lens, or never take pictures at low or awkward angles, you may wonder why some photographers prefer to use special viewing systems.

The reason is simple—the standard focusing screen is designed to work best with lenses that have a focal length of about 30 to 90 mm, and a maximum aperture of between $f/1.8$ and $f/2.8$. Outside these ranges, slightly different screens make focusing simpler. Different viewfinders are useful when the camera is to be used at a very low or high angle, or under difficult circumstances—when the photographer has to wear a safety helmet, for example, or when the camera is in an underwater housing. Special finders that greatly enlarge the image of the screen are available as well for high quality work.

Changing the screen
Not all cameras can take interchangeable focusing screens, and those that do may only offer a choice of two or three different types. On the other hand, some camera systems have as many as 20 screens available for their top models.

Focusing screens are changed in one of two ways. The camera pentaprism may be removable, giving access to the screen. The screen either rests in a

Viewfinders *Action finders (above) allow you to see the image from a distance. Other finders (below, l-r) have other functions: standard pentaprism; eyesight correction finders; swivelling eye and waist level finder; magnifier*

trough under the prism, or is clipped to the underside of it. Either of these two systems make screen changing quite straightforward. The alternative, which is adopted when the pentaprism is fixed, is to arrange for screen changing through the throat of the camera. The lens is first removed and the screen released by either moving a catch, or pressing back on it. The screen can then be lifted out. This system is considerably harder to use, and usually requires tweezers. Great care must be taken because dirt and fingermarks easily stick to the surface of the screen, and can prove impossible to remove.

Cameras that take meter readings from the surface of the screen may require compensation to the exposure indicated when a particularly transparent screen is fitted. Details of this are supplied with the screen.

If you have a camera that has a fixed screen, and you are not satisfied with the particular combination of focusing aids available, it is often possible to have the screen permanently changed for a different one. A competent camera repair shop should be able to do this.

Whether or not a focusing screen is easy to use is decided largely by the focusing aids which it incorporates. The simplest type of screen is just a matt surface backed by a fresnel lens, which provides even illumination over the whole area. Most cameras, though, have a split image rangefinder, or microprisms, or a combination of the two.

A split image rangefinder always takes

the form of a clear circle in the centre of the screen. A line across the diameter of the circle splits out of focus parts of the subject into two, but leaves in-focus parts unbroken. This split image is produced by a pair of tiny prisms, moulded on to the underside of the plastic screen. The slope angle of the prisms is very critical, and must be carefully matched to the focal length and maximum aperture of the lens with which the screen is to be used. If the angle is too steep, one half of the rangefinder circle will go black, making it impossible to focus. If the angle is too shallow, the accuracy of the rangefinder is reduced—rather like having too short a base length on a rangefinder camera (see page 202).

Microprisms are constructed in a very similar way to rangefinder wedges, but they are much smaller, and they can be fitted to any part of the focusing screen, and can even completely cover it. When an out of focus image falls on the microprisms, they shatter it, and break it up into tiny regular patterns. This has the appearance of a shimmering surface. When the image is in focus, it appears unbroken, and the pattern of the microprisms disappears completely.

Standard screens

Standard focusing screens are usually made with a combination of split image rangefinder, microprisms, and plain matt finish. When the subject has straight lines, or clearly defined contours, a split image rangefinder is ideal, as these are broken up by the central line. Microprisms, on the other hand, make it easy to focus on areas of even tone. For a rangefinder spot to break a subject clearly into two parts, the line on the subject must run at right angles to the direction of the break. Most cameras have a horizontal break, but a few break the subject diagonally. This is sometimes more convenient, particularly when the subject has no clear vertical lines.

Microprisms are usually placed in a ring around the central rangefinder spot, and this, in turn, is surrounded by another concentric ring of plain matt, free of fresnel lens circles which can interfere with focusing. A few of the newer cameras have such a fine fresnel pattern that this plain matt ring is dispensed with, and focusing can be done on any part of the screen.

This standard screen gives accurate, easy focusing under normal conditions and with a standard lens, but most photographers take pictures in a wide variety of different circumstances, often with a range of different focal lengths.

One of the options for cameras that accept interchangeable screens is a screen that has microprisms matched to the focal length of the lens in use. The Nikon F3, for example, has two different designs of focusing screen of this type, and both of these are available in four versions, suiting wide angle, standard, telephoto and super telephoto lenses. One of the two screens has a central microprism circle and a clear surround, and the other is totally covered by microprisms. The exact choice of screen for use with a particular lens depends not just on the focal length of the lens, but also on maximum aperture. If you use an ultra-fast standard lens such as an f/1.2, changing the screen for one fitted with steep angle prisms will result in more accurate focusing, particularly in poor light.

Conversely, if for some reason you are obliged to use a lens that has quite a small maximum aperture, such as a macro or perspective control lens, then a screen incorporating less steep prisms will enable you to use the focusing aids more easily—they do not blackout as they would on a normal screen.

Special screens

Some photographers prefer a screen which has no focusing aids at all, and so most cameras that accept interchangeable screens have one of this type available. Such screens are also useful if you frequently need to check depth of field. Although they darken when the aperture is closed, the image remains visible over the whole area of the screen, instead of

Split image focusing

The split image focusing screen is familiar to owners of many modern SLRs. With the standard lens, it works simply and efficiently—when the image is in focus, lines in the image in each half match up and when it is not in focus the image is split. But when a lens with a small maximum aperture is used, or if a faster lens is stopped down, one half goes dark and cannot be focused properly (below right)

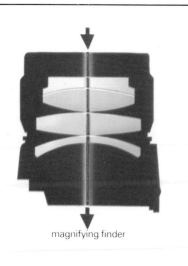

magnifying finder

folding hood

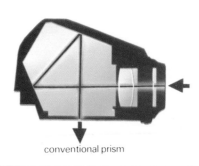

conventional prism

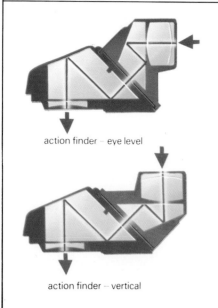

action finder – eye level

action finder – vertical

Interchangeable finders *Magnifying finders are used in close-up photography and when critical focusing is important; simple waist level viewfinders are valuable for shots in tight situations; dioptre correction lenses can be fitted to compensate for poor eyesight; action finders can be used at any angle from eye level to waist level*

blacking out in parts—as it does on a screen incorporating microprisms or a split image rangefinder.

In addition to these plain screens, there are a large number of special screens designed with very specialized applications in mind. These include *chequerboard screens* which are useful for architectural work, as they allow the photographer to check that horizontal and vertical lines appear that way in the viewfinder. *Graduated screens* have a scale in millimetres engraved on them, and these are useful for measuring magnification in close up work, or measuring size when the camera is attached to a microscope. *TV screens* are marked with the proportions of a television screen and are used when preparing colour slides to be broadcast on television. Other types include screens to be used with endoscopes in medical photography and telescopes for astronomical photographs. All of these screens are obviously of specialized interest, but if you use your camera in connection with your work, you may find that there is a screen available for your camera which is easier to use than the one that is fitted as standard.

Changing viewfinders

A number of 35 mm cameras can be fitted with interchangeable viewfinders, a facility that is almost universal in larger format cameras. A retaining catch on the camera prevents the prism from falling off accidentally, and when this is released, the standard prism can be slid off or lifted out of position, and replaced by an alternative viewing system.

Beside the basic pentaprism, most manufacturers offer an alternative prism that has an enlarged viewing window, through which the whole focusing screen can be seen, even if the photographer's eye is not pressed firmly against the eyepiece. The distance from the eye to the finder is called the *eye relief*, and on this large scale prism it is usually about 25 mm. Most pentaprisms have an eye relief of 15 mm.

Action finders, as these prisms are called, are ideal for fast moving sports subjects, and situations where it is impossible to get your eye close up to the viewfinder window. Goggles and safety glasses also often prevent this, and when the camera is in an underwater housing it is impossible to use a standard prism. Some action finders are fitted with a swivel joint that allows either a horizontal or vertical line of sight. This allows them to be used at awkward angles and very low levels.

An eye level view of the subject is not always the most convenient one. When the camera is very low down, it is much easier to look directly at the focusing screen, rather than sprawling on the ground to peer into the viewfinder.

Waist level finders make it possible to see the screen clearly through the top of the camera. Naturally, it is possible to do the same thing by simply removing the prism, but a waist level finder has a collapsible hood that keeps stray light off the screen, and is also fitted with a magnifier for critical focusing.

Chequerboard screen *One of the most useful alternative focusing screens has a square grid that helps to ensure that the picture is completely level— this is invaluable for architectural shots*

These hoods are good for copying, because when the camera is fixed to a vertical copy stand, a pentaprism viewfinder forces the photographer to clamber up above the camera in order to see the focusing screen. A waist level finder avoids this.

A drawback to this kind of viewfinder is that the image on the focusing screen is reversed left to right, as it is with a large format SLR.

Magnifying finders perform the same function as waist level finders, except that they give a greatly enlarged image of the focusing screen—typically six times bigger. They are most useful for really critical work where correct focus is specially important. Their usefulness for everyday photography is rather limited. Like waist level finders, they produce a reversed image of the focusing screen.

Viewfinder accessories
Many cameras do not have interchangeable finders, but this does not limit them to eye level use alone, as most systems have a *right angle finder* available. This fits on to the viewfinder window, either using a sliding action, or else screwing into place. It converts an eye level pentaprism into a reasonably good vertical type finder—similar to a magnifying finder, but with an image that is not enlarged. Some models give a right-way-round picture, but most right angle finders give a reversed picture of the focusing screen.

Focusing magnifiers can be fitted to the viewfinder in a similar way, and produce an enlarged view of the centre of the focusing screen. Since they do not show the whole screen, they are only useful for critical focusing, and are hinged to flip up out of the way when not in use. Most cameras can also be fitted with a *rubber eye cup* which fits over the viewfinder window. This excludes stray

light, and makes it easier to see the focusing screen in very bright sunlight.

Dioptres and eyesight correction
Few photographers, unfortunately, have perfect eyesight. The most common fault is short sight—the inability to see distant objects. Camera manufacturers recognize this handicap, and construct their viewfinders in such a way that the image of the focusing screen appears to be one metre away from the photographer's eye, or closer. If you have normal eyesight, you will have no difficulty in seeing this image, but if you are long sighted, or have very short sight, you may find that you need to wear glasses to see the screen clearly.

This brings problems, because it is not always possible to see the whole of the focusing screen when wearing spectacles. A better alternative is to use an adaptor lens which changes the apparent distance of the viewfinder image, either moving it out to infinity to

Graduated screen *Specialist screens like this are used if a camera is fitted to a microscope, as this stops microprisms and split image wedges from working. The graded lines help you judge the scale of the image*

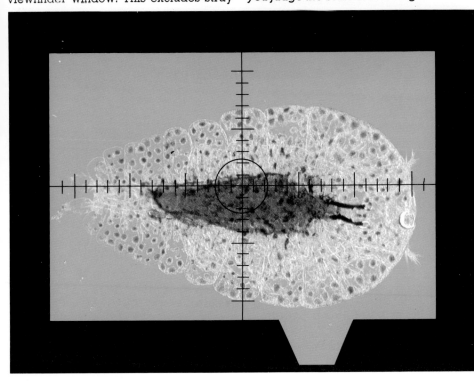

Viewfinder accessories *If your standard viewfinder is not interchangeable you may still be able to attach a flip-up magnifier (left) to your eyepiece, or a right angle viewer so you are not limited to eye-level viewing*

suit long sighted photographers, or bringing it closer in for short sight. The large camera manufacturers make adaptor lenses, calibrated in *dioptres.* The dioptre value is the strength of the correction lens, and can be positive or negative. Short sighted photographers need correction lenses with a negative value, and if you have very short sight, you may need a lens as powerful as —3 dioptres. Correction lenses for long sighted photographers, on the other hand, have a positive value.

Correction lenses are easily fitted to the camera—they either slide over the viewfinder window, or screw into it. If you normally wear spectacles, you may find that buying one of these lenses enables you to see the whole screen more clearly. Since the exact specifications of different camera viewfinders are not the same, it is important to buy such lenses over the counter, so that you can choose the one that best suits your eyesight—it may not have the same strength as your spectacles. If you have astigmatism, or similar eye defects, you may need a specially ground lens, and should see your optician.

The Pentax LX has built in variable dioptre correction, which is adjustable over a 4 dioptre range. This is the ideal solution to eyesight defects, and though it is still rare on modern cameras, it is likely to become more common.

Although the idea of special viewfinders may at first sound rather unnecessary, it is surprising how valuable they can be. Many people, for instance, consistently take out-of-focus pictures, not realizing that their eyesight is at fault. Other photographers may even buy a new camera with a different format simply because they want an eye level viewing system. If you do find problems with any area of your work, it may be worth investigating the possibilities of special viewfinders. And anybody who regularly carries out any form of technical photography may find that a camera with interchangeable finders and viewing screens is a worthwhile investment which makes life much easier.

TRIPODS

With shutter speeds of tiny fractions of a second, it may seem unlikely that camera movement during exposure can have any significant effect. Yet camera shake is still a very common cause of poor photographs—indeed, some people believe that camera shake can make a difference to quality even when shutter speed is as high as 1/500 second. Unfortunately, simply using high shutter speeds to avoid camera shake is no remedy—this only makes it impossible to get the best out of some shots—but there is a solution to the problem. A tripod, which holds the camera completely still during exposure, not only prevents camera shake but also enables the full speed range to be used to best advantage. A tripod is, therefore, a very valuable addition to your range of equipment, but what should you look for before you choose?

Travelling light

Tripods must be light enough to carry easily and sturdy enough to withstand light breezes or vibrations, so almost all modern tripods are built from aluminium alloys. The legs are made as tubes or as a U-chanelled, box-like construction. The circular tube style is generally more rigid than other types but is usually a feature of heavier and more expensive models.

For the photographer, the shiny, natural finish of aluminium tripods can sometimes be a disadvantage. In close-up photography, for example, or in copying work where you are focusing down on the subject through a sheet of glass, it is sometimes hard to avoid a reflection of the tripod appearing in the picture. And when photographing birds or other timid animals, a bright silvery

Leg locks *Channel section legs have either flip locks (top) or a threaded handle (centre). Tubular legs are locked by a threaded ring (bottom) which provides a very secure joint that is not prone to wear*

Tilt top *Many tripods have a pivoting camera platform. This is a valuable feature—it allows you to take both vertical and horizontal shots and the changeover can be made in a single action. Tripods without this feature are much less versatile*

Leg locks

There are two common methods of locking tripod leg joints into their extended position: screw threads and flip levers. The sections on tubular legs are normally locked by a screw thread mechanism —each section is pulled out to its full extent and locked into place by tightening the screw. U-chanelled leg sections are normally fixed by the flip lever type of locks.

Both locking systems have points for and against them. Legs fitted with flip lever locks, for instance, can be set up much faster than screw thread leg sections. But though this may seem a great advantage, in practice speed of assembly is of limited value, because tripods are rarely used in situations where time is pressing. Inner leg sections, on some tripods with flip lever locks, can wear loose and may drop violently to the floor when the lever is flipped open. The jolt can damage or knock off the base plate of the bottom leg section.

Screw locking, on the other hand, provides a very rigid joint. In fact the screw locks on some professional tripods are so sturdy that they can be used as footholds when a photographer climbs up the tripod to reach the viewfinder—but this kind of treatment is not to be recommended for most ordinary tripods!

Whichever kind of leg locks you have on a tripod, it is important to make sure they are securely fastened before fitting the camera to the top. If one leg collapses suddenly your camera could be ruined. To prevent such accidents, some of the more expensive tripods have air cushion devices, built into the legs, that make it impossible for the legs to retract suddenly. And should the leg locks come loose, the legs telescope together only very slowly—giving you plenty of time to catch the camera.

To stop the tripod slipping, the feet must suit the surface. Most tripods are equipped with both rubber feet for hard shiny surfaces and spikes for soft ground. On a few tripods the feet are reversible, but on most the spike is fixed and the rubber feet are screwed down when they are needed.

On the waterfront *For night-time pictures, a tripod is essential, as it allows you to use long exposures without running the risk of camera shake. Even at dusk, exposure times may still be too long for hand-held shots*

tripod might attract unwanted attention. In these circumstances it is better to use a tripod with matt-black legs. An anodised finish is preferable to black paint because paint can easily become chipped or scratched, revealing the shiny metal.

Leg length

Tripods vary enormously in size from small table-top models only 20 cm high to professional giants that can take a camera up to 3 metres off the ground. For portability and easy storage tripods need to fold up into a small space.

Rubber feet *In order to get a firm grip on soft ground, almost all tripods have spikes at the end of their legs. But make sure that the spikes have rubber covers, or, better still, are retractable, or they may slip on flat, hard surfaces*

The legs on modern tripods are usually telescopic with anything between two and eight sections, though most have three or four. The more sections a leg has, the smaller it is when folded up. Unfortunately, each joint in a tripod's legs is a possible source of unsteadiness and for maximum rigidity it is best to buy a tripod with as few sections as possible —even though this type may not pack down to as small a size as some others. It is better to have a bulky tripod that performs well than a compact type that may prove to be unstable.

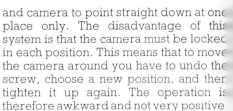

and camera to point straight down at one place only. The disadvantage of this system is that the camera must be locked in each position. This means that to move the camera around you have to undo the screw, choose a new position, and then tighten it up again. The operation is therefore awkward and not very positive.

Camera movement is made much easier and much more definite on a tripod fitted with a pan and tilt head. Not surprisingly, this type of head is the more popular. The direction of the camera is controlled by a long slim handle. With this the camera can be panned horizontally through 360°—and tilted backwards or forwards. Twisting the handle locks either the tilt or the pan, or sometimes both. In addition to the pan and tilt, some tripods allow the camera base to be turned up through 90° for taking photographs in vertical format.

Some of the more expensive tripods have one or more bubble levels fitted to the head. These work in the same way as a spiritlevel—when the bubble is in the centre of the tube or dish of fluid, the tripod head is horizontal.

If you are taking only a single picture levels are not important because the camera can be levelled with the pan and tilt or ball and socket head. Levels are more useful if you decide to take a series of pictures to show a wide panorama by panning the camera on the tripod between pictures. Unless the tripod is completely level, the camera moves up or down as you pan. You can judge whether the tripod is level by eye, but a bubble level makes it much easier.

On every tripod, the camera is locked on to the rubber-surfaced platform by a screw thread. This locking screw can often be very difficult to undo and a few tripods have a quick-release system consisting of a circular or wedge-shaped metal block. The block is screwed on to the camera base using the tripod socket,

Table-top tripods *If space and bulk are at a premium, choose a table-top tripod. Some of these are very simple, but others are like miniature replicas of their full size counterparts*

Centre column *A rising centre column is an invaluable feature. This one is geared, and winding a handle on the body of the tripod moves the head steadily up or down*

Holding the camera
One of the most important decisions to make when you buy a tripod is which of the two types of head to choose.

The ball and socket head uses a metal ball with a tripod-screw attached. The ball joint allows you to move the camera round through a full circle in the horizontal plane, and to tilt it up and down through about 40°. A narrow channel cut in one side of the cup allows the ball

Two heads *A pan and tilt head (left) has individual locks for each action. Ball and socket heads, on the other hand, are smaller and use just one knob to lock all movements of the camera*

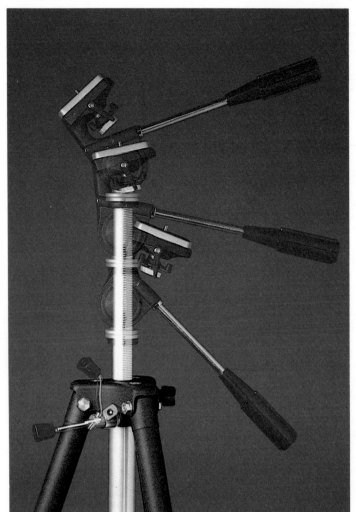

and the whole apparatus is then fixed into a recess on the tripod and locked into place by a lever or knob. A good quick release mechanism can make life much easier but a poor quality or worn device may fail to hold the camera rigidly. Since the main purpose of the tripods is to hold the camera rigidly, it may, therefore, be better to avoid cheaper tripods incorporating quick release heads.

Tripod heads are usually attached to a centre column which can be moved up or down through a boss at the top of the legs. On some tripods this column has teeth cut into one side and is raised or lowered by a small, geared crank handle. A non-geared centre column is moved simply by lifting or lowering the column to the appropriate height and securing it with the column lock. Crank handles, though convenient, usually prevent you inverting the centre column for copying, and low level photography.

Special tripods
If you cannot afford a full scale tripod it may be worth buying a miniature table-top version that holds the camera 20 cm or so above a surface. These are basic and can be very cheap and this is their main feature, along with ease of handling and portability, when viewed against full scale tripods.

One common type of miniature tripod has a hollow metal tube not much longer than a hand, with a ball and socket head at one end. When you unscrew the base

of the tube out come three legs, each pivoted to the base (often rather loosely). The legs unfold outwards and the base is screwed back into the main column to secure the legs. The height of these tripods is not adjustable.

Because of their size—when packed away the column is only about 10 cms high—table-top tripods can be carried anywhere. They can be placed on top of any convenient object such as a brick wall, a table-top or a car roof. The only limitation is that you must find something of the appropriate height on which to set the tripod.

Unfortunately, though relatively steady when set on a firm base, table-top tripods are not generally very stable. Any adjustment to the ball and socket must be made very carefully because they are very top heavy with the camera in place. A camera can easily topple over, especially if there is a long lens to help it over-balance. Nevertheless, the low cost and lightweight make these small tripods attractive alternatives.

A simple variation on the tripod is the monopod, sometimes called a unipod. This is really just a single tripod leg. Sometimes a tiny three-legged base is fitted in the base of the column and can be screwed into place when needed. More usually, it is stuck into the ground on a spike. Monopods cannot give the steadiness of a tripod but they can often be used in situations where a tripod cannot. With a single leg, they are much lighter to

Safari family *Long telephoto lenses are always difficult to use hand-held, and should be supported with a solid tripod whenever possible*

carry and do not need a large, relatively flat area to stand on. If, for example, you were going for a walk over hilly ground where a tripod might be awkward to set up and cumbersome to carry, then a monopod could be a useful accessory. Some sports photographers prefer monopods because they can move the camera much faster to follow the action than they could even on the smoothest pan and tilt head tripod.

A firm base
Though a light tripod is easy to carry, it can sway with the slightest breeze or vibration, so it may be worth spending the extra effort and money on a heavier model which will provide a firmer base. Remember, though, that some tripods are heavy because they have many leg joints and their weight advantage may be offset by the greater chance of eventual unsteadiness and trouble following wear and tear on joints. So, your final choice will probably be based on a compromise between weight, size and ease of use.

Finally, whatever tripod you choose, you should use a cable release or other remote control device for shutter control to gain the full benefit from the extra steadiness. Used properly, a tripod can make a substantial difference to the quality and range of your photographs.

HAND-HELD LIGHT METERS

In recent years, computer technology has so improved the versatility of built-in exposure metering systems in SLRs that a TTL reading will nearly always give satisfactory exposure, even with fairly unusual subjects. Indeed, advances like the Olympus OM4's Electro Selective Pattern (ESP) metering have made built-in metering as sophisticated as the majority of photographers can cope with. Such systems will even detect a backlit subject automatically and adjust the exposure accordingly. Nevertheless, there are many SLR photographers who still prefer to work with hand-held meters when they have the time. And for photographers shooting with medium and large format cameras with no built-in metering system, a hand-held meter is a must.

Hand-held meters may be less convenient to use than built-in meters, but they have a number of advantages. First of all, they make it much easier to take light readings from directly from individual areas of the subject. Secondly, handheld meters tend to give more useful readings in very low light conditions. And thirdly, hand-held meters make it much easier to make different *types* of meter reading, such as *incident light* readings.

Most modern meters, for instance, have a diffuser that can be placed over the meter's 'eye' to allow you to take incident light readings, readings of the intensity of light actually falling on the subject. This type of reading is normally impossible with through-the-lens (TTL) metering on an SLR.

Made from opaque plastic, the diffuser is normally dome shaped to include all the light falling on the front of the subject, but some meters have a flat diffuser. Because it has a narrower acceptance angle, a meter with a flat diffuser can also tell you the relative strength of a number of different light sources.

Some meters can be used with an accessory, to take spot readings—readings from a very small area of the subject. Indeed a few large and expensive meters, such as the Pentax Spotmeter, are designed specifically for this type of metering. With a spotmeter, you look through a viewfinder that takes in a wide view of the scene, but the reading is only taken from a small circle in the centre covering an angle of a few degrees. Spot readings are ideal for precise exposure readings from small areas, particularly at a distance,

such as a brightly lit figure on a dim, far away stage. But they must be used with caution because they are calibrated on the assumption that the spot they are aimed at is typical of average brightness.

Other facilities available on the more sophisticated meters are attachments to make exposure readings for either copying or enlarging. With a few meters, you can actually take readings from the

camera's ground glass focusing screen though this facility is usually only used with large format sheet film cameras which have a large screen.

More unusual features that you may come across are flexible fibre optic probes—for spot readings from otherwise inaccessible parts of the subject—and adaptors for readings through microscopes or telescopes. One meter, the

Spot or universal ? *A spotmeter (right) is of more specific use than other types (left), which can measure both incident and reflected light*

White tree *When a subject is very dark or light, as here, reflected light meters can be easily misled, but an incident light meter gives accurate exposure*

Gossen Profisix, can be converted into a colour temperature meter or a flash meter, and a few meters, such as those in the Calcuflash and Vivitar LX range, can be used for normal light and flash metering together.

With such a range of alternative facilities available, you may find the prospect of choosing a meter rather daunting, and unless you have any special need for a particular facility, it may be easier to select your meter on the basis of sensitivity and cost. Both of these factors partly depend on the type of photocell that the meter is based on.

Types of cell

Photocells for light meters are of three major types: selenium, cadmium sulphide (CdS) and silicon photodiode (SPD). Of the three, selenium cell meters are the most basic. They need no batteries, last for a long time and have a colour response similar to the human eye. However, they do not respond to low light levels and they tend to become less accurate as they age. Nevertheless, their low price and simplicity make them ideal for supplementing a built-in meter and one meter of this type, the Weston, has become a classic. If you are going to a remote spot where batteries are unobtainable, a selenium cell meter might prove invaluable.

For that extra sensitivity to meter low light levels however, you need either a CdS or SPD meter. CdS meters must

Meter dial *Although meter dials look confusing, operation is simple. Here a mid-tone reading gives a figure of 13 on the meter scale. The triangular index is aligned with 13 on the circular dial, and the aperture and shutter speed combinations are chosen from the concentric scales at the top left of the disc. Other markings are for shadow and highlight readings, and exposure values (EVs)*

have a battery but can be small and exceptionally sensitive. Unfortunately they are a little too sensitive to red light. They are also rather slow to respond and have a memory effect that makes them over read low light levels when metered shortly after exposure to a bright scene. Not surprisingly, CdS meters are now being superseded by meters with SPD cells which are equally sensitive and have no memory effect.

CdS and SPD cell meters are not only expensive to run, they are expensive to buy. But if you plan to do a considerable amount of night-time photography the extra sensitivity may justify the expense. Although you may have to make adjustments to exposure for reciprocity failure —the loss of effective emulsion speed during very long exposures—a CdS or SPD meter will at least give you a

Digits and dials *Some types of meter have a motorized dial (top), others a conventional needle display (left), or a digital display (right)*

reading in situations where many other meters would not respond at all. But sensitivity varies even between SPD meters, and it is worth checking that the meter gives the range you want.

Meter sensitivity

Conventionally, the maximum sensitivity of an exposure meter is given as an Exposure Value (EV) for a film of 100

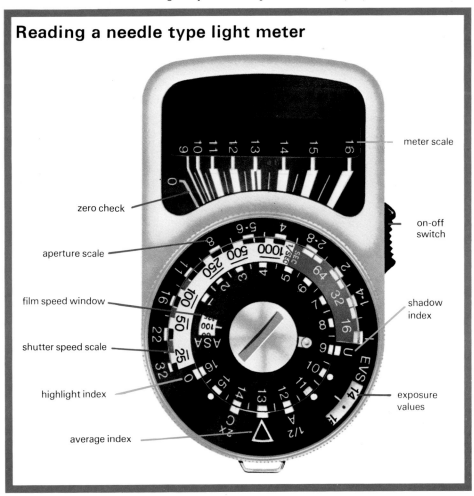

Reading a needle type light meter

- meter scale
- zero check
- on-off switch
- aperture scale
- film speed window
- shutter speed scale
- highlight index
- average index
- shadow index
- exposure values

In the spotlight *When the subject of a picture is inaccessible, a spotmeter may prove to be the only way of getting an accurate exposure meter reading*

ASA (ISO). Each exposure value is simply an expression of the various shutter speed and aperture combinations needed to give the correct exposure in particular lighting conditions. For EV of 10, for instance, exposure would be 1/30 second at $f/5.6$ or 1/60 second at $f/4$ or any equivalent combination. So the sensitivity of a meter in terms of EV is simply the correct exposure for the darkest conditions it can cope with.

While a few TTL meters on SLRs can operate at —6EV (the equivalent of two minutes at $f/1.4$ or a similar exposure), most cannot cope with EVs of less than 1 (one second at $f/1.4$, for example) and some do not operate below 3EV ($\frac{1}{4}$ second at $f/1.4$). Some selenium cell meters do not even work below 6EV (1/30 at $f/1.4$). CdS and SPD meters, on the other hand, typically give at least —2EV (eight seconds at $f/1.4$) and some give as good as —8EV (eight minutes at $f/1.4$) though for exposures this long reciprocity failure must be taken into account.

When ascertaining the sensitivity range of a meter, do not be misled by

Accessory kit *This meter is the basis of a system which includes spot, colour temperature, flash, copying, microscope, flexi-probe, and other sophisticated attachments*

the calibrations on the meter dial: they do not indicate the capabilities of the meter. For instance, some meter scales show exposures ranging from one hour to 1/5000 second, and $f/1$ to $f/128$. Many exposures in this range are not only impossible to put into practice: they may

also be beyond the meter's ability to measure. Such all-encompassing scales have little practical value and it is far more useful to have a reasonable range of values that are clearly legible and unambiguous even in dim light than rows of figures you never use.

Reflected reading *Reflected light meters work well for average subjects where it is easy to get close to take the exposure meter reading*

Scales and displays

Most selenium cell meters are permanently 'on' and do not need to be switched on to take a reading. CdS and SPD meters, on the other hand, must be switched on for every reading and often switch off automatically after a minute or so to conserve battery power. On both selenium cell and CdS/SPD meters, the reading is usually given by an artibrary number or light value. To find out the various possible exposure settings you must locate this light value on the calculator dial against the appropriate film speed.

The meter film speed scale may be in both ASA (ISO) and DIN, but increasingly nowadays it is in ASA only. The range of values given can sometimes be extreme—one meter shows anything from 0.05 to 800,000 ASA—but these extreme speeds are of little practical value. You will rarely need a film speed setting of faster than 3200 ASA and though the low values may be usable with printing paper and slow copying film, a much more restricted range is adequate. Ease of setting, a positive lock and legible numerals are again more important than extreme values.

Meter displays take two main forms: analog and digital. With analog displays, the reading is indicated by a needle that moves across a dial scale. Digital displays give an actual figure in a window either as a Light Emitting Diode (LED) or a low contrast Liquid Crystal Display (LCD). LEDs are luminous and can be read in the dark but are heavy on batteries: LCDs need far less battery power, but are not luminous.

Digital displays, on the other hand, only show values to the nearest third stop and disguise smaller variations, but give the reading in clear easy to read figures on a continuous scale. They also have a memory that can store a reading for later recall. On some meters this memory can be updated every second to allow a slow scan of a scene. A few meters have servo-operated calculator dials where the light value is automatically transferred to the calculator to give an exposure value, but this is really something of a luxury.

Meter displays can take other forms besides analog and digital, but these alternatives make up only a small proportion of the market.

As with all items of photographic equipment, your final choice of light meter must be a compromise between your needs and your pocket. A selenium cell meter is cheap and reliable and works well in good light, but for low light conditions you need the extra sensitivity of the more expensive SPD meters and, if you intend to use it at night it should have a digital LED display. Clearly, a diffuser for incident light readings is a valuable accessory.

Before you buy, you must decide exactly what your priorities are. But whatever your decision, you will find a hand-held light meter not only helps you to achieve the correct exposure but also gives you a tremendous feeling for the craft of photography.

Spotmeter *Using a spotmeter, a photographer can stand back from the scene and get a precise light reading*
Incident light meter *By measuring light falling on the subject, rather than the reflected light, the exposure will be absolutely consistent, and unaffected by subject and background tone*

REMOTE CONTROL SYSTEMS

Conventional releases *are either cable, electric or pneumatically operated*

There are many types of shots that cannot be taken by merely pressing the shutter release button on your camera. For these occasions, you must use some kind of remote control device. Some are available as stock items but others must be improvised.

At the simplest level, a remote control device, such as a cable release, helps to avoid camera shake when giving exposures longer than 1/60 second using a tripod. The problem becomes more complicated, however, if you need to be away from the camera, holding or manipulating equipment while the picture is taken, or if you wish to take candid shots or photograph shy wildlife at close range. In this case, various long distance triggering systems are needed.

The simplest remote control devices depend on a direct link between the photographer and camera, whether by cable, air line or electronic cable. The more complex—sonic and ultrasonic, radio, infrared and light—are genuinely remote and the photographer could work from across a wide river.

Cable releases

Perhaps the simplest and least expensive remote control device is the conventional cable release. These are available in a wide range of finishes—including fabric and clear plastic—and vary in length from about 250 mm to more than a metre. The shorter ones—costing little more than the price of a 20 exposure print film—are intended purely for long exposures when the photographer is close to the camera. If you buy one of these, make sure it flexes easily so that

there is no chance of vibration from your hand being transmitted through the release to the camera. Some releases, with metal-wound outer sheaths are durable but are in fact, quite inflexible.

You might also wish to make extra-long exposures, so a shutter release that is lockable is the best choice. A good design enables you to set the shutter release so that it stays depressed simply by pressing a lever. To close the shutter after a long exposure, the lock button is pressed. This has the advantage of being operable by one hand and so avoids the risk of shaking the camera which can occur with a screw-type lock.

Pneumatic releases

A pneumatic shutter release combines the advantages of smooth action, long reach and easy operation. The device can extend more than 5 m and does not cost much more than a cable release. The release mechanism at the camera end consists of an air-driven diaphragm, operated by squeezing a rubber bulb at the end of a thin connecting hose.

A pneumatic release can be operated by squeezing the bulb either by hand or

Electric release *This is merely a length of twin-core flex and a simple switch, used to extend the triggering circuit of a motor drive or auto winder*

nderfoot while it is on the ground. Most do not have a locking device but he shutter can be kept open if a weight s placed on the bulb.

If used carefully, a pneumatic release hould be no trouble. A common pro-lem is that the bulb does not recover its hape when you let go, so the shutter vill not close if the camera is on the B etting. This happens if the bulb is pres-ed too vigorously, causing air to escape rom the system. The best remedy is to letach and reconnect the hose at one nd, and apply only gentle pressure vhen you use the device. Greater ophistication and longer range can be chieved either by buying a suitable tock unit or by improvising.

Electrical triggering

Mechanical triggering methods using able and pneumatic releases are cheap ut restrictive. Much more flexibility is offered by electrical triggering methods. These range from very simple to quite advanced, and in some cases the equip-nent is not available off the shelf and you must make it yourself.

There are two main ways of taking a oicture by electrical triggering. The irst can be carried out using virtually iny camera, and involves triggering a flash only, to provide all the illumination. This can only be done at night or in a

A pneumatic release *is particularly suitable for taking self portraits or operating the camera while you are manipulating equipment in the scene. An electromagnetic plunger (below) gives you just as much freedom away from the camera, but it is more elaborate and expensive*

An ultrasonic trigger *has no connection between the camera-mounted and hand-held units, but its range is limited to the size of a large room*

A sound-operated trigger employs transistorized switching to achieve rapid response—it is used here to 'freeze' the cork being ejected from a pressurized bottle

dark room, but is useful for photographing shy and elusive wildlife. The other method, which is much more versatile, requires the use of a camera which has a motor drive.

In both cases, all that is needed to trigger off the exposure is to touch two electrical contacts together. Any flash unit can be operated by touching together the contacts of the inner and outer parts of a flash lead. This usually involves adapting an ordinary flash lead by cutting it and baring the wires. A motor drive unit usually has two contacts which will operate the shutter when they are touched together. The current and voltage within the circuit are low, so there is little danger involved, but losses in the cables could be considerable if the wires are particularly long—more than, say, 50 or 100 metres.

Sound-operated trigger

Sound-operated remote triggers are not widely available but they are simple in principle, and inexpensive. One design, made by the German firm Immo Drust, measures 30 × 60 × 105 mm and sells for about as much as three rolls of Kodachrome. Essentially, the unit consists of a miniature microphone, which detects ordinary sound frequencies. The electrical signal from the microphone is amplified by a transistorized unit which closes a circuit. The device can then be connected by means of an external cable to either a flash or a motor drive unit.

The sound-operated trigger is particularly effective in enclosed spaces because it works equally well by direct or reflected sound. At a distance of about 3 m, the sound of a spoon falling on an egg can trigger a shutter set to 1/500,

for example, to 'freeze' the falling spoon on the broken egg. But sensitivity falls off rapidly at greater distances, where louder sounds are required to trigger the device.

Infrared triggers

Another form of remote control uses infrared radiation, whose wavelength is close to the red end of the visible spectrum. This gives a beam that is deep red in colour but of an intensity which is too low to affect the film. The standard infrared triggers are two-unit devices, with a hand-held, pocket-sized transmitter, and a receiver mounted on the hot shoe or a bracket on the camera. Each unit is powered by its own separate battery, and incorporates an on/off switch and test facility. The only connecting lead is from the receiver to the camera motor drive unit. If you buy an infrared trigger, make sure the connector fits your make of camera, or you will need an adapter.

Some systems have up to three channels, so a single transmitter can be used to trigger more than one receiver. And a facility common to all is single frame or continuous operation— achieved by a two-way switch on the receiver. To use the system, each unit is switched on and channel 1 is slected on both. If single frame operation is selected, and the trigger button pressed, the receiver will pick up a single pulse of infrared signal and expose just one frame. Indoors, the two units need not be aligned because the receiver responds equally well to both direct and bounced signals. In the open, the signal can be bounced off objects—such as buildings and rocks—to a limited extent, but line-of-sight control is possible up to 60 m.

By selecting 'C' (for continuous) on the receiver, and pressing the trigger, a series of pulses is transmitted, each exposing one frame. In this mode, you can make time exposures (using the 'B' setting on the camera). The first trigger pulse releases the shutter, which stays open until it is closed by the second.

Some units are made as part of a camera system, such as Nikon's Modulite ML-1 and the Canon LC-1. The Nikon model has two channels, and the Canon has three. Other units, however, fit a more limited range of cameras, such as the three-channel Minolta IR-1, which is designed to fit the X-700 camera, motor drive and data back system.

It is also possible to buy units made by independent manufacturers. The Kenlock Beacon 200, with three channels, is one example. Connectors are available to suit a wide range of motor drives, and there is also a conventional flash socket.

Despite the sophistication and expense of infrared systems, they must be triggered manually. This is a disadvantage if your subject is unpredictable. For example, you might know the route taken by an animal or bird but could easily miss its appearance. This problem is best solved by adapting a security system, which raises an alarm when a beam is broken. One system sends out a pulsed infrared beam to a reflector (up to 50 m away) which throws it back. An alarm sounds when the beam is interrupted. Alternatively, it can be set to sound continuously once the beam has been broken, only while the beam is broken, or, for an extra ten seconds after a break. The signal that powers the alarm can be used, indirectly, to trigger a motor drive unit, and the choice of alarm modes gives a wide range of shutter operations.

A simple adaptation is to replace the alarm (usually sold separately anyway) by a miniature relay operating off the same voltage as the alarm, commonly 12V. The relay is a switch operated by a solenoid so that when current is applied, the switch closes.

When the beam is interrupted, the unit allows current to flow to the siren or, in this case, the relay or solenoid. This then closes the circuit to which you have attached either your flash leads or the lead to your motor drive.

If you are carrying out the work yourself, check with the camera manufacturer which terminals operate the motor drive. Remember that the system only needs to complete the circuit, and that you do not need an external power supply to the motor drive or flash unit, —this could damage it.

Radio control

The most advanced remote control equipment uses radio waves to operate the triggering device. Such equipment is not only expensive but must be licensed in many countries, including the UK, where controls on broadcasting are strict. But it is possible to adapt the systems used for radio-controlled models to operate a motor drive or flash. In the UK and some other countries, radio equipment is licensed to operate models only, so strictly speaking, its use for operating a camera is prohibited. But the rules vary from country to country so check with your licensing authority.

Radio control equipment consists of a hand-held transmitter and a receiver mounted on the model. Commands to the model—such as turn right—reach the receiver as coded radio signals, which are converted into mechanical movements by servo motors. The motors then operate linkages that carry out the commands. The linkages are arranged to move a throttle lever, shift a rudder or even depress a shutter release.

The problem, therefore, is to attach the receiver on or near the camera and mount a servo motor and linkages on the camera, without obscuring the lens or photo cells. Some experiments will be necessary to find the most convenient method of attachment. One technique is to bind the servo motor on with wire, twine or tape. Alternatively, you could clamp a rigid support on to the tripod and arrange for it to curve or angle towards the shutter release button. Whatever solution you find, care will be necessary with alignment and rigidity, but the problem should be well within the scope of a competent modeller.

Operating the shutter release button by mechanical linkages is probably the only means of remote control for many cameras. But if your camera has a motor-drive attachment, your choice of remote control is much wider. All that is required is a switch to close the circuit on the motor drive.

Light-operated switch

For the do-it-yourself electronics enthusiast, a light-operated switch to trigger a motor drive can be a most satisfying project. This can be constructed from a few readily available, inexpensive components using diagrams commonly found in most hobby electronics books.

The circuit for a typical light-sensitive switch is based on a *photoresistor*—a semiconductor device whose resistance varies with the amount of light falling on its surface. The change in resistance causes the circuit to activate a relay, which can be connected in the circuit of the motor drive unit via a jack plug. Either the relay connection or the photoresistor can be connected by a long conductor. The circuit can be made to switch either when the photoresistor is covered from daylight or when it is uncovered and exposed to daylight. And the sensitivity can be adjusted to compensate for ageing of components or for different ranges of light and dark.

Infrared triggers *are now commonly available. Contax were among the first manufacturers to build these devices; a current model has two channels*

Ultrasonic triggers

Sound at ultra-high frequencies can also be used for remote control. In principle, a transmitter similar to the ultrasonic device used to control TV receivers remotely is used to generate a signal, by pressing a metal trigger. This is no more than a metal strip that scrapes against a metal stud, all enclosed in a matchbox-sized case. In fact, shaking a bunch of keys will even transmit a suitable ultrasonic signal. In the camera's accessory shoe is mounted a receiver for the ultrasound. This converts the sound energy into an electrical signal, which energises an electromagnetic plunger, which in turn actuates a shutter release cable. The system is effective over a range of about 5 m and is more sensitive indoors due to reflection.

Improvised trigger *A typical announcer/alarm system transmits infrared beam pulses, which are reflected back. If the beam is interrupted, a 12 volt output triggers a motor drive by means of a relay (inset)*

BAGS AND CASES

While your photographic equipment consists only of a camera and a few filters, carrying it presents no problems. But as soon as you begin to acquire extra lenses, flashguns, light meters and other accessories, a proper carrying bag becomes a necessity unless you are prepared to take only the bare essentials on each assignment. Equipment can be simply flung in a cheap holdall, but for adequate protection a proper camera bag is needed. A proper camera bag also makes it easier to locate a particular item in a hurry.

Purpose-made camera bags are of two main types: soft 'gadget' bags and rigid cases. Soft bags are by far the most popular with both amateurs and professionals—except those who do most of their work in studios. Soft bags are usually equipped with a shoulder strap and are light and comfortable to carry around. Although they cannot be secured against theft and offer less protection against damage than a rigid case, they are ideal for the photographer who wishes to move around quickly and easily with the minimum of fuss. On the other hand, for photographers who work mostly in the studio and carry their equipment between locations by car, the awkwardness and weight of a rigid case make little difference and the extra protection is usually worth the expense.

Soft bags

Although light synthetic materials such as leatherette and vinyl have largely replaced more traditional materials, the range and quality of soft bags on the market is immense. For about the price of a roll of film, you can buy small bags that are little more than holdalls. They do not provide compartments for individual items and offer only the bare minimum of protection. If subject to any rough treatment, this type of bag almost invariably falls apart, but if you have only a few accessories and only take your equipment out occasionally, it may be perfectly adequate.

At the other end of the range, you can pay the price of a new camera and buy a bag that holds a considerable amount of equipment. Each item can be neatly stored in individual compartments and

Bags and cases *There is a huge variety of camera bags and cases to choose from but some are much better than others*

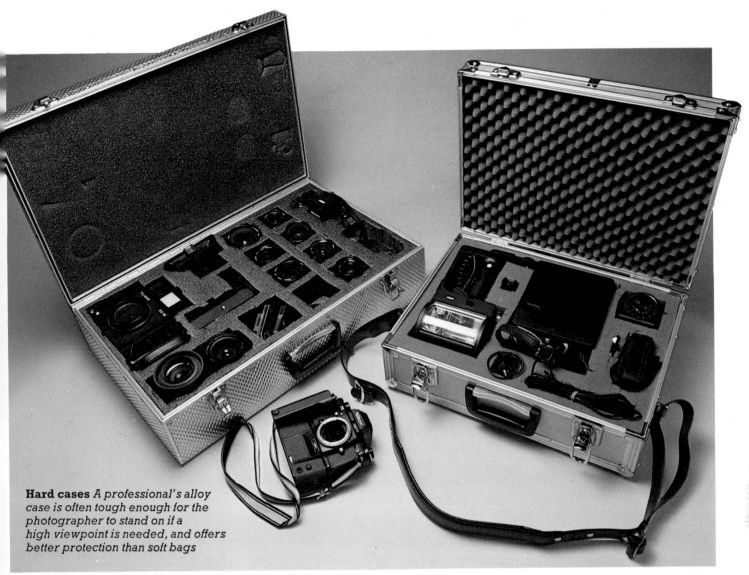

Hard cases *A professional's alloy case is often tough enough for the photographer to stand on if a high viewpoint is needed, and offers better protection than soft bags*

the whole bag is tough and durable and provides a considerable degree of protection.

Clearly, when choosing a bag you must balance the quality against the price you are prepared to pay. But if you use your camera frequently, it may be better to spend a little extra and get a good quality bag—in the long term it can work out less expensive.

Good quality bags are generally made from proofed lightweight and durable nylon weave—similar to the material used in the more expensive rucksacks—although other materials may be equally good and canvas is still popular. The outer walls of the more expensive bags are often double thickness, including a layer of shock-absorbing polyurethane in between each skin. The polyurethane also helps to prevent the bag losing shape, making it easier to get into the bag in a hurry. The better quality bags at the cheaper end of the range also have a double outer skin but the filling is usually cardboard which loses its stiffness rapidly after heavy use.

Like the double outer skin, foam makes a much better material for the compartment divisions but again tends to be found only in the more expensive bags. With the cheaper bags the divisions—if there are any—are made of cardboard covered with fabric.

The size and shape of the divisions vary from bag to bag. In some bags,

the divisions are fixed and there can be a variety of compartments designed to take specific items of equipment such as cylindrical tube for lenses. This can be a disadvantage if your accessories do not quite fit the divisions, but the alternative, with movable divisions, is often less satisfactory. Movable divisions may be altered to suit your equipment—the walls are often attached in each new position with the aid of Velcro strips—but because the division must be flexible, small items can creep underneath and get lost or damaged.

Many bags also have small pockets on the outside and these can be invaluable, allowing easy and rapid access in pressing situations. But these pockets should be well protected by firm fastenings or a flap to ensure that nothing can drop out.

Look for protection in the base of the bag as well. In some of the cheaper bags, the bottom is not padded or stiffened at all. This means that if you put the bag down sharply on a hard surface, you could do considerable damage. The best bags tend to have both padding and stiffening—often a wooden board covered in polyurethane foam. A rigid base not only protects the equipment from dropping but also helps to ensure that the bag does not fold in the middle when carried on the shoulder strap.

Shoulder straps are often a weak point with the cheaper bags and it is worth looking for a bag with proper

reinforcement around the strap fastenings. Sewn-on straps are generally better than the clip-on variety. Look also for a strap that is attached to bands stitched right the way round underneath the bag, so that the bag hangs in a cradle from the strap. This band should also continue over the top of the bag and provide the mounting point for the handles. If the strap is simply attached to the end of the bag, the strain on the bag wall and stitching is excessive. Straps should ideally be about 5 cm wide and have a non-slip shoulder pad if the bag is to be comfortable to carry.

When examining the bag, however, do not look only for the obvious features—try to establish how well it has been made; a bag made from the best materials will fall apart in use if it has not been put together properly. Look in particular at the stitching. Gently pull the seams apart—if the stitches appear in the gap, the stitching is loose and will eventually give. Look also at the zips; they should be tough and smooth running but not loose. Any gap at the end of the zip can let in rain and should be properly covered.

Weatherproofing varies from bag to bag but very few could be left out in anything but the lightest of showers. If you live in a wet climate or intend to visit such an area, you should look for a specially weatherproofed bag. This could also be valuable in very dry con-

Wide straps *It is always worth getting a bag with wide straps as these spread the load and make it more comfortable to carry*

Made to last *A well made camera bag is a work of art. Examine the fabric in detail for the use of quality materials. Look at the stitching, the zip and the way the strap is joined to the bag for signs of good workmanship*

ditions where blown dust would penetrate any normal bag. Impressive claims for weatherproofing have been made for bags such as the American Tenba Propack, which have been designed for Himalayan mountain expeditions. These have an external skin of PVC nylon canvas with a padded infill and inner waterproof liner. The top pulls down tightly over the edge and the bag is sealed with a fabric fastening and clasp so that it is completely weatherproof despite its low weight.

However, no soft bag will ever give your equipment complete protection, and if mobility is not important, it may be worth paying the extra for a rigid case with a gasket seal.

Rigid cases

Most rigid cases are made from aluminium alloy, although there are some plastic cases on the market. There are two different types of alloy case. The more expensive cases are manufactured from two shell halves of stress-formed aluminium. The interior is filled with a semi-hard foam giving much better protection than the cheaper soft foam used

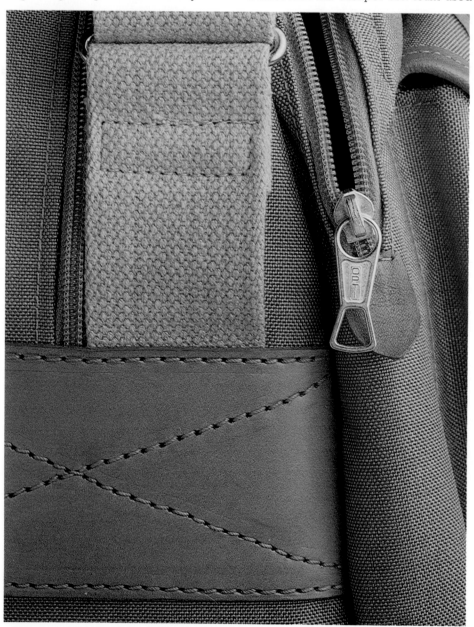

for upholstery, and the rim is fitted with a gasket seal, so that when the case is closed it is watertight and will float.

Cheaper cases use a wooden board structure covered in thin sheet alloy on the outside, with edge strips and corner protectors, and are lined on the inside with soft waffle foam on the lids and deep foam inserts in the body. Often the foam insert is divided into tear-off cubes, so that you can remove sections in crudely matched shapes to fit your equipment. However, the cubes tend to come loose, and you cannot 'rebuild' them easily. Some cases are bought complete with a block of foam and a knife to cut pieces suitable for packing your equipment. Unfortunately, any new equipment will not fit into these specially made shapes.

Alloy cases are used mostly by professional photographers who need rugged protection for expensive equipment.

Many cases are so strong that you could easily sit or stand on them without causing damage. A case could give you just the extra height you need to see over the crowd. The extra height could also be useful if you have a waist-level camera and want eye-level shots without going through contortions.

Although they may seem weak, plastic cases can actually be very tough and may be lighter than alloy types. You can find similar plastic cases made for the office briefcase market which are actually identical to the ones sold for photographers. You could buy foam to fit these, for less than the cost of the photographic version. The difference is that the photographic cases have side fittings for a shoulder strap and the office cases only have a carry handle.

Lightweight bag *Inexpensive bags are worth buying if your equipment is minimal*

Large bag *Some professional camera bags are as large as a holdall. This one has clip-on pockets for carrying extra equipment*

Which size ?
Once you have decided which type of bag to buy, you must decide what size you need. Obviously it is a mistake to buy a bag that can only take the equipment you have at the time of purchase but an overlarge, half empty bag can also be a nuisance. A compromise is necessary. If the make of bag you select has movable partitions or simply an empty main compartment, consider the longest lens you are likely to want to leave attached to the camera body when it is in the bag.

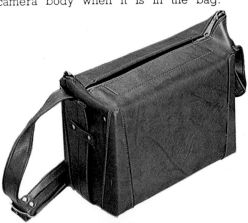

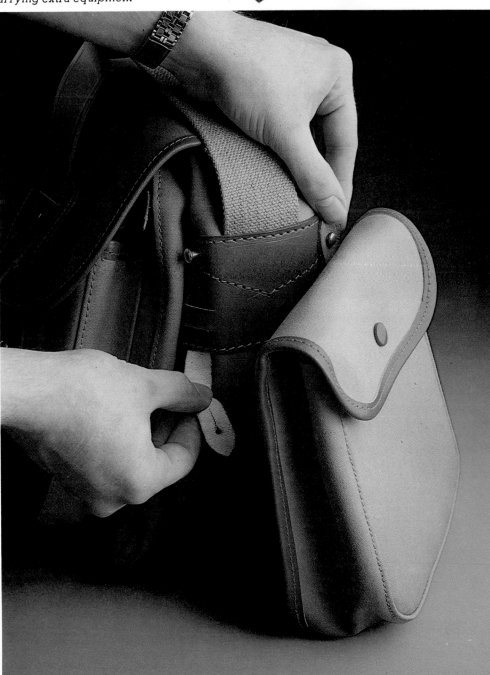

Packed for pictures *A well designed camera bag carries a surprising amount of equipment. You can even strap a tripod on to this bag*

Small bag *There is no sense in buying a large bag if you regularly carry only a single camera body and a couple of lenses*

Chapter 5
FILTERS
FILTERS AND LENS HOODS

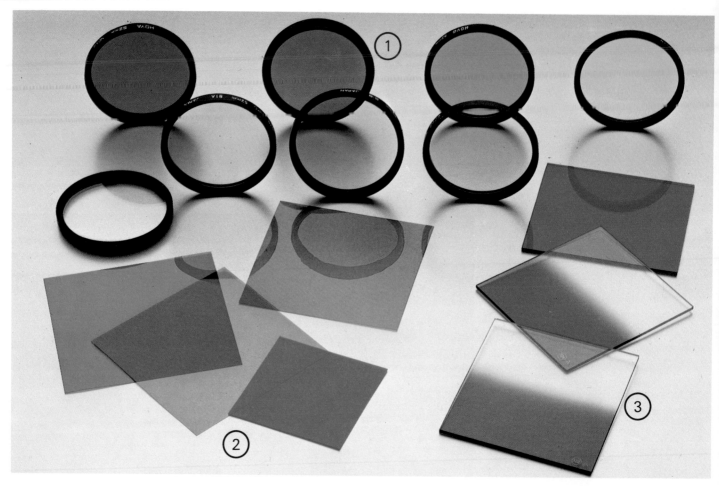

All but the simplest of cameras have lenses with threads or a bayonet fitting at the front to take a variety of accessories. Some of these accessories have very specialized functions and are of only limited use in day-to-day photography, but by far the most common and practical are filters and lens hoods. Both filters and lens hoods are designed to cut out unwanted light before it reaches the film. Filters are used in an enormous variety of ways, from colour correction to startling special effects, and some of the most important uses are described in following sections. This section concentrates on lens hoods and types of filter.

Lens hoods

When you look through a camera's viewfinder, you may only see light that is reflected directly from the subject—but light from sources outside the picture area also reaches the lens and, consequently, reaches the film on exposure.

Filter types *Screw-on filters* **1** *are best for colour correction; gelatin squares* **2** are available in more colours. Plastic filters **3** are best for special effects

This extraneous light may adversely affect the picture, veiling it with a light fog and reducing contrast. In extreme cases, a bright highlight, such as the sun just outside the picture area, can create flare on the film and spoil your pictures.

Most lenses have elaborate baffle systems that cut down unwanted light but these are not completely effective. By fitting a good lens hood, however, you should be able to overcome the effects of stray light in all but the most extreme conditions.

Ideally, a lens would cut off all light coming from outside the picture area but leave the picture unaffected. Unfortunately, this ideal is almost impossible to achieve. The hood would have to be precision made to suit not only the camera format, but also the angle of view of each individual lens. Even if this could be done, it would have to be

Lens flare *Without a hood, stray light from outside the frame can enter the lens and cause flare*

perfectly aligned on the lens for every shot and move in and out with every change in focus.

Understandably, lens hoods must compromise. By far the majority are round and made of metal, plastic or flexible rubber. While they do not cut out all unwanted light, round hoods cut out the worst of it, and are light and easy to use. Manufacturers usually supply round hoods for all their own lenses but you can buy independently made hoods in either wide angle, standard or telephoto fittings with thread sizes to suit your own lens.

In fact, the difference between a round hood for one lens and that for another is often not that crucial. Many telephoto hoods can be used on a standard lens without cutting off any of the frame, but since a telephoto hood can be longer than a standard lens itself, it may look rather odd. Round hoods for wide angle lenses are rarely of much optical value although they do help protect the lens—and sometimes a standard rubber hood for a standard lens will shade the lens just as effectively.

In some circumstances, particularly for shots where you want absolutely precise shading, you can use rectangular hoods which are often designed for specific lenses. A good rectangular hood cuts off nearly all light from outside the picture area while still allowing some margin for small changes or errors.

Rectangular hoods are of three basic types: metal hoods to fit particular lenses; bellows type universal hoods for all sizes and types of lens; and small plastic hoods which attach to universal filter holders such as the Cokin series.

Metal hoods are lens-specific and if one is not supplied with the lens it usually has to be ordered. Each of these metal hoods can only be used on one lens and indeed some lenses, particularly extremely wide angle lenses, need a hood so perfectly aligned that it must be permanently fixed to the lens.

Bellows hoods, however, are much more versatile and can provide accurate shading for a wide range of lenses.

Hooded lens *With a lens hood fitted you can reduce flare, and pictures will show a much sharper image*

Differences in camera format are accommodated by placing a mask of the appropriate shape over the front of the bellows. Differences in lens size are accommodated by moving the bellows in and out along a base rail—each camera format mask is marked with the focal lengths of lenses and corresponding settings on the rail. Makes such as the Ambico Shade plus, Ewa and B & W Compendium have an interchangeable mounting thread, a slot for filters, a base rail and a bellows hood that extends to 15 cm and collapses to 2 or 3 cm.

A bellows hood fitted with a mask cuts out unwanted light better than any other arrangement but can often be larger than the camera itself. Neither are such hoods robust, and for close-up work in particular they are too fragile and cumbersome. But for a zoom lens, they may provide the answer.

Hoods for zooms

Zoom lenses are, for a number of reasons, notoriously difficult to shade properly, yet with so many lens elements they need protection from stray light more than any other lens.

First, a normal hood could not give good shading for every focal length. If it were sufficiently deep for the longest focal length it would cut off the picture at shorter focal lengths. Secondly, the optical design of most zoom lenses means that anything close to the rim of the front element tends to appear in the final picture.

Unlike many fixed lenses, zoom lenses are often supplied without a hood attached and the hoods you can buy separately tend to be very much a compromise. Any lens hood, however, is

Lens hoods *Telephoto lenses often have a slide-out hood* **1** *permanently fixed. Bellows hoods* **2** *provide the most protection and can be used with any focal length lens. Slide-on metal hoods* **3** *and* **4** *are for use with specific lenses, and a collapsible rubber hood* **5** *will fit most standard lenses*

better than none at all, and even an inadequate one should be used if nothing better is available.

However, you can buy cutaway or scalloped lens hoods for some zooms. These have sections cut into the rim to allow for the picture corners, and are as good as rectangular hoods. They are also available for wide angle lens of less than 24 mm. But they must be perfectly aligned to avoid cut-off corners or unwanted intrusions into the picture.

Choosing a hood

Whichever lens you intend to use the hood with, it is worth making a number of tests before buying. Of these, perhaps the most important is to try the hood on the lens and check that it does not cut off or *vignette* the picture.

You can check for vignetting in two ways. If you have a manual exposure SLR or an automatic SLR with a depth of field preview, you can check through the viewfinder. With the lens focused on infinity, point the camera at a large, distant, plain area such as the sky and stop the lens down to its smallest aperture. If there is any sign of darkening in the corners of the frame when you press the preview button, the hood is cutting off the light from the picture.

Even if there is no trace of vignetting, a second check is necessary because

button catches. They are pushed into the filter thread and tightened a quarter turn. This makes it much easier to fit and remove them, and prevents the hood from becoming tightly locked to the lens.

You can also buy slip-on hoods. These can often slip off just as easily as they slip on, although a few slip hoods have a locking screw.

Filters

It is often said that a filter can add colour to a picture, or 'put the skin in'. In fact a filter cannot add anything; it can only take away. The purpose of a filter is to remove unwanted wavelengths of light. Other 'filters' may give soft focus or perhaps act as a close-up lens, but these are really special accessories, not filters.

A good filter should have no effect on the incoming light other than to remove the unwanted portion, so it must be thin, clear and totally distortion-free.

The best filters are sheets of coloured gelatin and you can obtain almost any colour density filter you are ever likely to need in gelatin. Kodak's Wratten range and the Hellma range of gelatin filters are both extensive.

Unfortunately, gelatin filters are not only expensive but fade quickly are are very susceptible to damage. They can be scratched easily and distort when touched. They also dissolve in water and cannot be used in the rain.

Understandably, most photographers prefer dyed filters of flat optical glass for everyday use. A single sheet of high-quality thin glass is made to the same standard as lens elements. Colouring is not achieved with an organic dye as used in gelatin, instead, chemicals are used. Such filters fade very slowly and

few SLR screens show more than 95 per cent of the total picture area. For the second test, once you have found a hood which seems roughly correct, take the camera into a darkened corner of the room and open the camera back. Set the shutter to 'B', and press the release. With your eye roughly where the film should be, look through the back of the camera through the lens at a small light source such as a single unshaded bulb. You should be able to see the light from any part of the film plane, even at the very corners of the frame. If the light source disappears as you move your eye from behind the centre of the lens, the hood is cutting off the corners of the picture.

If your camera is an automatic, you may not be able to hold the shutter open like this. Instead, take a photograph of a flat tone, and examine the negative or slide for darkening at the corners.

Once you are sure the hood does not produce vignetting, examine the inside

Standing stones *Using a graduated filter darkens one part of a scene, here the sky, to bring out detail interest elsewhere*

Windmill *With an orange filter fitted, you can increase the contrasts in a scene and create dramatic black and white pictures*

for any shiny surfaces that might reflect light. A good hood should have effective blackening with matt paint, ribbing to cut reflections, and absence of any chrome or bright areas inside the hood itself. Flock or velvet lining works very well, but if you ever clean the lens with a silicon cloth and have a flocked hood fitted, it can easily pick up bright yellow or blue fibres from the cloth. These are virtually impossible to remove and render the hood useless.

Because it can be difficult to use filters with a hood that screws into the filter threads, some hoods have small press-

Filter holders

Glass filters are normally held in brass rings that screw directly on to the front of the lens. Plastic filters, however, are held in *system holders*. System holders use a ring that is permanently attached to the lens. On to this ring clips a square holder. A lens hood, should you want to fit one, can be attached in front of the filter mount.

If you need to use gelatin filters frequently or you want to change plastic filters without disturbing the camera, a *technical filter holder* is a better choice. You can put several gelatin filters in this, though only one plastic filter can be inserted. The technical holder opens like a book, with a soft lining to avoid scratching the filters, and a central hole.

Filter holders *The technical filter holder (left) can hold several gelatin filters. The system holder (right) is for plastic filters*

Thread sizes

A feature that often proves confusing when buying filters is the wide range of filter thread sizes available. Obviously the filter must be wide enough to cover the front of the lens without any vignetting—and what suits one size lens may not suit another. Neither will a filter that fits one standard lens necessarily fit another. While some manufacturers make all their own lenses to take the same filter size, many do not, and if you use lenses made by various manufacturers it is unlikely that one set of filters will fit them all. Unfortunately, there is no easy solution to this problem.

However, you can buy step-up and step-down rings that allow you to use a filter on a lens with a different thread size. This means that even if you do have lenses with several different thread sizes, you may only have to buy one set of filters. But you must be careful not to introduce vignetting. Using conversion rings may also call for a new lens hood.

have good resistance to wear. A few glass filters are not dyed, but sprayed with a lacquer (graduated sky or 'chromo' filters, for example) and need treating with care.

Glass filters are usually, like many lenses, coated to reduce reflections. Most types are single-layer coated, which reduces flare a little. Some are multi-coated to cut down the risk of ghost images or flare marks further.

A recent development, *organic glass*, is a plastic material of good optical quality which is fairly scratch-resistant. BDB Filtran, Cokin and Filteck filters are of this type. Plastic filters are easy to engrave, emboss, spray colour, dye colour, and are very simple to make.

As a result there is a wide range of different plastic filters including most of the colour correction values which are available in gelatin and optical glass. However, plastic filters are not as accurate in colour values and are intended only for everyday use. For more precise filtering, you need either gelatin or dyed glass filters.

There are also cheap flexible acrylic and thick gelatin filters, made for the theatre and film industry, which fit on lights or windows. They may look perfectly flat and clear visually, but they blur the fine detail sharpness of pictures if you shoot through them. Only use them over lights or flashguns, or for special effects—not over lenses.

Special filters

Certain lenses require special filter systems, usually for optical reasons. Fish eye and ultrawide angle lenses sometimes have a large convex front element, and it is impossible to fit filters to them. These lenses have built-in filters which can be brought into place by turning a dial on the rim of the lens.

Lenses that have a very large front element—notably super telephotos—frequently have a filter drawer close to the camera body. Small filters can be fitted to this compartment, and the lens is sometimes sold with a set of the more commonly used filters. A disadvantage of this system is that the lens often has to be removed from the camera to fit the filter. Some modern lenses, though, have a front filter drawer.

Most lens hoods are simple and valuable additions to any camera outfit. They are relatively inexpensive compared with other photographic equipment. Most filters, and the cheaper hoods, cost about the same as one roll of film and a filter holder costs very little more. These simple devices are easy to use and can clearly improve the quality of many of your pictures.

FILTERS FOR COLOUR

Sheep in the snow *Light from a overcast sky has a blue cast. An 81B filter is needed for a neutral colour balance*

Many factors can affect the way a colour photograph looks. For one thing, there is no colour film which, even under ideal conditions, will produce pictures that have exactly the same colours as the subject. And the same subject photographed under identical conditions gives as many different results as makes of film. Even different batches of the same film can vary from one to another, although these variations are kept to a minimum by the manufacturers and are not usually very important. The lighting conditions have a great influence on the appearance of the final photograph. Sometimes the light from the subject is not recorded by the film in the same way as it is seen by the eye—fluorescent lights appear white or pink to the eye, but green on film, for example.

Considering how many ways there are of combining different films with different subjects and types of lighting, it is clear that some method is needed to control the eventual result, especially with colour slide film which cannot be colour corrected from a negative, as can a print. Colour control is the main reason for using filters over the camera lens. It is more important when using slide film than negative film, but even pictures taken on negative film will be improved by using the correct filter.

There are many different types of filter suitable for use with colour film. Apart from those for special effects (which are explained in the next section), the main types are *ultraviolet* and *skylight* filters, *neutral density* filters, *polarizers*, light-balancing or *colour conversion* filters, and *colour compensating* filters. These all affect the colours of your pictures without greatly changing the way your camera records the basic scene. In fact, under many circumstances, these filters make your pictures look more 'normal' than they would if no filter were used, because film is less tolerant than the eye of subtle changes in the colour of light.

Filters are often described by a standard series of numbers, such as 81A or 82C. The numbers relate to the 'Wratten' filters produced by an English firm which was later bought out by Kodak. Wratten numbers have become almost universally used, whatever the origin of the filter. Sometimes the letter W is used in front of the number. For example, W3 means the light yellow Wratten 3 filter. A letter following the number refers to the intensity of the filter—an 81B is a stronger orange than the 81A filter.

Colour compensating filters are called CC filters. Each filter in this range is described by a number and one of the letters Y, M, C, R, G, or B. The letters stand for yellow, magenta, cyan, red, green, or blue, and the numbers describe the density of the filter—a 40Y, for example, is a darker yellow than a 20Y from the same series.

Filters are available in a variety of forms. The commonest is made of glass with a threaded retaining ring that screws into the front of a camera lens. The diameter of the filter must match the lens: 49 mm, 52 mm and 55 mm filter mounts are the most common. Square

Winter landscape *Without a correcting filter, snow looks distinctly bluish under cloudy skies*

Without a polarizer *The skies over Brasilia are deep blue, but need some help for a dramatic effect*

With a polarizer *The filter's angle of polarization has been set to maximize the contrast between sky and clouds*

plastic filters are also available. These fit into holders which take adapter rings to fit into many different sizes of lens filter thread. The Cokin filter system is an example of this type.

Gelatin filters offer the greatest variety. Squares of dyed gelatin are available in a great range of colours at relatively low cost. Their main disadvantage is that they are extremely delicate and must be handled very carefully. Furthermore, they need a special holder to fit on a camera lens.

Filters are usually put in front of the lens, but some special lenses such as fisheye and mirror telephoto types take smaller filters mounted behind the lens. Wherever filters are placed in the light path between subject and film, they must be of high quality and kept scrupulously clean so as not to lower the image quality.

Except for the colour conversion and some of the colour compensating filters, filters for colour work are much less strongly coloured than those made for use with black and white film. Many filters that are important to colour photography have almost no colour at all.

Ultraviolet filters

Ultraviolet (UV) filters are examples of useful colourless filters. All photographic emulsions are sensitive to ultraviolet radiation. This type of radiation is stronger at higher altitudes, where it is less filtered by the Earth's atmosphere, than at ground level. In colour photography ultraviolet radiation can make distant views appear abnormally blue, particularly in photographs taken on mountains or from aircraft. This problem can be partially eliminated by using a UV filter which screens out ultraviolet radiation while leaving visible light wavelengths unaffected. Because UV filters are colourless, and because there are very few photographs that will benefit from including ultraviolet radiation, many photographers leave a UV filter on each of their lenses all the

time. This also helps protect the front element of the lens from dust and damage, at the cost of a slight loss in definition that can be expected whenever filters are used.

Putting an extra layer of glass, plastic or gelatin between your subject and your film will always cause some degradation of the image. You should keep this to a minimum by handling your filters with care, so as to keep them free of dirt and fingermarks without the need for constant cleaning.

Skylight filters

These are also designed to reduce the blue casts which often occur in outdoor photography, especially under a clear blue sky. Skylight filters—usually numbers 1A and 1B—absorb some ultraviolet radiation, but have a slight additional pink tinge. When a subject is in the shade under a clear blue sky it will not be illuminated by the white or yellowish direct rays of the sun. Instead, most of the light falling on the subject will have the blue colour of the sky. The pink tinge of a skylight filter partially

corrects this, and is particularly helpful when taking pictures that contain skin tones, such as portraits. While skylight and UV filters have an effect in clear air at high altitude, where the blue colour results from the strong UV content of the light, nearer sea level the blue colour of a distant view is often more due to scattered light than to ultraviolet. Skylight filters will have almost no effect on scattered light, and will not improve haze penetration.

Neutral density filters

UV and skylight filters have such little density that their effects on exposure can be ignored, but for some purposes you may wish to change your exposure with filters while leaving the colour rendering of your film unaffected. For example, if your camera is loaded with very fast colour slide film you may sometimes find under brightly lit conditions that you cannot set a small enough aperture and a

Unfiltered flash *Sometimes skin tones can look too cool when lit by electronic flash without a filter*

Flash with a filter *To give a natural warmth to the skin tones, an 81B filter was used over the camera lens*

fast enough shutter speed to give your film the correct exposure. Alternatively, you may want to use a wide aperture for differential focus effects.

In such cases you should use neutral density (ND) filters. These plain grey filters have no effect on the *colour* of the light—they simply reduce its quantity. They are available in a range of strengths. An ND 0.3 cuts the brightness of a scene to a half of its original intensity, an ND 0.6 cuts it to a quarter, an ND 0.9 to an eighth, and so on. Each 0.3 of density is equivalent to one stop.

Using polarizing filters

Polarizing filters are also neutral in colour. Their purpose is to reduce or eliminate glare and reflections. Rays of light are usually made up of waves vibrating at many different angles. However, light reflected from non-metallic surfaces such as glass, water, or paint is *polarized*—only the waves vibrating in one particular plane are reflected. The degree of polarization depends on the angle between the camera, the subject and the light source.

A *polarizing*, or Pola, filter will only transmit light that has been polarized in a particular plane. In practice, this means that you can use a polarizing filter to remove unwanted reflections in windows, if you are at an angle of 30 to 45° to the reflecting surface. Polarizing filters will not remove reflections from directly in front of a surface, nor will they affect reflections in mirrors, which rely on a metallic backing layer for the image they produce. Because polarizing filters reduce surface reflections from many subjects, they often increase the strength and saturation of colours generally.

Polarizing filters can have a spectacular effect on clear blue skies. When sunlight is scattered by the atmosphere it becomes polarized. The degree of polarization is strongest at right angles to the sun, and some polarizing filters

Woman with scarf *An 81C filter was used with slight underexposure to give richer, warmer skin tones and a more flattering effect*

have a small symbol on their rim that can be pointed at the sun to align the filter for the maximum effect. Skies photographed through a polarizing filter have a vivid blue colour that is extremely rich and striking in effect.

If you take your exposure readings with a separate hand held exposure meter, you will need to give an extra 1½ to 2 stops exposure above that indicated by the meter when you use a polarizing filter. Cameras with built in through-the-lens exposure meters will usually make the necessary allowance for exposure automatically, but there are some exceptions. Refer to your camera's instruction book: if your camera's metering system incorporates

any kind of beam splitter, it may give inaccurate readings through a polarizing filter. In such cases, you can use a more expensive circular polarizing filter which will work with all types of built in meters.

Polarizing filters are designed to be freely rotated when they are fitted to the lens, and they are therefore usually in thicker mounts than normal filters. When used with wide angle lenses, this may cause vignetting at the corners of the image. To avoid this problem some camera manufacturers produce polarizing filters in larger than normal mounts. Alternatively, you can buy a larger polarizing filter and fit it to your camera lens with a *stepping down ring.*

Matching light to film

The main purpose of the 81 series of light balancing filters is to make small changes to the colour of the light reaching the film so that it more closely matches the colour temperature for which the film is balanced (see pages 238 to 239). Most daylight slide films are balanced for a colour temperature of about 5500 K. The orangeish 81 series lowers colour temperatures over the range 5700 to 7500 K to approximately match film balanced for 5500 K. The blueish 82 series raises colour temperatures over the range of 4400 to 5200 K to approximately 5500 K.

What this means in practice is that you can use these filters to make your film give neutrally colour balanced pictures under a variety of common lighting conditions. For example, 82 series filters are useful in the early morning or late afternoon. The reddish colour of light at such times of day is very attractive with some subjects, but may be too strong for your taste. Adding a blueish 82C filter and giving an extra 2/3 stop exposure will give a more normal effect. The 82 series filters are also useful when using tungsten balanced

Hyacinths by tungsten *Photographed by the light of 500 watt bulbs on daylight balanced film*

Colour conversion *An 80A filter on the camera lens reveals the true colours of the plants*

lm with ordinary household light bulbs. Tungsten film is meant to be used with 500 W photographic bulbs, but 100 W bulbs have a lower colour temperature and call for an 82B filter with 2/3 stop extra exposure for accurate colour.

The 81 series is valuable when the sky is overcast. An 81C filter with 1/3 stop extra exposure will remove any blue cast under such conditions. An 81A filter will correct photoflood lamps for use with tungsten balanced film.

Because the colour temperature of light is very difficult to estimate, it is impossible to give precise recommendations for the use of light balancing filters under every circumstance. Expensive colour temperature meters are available to help you find out exactly which filter you need, but these are not usually necessary. As a rule, your error in colour balancing should be on the warm side, so that your pictures are a little redder than the ideal balance. Photographs that are too blue are usually less acceptable than photographs that are a little too red or yellow.

Colour conversion filters
These are similar to, but much stronger than, colour balancing filters. The 80 series of filters are a deeper blue colour than the 82 series, and allow daylight film to be exposed by tungsten light. The main practical problem with these filters is that they need a 1/3 to 2 stop exposure increase. With most colour films, used under the sort of light levels that are commonly given by tungsten light bulbs in ordinary interiors, this will mean that you must put your camera on a tripod and use a longer than normal exposure time. You cannot usually put an 80 series filter on your camera lens and take hand held photographs indoors.

Orange 85 series filters, which allow tungsten balanced film to be used by daylight, need less exposure increase—1/3 to 2/3 stop. Since daylight is usually much brighter than artificial light, taking pictures with a hand held camera and tungsten balanced film is quite practical if an 85B filter is used. Nevertheless, it is better to use film that is made to match the approximate colour temperature of the light you are photographing by.

Filters for skin tones
The eye will accept a considerable departure from natural rendering of skin tones if the added colour cast is warm. Warm brown skin tones are associated in most people's minds with health and cheerfulness. The 81 series of light balancing filters can remove the slight tendency towards cold pink tones found in many pale skins. The 81 series runs from the plain 81 filter, which has a slight warming effect, up to the 81EF, which produces an 'instant sun tan' and is popular with glamour photographers.

Magenta filters are also often useful for removing the green cast you often see in skin tones when there is a nearby expanse of grass or leaves reflecting light onto the subject. An 05M colour

Woman reading *Low-wattage household lamps give a result that is slightly too warm on tungsten film*

Colour balancing *A slight adjustment with an 82C filter gives a cooler, more neutral result*

compensating filter is usually strong enough for this job, but you may want to use a 10M filter if you are photographing a model who is surrounded by a large area of foliage.

Fine-tuning your colour
The colour compensating (CC) filters allow for small variations in colour balance when colour films are being used. All such films have three emulsion layers, sensitive to red, green and blue light. Each colour CC filter is designed to affect one layer only: the cyan affects the red, the magenta the green, and the yellow the blue layer. The range of CC filters allows an almost infinite variety of correction. In theory it is possible to reproduce many of the effects of other colour filters by suitable combinations of CC filters, but in practice it is not advisable to combine more than two CC filters in the image forming beam.

Most photographers who use CC filters

extensively keep an assortment of the less expensive gelatin type, but more durable glass CC filters are available.

Mireds and filters
Conversion filters can be given values on what is called the *mired* scale. The word mired—pronounced *my-red*—is short for *micro reciprocal degrees*. Any colour temperature has a mired value, found by dividing that temperature into one million.

The advantage of this is that a colour conversion filter can be given a constant mired value—for example, an 81B has a mired value of +27. This can be used to predict the effect it will have on a light source of any colour temperature: it makes it redder by 27 mireds. Such a scale is useful because if there is very little blue in the light, an 81B will have a comparatively small influence on the blue proportion of the light—that is, it raises or lowers colour temperature less

The Sixticolor meter *records colour temperatures through a metering cell on the back of the instrument*

than when there is a great deal of blue around. For this reason, it is usual to convert both filters and colour temperatures to the mired scale. On colour temperature meters, this is in the form of *decamireds* (units of ten mireds) —the +27 of an 81B is rounded off to +30, and called 3R. A similar strength bluish filter, with a negative mired value, would have a value of 3B. But few photographers would ever bother to remember the equivalent mired values of filters and colour temperatures.

This would require great powers of recall, because different manufacturers use different names for colour filters.

Colour temperature meters
Most colour temperature meters work simply by metering red and blue light separately and then comparing their intensity. The simplest, most popular and least expensive meter on the market, the German Gossen Sixticolor, illustrates the principle well.

The Sixticolor has two selenium cells, needing no battery. One cell is covered by a blue–green filter and the other by a red–orange filter. The outputs from both cells are fed to a meter in opposition to each other. So when the proportions of red and blue light are equal, the meter is exactly balanced and gives a zero reading. But if there is a greater proportion of one or the other the needle will be deflected, giving an indication on a scale of decamireds which can then be converted into filter values. It also has a colour temperature scale.

The Sixticolor measures colour temperature from 2600K to 20,000K—a range which includes at the red end the light from a 40W domestic bulb, and at the other end the bluest outdoor daylight, in which the subject is lit only by a blue sky with the sun behind a cloud.

When using the meter, there is no need to adjust for light intensity—it reads

A Profisix lightmeter *can, with a simple attachment, be converted into a colour temperature meter*

The Profi-color *attachment clips on to the Profisix, and a colour calculator is placed over the scale*

in all normal lighting conditions. First you set the film type, rather than speed— daylight, photoflood or tungsten. Then you point the meter directly at the light source, and note the meter reading in mireds—it will give a filter value of up to 21B units (indicating that a bluish filter is needed) or 24R units (a reddish filter). A table supplied with the meter gives the appropriate conversion filter, or pack of CC filters, for each reading. There are differences between the reference numbers used by Kodak, Agfa and some filter makers, so the tables are essential.

It is also possible to convert the Gossen Profisix light meter to read colour temperatures. The Profi-color attachment includes a meter cell and dial which clips over the normal light metering scales.

Minolta Color Meter II
A much more elaborate and expensive meter, the Minolta Color Meter II works on the same basic principle as the Gossen Sixticolor, but instead has three cells, covering red, green and blue parts of the spectrum, and uses micro-electronics to compare their outputs and give a reading. It has a switch to program daylight (5500K) photoflood (3400K) or tungsten film (3200K), but can also handle any other setting. Nevertheless, some films usually balanced at 5350K might actually be balanced at 5350K. So if you wish to take full advantage of the meter, you must test the film batch to establish its true bias, using the meter and a series of filter combinations on a test film.

Readings can be taken in kelvins, mireds (called light balancing or LB values) and CC filter values in deca-

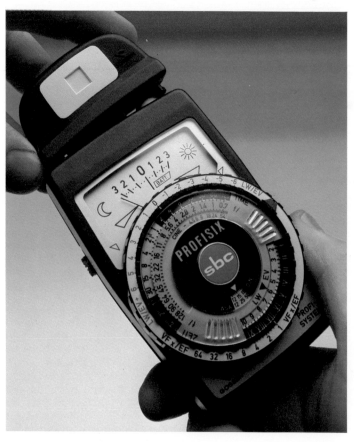

mireds. A scale on the back of the meter converts the mired values into Wratten filter descriptions, and CC decamired values into magenta or green filter numbers.

To use the meter, a button is pressed to select the type of film being used. Then a large metering button on the side is pressed for a few seconds to record and stabilize the reading—the liquid crystal display stays blank until the reading is computed and stored in the memory. You can then press the required function key for light balancing filter, CC filter or kelvin reading repeatedly, and the appropriate value will be displayed from the meter's memory.

For example, a reading taken in a tungsten lit office with daylight (5500K) film was 3270K, -2 units CC, -123 units LB. The scales on the back indicated an 80B plus an 82 blue light balancing filter, and a 05G green CC filter. Factors on

the scales showed an exposure increase of 2⅓ stops necessary with this filter pack.

In a room lit by fluorescent tubes with a magnolia painted ceiling, the reading was 4700K, +9CC, -31LB. This resulted in a filter pack of 82B plus 20M for daylight film, with one stop exposure increase. Switching to Type B film, the meter displayed +99 LB, +9 CC, which converted to 85C plus 81A and 20M: exposure increase was one stop. A

colour temperature meter's readings are, however, likely to be inaccurate in any form of lighting which consists of a discrete line output (see page 199), and the readings may be untrustworthy.

A reading taken in bright, overcast daylight gave +15 LB and -2 CC at 6000K. The recommended filters were 81A plus a 05G CC. The 81A is the usual filter to 'warm up' an overcast day, but the 05G is unexpected. It was needed because red-brick buildings surrounding the subject reflected a high proportion of red light.

The Minolta Color Meter II is the only popularly available meter of this type and will give readings for almost any film stock and light condition.

Using the Minolta Color Meter II
Select the type of film being used and press the metering button on the right hand side of the meter long enough for the reading to be recorded and stored in the electronic memory.
The LB key is pressed to display light balancing filter values; the CC key for colour correcting filters and the K key for colour temperatures. Filter numbers are tabulated on the back of the meter

Controls *for selecting film type and preset or variable colour temperatures, are a feature of most meters*

Example reading *The Minolta Color Meter II here gives a light balancing filter reading of −179 for daylight film in tungsten light, and indicates the use of a Wratten 80A filter*

SPECIAL EFFECTS FILTERS

Most amateurs are familiar with the use of filters to modify a light source or to achieve faithful rendition of colours. Also intended for the amateur market are filters for special effects, ranging in complexity from simple coloration, through selective magnification to distortion of the image. Before you attempt to use these, it is best to know what effect they give and how easily it is achieved.

Special effects filters are available separately or in kits, and vary in price according to the construction. In the Cokin range, for example, a coloured diffuser costs less than a plastic lens cap, and a 'diffraction universe' costs about the same as a 36 exposure roll of Koda-chrome. For about four times as much you can buy a Hoyarex starter kit, complete with Hoya filters and acces-

sories for attaching them to the camera lens.

The basis of the various special effects filter systems is a filter holder, which is attached to the camera lens by an adapter ring that screws into the filter thread. A range of adapters is supplied with some filter systems, but with others you must ensure you buy the correct adapter for your lens.

Filters are slotted into the holder in grooves, which vary in distance from the front of the lens. Filters from one system will not fit into a holder from another system, so it is a good idea to decide on one make only.

Some filters are no more than a shape cut out of black cardboard to form a mask. You can make these simply, to your own design, but the effect is

Filter kits *include a range of basic filters and accessories—some of which are not strictly necessary*

probably not worth the effort. Most special effect filters are outside the scope of the do-it-yourself enthusiast, but you can appreciate the effects better by studying how the filters work.

Probably the most sophisticated filters work by diffraction. These are gratings made from high quality optical glass ruled with parallel lines in one or more directions—they give a star or coloured spot effect. Easily the most creative filters are the Coloured Vaseline and Coloured Varnishes, with which a wide range of coloured effects can be achieved. But they can be a little difficult to handle.

The rainbow effect *is most prominent when this type of subject (a bright sky and reflective water surface) is underexposed. At the correct exposure, the rainbow is 'washed out'. In a real rainbow, the colours occur in the reverse order*

Spot in violet *Essentially this is a diffuser with a clear central spot. There is a choice of several different colours, and the filter can be combined with others, such as a starburst. Focusing through the filter can be a problem*

A split field filter *is merely half a lens in a mount, used as a close-up lens for half the field of view. The edge of the lens causes blurring, and the non-uniform magnification causes distortion, as can be seen in the upper shot*

Coloured diffuser *This is supplied as two squares of crumpled plastic, which vary in colour according to the angle of view you use. Shown above are shots with and without the filter*

Spot in plain diffuser *This is particularly suitable for combining with coloured filters of various densities*

Dreams *The effect varies enormously according to the aperture used and the filter to lens distance*

Diffraction universe *These are plain in appearance, but are in fact extremely fine gratings of various designs*

Coloured varnish, *smeared on to glass, gives a varied effect. Here it is used to tint the night sky*

Starburst *filters for point light sources—available for two, four, eight or 16 rays*

Masks *come in a variety of shapes, but you can easily make them yourself*

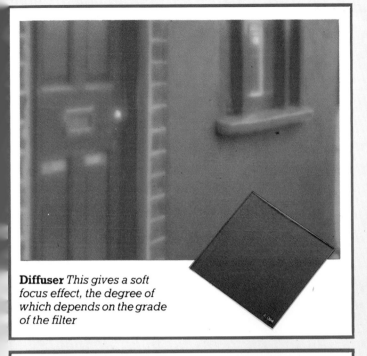

Diffuser *This gives a soft focus effect, the degree of which depends on the grade of the filter*

A graduated diffuser *leaves part of the image sharp, so it is easily combined with other coloured filters*

Coloured vaseline, *smeared on to glass, allows you to filter areas of the picture just as you wish*

Fog filters *are similar to diffusers. Their effect varies according to the density of the coating on each filter*

Linear slit *This is probably the most difficult filter to use but the easiest to make yourself. Results depend on how smoothly you wind the film*

Chapter 6
FLASH EQUIPMENT
ELECTRONIC FLASHGUNS

For situations where there is little or no light available, the flashgun is an invaluable addition to your range of equipment. With fast films and long exposures you may just be able to get your shot, providing that the subject is perfectly still. And you may get better control with elaborate photographic lights. But for impromptu shots, the sheer simplicity, portability and low cost of the flashgun is unbeatable.

Although with some cameras, such as the cheaper 110s, the only form of flash on the market is the standard flashcube—just a more convenient modern version of the traditional magnesium flash bulb—there is now a tremendous range of electronic flashguns available for use with 35 mm and large format cameras. Flash bulbs can only be used once and then have to thrown away, but you can fire an electronic unit again and again, many thousands of times. Though electronic guns are a great deal more expensive than a single flash bulb ever was, they are much more convenient and probably work out cheaper in the long run. Modern flashguns are also very reliable compared with the old bulb types.

Flashgun choice *The large gun at the back would be ideal for a press photographer, but for family snaps, the two small units at the front would be more suitable*

Manual or automatic?

Although there are many individual types of electronic flash, they fall into two distinct categories: the manual type and the computer or automatic types. In the past, manual flashguns were far cheaper, but over the past decade the price of the automatic type has been brought down considerably and the difference in cost between the two types is now virtually negligible.

With manual units the intensity and duration of the flash is fixed and cannot be changed to compensate for the reduced amount of light reaching distant subjects. So with the flash attached to the camera, the photographer must compensate manually by adjusting the exposure according to the distance of the subject from the camera. Because the flash always has the same duration, changing the shutter speed will not significantly affect the amount of light falling on the film and exposure adjustments can only be made by altering the lens aperture.

However, the shutter speed does affect the use of flash: you can only use shutter speeds slower than a certain value the synchronization speed. If this is exceeded, the flash will fire when the shutter is not fully open. The fastest synchronization speed is generally 1/60 or 1/125 sec.

Synchronization is usually achieved by making an electrical connection between the camera and the flashgun. Most guns are designed to fit into the *flash shoe* on the camera, usually above the viewfinder. Contacts in the shoe align with contacts in the flash unit, to operate the flashgun when the shutter release is pressed—the *hot shoe* arrangement. The alternative is to have a separate cable that runs from the flashgun, and is plugged into the camera.

The correct aperture is usually found by consulting a table printed on the back of the flashgun. Though this takes a little time, it is a very simple operation. You either measure or guess the distance of your subject and then read off the aperture in the column appropriate to the speed of the film in your camera.

If you feel such calculations would interfere with your shooting, you may prefer an automatic flashgun. With an auto unit, the aperture is simply set according to the film speed, and provided the subject is not too far from the camera the flashgun does the rest. The intensity of light reflected from the subject is measured by a photocell, set in the front of the flashgun, and the duration of the flash is automatically varied accordingly. If you intend to take pictures of very distant subjects, or out of doors, it is a good idea to check the

upper limit of the auto range on the flashgun you plan to buy.

An additional advantage of this system is that it takes into account the brightness of the subject as well as the distance. Understandably, automatic flashguns are now the most popular

To generate the bright light a flash must give requires a considerable amount of energy and the flashgun's energy system must play an important

Auto and manual *The unit on the left is an automatic 'computer' flash, and would cover most people's requirements. While the manual gun on the right is suitable for straightforward uses, it does not have as much power or versatility*

part in your final choice of gun. If you buy an automatic gun, for instance, you will have to choose between basic units and the more expensive *thyristor* type. With the basic units, some shots will use less energy than others but the gun will still consume the same amount of power and the excess energy is simply wasted. With the power-saving or thyristor type, the unused energy is retained for the next flash.

Although thyristor guns initially cost more than the conventional automatic units, they greatly extend the life of the batteries by using the minimum energy, and may be cheaper in the long term. More importantly, thyristor guns give a substantially shorter recycling time. This means that after each flash, they are ready to fire again very rapidly.

In most cases the energy is provided by a battery, although a few of the more expensive units have a mains adapter facility. Some flashguns accept only one type of battery or require a lot more power than others. It is worth looking at all the available options and deciding

Bounced flash *The photographer bounced the light of his flashgun off the ceiling of the room to get the natural looking lighting for this picture. Direct flash (right) gives harsh lighting, and forms a dark shadow to one side of the subject. By bouncing the light, (far right), the hard shadow goes and the light becomes softer. Automatic flashguns with tilt heads make bounce flash simpler*

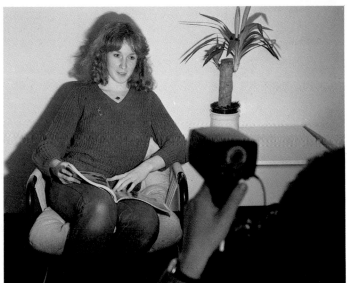

which suits your needs best.

There are two kinds of battery used in flashguns: rechargeable and non-rechargeable cells. Of the non-rechargeable batteries, conventional dry cells like those used in torches are by far the cheapest form of battery. Dry cell batteries are probably the most economical source of power, even though they have a relatively short life. Unfortunately, this type of battery tends to leak and if you use your flashgun rarely, it is worth removing them during long periods of storage.

If you take flash pictures regularly, but still not frequently, you will probably appreciate the virtues of the manganese alkaline cell. Non-rechargeable batteries of this type are made by most manufacturers, but perhaps the most familiar are the Mallory Duracells. Manganese alkaline cells are more expensive than ordinary dry cells but have a longer life. Fortunately both the main types of non-rechargeable battery are almost always interchangeable and you need not decide between the two when you select your flashgun.

If, however, you intend to take large numbers of flash photographs, it may be

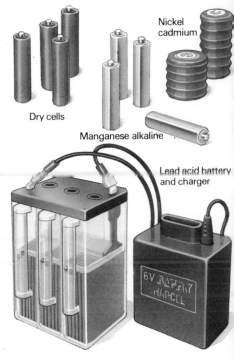

Battery power *The more costly guns offer several alternative power sources*

Professional flash *Although this gun has high power and many features, it sacrifices portability and compactness*

worth considering buying a flash unit that will accept rechargeable batteries. Many professional portable units will only accept rechargeable batteries.

Rechargeable batteries

There are two kinds of rechargeable battery available: the *lead–acid* type, which is a smaller version of the car battery, and the *nickel–cadmium* cell.

Lead–acid batteries are heavy and bulky, and must be carried in a pack over the shoulder, separate from the gun. This may seem terribly inconvenient, but it is an arrangement preferred

by press photographers because lead–acid cells are the most powerful of all batteries, giving far more flashes per charge, and halving recycling times.

For the non-professional user, though, the nickel–cadmium type is less bulky and is a much more practical option. Nickel–cadmium cells are often made to fit exactly into the place of ordinary non-rechargeable cells, or they may be quite different in size. Some flashguns can accept a cluster of small dry or manganese cells or a single large nickel-cadmium battery.

Whatever the shape, the principle of

a rechargeable battery is the same. When the battery runs down (this can be judged by when the recycling time rises to 30 seconds or a minute) a special charger is plugged into the gun, or the cells are removed and inserted into the charger. The charger is connected to the mains supply, and after several hours, usually between 3 and 14, the batteries will be up to full power.

Since the cost of rechargeable cells and a compact charger is so high, it is perhaps a good idea to buy a flashgun that accepts both rechargeable and non-rechargeable types. Then if you find

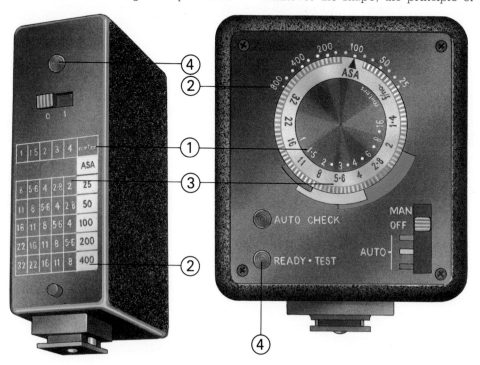

Exposure calculation *All flashguns have some sort of chart or dial on the back or side, to help the user work out the correct aperture. On a manual gun, such as the one at far left, the photographer looks along the line adjacent to the film speed that is being used (2). The distance from the flash to the subject is read from the scale at the top (1), and where the two rows meet, the appropriate aperture can be found on the aperture scale (3). Automatic guns are easier to use. This typical gun allows the user to choose one of three apertures. The choice is indicated by the right-hand end of each of the three coloured bars. For the film speed that is in use (set on scale 2), the photographer can choose f/2, f/4, or f/8. The switch at bottom right enters the chosen aperture into the flashgun's 'computer'. Automatic guns can be used only over a limited range (indicated on distance scale 1). Both guns have a ready light that comes on when the unit is ready to be used*

yourself taking so many flash pictures that you get through non-rechargeable batteries at an unacceptably high rate, you can simply purchase a nickel-cadmium cell and a charger rather than a new flashgun. It will cost you less in the long run.

Flash power

Another important consideration is the power or brightness of the flashgun. A distant subject needs a more powerful flash to illuminate it properly than a nearby subject. So if you are often likely to photograph distant subjects by flash, you will probably need a more powerful unit than if all your flash pictures are going to be close-ups.

A figure that simply told you the power of a flashgun would be of little value—you need to know how it will affect exposure. This is what *guide numbers* (GNs) do. Guide numbers indicate the amount of exposure needed with a specific film speed for a certain distance. Usually, the GN for a particular flashgun is given for ISO 100/21° film, but for other film speeds a simple table is provided, from which you can read off the correct aperture alongside the distance from the camera to the subject. The illustration opposite explains this.

The higher the GN, the more powerful the flash unit and the greater the distance over which it is effective. Unfortunately, more powerful flashguns tend to cost much more and you must balance your requirements with your pocket. A typical low-cost unit will have a GN of 18 (metres/100 ISO), while larger guns have guide numbers of 45 or more.

Some units offer a choice of guide numbers, which allows for photography under a range of conditions. There is certainly no point in buying a more powerful unit just for the sake of it—a powerful gun can sometimes be positively awkward to use, particularly if you take a lot of close-ups by flash.

Tilt heads *This triple exposure shows the way that the heads of some guns tilt up to bounce light from the ceiling*

Flash for impact *American master photographer Weegee used direct flash for this picture of two theatre critics on the steps of the New York opera house*

Tilt and swivel heads

A flash pointed straight at the subject from the top of the camera often produces horribly flat, washed-out results. The solution to this problem is to 'bounce' the flash off a ceiling or wall so that it is much more diffused, giving a softer effect than direct flash. This means that the gun must be tilted towards the reflecting surface.

One way of doing this is to remove the flash gun from the camera and, holding it in one hand, or on a *flash bracket*, point it at the ceiling. Unfortunately, with an auto flashgun, this upsets the exposure because the photocell measures the light reflected from the ceiling rather than the light reflected from the subject. So the photographer has to set the exposure manually after some complex mental calculations.

Units with tilting heads go some way towards solving this problem. With this type of gun, the flash head can be tilted to point up at the ceiling while the photocell remains directed at the subject. Because the photocell sees exactly the same reflected light as the camera, the automatic flash control still works.

With some of the more expensive flash units, the photocell can be removed from the gun. This means that you can leave the photocell directed at the subject while taking the flashgun off the camera and pointing it in any direction. The photocell is usually mounted on the camera hot shoe and the flashgun is secured to a bracket on the side of the camera. This feature is more versatile than a tilt head because you can bounce

the flash off a wall or the ceiling, whenever appropriate.

A more convenient solution, though, is a flash head that both tilts and swivels sideways. These are more expensive, but may justify the outlay if you do a lot of flash photography. If you regularly use bounce flash, though, it is worth getting a more powerful unit, because the amount of light falling on the subject is greatly reduced, and you may find yourself working at a very wide aperture.

Dedicated units

Most camera manufacturers now offer guns designed specifically for their own cameras, referred to as *dedicated units*. The idea behind these is to make life easier for the photographer by automatically setting the correct synchronized shutter speed and by incorporating the flash ready signal in the viewfinder so that there is no need to look at the back of the gun. Unfortunately, such units cannot be transferred between cameras of different makes. This means that if ever you change your camera, you will have to change your flashgun too.

Whatever gun you select must suit your needs. So before you commit yourself, work out just how you will use the flashgun and avoid buying redundant features. In particular, you should think about the sort of power you are likely to need: a whole range of sophisticated features will not make up for a basic lack of power, while a flashgun that illuminates your sitting room like the floodlights at the international sports arena will be equally awkward to use

DEDICATED FLASH

A huge number of photographs are taken using flash. Unfortunately, flash is notoriously difficult to handle, and many pictures are spoiled because the photographer made a simple blunder. Two common mistakes are setting the wrong shutter speed and using the wrong aperture for the subject's distance.

These two features are often (on modern cameras) under automatic control. It is therefore feasible to arrange things so that as soon as the flashgun is attached to the camera, the correct shutter speed is set automatically and, in some cases, the camera is automatically set to the correct aperture. Such a system, where the automatic systems of the flash and camera are linked, is called dedicated flash. The word 'dedicated', used with reference to equipment, means that the unit is designed specifically to work with a particular model—it cannot be interchanged with others. This inevitably means that a dedicated flash unit must be bought with your camera in mind, to suit its special features.

Dedicated flash can only work with cameras that have electronically controlled exposures, and which have been designed with dedicated flash in mind. These will have a means of electronically linking the film speed, shutter speed and aperture between the camera and flash. This is usually achieved by means of contacts on the camera's hot shoe.

Most units are 'dedicated' to one or two cameras from a manufacturer's range. They can be used only with the cameras for which they are intended. In addition, several independent flash manufacturers make units that will suit particularly popular models of camera.

A dedicated unit looks much the same as a non-dedicated unit of comparable power, but it will cost 20 to 30 per cent more because of its more sophisticated electronics.

What can a dedicated flash do?
Different units have different facilities but one function performed by even the most basic dedicated unit is that of setting the camera's shutter speed to the flash synchronization speed. This is only possible on cameras with an automatically set electronic shutter—either those with aperture priority automation, or with a manual dial which is nevertheless an electronic control. To achieve this, a

Quick snaps *Dedicated flash is very useful if you must compose pictures quickly and do not have time for flash calculations*

contact on the flash hot shoe either completes a circuit on insertion, setting the shutter speed to the correct one for flash (usually 1/60 or 1/125), or feeds a current through to a circuit which does the same only if the flash is switched on as well as inserted.

A slightly more advanced unit will both set the speed and indicate when the flash is ready for use by a light signal in the viewfinder. This means that you can keep your eye to the viewfinder and shoot as soon as the flash is ready, without the need to look at the flash for the ready light. When the ready light on the flash comes on, a similar light in the camera does the same.

More sophisticated dedicated flash units set the flash speed only when they are ready for use. Until the ready light comes on, the shutter speed display scale continues to work as normal and will give auto exposure readings for the prevailing light. As soon as the flash is ready, all systems switch back to the fixed flash speed. If you have forgotten to switch on the flash, therefore, your picture will be correctly exposed though probably blurred as a result of a long exposure time.

Dedicated flash units may have a number of further features. Aperture signalling displays in the viewfinder the f-stop which the flash requires for good exposure using its auto sensor. On aperture priority cameras, the photographer must remember to set this. In this case the photographer must also set the speed of the film in use on the flashgun, as normal. However, if the dedicated unit has ASA film speed setting, it will transfer the film speed set on the camera directly to the flash.

On a shutter priority camera, however, the f-stop itself is normally set on the basis of electronic signals from the light meter, shutter speed control and film speed dial. This makes it possible to set the aperture to that required by the flash unit, as well as provide the other functions. The shutter speed set on the dial is electronically overridden by the dedicated flash. This facility is called auto aperture setting.

Not all shutter priority cameras, however, can offer this. Some cameras, such as the Minolta XD and Fujica AX series, monitor the light continuously even as the

lens iris closes, firing the shutter at exactly the right moment. These cameras therefore do not control the aperture in the same way, and auto exposure setting is not possible.

Most flashguns offer automatic exposure only at one or a few *f*-numbers, to which the camera must be set. The correct amount of light is metered by a sensor on the gun itself. But on many cameras now, such as the Olympus OM-2, the Canon T70, the Contax 137 and the Pentax LX, the flash reading is metered off the film during the flash discharge itself, and the light is cut off as soon as enough has been received by the meter cell. Such a system demands a dedicated flash offering TTL auto flash metering. This eliminates completely the need for fixed aperture settings, as opening up a stop simply halves the light output of the flash and vice-versa.

Fill-in flash by daylight—synchro sunlight—is best handled by systems which meter off the film, and only works on an SLR when the shutter speed required for the conditions is longer than the flash sync speed.

Some dedicated flashguns have a special low power switch. This is intended for use on a camera with the manufacturer's own motor drive, which has a set shooting rate. It limits the power of each shot. This necessarily means wide apertures, but the facility allows you to freeze action very successfully.

Independent dedicated guns

The major independent flash manufacturers make guns which may be switched or adapted to fit a whole range

of different cameras, as in the way that independent lenses may be made to take different mounts. The changes from one camera to another are achieved either by different interchangeable hot shoes, or by a universal hot shoe with several contacts and a switch on the unit.

Not all independent guns offer the same facilities as a maker's own guns. Some will perhaps only switch the shutter to the correct speed and not operate other functions. Some independent units may have features not found on the camera. Because of the need to allow for all the features of every maker's cameras in one gun, future dedicated multi-fit flash units may have far more features in total than some of the true dedicated units.

Flash systems

Most dedicated flash units are not part of a true 'flash system' and you cannot, for example, use a series of flash heads simultaneously in a dedicated fashion. The Olympus T32 and T20 can, however, be linked to each other and, via a central control box, to the camera. A ring flash can also be used.

The OM-2 meters only the light received on the film, in the ratio delivered by the guns, and it cuts off the flash from all guns simultaneously. With the T32 and T20 systems, unlike other auto-computer guns when used together, the exposure should be accurate.

Disadvantages of dedicated flash

Used properly in the appropriate situation, dedicated flash can reduce the risk of errors and help you get better pictures, but the degree of automation can also make you lazy. You might, for example, trust the automation so much that you forget to set other camera controls or adjust other things which need attention. The main failing is the temptation to use the system which overrides the flash when it is not charged, and to shoot haphazardly mixed ambient and flash exposures.

The other major fault is that nearly all dedicated flashguns are very low in power, intended for the family snap market and not for the serious amateur. Most offer a bounce facility, but are so weak that you would have to work at *f*/2 in a normal room with slow film to be sure of getting acceptable exposures.

When buying dedicated flash, remember to consider whether or not you may want to use the gun on another camera as a purely manually set flash, or use it off the camera for lighting effects. You may not be able to ; some models can only be switched on by inserting them into the correct dedicated shoe, and have no other switch. Some cannot be set manually, test fired on open flash, or removed from the camera (because no extension cord is made). Others do not allow you to override the X synchro speed set by the flash when you want to give a longer background exposure for special effects, such as fill-in flash or 'synchrosunlight'.

Olympus T32 *You can use the T32 as an ordinary automatic flash, or it can be linked to the OM2's meter which takes a flash exposure reading directly off the film*

Versatile gun *Independent makers produce guns that are fitted with different hot shoe adaptors to suit different cameras*

Nikon Speedlite *This unit is dedicated to the FE, but will also work with other Nikons as an ordinary flash. It is quite expensive, but makes flash photography very simple*

PROFESSIONAL FLASHGUNS

Hammerhead *A typical powerful flashgun, mounted on its sturdy adjustable bracket. The powerful main head swivels up (below), allowing the photographer to bounce light on to the subject, while the fixed secondary head, located beneath it, provides fill-in light to prevent unpleasant shadows under the chin and nose*

For shots of the family at home, the illumination provided by a small amateur flashgun is usually adequate. But if you wish to do anything more ambitious, you may have to buy one of the guns designed for the professional. Professional units are much more powerful and versatile—they recycle more quickly and deliver more flashes per set of charge of batteries. They can also cover wider angles, and are adjustable over a greater output range.

The extra power of a professional unit is particularly valuable. While an amateur unit may have a guide number of 20 with 100 ISO film, the GN for a professional unit may be 70 or more. This is the difference between having to use an aperture of f/4 at 5 m and being able to use it at 15 m or more.

Power is especially useful in automatic flash photography—the photographer is left free to concentrate on the subject, knowing that most situations are well within the range of the flashgun. Also, for bounced flash, which requires an increase in exposure of two to four stops, power is essential. The greater the power of the unit, the more chance there is of using a small enough aperture to obtain good depth of field even with the most difficult subject.

Types of unit

Most small amateur units are light enough to clamp on the 'hot shoe' of the camera without placing strain on the camera body. Professional units, however, are considerably heavier, and the flat lighting given by the centrally mounted flash is rarely that desired by professional photographers. For these reasons, professional units are generally mounted on a bracket bolted to the camera, which positions the flash head above and to one side, giving some modelling to the subject and avoiding 'red eye' effect.

Brackets come in different shapes and sizes, but usually incorporate a grip. The *hammerhead* type of gun, sometimes known as the 'potato masher' because of its shape, incorporates a tube which contains the batteries and acts as a grip. With the more powerful units, the battery pack is contained in a separate unit, suspended from the photographer's shoulder and connected to the flash head by a cable.

As well as the true professional units, some small but very powerful amateur units are available. These are light enough to be fitted to the hot shoe, but can be mounted on a bracket if desired. The Olympus T32, for example, clamps on to the hot shoe of the camera, but, with he addition of a combined grip and battery housing, it converts into a hammerhead type. With a guide number of 32 (see page 135) it provides more power for amateur units.

Automatic flash

Most modern professional flashguns are automatic and have a sensor which measures the light reflected from the subject, cutting off the flash when exposure is correct for the stop being used. Most are also thyristorized, which means that after each flash, unused power is stored in the capacitors and used for the next flash.

The flash duration of powerful automatic units varies greatly. At full power, it may be as long as 1/200 second. With this duration, rapid movement might be blurred, so bear this in mind when shooting moving subjects at medium distances. When working on automatic, however, flash duration is unlikely to be longer than 1/1000 second, so you should not have any problems with moving subjects. At close range, the duration is much shorter, and may be as

Power pack *Although this unit has a grip, its batteries are very bulky and must be housed in a separate power pack. Many of the more powerful guns use this system, which is convenient and manoeuvrable.*

Wide angle diffusers *are used to increase the angle of coverage of flashguns. Some are incorporated in the unit and swivel over the reflector (left), while others are separate and can be clipped into place when required (right)*

little as 1/25,000 second, freezing the fastest action.

Professional units recycle much faster than amateur guns—even at full power, recycling time should not be more than three or four seconds. This can be invaluable in situations where you wish to take many shots in quick succession. On automatic operation, recycling time is much shorter, and when shooting close can be as little as ¼ second.

With nearly all professional units, you can choose between a much wider number of apertures for every film speed. With most cheaper units, the range is rarely more than two stops but with the professional guns, there is a choice of four or more stops. As you set the film speed on the gun, a counter moves to show the different apertures that you can use with that film speed. You

then simply set the desired aperture on both the flashgun and the lens: the flashgun automatically adjusts the intensity of the flash to suit the aperture which has been set.

There are two advantages to this wide range of aperture settings. First, it allows you to choose the aperture to obtain exactly the depth of field you want, though with a fast film you may still not be able to open up the lens quite far enough to blur the background completely.

Second, it means that you can set a wide aperture so that the flash functions at low power. When the gun uses less power, it recycles faster so you can set a wide aperture when you want rapid recycling time. This can be particularly valuable when you use flash with a motor drive. Some units also have a facility for

working at half power in the manual mode, which also saves batteries—however, automatic operation is the most economic way of working over all.

Bounced flash

Since a great deal of flash photography is done with bounced flash, it is important that an automatic gun should be able to read the light off the subject, even though the head is tilted in another direction. The most useful type of gun is that which allows you to tilt the reflector in as many directions as possible while the sensor remains pointing at the subject, such as for example the Metz Mecablitz 60 CT1.

A remote sensor, separate from the flash head, is especially useful when you are using a hammerhead unit, because it is near the lens and reads roughly the same area of the subject. The Braun remote sensor is very versatile, allowing 22 different aperture settings at a third of a stop intervals.

Beetle *For close-up shots where detail is important, a conventional flashgun is unsuitable because it casts heavy shadows at close range, hiding detail; ring flash cancels out these shadows by casting light from all sides at once*

Remote sensor *When the flash head is used at a distance from the camera, it is important to have an exposure reading from the camera position. This sensor has a facility for 22 different aperture settings at intervals of one third of a stop*

Most advanced flashguns will illuminate the subject over an angle of about 50°, but the coverage can be increased for wide angle lens shots in one of two ways. With units such as the Braun, there is a special built-in diffuser that can be pulled down over the reflector to spread the light out more. Others have a flash tube that is reversed to give extra coverage when the gun is set on 'wide angle'. Both these methods increase the angle of illumination to 65–75°, enough for a 20 mm or even 24 mm lens on a 35 mm camera.

Another common feature on professional flashguns is the facility to swivel the head for bounced flash—reflected flash. The more positions the head allows you, the better. If, for example, you are bouncing the flash off the ceiling, the head is tilted upwards. But if, with the head in this position, you turn your camera to shoot in the vertical format, the flash will bounce off the wall. With a fully tilting reflector, you can keep the flash unit pointing at the ceiling.

Some of the recent hammerhead units incorporate a secondary flash head below the main one and this could be a valuable feature if you anticipate using bounced flash frequently. Without the secondary flash, light bounced from the ceiling falls on the subject from above, and may cause sharp shadows under the eyes, nose and chin. The secondary flash head points directly at the subject and fills in these shadows giving much more acceptable results for lighting most types of portraits.

It is also an advantage to have a flash unit which can easily be detached from its bracket, so that you can hold it away from the camera. When using bounced flash, the more freedom you have in adjusting the angle and position of the flash head, the more control you have over the amount and quality of the light.

Extension heads

Many advanced units allow extra flash heads to be connected to the power pack by cables. This greatly increases the control you have over lighting and modelling. The extra heads are powered by the capacitors either in the main gun or in the extra head.

With the capacitor in the main gun, there is no extra power to fire the extension heads so power from the main gun is split between all the heads. If you are using three heads, for example, each will give out one third as much power as the main head would on its own. Using a capacitor in the extra head, each head operates at the same power so you exhaust the batteries sooner, but have more light at your disposal and this can often be a great advantage.

Since both arrangements make use of cables to connect the units, triggering is more reliable than when using slave units. There is a limit to the distance at which you can place the heads, but for most purposes this should not be a problem.

Ring flash *This type of gun is useful in portraiture where gentle lighting is desired.* **Hair** *can be given a 'soft' look, while other details of the face remain distinct. This effect is most pronounced at fairly close range*

Ring flash

Even when a flash unit is used in the hot shoe of the camera, it produces small but sharp shadows on the subject. The closer the subject is, the more noticeable these shadows become, until at macro distances they become excessive and mask parts of the subject.

If you do a great deal of macro photography, you might consider using one of the ring flash units designed for close-up work. These fit around the lens, usually screwing into the filter thread. When you shoot a close-up subject with one of these units, the light falls from all sides, cancelling out all shadows. Shooting from further back, though, casts shadows.

These units are powered by a separate pack, connected to the tube by a cable.

Power sources

Several different types of power source are available for professional flashguns, each with its pros and cons. Lead-acid accumulators need constant attention and must be kept permanently charged, but have a greater capacity and recycle faster than nickel-cadmium cells, which are also more expensive. Nickel-cadmium cells, however, are sealed and need no maintenance other than charging.

Zinc-carbon batteries are inexpensive but cannot be recharged, so if you plan to take many flash pictures they are not practical. Manganese alkaline cells, though they have a longer life, are more costly. The new Barix Dry Cells combine the capacity of the lead-acid accumulator

nickel-cadmium 510 volt pack.

Professional units can also be powered by the mains, but this is only practical if you are not moving about very much—indoor flash photography is the obvious choice for this source. Your choice of power source must depend on the type of photography you intend to do, as well as the amount you want to spend.

Choosing a unit

The professional gun you choose depends on the amount of flash work you plan to do. To a certain extent, your choice is determined by the 'feel' of the unit—you may find a particular grip more comfortable than another. Look at the bracket, also—it should be as rugged as possible, and made in such a way as to

A reflector *is an asset when working with bounce flash*

Direct flash *gives sharp, unpleasant shadows to faces*

Bounce flash *gives diffused light from one side only*

Combining *bounce and direct light gives best results*

They are normally used for medical photography or technical work, but they can also be used for fashion photography when shadow-free results are desired. However, they do not usually have sufficient power for studio work except at close range. For macro work, their power is ample. Some units, such as the Olympus ring flash, have the added advantage of TTL metering automation which measures the field covered by the lens for accurate exposure in close-ups.

with the convenience of the nickel-cadmium type, and cannot be over-charged, as some other cells can.

Some flash units can be powered by a High Voltage Dry Battery Pack, such as the Vivitar, which supplies 510 volts. These cells recycle the unit rapidly, and deliver many flashes before being exhausted, but they are costly and heavy. Most cannot be recharged either, although for some units, such as the Sunpak range, there is a rechargeable

prevent the camera from twisting. You should be able to hold it comfortably and steadily at all times.

If power is your primary concern—and this is the greatest advantage of professional flash—then buy the unit which gives you ample reserves of power, the most powerful you can afford. Bear in mind, also, that if you are to do much bounce flash work, a head which can tilt in any direction is a great advantage for control over modelling.

Chapter 7
STUDIO LIGHTING
LIGHTING ON A BUDGET

Light is essential to photography. Without it, you would be unable to take pictures. But whereas the use of available light will normally give satisfactory results out of doors, you will often require artificial light if you wish to take good photographs indoors.

Full studio lighting can cost a lot of money, but if you choose carefully from the range of budget equipment available, you will be able to create excellent and easily controllable sources of artificial light for a relatively modest outlay.

There are basically two methods of providing light for an indoor subject—flash and tungsten lighting.

Bulbs
The term *tungsten lighting* is generally used to describe sources of light that are illuminated continuously, rather than lighting up for a very brief instant

in the way that a flashgun does. Because it is a general term, tungsten light is used to refer to all sorts of light sources, ranging from ordinary household bulbs to football stadium floodlights. For photographic purposes, the type of tungsten lamps that are most commonly used range from 275 watts to 1000 watts, though for the home studio anything brighter than 500 watts is rather unmanageable. Lamps dimmer than 275 watts emit light that is too yellow in colour, and are therefore not really suitable for colour photography.

There are many different types of lamp which are made specifically for photography, but the most useful of these, as far as the non-professional user is concerned, is the photoflood bulb.

Photofloods are made in a variety of sizes and power outputs, the outputs of the most popular sizes being rated at

Schoolboy still life *For this sort of still life, a cheap, simple lighting set up is perfectly adequate to achieve well lit pictures*

275 watts and 500 watts. Although photofloods look very similar to domestic light bulbs, they are made with a different electrical element within the glass globe. But photofloods get much hotter, shine brighter and last for less time than conventional light bulbs. Their most important advantage, however, is that they burn with a bluer light.

Photofloods have a colour temperature of around 3400 kelvins, (see pages 238 to 239) which makes them much more suitable for use with tungsten balanced colour slide film than conventional light bulbs. Some filtration must still be used, though, because tungsten film is balanced for light with a colour temperature of

200K (see films and filters, below).
The cap fittings of photofloods are the same as those of ordinary domestic light bulbs, so they could be used in place of ordinary bulbs. Although this is feasible with the smaller bulbs for short periods, it can be dangerous to use large photoflood bulbs in fittings that have not been specifically designed for this purpose. The bulbs heat up very rapidly, and could damage light fittings in a few minutes. A burnt out lampholder may just mean a blown fuse, but there is a serious risk of fire if the bulb touches flammable material. Photoflood bulbs, particularly the larger ones, should be used in ceramic lampholders with metal fittings.

There are other types of tungsten lamp available, some of which offer significant advantages over photofloods. Photopearl lamps, also called Argaphoto bulbs, are in many ways similar to photofloods—they consume either 500 or 1000 watts and have a colour temperature of 3200 kelvins, which means that they can be used with tungsten film without the need for filters. The major difference between photofloods and photopearl lamps is in burning time: photopearl bulbs burn for 100 hours or so, while photofloods will burn out after only 3 to 6 hours. Although the cost of the longer lasting bulbs is as much as five times greater than the cheaper photofloods,

they cost less in the long run.
Photoflood lamps are now commonly called 'photolamps' and photopearl lamps are generally known as 'tungsten (3200K) lamps'. Without the colour temperature in brackets the term tungsten is virtually meaningless because all filament lamps have tungsten filaments.

Lampholders and stands
On its own, a bulb is useless—it needs to be supported and its light directed. There are a variety of lighting systems on the market which provide a good selection of stands and lamp-holders, and can be fitted with a number of different reflectors.

There are three common types of lamp fitting available for photographic purposes—one is a bayonet cap (BC) fitting, and the other two are Edison screw (ES) fittings. Some photographic lamps are available in a choice of fittings, but all photoflood and photo-pearl lamps that are likely to be used at home are available in the smaller of the two Edison screw fittings. It makes sense, therefore, to base any home studio around this one standard size, which is also the size most commonly used in domestic screw-thread light fittings in Europe and the USA.

Most domestic light fittings are made of plastic, and while this is a perfectly

Photographic lamps *The opal bulbs are photofloods—two are 375W, one 500W. The clear bulb is an ordinary 60W lamp*

suitable material for bulbs up to 200W, it will probably char or melt if used with powerful photographic lamps. If you plan to use one of the more powerful bulbs for extended periods, make sure that the lampholder you buy is made of metal, and that the insulators inside are made of a ceramic material—you should be able to see these insulators by looking into the lampholder with the bulb removed.

Lighting stands for the lampholders are available in a wide variety of shapes and sizes. They are usually collapsible, and fold up quite small for ease of transportation. The more portable stands are made of aluminium alloy—this makes

Budget lighting *Even unexpensive lighting systems offer a choice of stands and reflectors. Some allow you to use your electronic flashguns as a light source*

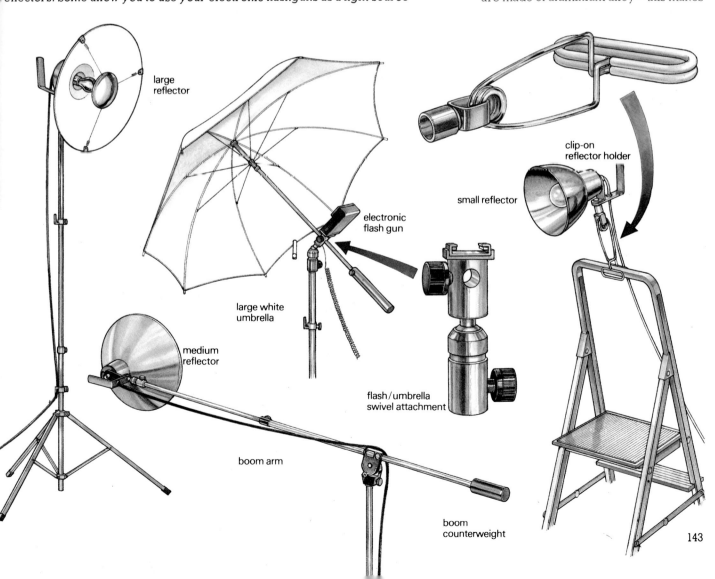

large reflector

large white umbrella

electronic flash gun

small reflector

clip-on reflector holder

medium reflector

flash/umbrella swivel attachment

boom arm

boom counterweight

143

them a lot lighter to carry around. Unfortunately, aluminium is both expensive and rather soft, so the better makes of aluminium stand are quite substantially built, and therefore tend to be quite costly. If you intend to use your lighting frequently, or if you will have to carry it around a lot, it is probably a good idea to spend your money on heavy duty types.

On the other hand, most amateur lighting set-ups are used infrequently, being stored in a cupboard when not in use, and in such a case a strong aluminium stand would be a waste of money.

The most rigid types of stand are those made of aluminium tubing. Although the stands constructed from aluminium extrusions are adequate for most purposes, they can be more difficult to assemble, and are not usually quite as steady as the tubular type.

Cheaper stands are often made from pressed steel—they have telescopic steel tubes in the centre, and flat metal strip legs. These stands only extend to about 2 m, but this is usually adequate for portraits and still life photography in the home. When these are not being used they can be stored in boxes which take up very little space.

It is very useful to be able to get a light down low, almost at floor level. This is sometimes necessary when lighting a portrait, because a low light can be used for backlighting—it will come from behind the subject, but will not be visible in the picture. In such cases you can buy a small tripod attachment which will take the lampholder. Some manufacturers produce a clamp that can be fitted to one leg of a lighting stand serving the same purpose.

Lighting stands are not the only means of fixing lamps into position. Strong spring clips are available that have a lampholder and reflector attached. These can be fixed to the back of a chair or onto a shelf, and usually have a ball and socket joint which allows the lamp to be pointed in a number of different directions. These devices work well for improvised lighting set ups, and can be usefully pressed into service as extra reading lights when not in use for photography.

Another useful accessory that comes in handy for occasional photo sessions is a small steel bracket that hooks over the top of a door. Most internal doors have a small amount of clearance at the top, so the door can often be closed with the bracket in place. The light is then fixed onto the bracket, which again has a ball and socket joint so that it can be pointed in the required direction.

Getting a lamp above a subject is often a problem, particularly for portraiture where a dark haired sitter will need extra light on the hair for good results. A long horizontal bar is usually used for this purpose, with the lamp fixed to one end. A counterweight is attached to the other and the whole arm, called a *boom*, is clamped to the upright of a lighting stand. The lamp hangs above the sitter's head, but does not appear in the picture.

Reflectors

Even the most inexpensive lights can be used with a range of different reflectors. As a general rule, the smaller the reflector, the sharper and harder the light source will appear to be. A bare light bulb is the most extreme example, forming very hard, abrupt shadows. It also wastes a lot of light.

A small shiny reflector directs more light from the bulb onto the subject, but still forms fairly hard shadows. A larger reflector is less efficient in concentrating the light from the bulb, but produces less harsh shadows. Very large reflectors give extremely soft illumination, with very gentle shadows, but the light is spread out so that it is much dimmer.

These three types of reflector can be fitted to most types of economical lighting units. They are generally made from spun aluminium, which makes them light, reflective, and easy to move around. The smallest reflectors are usually about 17 to 18 cm across, and are highly polished inside. They are best used for backlighting, where a small source of light is required, or for a dramatic main source of light. They produce narrow beams with little spread.

General purpose reflectors are not so highly polished, measure about 24 cm across, and produce a softer, wider beam of light. This is the type of reflector that is supplied as standard with many lighting units.

Hard light *The smallest reflectors produce a concentrated, harsh beam*

Fill in reflectors are much larger—40 cm or bigger, and are painted matt white on the inside. They often have a cover which prevents light from reaching the subject directly from the bulb. These reflectors are used to fill in harsh shadows in a picture, without forming disturbing secondary shadows themselves. They are also useful as a soft, flattering main light for portraiture.

Some photographic lamps also have a reflector built into the bulb. Since the reflector is fixed in place these bulbs are of limited use. They produce fairly narrow beams of light, and can be pressed into service as a last resort.

Slightly softer *Medium size reflectors form a beam that is marginally softer*

Big and soft *Large white reflectors are much more suitable for portraits*

Lighting accessories

The most expensive lighting systems have custom built systems of accessories available, such as *barn doors* and *snoots*. Barn doors are black metal flaps that control the area of the subject that is lit by the lamp, and can also be used to prevent light falling directly on the camera lens.

Although these are rarely made for the cheaper lighting systems, a substitute can be improvised using pieces of black card and a pair of spring clips.

A snoot is a long cone-shaped cover that is fixed to a lamp to produce a small spot of light on the subject. Some of the cheaper lighting systems have snoots available, but you can easily make snoots for lights without them from black card and adhesive tape.

Dimmers and cost-cutting

Tungsten lights are expensive to run—the bulbs are costly and use a lot of power. The lives of photoflood bulbs are very short, and towards the end of their working life the colour of the light they emit becomes redder. For this reason, many photographers use a dimmer in the lighting circuit. This is set to a low level for focusing and composing the picture, and is turned up to full power for the exposure itself. Since the power to the lamps is reduced, they consume less electricity. The life of the bulbs is prolonged considerably—an eight per cent cut in voltage to a photoflood doubles the life of the bulb. It is easy to see that the use of a dimmer can halve the number of bulbs used.

Cutting the voltage to a bulb also lowers the colour temperature of the light, so it is important to remember to turn up the power before pressing the shutter release on your camera.

The same effect can be achieved by using a series/parallel circuit. This has a two-position switch with one position for exposure, and one for focusing. Un-

Solitary apple *The lighting for this picture was very straightforward—just one lamp in a large white reflector on the left of the subject, and a reflecting sheet on the right to put some light into the shadows*

Flattering flash *Best results are produced by flash and an umbrella*

fortunately, it can only be used with even numbers of bulbs, and will not work if one, three or five lamps are in use. Some manufacturers produce ready made units of this type, and even if they are unobtainable, any competent local electrician should be able to make one up to order for minimal cost.

Flash for the home studio

A lot of professional photographers prefer to use electronic flash for studio work, and it is easy to see why. Electronic flash does not heat up in the same way that tungsten light does—and it freezes all movement in the subject. Daylight balanced colour slide film can be used with electronic flash, which is an advantage, because there is less choice of film balanced for tungsten than there is of film balanced for daylight.

Professional studio flash units are often very powerful, and they can often be extremely costly, and so quite out of reach of the amateur photographer. When there is no suitable hire shop nearby, photographers may be tempted to use small portable flashguns as light sources for portraiture and still life indoors. The biggest drawback to this is that you cannot see the effect that the flashes will have until you develop the film, and you cannot use a conventional meter to measure the light. Studio flash-units avoid these problems by using *modelling lights*—small halogen bulbs placed

close to the flash tube to simulate the effect of the light—and by using flash meters. Polaroid test shots are also used as lighting checks.

Few of these possibilities are open to the amateur, and a portable flashgun is a poor substitute for a custom built studio unit. However, the versatility of a small flashgun can be increased by using accessories designed to direct and control the light. The most useful of these is a bracket that enables a portable flash gun to be directed into a reflective white or silver umbrella or *brolly*. This produces a much more diffuse source of illumination than direct flash, though much of the flash's power will be lost.

The advantages of a brolly are that it is the correct shape for a directional reflector, with the flashgun at its focus pointing into the umbrella, and that it can be folded up for convenient storage.

Umbrella brackets are usually quite cheap, and are made to fit either onto a tripod, or onto a conventional lighting stand. Since the area of the umbrella reflector is quite large, the light produced by such a unit is soft and gives gentle shadows. Quite acceptable portraits can be produced by using just one umbrella and a fill-in reflector.

Films and filters

Most colour films are carefully balanced to give perfect results in sunshine—light with a colour temperature of 5500 kelvins. Electronic flash emits light with this colour temperature, so daylight film will give good results with flash without any filtration on the camera lens being necessary.

If daylight balanced colour slide film is used in tungsten light, the pictures will have an orange cast. This can be prevented by the use of an 80B blue filter over the lens, although even this precaution may not result in perfect colour reproduction.

The best solution when using tungsten lighting is to use film that is specifically balanced for this kind of light. Tungsten balanced film, such as Ektachrome 160 Tungsten, will give accurate colour when used in light with a colour temperature of 3200 kelvins. Photopearl lamps have this colour temperature, so they can be used without filtration when the camera is loaded with tungsten film. Photoflood lamps are slightly bluer in colour. They have a colour temperature of 3400 kelvins, and if they are used without filtration, they will give a pale blue cast to pictures on slide films. The solution is to use an 81A or an 81B filter. Either of these filters will eliminate the blue cast from the picture, but the 81B has a more pronounced effect.

. Colour print film is only available in a daylight balanced version and, though correction can be made at the printing stage if the film is exposed in tungsten light, it is better to use an 80B blue filter over the lens for photofloods or an 80A for photopearl lamps. This will give better colour reproduction, and make printing the negative that much easier.

STUDIO FLASH

If you are planning to adapt a room in your home for use as a studio, you must give careful consideration to the lighting you buy. Since the greatest advantage of a studio is that you can create the conditions you want, the first requirement for studio lighting is that it should be as versatile and easy to control as possible.

Although you can sometimes use light from a window, this has the great drawback that you cannot control either the direction or the quality of the light. You have no control over timing, either, and you will often find that the light is lacking just when you want it most.

There are two ways of obtaining lighting as and when you need it—tungsten light and electronic flash. Each has its advantages and disadvantages.

Tungsten lighting is comparatively cheap and gives excellent results, but it can sometimes be unreliable, and the bulbs get uncomfortably hot. Portable flash, on the other hand, can give good results if used off the camera and bounced, but it has the great disadvantage that you cannot see the quality of the light before taking the shot, forcing you to rely on experience or guesswork. As most electronic guns are of comparatively low power they are not suitable for repeated flashing into a diffuser or reflector and the batteries tend to run down very quickly.

Studio flash

The solution to these problems lies in flash which has been designed specially for use in the studio. Studio flash units are mains powered and have very short recycling times—between one and four seconds—with a ready light to show when the flash is ready to fire again.

One of the great advantages of studio flash units is that they always have built-in modelling lamps. These are mounted next to the flash head, and shine continuously, giving off a light whose directional properties are very similar to that of the actual flash unit. In this way you can see the effect of a given light combination.

Many modelling lamps are switched to suit the power output of the flash. The higher the flash setting, the brighter the modelling light. This is an invaluable feature, especially if you are using two units, because by switching off all other

Girl in red *Sophisticated, professional looking lighting arrangements are possible even with the most basic electronic studio flash units*

ght sources you can adjust the light balance visually with the modelling lamps. The flash units then give out the light in the same proportion, giving the modelling you want.

Some units have a special device which switches off the modelling light just before the flash fires, and turns it on again afterwards. They also have a socket for a synchronization lead, allowing you to use them at any distance from the camera. Others include built in photocells or 'slave' units, which are connected to the circuit of the flash unit and trigger it off as soon as another unit is fired. In this way you can synchronize any number of flash units. Slave units can be bought separately and plugged into flash units which do not already have them built in.

Most flash units are built on the *monobloc* system, with the power pack and the flash head together in one unit. At one end there is the flash head with the modelling lamp, while the power socket, sync socket and the controls are at the other end. Most studio flash units can be combined with all kinds of accessories, so you can build up your own flash 'system', with facilities for controlling the light in many ways.

All manufacturers offer a range of accessories, designed to direct the light as required. Umbrellas are used for bouncing flash, and snoots have a similar effect to a spotlight, while honeycombs provide large areas of concentrated light. Barn doors are flaps which prevent light from going into unwanted areas.

Flash power and exposure

The power output of studio flash units varies from model to model, and in addition each one can generally be used at half power or quarter power. For a single unit, the exposure may be calculated using the guide number supplied by the manufacturer. However, when using umbrellas, diffusers or more than one flash head, these numbers become useless, because so many factors are involved.

Some manufacturers only give a power

Flashmeter
Manufacturers' recommendations cannot always give the accuracy needed for exposure and a proper flashmeter can be an invaluable extra. Unlike some, this Minolta meter gives a reading directly in f-stops.
Studio flash
The Bowens Bo-lite 200 is an inexpensive unit that comes with reflector and modelling lamp. A wide range of accessories is also available

rating for their units in joules or watt–seconds, and with these units you should follow the manufacturer's instructions for calculating exposure. (A joule is a unit of energy equivalent to one watt of power flowing for one second—the higher the joules or watt–seconds rating, the brighter the flash.)

The smaller units have a maximum output of 100 joules, while the more powerful ones go up to 500 joules, though this is far from the most powerful flash available as some professional units

go up to 20,000 joules. All units have variable power output, an essential feature when you are using them for fill in or for close-ups, where full power would be too bright.

There is no simple conversion between joules and guide numbers. While the joule rating gives an indication of the overall power of the unit, it is of no use in calculating the exposure, as the light output depends on other factors. These include the type of reflector behind the flash tube, and the degree of spreading of the flash. In fact, a 127 joule unit from one manufacturer has a similar guide number to a 100 joule unit from another.

The only way to ensure completely reliable exposure calculation is to use a flashmeter. This device measures the brightness of the flash, and either gives you an index number which you then convert to an f-stop, or it gives you a direct f-stop readout. This is an essential piece of equipment to accompany studio flash, and well worth the extra expense.

Flash systems

There is a wide range of flash systems available, and your choice depends on the type of work they are intended for as

well as on how much you can afford.

At the inexpensive end of the scale, a unit such as the Bowens Bo-lite costs about three times as much as the average on-camera electronic flash, or about the same as a budget SLR. The Bo-lite has a built in reflector and modelling lamp at one end, with clearly laid out controls at the other. Its power output is 100 joules, giving a flash factor of 33 (metres with 100 ISO film).

The accessory kit consists of a four panel barn door, a silver and black honeycomb, and a 'softlite', which is a 36 cm square diffuser panel. All these attachments are easily fitted to the flash head, and the unit can also be used with an umbrella. All studio flash outfits require a sturdy lighting stand, and the Bo-lite can be bought as a complete kit which contains all you need for basic studio flash. This consists of a carrying case, two Bo-lites with stands, two umbrellas and other accessories, a slave cell and all the necessary leads.

Another low priced system is the Courtenay Colorflash 2 and 4 series. The Colorflash 2 has a similar power output to the Bo-lite, giving a guide number of 27 to 34 with 100 ISO film. The Colorflash 4 is more powerful, with a guide number of 38 to 46 with 100 ISO film. Courtenay also supply a full range of accessories, all of which can be fitted in their specially built carrying case.

More expensive are units such as the Multiblitz Mini Studio 202, which has an output of 200 joules and a recycling time of 2 seconds at full power and only 1½ seconds at half power. The accessories

are fundamentally the same as those for the other makes mentioned, namely a soft box or diffuser, honeycomb, reflectors and umbrellas. The 202 system can be bought as a complete kit, with three heads, lighting stands and accessories, all in a compact carrying case. The flash heads have built in slave cells.

Another system, the Multiblitz Profilite system, combines the advantages of both portable and studio flash, constituting a multi-role system suitable for both studio and location work. The unit consists of a power pack, flash head and power source adaptor. The essential feature of this system is that it can be used as a portable flash when fitted with a battery pack and a flash head without a

Studio flash systems *Like the Bo-lite the Courtenay Colorflash (above) is an inexpensive unit with a power output of 100 joules giving a guide number (in metres) of around 30 with 100 ISO film. The Multiblitz Mini Studio 202 (left) gives twice the power and recycles rapidly, but costs a little more. The sophisticated Bowens Monolite system (right) is even more expensive, but it can be built up gradually rather than purchased outright*

modelling light. Alternatively, it can be used as a studio lighting system when the flash head is changed for one with a modelling lamp, and a mains adaptor attached. There is even an adaptor available which allows the unit to be

powered by a car battery, and the full range of accessories is available, including a carrying case.

Among the more sophisticated units is the Bowens Monolite series. The Monolites are cylindrical monobloc units with built in modelling lights. These are switched on in proportion to the flash power output. There is also a control for switching the modelling lamp to full brightness, which is very useful when focusing, and a device which extinguishes the modelling light as the flash fires, switching it on afterwards. The Monolite 200 E has a rating of 127 joules and a guide number of 34 with 100 ISO film.

A more powerful version, the Monolite 400 E, gives a maximum power of 254 joules, and a guide number of 50 m with 100 ISO film. Top of the range is the Monolite 800 E, with a power output of 508 joules, and a guide number of 67 m with 100 ISO film. This model also has a recycling time of 1½ seconds and a four power output selector.

The Monolites have sockets for flash

On the bench *Some systems can be used outdoors as well as in the studio—the Profilite runs off a normal 12 volt car battery*

slave cells, and an overheat cutout device. The accessories available form a very comprehensive range, and there are a variety of reflectors and devices for controlling light. The stands available run from lightweight to heavyweight, with a boom type stand also available.

Similar to the Monolites is the Courtenay Sola studio flash. There are three models in this range—the Sola 2, the Sola 4 and the Sola 8, giving guide numbers identical to the Monolite units.

Choosing a system

The first thing you must consider when you buy studio flash is the power output you are likely to need. If, for example, you only intend to shoot close-ups or head and shoulder portraits on fast or medium speed film, then an ordinary amateur flash or one of the less powerful studio units, say one with 100 joules output, should be quite adequate for your needs. On the other hand, if you want to photograph groups, then you need a much more powerful unit. It is better to buy more power than you need than to buy less, because you can always turn a unit down if necessary, but you cannot increase its maximum power output.

The number of accessories you buy depends on the amount of work you intend to do, as well as on the type. The range of accessories is vast, and not all of them are essential, at least at first, while others can be improvised. An umbrella is probably the most useful item, but diffusing screens can be made with tracing paper, while you could make snoots from heavy black paper or card.

Bear in mind that the more accessories you buy, the heavier the equipment will be, and it can become very troublesome to carry around. If you do not intend to move about too much, this is not too important, but you should still avoid buying items you do not really need. The best method is probably to build your system up slowly, starting with essentials and adding things you need one at a time.

You might also try looking at what is available on the secondhand market, as a system in good condition might be much cheaper than a new system, and is certainly an alternative worth considering if you are working on a budget.

Although not all the units described are as powerful as some of the more expensive hand held guns, and they are also much more cumbersome to use, the advantages far outweigh the disadvantages if you intend to do studio work at all seriously. The control you can achieve over the direction and quality of the light gives you a far wider range of possible modelling effects.

For a photographer who plans to do studio work regularly, a studio flash system is essential equipment. If you decide that studio work is for you, then you must decide what power output you require, and base your choice on this consideration. If you choose the right studio flash system, it should prove to be a very worthwhile investment.

FLASH METERS AND SLAVES

For many shots, particularly studio portraits and close-up work, you often need to use several flashguns at once. Obviously this is more complicated than using a single gun and if you use multiple flash frequently, it may be worth acquiring a flashmeter to make exposure calculations easier or slave units to synchronize the firing of the flashguns without having trailing leads.

Slave units

The basic slave unit is essentially a light-sensitive cell which activates a tiny switch linked to the extra flash unit by a normal flash lead connection. The cell reacts to the fast burst of light from a flashgun but it is unaffected by sunlight or any other continuous light sources. So when the 'master' flash linked to the camera is fired, the slave reacts instantly and triggers the extra flash unit. In fact, the master flash need not contribute to the exposure at all but can simply serve to trigger off the other flash units via slave cells—it can be a small unit fitted to the camera's hotshoe.

The slave does not usually have to receive direct light from the master flash. Most units can be triggered by flash light reflected from walls, ceilings or surrounding objects. A great deal

Creative lighting *In pictures using more than one flashgun, a flashmeter is essential to help balance the illumination from the units*

Plug-in slave *Many studio flash units, such as this Monolite, have special sockets which take both normal slaves (as in this case) and infrared units*

150

guns which do not have flash lead connections but must be fired using the hotshoe.

Some studio flashguns have slave cells built in. Others, such as the Bowens Monolites, have sockets into which a slave cell can be plugged. And some of the more advanced units can be fired using special infrared devices. With these the master or main flash is replaced by an emitting device which fires a synchronized pulse of infrared light. This triggers the special slave units attached to the flashguns. The main advantage of this system is that none of the flash units need to be connected to the camera, so dispensing with both the flash leads and the flash on the camera.

Making use of slave units gives the maximum possible flexibility with flash lighting. The flashguns can be positioned freely, enabling you to create any lighting effect you want. In particular, separate areas of the subject can be lit by separate light sources, a small gun can be introduced to provide back-lighting, and so on.

Metering the flash

Employing several units together creates one major problem, however, in that the correct aperture to use with a given set-up is almost impossible to calculate using normal guide numbers. The scales on the majority of portable flashguns, and the guide numbers quoted for them, are usually approximations. They take no account of the reflective properties of the surroundings—a subject receives more light from the flashgun in a small white room than it does in a large dark hall because of the light reflected from the walls and ceiling. So these guides are inadequate for really critical exposures, especially in close-up work.

With several flashguns used at different flash-to-subject distances the situation becomes more difficult. And a further complication occurs when the flashguns have different power outputs, especially if the light from the units overlaps in varying amounts.

All these factors make it almost essential to use a meter to find the correct exposure. Conventional meters do not respond to the brief duration of flash so it is necessary to use a special *flashmeter* or attachment. These use a fast responding light sensor, such as a silicon photo diode, and help you to determine the correct aperture quickly and easily.

The simpler flashmeters, such as the Courtenay 303, are connected to the flash by a normal flash lead. Pressing a button fires the flash and a needle on the meter indicates a number. This number corresponds to an aperture shown on a dial. Such meters are inexpensive and are suitable for most flash situations. They are used like a standard incident meter (see page 197) with spherical diffusers giving an acceptance angle of 180°. A few models have flat diffusers with an acceptance angle of 60° and so allow slightly more selective metering.

Meter readouts *The range of readouts available includes simple meters (top left), LEDs (top right), LCDs (bottom left) and illumination arrows*

Invisible link *Infrared slaves can be fitted to the flash. The transmitter is triggered either by hand (for cordless metering) or by the camera*

depends on the sensitivity of the unit—some will operate at distances of up to 30 m—though it is almost impossible to tell how sensitive a unit is without actually using it. As a general rule, the more expensive the slave, the more sensitive it is likely to be.

Some basic slave units can be very small—about the size of a thumbnail—while others designed for professional studio flash outfits are quite large. For the amateur the small units are perfectly adequate, and their size can be a great advantage in situations where fixing a larger unit in place is difficult. In fact some of the small units have rubber suction pads by which they can be attached to any smooth surface, such as the flashgun itself. Other units incorporate a tripod bush and a hotshoe. This allows large flash units to be fixed to tripods and also permits the use of small

Many flashmeters also allow reflected light readings. This is achieved by replacing the diffuser dome with a lens unit, or by simply sliding the dome out of the way. This facility is useful when it is impossible to get right up to the subject to take a normal incident reading.

Unfortunately, for a long session with many readings, the lead between flashgun and meter can be very inconvenient involving constantly switching the lead from the camera to the meter. So many flashmeters offer cordless operation. With this method a button is pressed to activate the meter and the flash is fired manually. Most meters of this type remain activated for 30 to 60 seconds so that there is no rush to fire the flash after pressing the button. For maximum versatility some meters, such as the Calcuflash, offer both types of operation —cord and cordless.

Light level readout
The Calcuflash, in common with many of the more modern meters, has another advantage over the simpler models in that it uses an LED (Light Emitting Diode) readout—like a digital watch—rather than a moving needle. This type of readout is more robust as there are no moving parts involved.

A few models, including those made by Vivitar and Minolta, have Liquid Crystal Displays (LCDs) which have all the benefits of LEDs plus the advantage of using less battery power. As some meters take up to four hearing-aid type batteries this can be an important point.

Another valuable feature of some of these meters is that they give readings in actual f-numbers rather than index numbers. This means that you can tell at a glance what the aperture setting must be. This can save a considerable time and effort when you are adjusting the flash power or position to give a particu-

lar f-stop, rather than adjusting the f-stop to suit the flash. Most meters of this type have symbols to indicate settings between the main f-numbers in steps of one third of a stop. This is probably the clearest and easiest to understand of all the types of readout, and the one third stop settings are accurate enough for any film. Even so at least one meter gives readings in precise f-numbers, such as f/19 or f/7, though this type of accuracy is rarely needed by the amateur.

One variation on this idea is employed by the Bowens SSR. This has an array of 15 LEDs arranged in a semicircle around a dial numbered with the aperture values. The correct aperture is indicated by the LED that lights up.

Just as important as the type of readout is the range of the scale. Many of the more expensive meters have aperture ranges running from f/1 to f/128 or even f/180. These extremes are rarely needed, even by professionals, and for amateur use a range of f/2.8 to f/45 is ample. However, when choosing a flashmeter it is worth checking that it will give this range at all film speed settings. Even this aperture range may seem extreme at first sight, but in close-up work where extension tubes or bellows are being used it is possible that effective stops of f/32 and f/45 could be needed.

Although your flashgun may not be powerful enough to give an aperture this small when used normally, it is often possible to build up the exposure with multiple flash. In a totally dark studio or room, with the camera shutter open on the B setting, the flashgun is fired manually several times until the required exposure level is reached. The effect is like using a much stronger light and it is very useful for still lifes as it gives greater depth of field. However not all flashmeters allow readings to be built up in the same way, so this is a feature

worth checking for.

One point to note is that the whole aperture range may not be contained in one scale. Like many normal exposure meters, flashmeters often use two scales —'high' and 'low'. It is worth trying the meter to see how easy it is to change between the two. The Courtenay meter for example, simply uses a slide which is pushed one way for high and the other way for low. This system is quick and easy to use and can save a lot of fuss.

In addition to measuring the amount of flash light some of the better meters measure the ambient light. This is a very valuable feature when using the flashgun for fill-in work or when using slow shutter speeds. On such meters, there is usually a dial with a range of shutter speeds. The meter automatically takes the shutter speed into account when it gives the suggested aperture setting. The range of speeds is usually just those which you are likely to encounter in normal flash photography—from 1/15 to 1/500 second. But very advanced meters like the Minolta have a huge range and so can be used as normal exposure meters.

Additional features
One extra design feature to look for is the positioning of the meter cell. Many meters have the cell on the front edge so that, when the meter is in the hand, the cell is pointing forwards. This is perfectly adequate for most situations, but in copying work, for example, it is often better if the cell is on top so that the meter can be placed flat on the surface being copied with the cell still pointing towards the camera. With the Minolta Flash Meter III the cell is not only on top but also mounted in a rotating head so that it can be turned in practically any direction. The Calcuflash and Vivitar meters have accessory diffuser domes

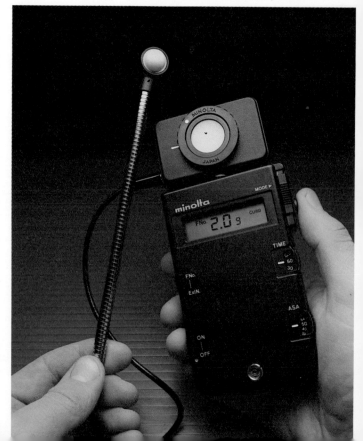

Metering using a flashlead

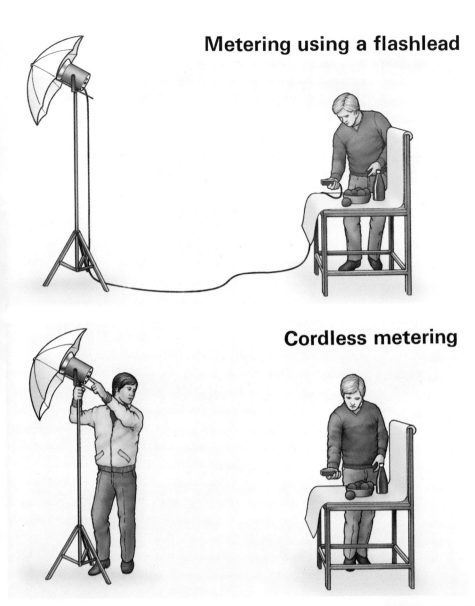

Cordless metering

which provide a similar facility.

Multidirectional metering is an extremely valuable feature when photographing small objects, such as still lifes, because the cell can be placed right next to the main subject. But, even so, there are times when there is insufficient space to insert the meter near the part of the subject you want to measure. So some of the more advanced meters include a meter 'eye' attached to a fibre optic cable. The 'eye' itself is small enough to fit in tiny spaces and the light is passed to the meter by cable.

For reflected light readings of small or inaccessible areas the top models also offer spot reading accessories. These take the place of the diffuser dome and usually incorporate a viewfinder so that the precise area being measured can be seen. The angle of view varies between 1° and 10° according to the model.

An even more sophisticated accessory is the Minolta Booster which connects to the Flash Meter III via a normal cable. This unit allows direct flash readings to be taken from camera focusing screens, viewfinders and even from the film plane of 35 mm cameras.

These sort of accessories are quite specialized and it is unlikely that the average photographer would ever need them. But if you do a great deal of close-up work or copying then something like the booster could prove useful.

Your choice, therefore, depends on the features you are likely to need. With a studio or room—even the simplest meter is perfectly adequate. But if you are interested in experimenting with flash, or using it in more difficult circumstances, then a more sophisticated meter is probably the best choice.

Metering methods *Using a meter with a flash lead is very simple but involves trailing wires and constant switching of the lead between the meter and the camera. Cordless metering is often more convenient, especially if you get someone to fire the flash for you*

On the spot *Some of the more sophisticated meters allow selective reflected light readings to be taken by the addition of a spot metering attachment (far left)*

Meter probe *This probe is a useful accessory for taking incident readings in situations where the complete meter would prove clumsy or be impossible to position*

Shutter dial *A few meters allow you to set the shutter speed in use so that the reading given automatically compensates for the existing light (left)*

Meter cell *The cell position can affect the versatility of the meter. The best type uses a rotating head*

Chapter 8
SLIDE PRESENTATION
SLIDE PROJECTORS

The first widely available colour film produced colour slides which had to be viewed by transmitted light or projected onto a screen to be seen clearly. Although nowadays colour prints are much more popular than transparencies, colour slides are still widely used, and the need for projection remains.

Colour transparencies offer a number of significant advantages over colour prints, primarily because the brightness range is much greater than in prints. Many photographers prefer to use slides because the quality of the colour is better and they are in some respects easier to print at home than colour negatives. Professionals like to use them because they give better results when printed in a magazine or book. Most of the pictures in this book are reproduced from colour transparencies, many of them of the standard 35 mm format.

Basic features

A slide projector is essentially an enlarger turned on its side. It has a light source to illuminate the slide, condensers to concentrate the light into a narrow beam, a carrier to hold the slide, and a lens which can be focused to throw an enlarged image of the slide onto a screen. All slide projectors have these same features and differ only in the degree of automation with which the slides are projected.

The lamp in almost all slide projectors that are currently available is a low voltage quartz halogen type. The lamp normally takes 24 volts and is fed with power by a transformer which is built into the body of the projector. It generally has an output of 150 watts, but some projectors are available in a higher power version, usually 250 watts, for use in large halls.

Projector bulbs get extremely hot in the course of operation. All but the cheapest projectors have a fan to draw air over the bulb and cool it down. The most basic type of projector relies on convection currents to cool the bulb, but this method is not as satisfactory as a forced supply of air.

Light from the bulb is reflected forward by a concave mirror. This is often specially coated to reflect only visible light and to absorb infra-red radiation, which would otherwise heat the slide in the gate. This keeps the operating temperature down.

To produce a concentrated beam of light, all projectors incorporate two or more condenser lenses. These collect the light from the bulb and reflector and focus it in the projector lens. Somewhere in the light path, usually between the condensers, there is a heat filter. This erforms the opposite function to the reflector, allowing visible light to pass through, while stopping infra-red.

The lighting system of a slide projector is very much the unglamorous side of the machine. Unfortunately, it is often overlooked by potential buyers because it is concealed inside. The quality of the light system decides how well the projector will work. A cheap optical system which uses unsuitable condensers, and perhaps an inadequate fan, can lead to uneven screen illlumination with dark corners, and also to premature bulb failure. Since replacement bulbs are very costly, a cheap projector can turn out to be a false economy in the long run.

Immediately in front of the condensers is the slide carrier itself. The design of this varies considerably. Different projectors use different methods of positioning the slide for projection and holding it steady once in place. All 35 mm slides are mounted in holders which are 50 mm square, so the slide gate is always made to fit this standard size.

The slide carrier should be kept cool, because if the slide gets too hot during projection it can buckle in the heat. This is known as popping, causing the slide to go out of focus on the screen. Extremes of temperature can lead to permanent damage of your slides.

A specially computed lens forms an image of the slide on the projection screen. The standard lens for 35 mm projectors usually has a focal length of 85 mm and an aperture of f/2.8 or f/2.5. The lens is mounted in a threaded tube. Turning the lens moves it closer to the slide in the gate or further away from it. This focuses the image on the screen and allows the projector to be used in rooms of various sizes.

At a distance of three metres, an 85 mm lens forms an image that is 1.2 metres in width, if the slide is horizontal. If a larger picture is needed, a lens with a shorter focal length provides greater enlargement without moving the projector away from the screen. Most projector manufacturers make a range of lenses. Longer focal length lenses are useful for projection in large halls where an 85 mm lens would form an image which is too big. The chart on this page shows how far apart the projector and screen must be placed when using different focal length lenses, if the projected image is to be 1.5 metres wide.

If it is likely that you will be using the projector in many different size rooms, a 'zoom' projection lens makes it easier to frame the image to fit the screen. These lenses are not, strictly speaking, zoom lenses as they need refocusing each time the focal length is changed, but they can sometimes eliminate the need to buy different lenses for large and small rooms.

In recent years, considerable effort has gone towards making projectors more automatic in operation. Both transporting the slides and focusing the lens can now be done automatically. All complex mechanisms are necessarily

Lamp changing *This projector has an easily removable cover that makes changing the bulb an easy matter*

Projection distance *In large halls, long lenses must be used, or the picture is too big. To find the lens needed for a 1.5 m wide image, read the projection distance on the left, and where this meets the red line, look down to read the focal length on the bottom scale of the graph*

expensive, though, and many people are perfectly happy with a simple projector and neither want nor can afford the sophistication of a fully automatic model.

Slide changing

The simplest slide changing mechanism is a metal carrier with two apertures to hold the standard 50 mm square slide. The carrier slides back and forth in front of the light source. While one slide is being projected, the opposite end of the

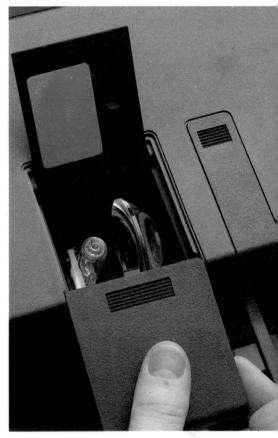

carrier protrudes from the projector so the other slide can be replaced by a new one. Only the simplest projectors use this shuttle change system, but it does have the enormous advantage of being foolproof and unbreakable, while many of the more complex slide changing systems are prone to jamming and sticking. On the negative side, slide changing has to be done manually. This is tedious, and a slide can easily be wrongly inserted in the dark.

Most projectors use magazines. These are made of plastic and are loaded before the slides are to be projected. This is a more satisfactory system, as you can examine the pictures and plan the show at your leisure, instead of scrambling round in the dark.

There are two basic types of magazine: straight and rotary. In straight magazines, the slides are lined up in a row in individual slots. As the slides are changed, the magazine moves forward so that a new slide becomes available. A rotary magazine is similar, but the slides form a circle and the capacity of the magazine is higher. With the rotary magazine continuous shows are possible, which is convenient for automatic

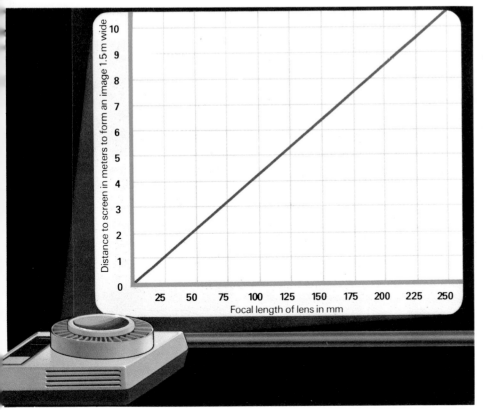

Projector lenses *Most projectors have a choice of lenses. The 60 mm lens on the left forms a bigger picture than the 85 mm on the projector at the same projection distance. The 'zoom' lens on the right gives a variable picture size*

Slide editing *If a slide is loaded into the magazine the wrong way round or upside down, it is possible to lift it out and correct it when using this projector. This useful feature also lets you project single slides*

Slide-tape presentations

Slide projection does not have to be confined to a series of images projected individually, with a spoken commentary. Most slide projectors which have a socket for a remote handset can also be operated by electronic devices which change the slides automatically.

The most common way of using this facility is to record pulses onto ordinary magnetic tape which, when the tape is replayed, change the slides at preset points. Using a stereo taperecorder, the other channel can be used to record a sound track or a 'voiceover'—a spoken decription of the slides on the screen, or remarks to clarify what is seen.

Using a slide projector and tape recorder combined in this way is called audio–visual, or slide–tape presentation, and makes slide projection much more versatile. Although in its most simple form, slide–tape features need only one projector and a tape recorder, many photographers use a slightly more sophisticated set up. This uses two projectors, and a device which makes it possible to dim the image of one of them while the image from the other projector is made brighter. By careful superimposition of the two images, the impression is given of one image dissolving while the other one appears. This eliminates a dark gap between slides and lends a professional gloss to the show.

When purchasing a projector it is worth bearing this possibility in mind, and finding out whether the machine you are thinking of buying can be used with a slide–tape synchronizer.

Often, a projector with this facility costs no more than one without it, and there is little point in buying a model which limits the further development of your photographic activities.

displays and presentations in shops, museums, and craft exhibitions.

Different manufacturers produce different types of magazine, although there is a degree of standardization in the case of straight magazines. When buying a projector, ask the price of extra magazines. If they are cheap, use them to store slides between shows.

A variety of mechanisms are used to get the slides out of the magazine and into the gate of the projector. Some projectors use a gravity feed mechanism with the tray of slides on top. This has proved a simple and reliable system and less prone to jamming than most other mechanisms, but the projectors are quite expensive.

The alternative which other manufacturers have adopted is a sliding or swinging arm that pushes the slide into the gate. This is done manually on the cheaper magazine loading projectors and the user slides a knob in and out, but even on quite cheap projectors a motor does the job instead. The 'command' to change the slide is given by pressing a button either on the projector, or on a separate remote hand set. The slide is removed from the gate and replaced in its slot in the magazine, which then advances to the next slide. This in its turn is removed from the magazine and inserted in the gate.

Focusing

Since different types of slide mount hold the transparency in slightly different positions, a tray of mixed slides often needs constant refocusing. This can be irritating if you are not near the projector, so projectors often have a motor operated focusing device, which by pressing a button on the handset or sliding a switch, causes the lens to be

racked back and forth. When correct focus is achieved, the button is released. Even this small task is made unnecessary on the most expensive projectors, which have automatic focus maintenance. Once the first slide in the magazine has been focused, the projector automatically adjusts to focus all the others. This is done by clever arrangement of photocells and an infra-red beam, which is bounced off the slide in the gate. The focus adjustments are made almost instantaneously. Even when a slide pops, it is rapidly returned to correct focus.

This feature is very useful, and definitely worth paying extra for.

Which model to buy

When comparing projectors, remember that all projectors perform basically the same function, regardless of price. A very elaborate automatic projector probably produces a picture on the screen that is completely indistinguishable from that produced by a projector costing only a fifth of the price.

Paying more for a projector does not necessarily mean better quality. It does often mean more features, though there are exceptions to this rule. Some of the very expensive models which are designed for continuous running in audiovisual displays have few extra features, but they are very solidly built.

There is no substitute for actually going and looking at projectors if you can. Although it is often cheaper, buying by post can lead to disappointment. Advertising brochures give only an idea of appearance and specifications, and rarely an indication of what the performance of a projector is like.

Take a decision about what type of projector you want—auto, manual, or semi-automatic—before you start comparing the different models on the market. Decide also whether or not you need auto focus or remote focus. If you take basic decisions like this quite early on, the wide range of projectors on the market is less likely to confuse your choice of model.

Do not buy a projector without trying it out, or at least trying an identical one. Take a selection of your own slides to the shop, including a very thin slide mount and a thicker one, since some projectors jam easily on the two extremes of slide thickness. Ask the assistant to show

you how the bulb is changed. On many projectors this is very difficult and involves removing the whole projector casing. Since projector bulbs usually blow in the middle of a slide show, the process of changing bulbs is complicated still more by the area around the bulb being very hot indeed. The most modern projectors sometimes have a standby bulb which can be quickly swung into position, but this is not a common feature.

It is difficult to judge the quality of a projector lens merely by looking at the image that it forms unless a special test slide is in the gate of the projector. Some high quality projectors are actually supplied with such a slide. Unfortunately, such self-confidence is rare. A poor lens will not resolve fine detail in the corners of the picture. Slides often suffer from distortion, so that straight lines in the original slide appear bowed either in or out. Further faults include inadequate coverage, where the corners of the

projectors with a sound track recorded on tape is quite important. It can add life and pace to an otherwise mundane show (see opposite). Almost every projector that has a remote control socket for slide changing can be used with a synchronization device. Those that do not may be adapted to accept the necessary inputs to fade the slides and change them at the right moment.

Other points to look for include *infrared remote slide change*. This is a cordless handset similar to a remote control for a television. *Variable light intensity* allows the bulb to be dimmed to suit the level of ambient lighting, and incidentally can increase the life of the bulb. A *safety cutout* switches off the projector if a slide jams in the gate. A *slide timer* changes the slides at preset intervals. A small lamp incorporated in the remote handset projects an *arrow pointer* onto the screen to draw attention to objects in the picture. With a *single slide projection/edit facility*, the slide being

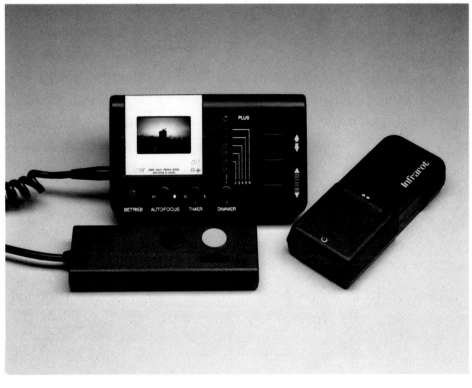

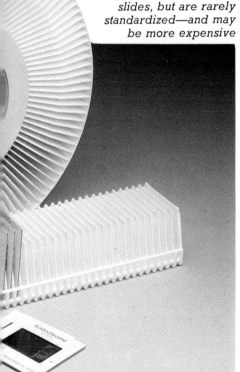

Round and straight slide magazines
Straight magazines have a low capacity, but are often of a standard design. Round magazines hold far more slides, but are rarely standardized—and may be more expensive

Remote control *Handsets vary from basic, which only has forward, reverse and focus (front) to total control (back). This one also has dimmer, timer, autofocus on/off and preview screen. The cordless unit (right) uses infrared pulses*

picture appear cut off, and vignetting, when there is a hot spot in the centre of the picture. Vignetting can also be caused by a badly designed condenser system or a wrongly aligned lamp.

Trying out a projector also gives an indication of noise levels. An induction fan can be very noisy, particularly in a small room, and the changer itself can make a noisy clatter.

Optional extras

Minor selling points usually separate similar models in the range of any one manufacturer. Most of these small features are quite insignificant details, but the ability to synchronize one or more

projected can be lifted out of the gate, if it is accidentally loaded into the magazine upside down or back to front, and reinserted correctly. This feature is also useful for showing individual slides, since it makes loading into a magazine unnecessary. A *preview screen* is a small, slide-sized screen, lit from behind, that allows you to examine a slide in the dark without lighting the whole room.

All these facilities are useful from time to time, but are hardly essential to the smooth running of a slide show. They might, perhaps, be the only difference between two otherwise identical projectors. Choose your projector for the features that suit your needs.

SLIDE MOUNTS

that card or plastic mounts cannot be used for general handling or storage purposes. On the other hand, overlay mounts cannot be used for projection.

Your choice of mount basically depends on how much you want to pay, what sort of use they will have and how long you want them to last. By far the most popular and commonly used, though, are the card and plastic mounts.

Card mounts
The simplest mount is the card type —usually white or grey in colour. The two sides of the mount are folded over with the slide sandwiched between and either heat sealed or stuck together with a self-seal adhesive.

Heat sealed card mounts are the kind usually used for most commercially processed slides because they are cheap and well suited to large scale mechanical mounting. They are not generally available to the public, however, and attempts at DIY heat sealing are rarely completely successful.

Removing dust *Glass mounts tend to trap dust so a blower canister should be used when mounting slides. Failing this, a blower brush is adequate*

With some slide films, you have little choice in the way your slides are mounted—the initial cost of the film includes processing and mounting in the manufacturer's normal manner. With films for which processing is paid for separately, however, you must specify the type of mount you want or cut and mount you own slides.

While professional mounting is undoubtedly convenient, doing it yourself has its advantages: there is less risk of damage to irreplaceable film by the mounting machines now used in modern processing labs; you choose exactly which slides you want to mount— which saves the cost of having poor images mounted automatically; you can also crop images to your own taste and may even be able to correct mistakes in particular shots.

Range of mounts *A wide range of mounts is available for most formats. White card mounts (1) are the **cheapest** and are easy to write on. A transparency stands out clearly in a black card mount (2). Sturdy plastic mounts (3) can be bought either plain or with two glass sheets to hold a slide flat. Creative mounts are available (4) for decorative mountings and masking*

Types of slide mount
There are many types of slide mount but most can be divided into one of two broad categories: those for projection— which is the most important category, certainly for amateur use, and which includes card mounts, plastic mounts and glass mounts; and those for handling or display—which consists mainly of overlay mounts. This is not to say, however,

Self-adhesive type card mounts are widely available and much more suitable for home mounting. Unfortunately, the adhesive often comes apart after a lot of handling, and it is difficult to align the film and the two halves of the mount accurately. Crooked slides look odd in a slide show and a badly sealed mount may jam in the projector.

Jamming may also occur when projecting card slides that have become dog eared or battered by overhandling. If the autochange mechanism on the projector is very fierce, buckling may be severe enough to damage the film itself. A further problem with card mounts is that they tend to show rather ragged edges on the framed area of the projected image. Even if they are crisply cut to begin with (and many are not) the adhesive picks up hairs and dust which always show on the screen.

The advantages of using card mounts, however, usually outweigh the problems as far as slides for general handling, if not for projection, are concerned. And this is borne out by the fact that most professional users use them for mounting and showing slides intended for publication. They are cheap; information can be written or printed directly on the mount; and they can be cut or marked for identification.

Plastic mounts

Plastic slide mounts are an alternative to card types, are only slightly more expensive and a wide range is available.

The cheapest are the fold-over types which are simply plastic versions of the card mount. Press-together type mounts come in two halves with snap studs to hold them together. Moulded-in guides help you locate the slide correctly. More expensive are the slip-in type where the slide is fitted into a hinged section which swivels into the mount casing.

Plastic mounts are rather better for projection than card types. The problem of dirt and dust around the image edge is eliminated. They are rigid and therefore less likely to cause jams and they are much easier to use. Further, they come in a variety of thicknesses, the range being approximately 1½ mm–4 mm. Some projectors work better with one type or the other. A good test of your projector is to try it out with a variety of mounts of different thicknesses and see which type works best.

Specific disadvantages, when compared to card mounts, are that plastic slides are difficult to write on and cannot be cut for identification. Storage, if you have many slides, is also less economical as the mounts are much thicker than card types and, therefore, fewer fit in a box of a given size. A rather minor point is that stacking plastic mounted slides, for example, while you have them out on a table top, is tricky—they tend to slip around and this can prove most irritating.

Card and plastic mounts suffer from two major drawbacks. The first is that they offer no protection to the surface of the transparency. It can easily become marked with fingerprints or stains from careless handling. Unless these marks are removed promptly, they can become permanent. The problem can be minimized of course by storing the slides in magazines and handling them as little as possible.

The second drawback of simple plastic and card mounts is less easily overcome. Because film has a slight natural curvature, these mounts grip the slide firmly by the edges to keep it flat. Unfortunately, this means that the film cannot expand sideways when it is heated in the projector and consequently it bulges outwards either gradually, as it warms up, or quite suddenly causing it to 'pop' out of focus. This is irritating enough in an autofocus projector but on a manual version it can be infuriating.

Card mounting *requires a little care. Making sure that both mount and transparency are free of dust, align the slide in the adhesive mount using a pair of tweezers. The mount can then be firmly folded over*

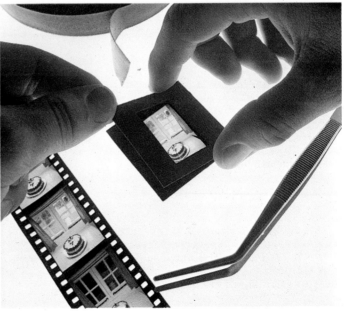

Other types of mount reduce the problem of popping by securing the film at only one point so that it can expand sideways as it heats up. However, this means that some of the film's natural curvature remains causing projection problems, since most projector lenses are designed to project a flat slide. If the slide is curved, they cannot hold it all in focus at once, so either the centre or the edge of the image is out of focus. The problems of slide protection and popping, though, can be solved by using glass mounts.

Glass mounts

Glass mounts have a plastic body but contain two small pieces of glass set into the cut-out in the middle. They both protect the film and hold it flat. Fingerprints or other marks can be wiped off the glass, or at worst the slide can be remounted in a clean mount. Because the slide is sandwiched, it cannot pop either—it must expand sideways instead.

Glass mounts are the type most often used in professional audio–visual presentations because they hold the film in more precise vertical and horizontal alignment than glassless slides. This is particularly important if fades and dissolves are being used to add effect. For perfect precision, special registration mounts are available which locate the film by means of the sprocket holes. Such mounts are very expensive, however, and are only worthwhile if the camera used for shooting the film, and the projector, are of top quality.

The main drawback with glass mounts

is that the glass can break. Though this rarely happens in ordinary use, it can pose problems if the slides need to be mailed—indeed you should not do this. Should a slide break in use, the pieces of broken glass may be ground against the image and ruin it.

Glass mounts also require more care at the mounting stage. Instead of two surfaces to attract dust, there are six.

Another problem with glass mounts is that they can produce an optical phenomenon called Newton's rings. These arise when two transparent surfaces are held in slightly less than perfect contact. If they are separated by a distance about equal to the wavelength of light, coloured

rings appear as a result of optical interference. Newton's rings can to some extent be prevented by using special glasses, although these add more to the cost of the mounts and in any case are not completely effective.

Mounting press *This device makes accurate mounting much easier. A small built-in light box illuminates the transparency to facilitate alignment in the mount. When the lever is pressed down, the mount is snapped shut neatly and accurately. Since you need not handle transparencies, the machine ensures cleanliness as well as accuracy —it should, however, be kept clean*

Overlay mounts *Where several slides are to be examined but not projected, these mounts are ideal. They can be handled without risk of damage*

Cropping *Part of a transparency can be masked off with thin black tape. Ensure that the slide and mount are clean, and trim off any excess tape before folding*

Overlay mounts

If you want to mount your slides purely for easy handling or for examination, for example on a lightbox, rather than for projection, you can use overlay mounts. These are simply black cards, folded double, with a cut-out, behind which the frame of film is taped. Overlay mounts are much larger than the transparencies they contain and are enclosed in a vinyl envelope which is clear at the front and frosted at the rear. They are easier to handle than projection mounts, provide good protection and allow transparencies of different sizes to be presented in a uniform way. Picture agencies often use them because the black frame enhances the quality of the image.

Slide mount formats

Two dimensions are used to describe slide mount size—the outer measurement along each side, and the inner or frame size. The frame size of the mount is always slightly smaller than the actual image size of the transparency. On 35 mm slides, up to 1 mm may be lost all round, while on 6 × 6 cm slides, the loss may be as great as 3 mm all round. This point is worth bearing in mind if you like to compose your pictures right up to the very edges of the frame.

The most common size of mount is the 5 × 5 cm with a 23 × 34 mm image area. If you own a 35 mm camera, this is the mount into which your film is normally fitted. Other film sizes which can be mounted in 5 × 5 cm mounts and used in all projectors designed to accept this size are: 110 format, 16 mm, 18 × 24 mm, 24 × 24 mm, 28 × 28 mm and 40 × 40 mm. The frame areas, of course, vary in size

to suit the type of film. Most of the major mount manufacturers offer all these formats although it is often difficult to buy them in the cheaper ranges.

There are two other standard outer sizes—3 × 3 cm (which is sometimes used for mounting 110 and sub-miniature format film) and 7 × 7 cm (used for rollfilm sizes up to 6 × 6 cm). Picture agencies and photographers who frequently lend their transparencies to publishers, and advertising agencies, often mount their slides in the large format type but because of the difficulties involved in projection neither format is widely used by the amateur.

Obsolete mount sizes include the old 3¼ × 3¼ inch lantern slide, various stereo formats and those peculiar to particular manufacturers.

There are also a number of so-called 'creative' mount formats. Usually these are made to fit only full frame 35 mm film. They consist of masks of various shapes —long, thin, panoramic types, small squares, circles and ellipses, TV screen shapes and even hearts, stars and

keyholes, through these are no substitute for creative images.

Should you wish to crop your slides, to get rid of unwanted details, or perhaps to strengthen the composition, you can use very thin black tape. This is applied to the actual film so it is important not to use tape where the adhesive spreads as this attracts dust, making the edges of the picture look very ragged. After masking, the tape can then be trimmed and the slide mounted normally.

Mounting accessories

Slides can be cut and mounted using little or no special equipment but some items make the job much easier. A lightbox helps you to judge exactly which slides are worth mounting and makes them easier to cut accurately.

For most mounting jobs, scissors perform perfectly adequately as a cutting device. But if you have a lot of mounting to do, then mechanical cutters and mounting presses may be worth considering. One manufacturer produces a mounting press which includes a built-in lightbox for highly accurate transparency positioning.

A problem involved in using any mechanical equipment for slide mounting is that it gets dirty. Slides and equipment should always be kept meticulously clean during all the stages of cutting and mounting. For glass mounting a soft duster is ideal for removing dust. Preferably it should be antistatic. A blower canister is also extremely useful. For perfect cleanliness, thin cotton gloves should be worn and hands should be washed with watchmakers' soap.

If you follow these simple precautions, there is no reason why your slide mounting should not be every bit as good, if not better, than that obtainable from the processing laboratory. All slide mounts are relatively cheap but for best protection and projection it is worthwhile paying a little extra for plastic or glass mounts.

VIEWERS AND LIGHTBOXES

Whether you are editing a selection of transparencies for a show, or simply searching through your collection for a single image, there are usually occasions when you wish to look at your slides without setting up your projector with all its associated bother.

Although projection shows transparencies to their best advantage, it is certainly not the best method of viewing a large number of images in a short time. So when you want to preview rather than view transparencies, it is much more convenient to use one of the viewing aids available.

Viewing aids vary from the simplest of viewers—little more than plastic boxes to hold transparencies—to the most sophisticated colour corrected lightboxes. In addition to these, several types of magnifiers are available which can be used in conjunction with viewers to make detailed examination of transparencies even easier.

Viewers

The simplest viewer consists of a small plastic box with a focusing lens at one end and a diffuser at the other. The transparency is inserted in front of the diffuser and by holding the viewer up to the light and looking through the lens, you can see the transparency, usually magnified.

This type of viewer is small enough to fit into a pocket, and is inexpensive—about the price of a roll of black and white film. However, the image it shows is usually not of the best quality. Also, you have no control over the colour temperature of the light used to illuminate the image—and this is important for assessing the true colours of the image as well as for displaying it to best advantage. In bright daylight illumination should be satisfactory, but by artificial light the image will not be bright enough, consequently the colour temperature will be too warm and the image will appear dim and yellow looking.

The ideal colour temperature of light for viewing transparencies is about 5000K (see page 246), which is roughly equivalent to bright sunlight at midday—you cannot always obtain this if you depend on available light.

The problem of brightness—though not that of colour temperature—is solved by using an illuminated viewer. These take the form of a plastic box with a large magnifier at one end, and a small torch-type tungsten bulb behind the diffuser at the other. The viewer looks rather like a very small television, and you

view the transparency by inserting it in to a slot at the top, which automatically turns on the light source.

These viewers have a magnification of between ×2 and ×12—at least ×4 is necessary for comfortable viewing. Some viewers have a switch which varies the light intensity and this compensates for transparencies of different densities. Viewers of this type are available for different formats, from 110 to 5 cm × 5 cm transparencies—some accommodate more than one format. Most have a facility for retaining the

Loupes *include the linen tester (bottom) and the sophisticated Schneider. The pocket Agfa viewer (top right) can also be used as a loupe*

slide in the slot—some sort of clip—and for keeping the light on for an extended viewing time. The most sophisticated types take up to 36 transparencies at a time, which can be viewed in rotation. The majority of viewers plug into the mains, which is convenient and economical when the viewer is to be used for a fairly long period.

Viewers *Except for the Agfa pocket viewer, these all have their own light sources. The Unomat has a motorized facility for viewing a series of slides*

The advantages of this type of viewing aid are magnification and portability, as well as the fact that the light source is of constant brightness. However, they suffer from a number of disadvantages. Only one person at a time can see the transparencies comfortably, which can make selection slower and more tedious. A greater disadvantage, though, is that the tungsten bulbs are not colour corrected, and the light they give out is too warm, even though it is constant.

Lightboxes

If you want to look at several transparencies at once, for example when you are planning a sequence for a show, a lightbox is by far the most convenient way of viewing. Not only does it allow you to compare density, composition and other aspects directly, but more than one person can see the transparencies at the same time.

A lightbox consists of a wooden or metal frame with an opal glass or acrylic sheet top. Inside is the light source, which usually consists of one or more fluorescent tubes, according to the size of the box. These are normally switched on by means of a rocker switch on the frame or side of the box.

The screen on the top of the box acts as a diffuser, giving even illumination all over the top of the lightbox. Both glass and acrylic screens are equally suitable. Glass, however, is more fragile, and if

On the screen *The Agfa Diastar viewer projects a full, clear image on a translucent screen*

you plan to carry your light box around a great deal an acrylic screen might be a safer choice. Though tougher, these require more care in use because they are more easily scratched than glass.

The fluorescent tubes of the light sources are available in a variety of colour temperatures, and under different names. They may be described as 'white', 'cool white' or simply 'daylight'. These all have different colour temperatures, so you should always check the temperature rating before you buy. Again, the ideal colour temperature is 5000K, and the lightboxes which have tubes described as 'colour matched' or 'colour corrected', such as Philips Graphic A tubes, give light of this colour temperature. Such tubes are more expensive than other white tubes available, so if cost is a limiting factor you may have to consider looking at other tubes of less than ideal colour temperature.

The colour temperature of tubes should remain constant for a minimum of 1000 viewing hours, but should it change after a long period of use tubes can be easily changed. However, for all practical purposes you can regard

colour temperature as permanent.

Some lightboxes are available which incorporate tungsten bulbs or tubes. You should avoid these—not only is their colour temperature far too low for viewing transparencies, but they generate a great deal of heat, which can damage the film emulsion and cause warping.

Lightboxes are available in a variety of different sizes, usually measured in standard paper sizes, from A4 (approximately the same size as one page of this magazine) to size A0 (16 times larger). Larger models are available and some manufacturers build to order. Generally speaking, a good all round size is A2—large enough to accommodate a good number of transparencies, yet still small enough for easy storage.

Most lightboxes are horizontal, and you view transparencies from above. One type, though, known as an 'audio-visual editor', has a screen which is angled towards the viewer. Channels running across the screen are fitted to prevent transparencies sliding off. This is a comfortable way to view slides and very convenient too, but the channels are fixed which means that you can only work with one slide format.

Other types of box are manufactured as well—one is built into a small table with legs, so that you can sit at it like a desk. Another type is built into a small case and can be carried around.

Lightboxes vary widely in price, so the amount you spend should be proportional to your collection of transparencies and the amount and type of work you plan to do. A small box, A4 size or thereabouts, should cost about as much as a lower to medium price telephoto lens, while a larger box, say A2, is around the price of a medium price SLR camera.

As well as for viewing transparencies, you can use a lightbox for retouching film and paper negatives, or transparencies. If you envisage doing this type of work, you might consider buying a lightbox with a dimmer control—you can then turn the brightness down for more comfortable viewing levels when working over long periods.

You can use a colour corrected box in conjunction with colour corrected tubes, mounted above the bench, to assess the colour accuracy of prints made from transparencies. By placing the transparency on the box, and the print under the fluorescent tubes, you can compare the two.

Magnifiers

To see all the detail in a transparency viewed on a lightbox, you need a magnifier. The best choice is one of about ×8 magnification, and many such glasses are specially made for photographers.

Some of these, known as 'loupes', consist of a lens in a short tubular mount, which may be of black or clear plastic. These are placed over the transparency, leaving the viewer's hands free. The

Portable light box *featuring a carry handle and mains lead. The colour temperature of 4300 K gives adequate colour balance and extra brightness*

Audio-visual editor *This compact unit is very light and is ideal for editing series of slides. The grooves stop slides from falling off the box*

cheaper ones cost about the same as one of the simpler viewers. Some have very high quality lenses and a focusing device, and may cost twenty times the price of the more inexpensive types.

Another useful magnifier is an ×8 linen tester used for checking the quality of fabrics. This type folds flat, but opens out so that you can view in the same way as with a loupe. You can buy a linen tester for about twice the price of the cheaper loupes.

Before buying a glass, make sure that you check the quality of the lens. Many of the cheaper models do not show the whole transparency, or show severe distortion round the edge of the image. Avoid those which show colour fringes at the edges of the frame.

Larger size magnifiers are also available. These consist of a lens on a flexible stem, mounted on a heavy base or clamp. These are particularly useful for retouching work, as the space between the transparency and the glass allows you access, with a brush, to the image.

Which of these items of equipment you buy depends on your commitment to transparency work. If you just want to look casually over a few at a time prior to, or instead of, projecting them, then a viewer should suit your purposes. If, however, you plan to give many slide shows, or do a great deal of selecting, editing and retouching work, then a lightbox and high quality magnifier should suit your requirements.

Lightboxes *are available in various shapes and sizes, from the size of this page (foreground) up to that of a medium sized table*

Loupe in use *A magnifier and a lightbox are the ideal combination for viewing and selecting a large number of transparencies quickly and conveniently*

Chapter 9
EQUIPPING A DARKROOM
BASIC DARKROOM OUTFIT

Setting up a home darkroom requires a large range of equipment besides printing paper and chemicals. Most of it is fairly cheap and simple, and it is easy to buy the first things you see in the shop. But for even the most basic items there are alternatives, and making the right choice makes life in the darkroom much easier and can make the difference between consistently good and variable results from your negatives.

Some manufacturers market 'complete' darkroom kits and many of these are good value for money. Not all of them, however, offer all the equipment or quality you require, and a few offer too much. To evaluate each kit and decide which is best for you, it is essential to know a little about each individual item. Indeed, you may find that the only way to obtain the exact range of equipment you want is to purchase each item separately.

Essential darkroom equipment falls into three main areas: film processing equipment, print processing equipment, and equipment for monitoring time or temperature and for measuring and storing the chemicals for both processes.

Processing film
Rather than plunge in at the deep end with enlarging and printing, many photographers start off in the darkroom by processing film only. To save expense, some photographers process film with a bare minimum of purpose-made equipment and improvise the rest from things around the house. Quality often suffers from this casual approach, however, and it is better to buy the proper equipment. The most important piece of equipment, the developing tank, cannot be improvised.

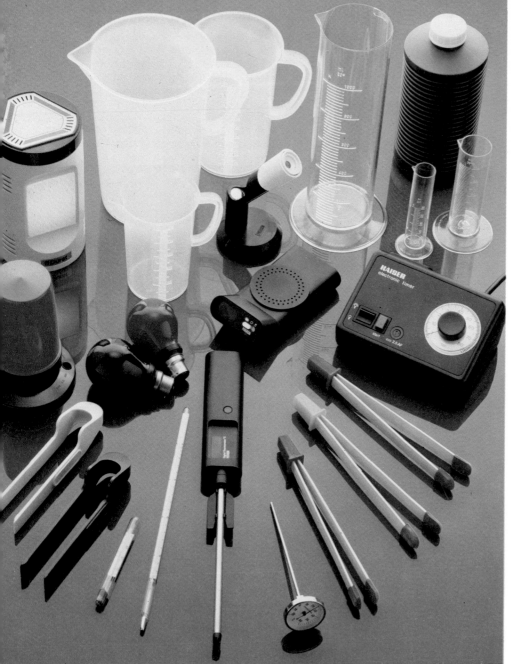

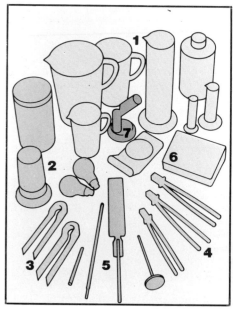

Darkroom essentials *Key to photograph*
1 *Measuring cylinders*
2 *Safelights and safe bulbs*
3 and 4 *Print tongs, plastic and bamboo*
5 *Thermometers*
6 *Timers, with seconds bleeper at left*
7 *Focusing magnifier*

Developing tanks Although an important and often expensive piece of equipment, the developing tank is simply a container to hold the film and chemicals during processing. Unfortunately, the perfect developing tank is yet to be invented. It must, obviously, be completely light-tight to allow development in normal room light. It must also be water-tight, except when you want to change chemicals during processing and then it must be possible to empty and fill it very quickly.

Tanks are usually made of black plastic or stainless steel. Stainless steel tanks conduct heat well and are easier to warm up in a water bath. But they also lose heat very rapidly as soon as you remove them from the bath. A plastic tank, though harder to heat up, retains heat for longer. Since with fast modern processing times many photographers dispense with a water bath and rely on prewarmed chemicals retaining sufficient heat during processing, the extra insulation of a plastic tank might be an advantage.

Stainless steel tanks are unbreakable, but they may bend when dropped heavily so that the lid will not fit properly. Plastic tanks, on the other hand, are very robust, but can be cracked if mistreated. They are also very sensitive to heat and some crack even if washed in hot water. On the other hand, you can even dry out a stainless steel tank in the oven if you wish to re-use it in a hurry.

When starting out, most people buy a tank that has a single film spiral, but if you frequently have many films to develop, you may find a *multi roll* tank more useful. Multi roll tanks will take three or more spirals and allow you to develop a number of films together.

Plastic tanks usually have nylon spirals; metal tanks have metal spirals, although they are sometimes interchangeable. Neither has any marked advantages over the other. Some people find it easier to load metal spiral: others find it easier to load a plastic spiral. The best way to decide which suits you best is to take a fogged film with you when choosing a tank, and try out a number of spirals. The methods of loading each type can be rehearsed with an old roll of film.

An important feature of plastic tanks is that they generally fill and empty very quickly. This is an advantage when it comes to timing processes—many stainless steel tanks take 15 to 20 seconds to drain and fill, and when judging development times you must remember this. The most recent colour processes use very short development times, and drain and fill times might well account for 20 per cent of the whole development time if you are using a steel tank.

Since it is impractical to check the leakproof qualities of different tanks in the shop where you buy—some tanks dribble large quantities of solution when inverted—we ran a test ourselves. Fill and drain times were also tested, as was the minimum quantity of solution needed to develop one roll of 35 mm film. Tank brands are named, but the tanks may be sold under different names by different suppliers (see page 492).

Washing film When a film has been processed it has to be washed and dried. Although it is possible to wash a newly developed film in an open tank under a stream of running water, specially designed film washers do the job more efficiently and more quickly.

The simplest kind of washer is a short length of rubber or plastic tubing that takes water from the tap to the inside of the developing tank. This forces water to flow under pressure from the bottom of the tank upwards, past the film and out through the top of the tank. Manufacturers of some of the more expensive types claim that their washers will wash films in as little as five minutes.

Some washers use water pressure from the tap to spin the spiral holding the film round and round. Another, called a *turbo-washer* mixes air with the water and so sends bubbles as well as water through the developing tank. This is supposed to speed up the washing process still further.

Drying film Film dries much more quickly if surplus water is removed before hanging. You can do this lightly with your fingers, with a piece of chamois leather, a sponge, or a pair of specially designed film wipers. Whatever you use, it must be kept scrupulously clean, because dirt can make tram line scratches down the film.

The blades of most film wipers, which look like car windscreen wiper blades, are often heavy and stiff. If you decide to buy a pair, look for the kind with very lightweight flimsy blades. Despite their fragile appearance, they work well, and are less likely to scratch the film.

You can use clothes pegs to hang up the film, but they tend to leave drying marks and dirt. It is worth spending a little extra to buy a pair of film clips. One type is weighted to prevent the film from curling, and most clips hold the film in such a way that no water is retained. This more or less eliminates streaks and marks in drying.

Print processing
After leaking developing tanks, poorly made masking frames are probably the greatest source of irritation in the darkroom. To work well, a masking frame must hold the paper perfectly flat, and in exactly the right position. Many cheap masking frames fail to do either of these things, and the result is unsharp prints with crooked borders.

The basis of a masking frame is simple. It is a flat wood or metal board with a hinged framework that lifts up for the insertion of printing paper. It has adjustable arms to accommodate different paper sizes and to vary the width of border. When lowered, the framework holds the paper flat and it should be impossible to slide the paper around underneath it. A masking frame that does not hold the paper firmly flat is not worth having.

The more you pay for a masking frame, the more solidly it is likely to be built. The large sized, heavy duty models can cost as much as an enlarger. Cheaper frames have non-adjustable border widths, and only take small sizes of paper. However, if you rarely make very large prints, and trim off borders after printing, a cheap frame should be adequate.

Besides the basic frame, there are several special types on the market. The most common are designed for making borderless prints. Professional printers use a *vacuum easel* for this purpose—a pierced board attached to a suction pump, which sucks the paper down flat. Unfortunately, these are very expensive. Manufacturers have adopted a number of cheaper systems, as a result, though some of these may prove to be less than satisfactory.

One type uses a *low tack* adhesive which is supposed to hold the paper flat. This is not very satisfactory, as the adhesive layer collects dust and has to be renewed periodically. A second system holds the paper flat under glass, but this collects dust which shows up on the print. A third alternative holds the paper by the corners, but this often fails to keep the paper flat. The best solution is probably to print with white borders, then trim them off.

Focusing devices It is not always easy to focus the enlarger, particularly when a dense negative is in the carrier. Focusing magnifiers make this task easier. They stand on the masking

Thermometer choice *A simple spirit thermometer is cheap and is more accurate than floating or dial types. Electronic models are very precise*

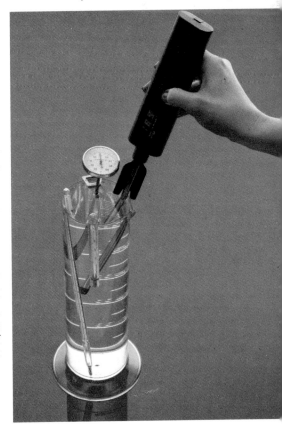

Tank test *We tried out six different tanks, testing them for filling and draining times, and checking the minimum volume of solution needed to cover a 35 mm film. No tank was leakproof, but some were more watertight than others*

Dixons stainless

Fill time—7 secs
Drain time—8 secs
Min vol—293 ml
Solidly made 'own brand' tank for 120 and 35 mm, but leaked badly

Jobo daylight tank

Fill time—12 secs
Drain time—6 secs
Min vol—393 ml
This tank needed no darkroom for loading film, but filled very slowly indeed, leaked a lot during processing and used more chemicals than any other tank

Kaiser

Fill time—5 secs
Drain time—5 secs
Min vol—323 ml
Neat looking tank that was reasonably watertight and filled and emptied quite quickly

Paterson Universal

Fill time—5 secs
Drain time—4 secs
Min vol—290 ml
Very popular brand of tank with wide mouth, making pouring easy and quick. It leaked a lot of solution when we tested it

Durst

Fill time—8 secs
Drain time—5 secs
Min vol—267 ml
Almost watertight tank—it only leaked one drop. It also used the absolute minimum volume of solution

Ilford 72 tank

Fill time—8 secs
Drain time—6 secs
Min vol—353 ml
This was a special tank for Ilford's 72 exposure film. It leaked badly, but frame for frame it used less solution than any other tank

frame, and consist of a small mirror, which reflects the image of the negative up to an eyepiece—actually a simple microscope. The eyepiece is adjustable to suit the eyesight of the user, and when the enlarger image is correctly adjusted, a clear picture of the grain of the negative snaps into focus in the eyepiece.

A second type of focusing aid is simply a mirror which reflects the image of the negative onto a ground glass screen where it is easier to see than on the paper itself. These devices are not as precise as enlarging magnifiers.

The wet bench Developing trays are one type of darkroom equipment where it is possible to make economies without adversely affecting picture quality. Many photographers successfully improvise trays from greenhouse seed trays, cat litter trays or window troughs.

Proper darkroom trays do have a number of points in their favour, however. They are rigid, making spillage less likely when they are full of chemicals, and they have spouts for pouring solutions. The better ones have small indentations in the bottom and sides to hold a thermometer in place.

Purpose built troughs come in several

colours—usually red, grey and white—and most photographers buy three colours and use the same solution in each one every time they are used. Clear plastic trays are also available, and these are useful when processing certain types of sheet film—you can shine a red light through them to see how development is progressing.

Print tongs are a good idea, even for a beginner, because they avoid chemicals coming into contact with your skin and stop cross contamination of the processing solutions. Two pairs are needed: one for the developer, and one pair shared between stop and fix.

Whatever kind of tongs you use, they must have a firm enough grip to hold large slippery sheets of paper, and yet not scratch the surface of the paper. Plastic tongs range from poor to reasonably good, but even the best of them break very easily. The most resilient tongs are rubber tipped, and made from stainless steel or bamboo strips. Bamboo tongs stain quite quickly, but they are colour coded like trays, and the staining does not seem to do any practical damage to processing solutions.

Safelights Black and white printing

paper is sensitive only to blue light, and can be handled quite safely by dim yellow or red light. Consequently, darkroom lights are usually of these colours.

In their simplest form, they consist of ordinary light bulbs dipped in a special red dye—ordinary decorative red light bulbs must not be used. They have a rubber ring where the glass meets the metal cap to stop light leaks. These bulbs are much cheaper than even the least expensive safelight, and are perfectly adequate for most purposes.

There are many other designs for safelights and most of them are quite satisfactory. The only point to look for is the light seal. A safelight that leaks white light will ruin your prints. Some safelights have interchangeable coloured filters, but if you buy a red safelight, this should be unnecessary because it can be used both with paper and orthochromatic film. A yellow light can be used only with paper.

Measuring equipment

For good results in the darkroom, both film and print processes must be measured accurately. Solutions must be made up to the right concentration, rocesses must take place at the right temperature and development must be timed accurately.

Measuring Cylinders To mix up solutions in the correct proportions and to ensure that exactly the right amount of solution is used in the process, you must have some way of measuring liquids. Some photographers improvise with cheap kitchen measuring jugs but these are not sufficiently accurate—many films have been ruined by such crude methods. Indeed, using kitchen containers for mixing chemicals is to be positively discouraged since someone may accidentally use a contaminated container for food.

Proper measuring cylinders are generally made either of semi-opaque polypropylene or transparent polystyrene. The semi-opaque cylinders are almost unbreakable but stain easily and their markings become difficult to read.

Clear plastic measuring cylinders are cheap and fairly durable. But you should check that the graduations are moulded into the plastic and not just printed on the outside, as these may be scratched off or fade. Some clear plastic beakers are not resistant to the concentrated acetic acid found in some stop baths. The acid etches the inside of the cylinder, making the graduations difficult to read. As a result, it is worth buying a small cylinder purely for stop bath concentrate.

Although it is possible to measure any quantity of liquid in a large cylinder, small quantities cannot be measured accurately and it is necessary to buy a range of sizes. A very small cylinder is particularly important if you use concentrated negative developers like Kodak HC-110 or Paterson Acutol A good choice is 1000 ml, 250 ml, and 50 ml flasks.

Measuring temperature Accurate temperature measurement is important because the temperature of almost all the solutions used affects the rate at which the chemical processes take place. If the developer is too warm, film will be overdeveloped even if the processing time is correct.

The cheapest thermometers are filled with a thread of alcohol, often coloured blue so that it can be clearly seen under the safelight. Although a cheap thermometer is better than none at all, it is worth spending a little extra for something more accurate. Most spirit thermometers are accurate to within about half a degree Centigrade, which is quite adequate for black and white work, though not for colour.

Greater precision is obtainable from mercury thermometers, though these are generally expensive. They are often accurate to within 0.2°C. Since thermometers are easily broken, some

photographers keep a mercury thermometer safely locked away to provide a check, and use cheap spirit thermometers for their darkroom work.

There are several other types of thermometers apart from the traditional straight glass variety. Some are crooked, so that they do not roll around in the bottom of a dish, and some thermometers float—this can be useful when you are mixing large quantities of chemicals. *Dial* thermometers have a clock-like dial about 5 cm in diameter attached to a long metal stem. Although they are very easy to read, dial thermometers are not usually as accurate as straight mercury thermometers, and are often expensive.

Electronic thermometers have been used for many years in processing laboratories. These are ideal for a club or for a semi-professional photographer because they have a large digital display which indicates the temperature with great precision. Unfortunately, they are very expensive compared to ordinary mercury thermometers.

When buying a thermometer, do not forget to check the range of temperatures that it covers, particularly if you anticipate developing colour films, which frequently need to be processed at temperatures in excess of 41°C. Even some black and white developers have to be mixed from crystals at similar temperatures.

Measuring time Although a clock with a sweep second hand is adequate to begin with, it is not sufficiently accurate for times shorter than about 12 or 15 seconds. When printing pictures, it is a great help to have one of the many

electronic timers that are on the market, and if you are printing a number of identical copies from one negative, a timer is essential.

Most timers can be preset to the required exposure time, and when a button is pressed, the enlarger light is switched on for the required period. The most modern type, which has a digital readout of the time that has elapsed since the enlarger was switched on is particularly useful, as it makes dodging of a print much easier—you know when to start and stop without having to look at a separate clock.

Basic timers only switch the enlarger on and off, but the more sophisticated models also do other things. Some turn the darkroom safelights out while the enlarger light is on. This makes it easier to see the image on the baseboard and shading the picture is made simpler. A very useful point to look for is a footswitch—turning the enlarger on with your foot leaves you with both hands free.

Try to avoid the type of timer that has two ranges, such as one to nine seconds and 10 to 90 seconds. It is easy to forget to change the range and this can waste a lot of paper and time. Timers that have one continuous range eliminate this simple mistake.

A lot of photographers do not use a timer at all, but time prints using a metronome or a flashing light. Although these are not suitable for short exposures they are sufficiently accurate for exposures exceeding 12 seconds. They save looking at a clock. And they are also comparatively cheap.

Masking frames *Large masking frames are very costly so, if you rarely make big prints, a smaller model should be quite adequate. Look for solid construction, adjustable borders, and the ability to hold the paper perfectly flat*

THE FIRST ENLARGER

If you decide to set up your own dark-room, whether it is improvised or a permanent arrangement, its' central feature will be an enlarger. As your skill increases, many hours will be spent using this piece of equipment. To ensure that your time is not spoiled by irritating minor frustrations arising from awkwardly placed controls or badly designed features, it is advisable to take a particularly close look at the alternative enlargers on the market.

All enlargers work on the same principle. They have a light source which illuminates a piece of film. The emerging rays are focused by a lens, which forms an image of the negative on a sheet of light-sensitive printing material. In most enlargers these components—the light source, negative stage and lens—are incorporated within an 'enlarger head' which is supported by a metal column. The column is fixed to a baseboard on which the printing paper can be placed.

The light source

The design of the optical system is a particularly important consideration. For most basic 35 mm enlargers, an opal photographic lamp between 75 W and 150 W is the light source. The image on the enlarger baseboard must be illuminated evenly, so before the light reaches the negative it is either con-centrated by an arrangement of simple lenses called condensers or diffused by a translucent sheet.

Most basic 35 mm enlargers use the condenser system. To make the most efficient use of the lamp light, condenser systems are matched to specific negative sizes. In a 35 mm enlarger, the condensers concentrate all the light from the bulb over the small area of the negative. Light rays from the bulb are, therefore, almost parallel when they pass through the negative, but come to a focus within the enlarger lens. The benefits of this system are relatively short printing times with crisp, contrasty detail. The disadvantage is that con-denser illumination emphasizes all the imperfections of the negative, such as scratches and dust.

Diffuser light sources work in a different way. They substitute an opal or frosted sheet for the condensers. This scatters light in all directions so the light rays approach the negative at several angles. This diffused light re-duces the effect of surface imperfections of the negative, but also tends to reduce the contrast of the image. Diffusers, unlike condensers, do not direct light efficiently through the film, and they therefore tend to give a dimmer image unless they are fitted with a more powerful lamp. For these reasons, diffuser light sources are most commonly found on enlargers designed primarily for colour printing—and are fitted with colour filters and powerful tungsten-halogen lamps.

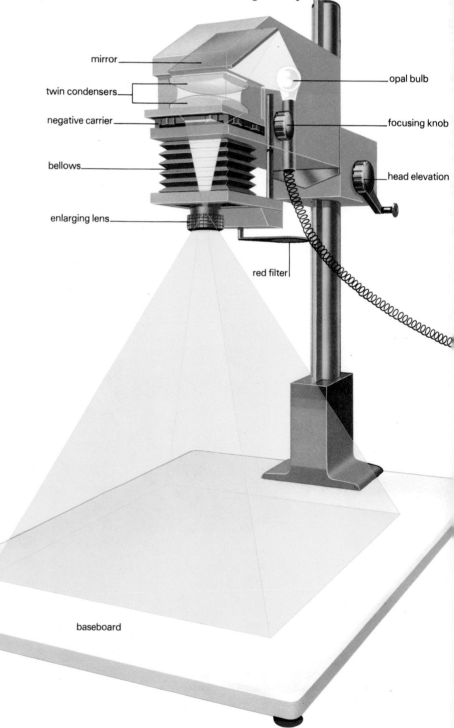

Enlarger construction *All simple black and white enlargers work in much the same way. This cutaway picture shows the path of the light from the lamp, via a mirror (omitted from some enlargers) through condensers and negative, and finally through the lens to form an image on the printing paper*

mirror

twin condensers

negative carrier

bellows

enlarging lens

red filter

opal bulb

focusing knob

head elevation

baseboard

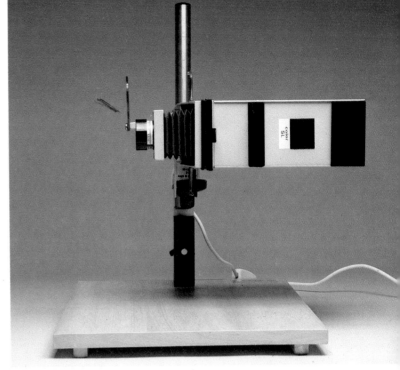

The column and chassis

The purpose of the column is to support the enlarger head above the baseboard. It should be constructed so that the head is completely free of vibration during exposure of the paper.

Most columns are vertical although some longer ones are inclined at an angle of about 30°. This allows very large images to fall clear of the base of the column.

The columns on the simplest enlargers are usually single tubes of plated steel. The height of the column varies considerably from model to model but is usually from 60 cm to one metre. The height of the column is important, because it dictates the maximum print size that can be made. If you intend to make a lot of large prints, buy an enlarger with a long column.

Other types of column include double tubes, which give a firmer support, and box columns, which are usually rectangular in cross section and give a very firm support. The flat front surface of a box column is often calibrated on more expensive models, and this enables various image sizes and exposure calculations to be made without direct measurement of the height of the enlarger head.

As the enlarger head is heavy and carried clear of the column, the bracket that supports it must be robust. This bracket normally incorporates a mechanism by which the head is positioned at the selected height. On most enlargers this is a friction brake. It is secured by either a locking screw or a spring loaded lever. More advanced models sometimes use a rack and pinion mechanism which raises the head up the column when a crank is turned. This method of head elevation is the most positive and secure, and allows the most accurate positioning of the head.

For occasional large prints, many enlargers allow the column to be swivelled to project onto the floor, and a few have an adjustable bracket that lets the head turn so that the image falls on the wall of the darkroom. Both these methods produce larger images, but are inconvenient if many giant prints are to be made.

The negative carrier

The negative to be printed should ideally be held perfectly flat, and parallel to the printing paper. This is usually achieved by placing the film between two plates of metal, hinged together at the back. This arrangement is called a *bookform carrier*, because inserting the negative into the carrier is rather like putting it between the pages of a book. The carrier slides into a slot in the enlarger head where a spring mechanism, or the weight of the head presses the film flat.

Rectangular holes are cut into the metal plates, and registration pins hold the negative in position so that the negative to be printed is visible through the holes. Some carriers have pieces of glass over the hole, which press the film flat. Others—*glassless carriers*—hold it flat without using glass. Glassless carriers have the advantage that they accumulate less dust, but they do not hold the negative quite as flat as those carriers which use double glass plates. A good compromise is the use of just a single glass plate. This holds the

Inside the head *Large glass lenses, called condensers, collect the light from the bulb, and channel it down to the negative, which is held in a carrier located directly below*

Turning the enlarger *The largest size of print that an enlarger can produce need not be limited by the height of the column—often the head turns to project the negative on to the wall*

Negative carrier *Some carriers can be used with several different film formats, and this one has four sliding masks which allow the printer to mask off those areas of the negative that are not going to appear in the print*

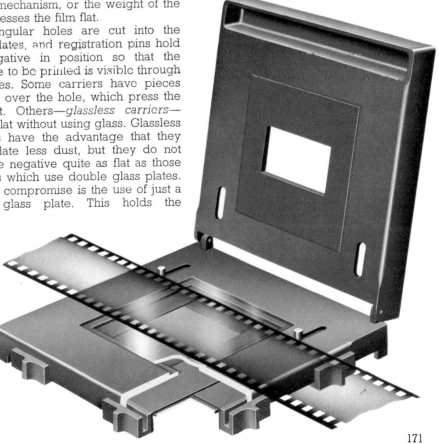

Filter drawer *You do not need a colour head to print colour pictures on your enlarger, because you can insert individual filters into the small drawer that is found on almost all enlargers, above the condensers*

negative flat but does not gather as much dust as two sheets of glass.

A further difficulty with glass carriers is that where the negative is pressed closely into contact with the glass, a pattern of concentric rings appears in the picture. These are called Newton's rings, after the scientist who first noticed them. They will show up on the print, and if they appear in the sky, or some other area of flat tone, they can be very unsightly. The glass plates of the carrier can be acid etched to prevent Newton's rings, and such glass is called *anti-Newton glass*. This is expensive, and many enlarger manufacturers opt for the cheaper alternative of glassless carriers.

Not all carriers are of the bookform type. A few enlargers use a simple plate upon which the film is placed and held flat with the weight of the lower condenser. This is not just a cheap alternative—some of the best enlargers ever made have used this system.

When buying an enlarger, it is a good idea to pay particular attention to the negative carrier. A good carrier is a pleasure to use, but some of the worst ones can make darkroom work a nightmare. A few carriers have useful features that will improve the quality of your prints. The most important of these is a system of sliding masks, which move across the frame just below the film. When printing a small section of a negative, the masks can be moved to block off those areas of the picture that are not going to appear in

the final print. The purpose of this is not to compose the picture—the masks are not usually quite in focus—but to block off scattered light that would otherwise be reflected back onto the print, thereby reducing contrast.

Things to avoid in negative carriers include fiddly methods of construction—some carriers consist of four plates of metal which have to be assembled in the correct order each time the carrier is removed from the enlarger. This can be very annoying. Another point to watch is the area of the aperture through which the film is visible. If the hole in a glassless carrier is too big, the film will not be held flat, and light will spill into the picture from the edges of the negative. If it is too small, not all of the negative will be visible, and you will not be able to print the whole frame. If the carrier is glassless, a few minutes work with a file will cure this, but if it is not, there is very little that can be done.

Lenses and mounts

Most enlarging lenses are attached into the head of the enlarger by a screw thread fitting. This is generally a standard size—39 mm—so most enlarging lenses are interchangeable.

The lens is threaded into a mounting plate. On a single format enlarger, for example, designed to be used with 35 mm film only, the plate is usually fixed permanently into the head. When the enlarger is made to print more than one size of negative the lens screws into a special plate which is then fixed to the enlarger, often with a quick release device. There is a simple reason for this—different lenses must be held different distances from the film, so that while the lens mount for a lens that covers the 120 roll film format will simply be a flat plate, the mount for 35 mm is recessed so that the lens sits closer to the negative.

If you print your own photographs, then the quality of the final picture will be limited by the weakest link in the image forming chain. If you buy a cheap enlarging lens, then however good the lens on your camera is, the print quality will never be first rate. The quality of lens on the enlarger is therefore of great importance.

Enlarging lenses are generally much cheaper than camera lenses because they are much simpler in construction both optically and mechanically. The diaphragm mechanism is simpler, and the job of focusing is done by the enlarger, not the lens. Enlarging lenses come in a variety of maximum apertures, just as camera lenses do, but in the darkroom maximum lens aperture is less crucial. The only virtue of a lens with a wide maximum aperture is that it makes focusing easier because the image is brighter. Unless you plan to make a lot of giant enlargements with images that are dim and hard to focus, the extra cost of a lens with a wide maximum aperture is not justified.

For a 35 mm negative, the normal

focal length of the enlarging lens around 50 mm. For roll film, it is 80 mm. Although these focal lengths are standard, it is possible to buy wide angle lenses for enlargers. These will produce a larger image on the baseboard than the standard enlarging lens when the head is a fixed height up the column, but are usually specially computed for big enlargements, and do not give their best performance on prints smaller than 25 to 30 cm wide. The apertures on enlarging lenses are marked by click stops. When a lens is used in a recessed mount, this might be the only way of determining which aperture is in use since the markings are frequently difficult to see. For this reason, it is essential that the click stops are firm and positive.

The quality of an enlarging lens is difficult to judge until it is actually used for making prints. The only real guide to quality without actually testing a lens is to buy a brand that is well known for producing top quality results. Schneider, Nikon, Soligor, Vivitar, and Minolta all make enlarging lenses that can be relied upon to produce good results.

ocusing methods

s the enlarger head is moved up and own the column to change the size of e picture, the lens must be moved oser to the film or further away from to bring the image into focus. The lens ount on many enlargers is fixed to the ead by a pair of rods. These are driven y a handle which racks the lens in and ut when turned to focus the image. A ellows or sliding tube arrangement revents stray light from spilling out f the enlarger. Alternatively, the lens ount is fixed into a helical screw echanism, and the lens is focused as is in a camera—by turning a focusing ng. Both these methods work equally ell, though helical focusing is the less ommon of the two methods.

A few enlargers have automatic ocusing. When this system is perfectly djusted it can save a lot of time, but e manufacturing tolerances involved n making such a system are small, and e enlarging lens has to be precisely atched to the enlarger. Consequently, ood autofocus enlargers tend to be ery expensive. The cheaper ones ould be avoided.

Man's best friend
Even a cheap enlarger will give good b & w prints. The quality of the enlarging lens, however, is the vital factor for print sharpness

Enlarger choice
All these three enlargers are basic b & w models. Any of them would be suitable for a beginner

Other features

If you plan to do any colour printing on your enlarger, make sure that it has a *filter drawer*. This is a small drawer located above the condensers, in which coloured filters can be placed to change the colour of the light from the enlarger. This is essential for colour printing, and is also useful for black and white, where filters can be used to change the contrast of certain types of paper.

Instead of a filter drawer, many enlargers are available with a *colour head* fitted. This is a light source with continuously variable filtration in yellow, cyan and magenta colours. Although not essential for colour printing, it does make life a lot easier.

If economy is a priority, but the idea of colour printing in the future sounds attractive, many enlargers have colour heads available as an optional accessory which can be purchased later.

Which model ?

The most suitable enlarger is the one that fits your needs and your wallet. There is nothing so frustrating as having an enlarger that limits your creativity in the darkroom, but on the other hand it is senseless to spend so much on an enlarger that there is no money left to buy photographic paper.

If you only expect to do a small amount of darkroom work of a fairly limited nature—no large prints, and no colour, for example—your choice of equipment will be very broad. The more specialized your need, the narrower will be the choice. Think carefully about the largest size of print that you expect to make frequently, and make sure the enlarger is able to print pictures this big. Check that the head will turn or the column swivel for the occasional giant blow up. Examine the negative carrier carefully, and make sure that it is easy to use. Be certain that if your photographic horizons are likely to expand, the

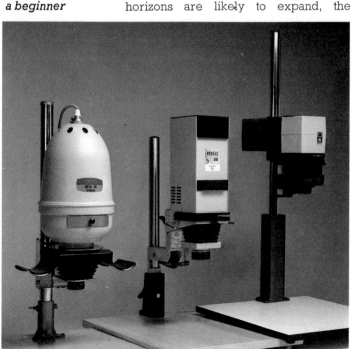

enlarger can expand with them. It is no use buying a roll film camera, and then finding that you cannot adapt your enlarger to take the film format.

If you have special needs, remember that all enlargers are made to suit the average user. Left handed photographers often have problems with controls designed for right handed people. Some makes of enlargers have head elevation and focus controls on both sides of the head, which gets around this problem. If you expect to store the enlarger in a cupboard, bear this in mind when buying, and check that the unit can be dismantled and reassembled easily.

Above all, make sure that the enlarger you buy is built to withstand the wear that it is likely to get. If more than one person is likely to use it, make sure that it is very well made, particularly for young or inexperienced photographers.

Enlarging accessories

Certain important accessories can be bought to make many aspects of darkroom work either easier or more straightforward. On the enlarging side, top of the list of desirable items is a timing device which is used to switch the enlarger on and off in place of a conventional switch. A timer leaves both hands free during exposure (which may be important if you have to dodge or burn-in a print), and is a far more satisfactory alternative to other methods of counting the seconds for the exposure. This accuracy enables meaningful test prints to be made—and is also particularly useful when a long run of prints of the same exposure has to be made and where consistent print exposure is required.

Various types of printing easel are available. This is one of the more basic accessories which you do need to obtain. In any form, a printing easel (also called an enlarging easel, or a masking frame) exists simply to hold paper flat during exposure. The conventional type employs sliding arms in conjunction with a border-masking frame arrangement which keeps the paper flat. The arms are, in fact, masks which can be adjusted to different print paper (or image) sizes. Another type uses magnetic corner pieces to hold the paper firmly in place but gives a borderless image. Other borderless easels use either a tacky surface coating or tape to keep the paper flat. At least one type of easel permits a variety of fixed print sizes to be printed on a single sheet of paper.

Often the negative image on the easel is dim, making it difficult and tiresome to focus. This can be made easier by using a simple device called a *reflex focus* aid. This has a mirror magnifier which enables you to see the grain structure of the enlarged image large and bright for easy focusing. You simply place the magnifier on the easel, inspect the image, and adjust the focus of the image until it becomes crisp—a simple but effective device.

DARKROOM TIMERS AND METERS

High quality darkroom work calls for a considerable degree of precision at every step. In particular, accurate exposure and close control of process times are essential, and for this kind of precision, proper darkroom meters and timers are invaluable.

A darkroom meter is a light meter that indicates the exposure needed for a particular negative. Darkroom timers are elaborate clocks that allow you to time exposures and processing accurately.

There is far greater margin for error with black-and-white processes than with colour and many experienced darkroom technicians will work quite happily without any form of timer or meter whatsoever for black-and-white processes. However, timers are all but essential for colour processes and, for the inexperienced, print exposure meters certainly save a great deal of wasted, expensive colour printing paper. And they help ensure consistent results with all processes.

Darkroom timers
Most darkroom timers are designed specifically either for processing or enlarging exposures but there are very basic timers that can be used for both enlarging and processing. These simple timers are resettable, and count both minutes and seconds. They may be either clockwork or electronic. The clockwork timers generally have a simple clock face with a minute hand and a second hand. They are controlled by two levers, one for stopping and starting the mechanism, and the other for resetting the hands to zero.

Basic universal timers are usually reliable, versatile and easy to operate but they cannot give the great precision of a special timer. It can also be awkward to switch on the enlarger and the timer at the same time—accurate dodging and burning-in are particularly difficult with this type of timer. For more complicated exposures, it is better to have a timer designed specifically for enlarging. And for the extra facilities offered and the greater accuracy, it may also be worth paying the extra for a special processing timer.

Processing timers
Timers especially designed for processing vary enormously in sophistication, but all have facilities for timing a series of processing steps of different lengths.

The simplest timers have a clockwork

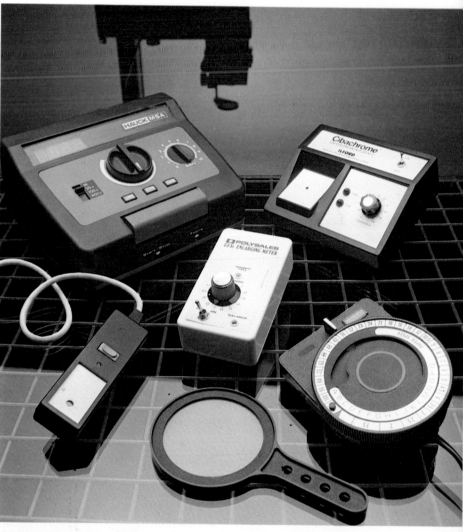

Darkroom meters *vary in complexity between the simple spot and integrating meters and the more sophisticated combined timer–meter*

mechanism, with a removable dial into which small index stops can be inserted. As each stop turns against a feeler on the dial a bell rings and the clock stops. On this type of timer you can see when the time is up for a processing step but you have to reset the timer for the next step. More expensive versions use electronic circuits to display a series of times, and are usually very accurate, though this facility may not be needed.

Enlarging timers
Timers designed especially for enlarging not only time the exposure, but also switch the enlarger on and off automatically. Unlike processing timers, they

usually only time intervals of up to one minute. A wide range is available, both clockwork and electronic, and all have luminous or dimly illuminated dials that can be set in the dark. The level of illumination is bright enough for you to see the dial setting, but not so strong as to affect light-sensitive materials.

Although electronic timers have become increasingly popular in recent years, they do not show how much exposure time is left. With dial-type faces, however, you can take in this information at a glance, and dodging or burning-in is much easier because you can gauge exactly when to stop masking the print.

Some enlarger timers have an added feature which makes print dodging easier. A foot switch leaves your hands free while switching the enlarger on or off. You can thus position your hands

over the easel before you start the exposure, and this makes complicated burning-in or dodging much easier.

Dual purpose timers

There are some timers available that can be used both for printing and for processing. These dual purpose timers may be either electronic or electromechanical, and their main distinguishing feature is a dial which counts both minutes and seconds. They also have switched outlets into which an enlarger or other device may be plugged.

Although these timers are the most versatile type available, many of the electromechanical types do not incorporate automatic resetting. This means that you must set the enlarging time every time you make an exposure. This can be especially inconvenient if you are making several prints from the same negative.

Another disadvantage of dual purpose timers is that they are considerably more expensive—a good dual purpose timer can cost as much as an enlarging timer and a processing timer put together.

One other type of timer deserves mention—the metronome. Metronome timers do not show how much time has elapsed—instead, they click at regular

Four programs *This timer can be programmed to indicate up to four different time settings. Foot switch operation leaves your hands free*

Clockwork timers *are accurate enough for most processing and enlarging work. The Durst is useful for timing the different stages of colour processes*

Bleep timer *This battery-powered metronome timer either bleeps or emits a flash from its red light emitting diode at one second intervals*

Digital timer *The Philips PDC 112 plugs directly into the enlarger and switches it off automatically when the programmed exposure time has elapsed*

The Jobo B-timer *is set by the two illuminated dials on the front. It is directly connected to the enlarger and has a time range of 0.5 to 99 seconds*

intervals, usually of one second. Print exposures are timed by counting the clicks. Some timers of this type give very faint flashes at one second intervals. These flashes are bright enough to see but not bright enough to affect paper or film. Metronome timers are not really suitable for timing processing, but they are cheap and simple, and if you only undertake a small amount of darkroom work, this kind might be a wise choice.

Enlarging meters

Experienced printers can often tell exactly how much exposure a negative needs for a given grade of paper simply by glancing at it. Few amateur photographers, however, are able to do this reliably and a test print is usually necessary. An exposure meter makes life considerably easier.

The cheapest enlarging exposure meters do in fact use a variation of the test strip principle. A sheet of plastic film bearing calibrated areas of different densities is laid on a piece of enlarging paper, and given a one minute exposure through the negative to be printed. The processed print shows a range of different exposures, usually with a corresponding exposure time printed by each strip. The time which gives the best

density is then set on the enlarger timer, and should yield a satisfactory print.

Even the more sophisticated versions work on a similar principle, but have a 'memory' which stores the degree of density you decide upon so that you can achieve consistent density in your prints.

To programme or *calibrate* the memory, a print with the desired density is made, and the exposure given to it is recorded. The meter can give a reading for the paper speed, and once this speed is set on the meter, it will give exposure readings to produce prints of the same density from a given batch of paper whatever the density of the negative used. The technique for calibrating

exposure meters for darkroom work is covered fully in a subsequent article.

Some meters have indicator lights which give a readout, others have a needle indicator that points directly to the correct exposure. The simplest meters have only one indicator lamp, which lights up when the correct exposure time is set on the meter scale. With some exposure meters, you work at a fixed time, and achieve correct exposure by adjusting the aperture.

Enlarging exposure meters are invariably electronic, but there are two different kinds available: integrating and spot meters. Integrating meters use a sheet of diffusing material held under the enlarging lens to completely diffuse the projected image before it reaches the light sensitive cell in the meter. Spot meters have a small light sensitive cell for reading just a small part of the image and give a spot reading.

Generally, the integrating type of meter is easier to use because it does not need to be calibrated quite as carefully but it may give less accurate results.

With a spot meter you can obtain a correctly exposed print from a 'difficult' negative, by positioning the meter cell on a part of the image which has the density you want to expose for. Spot meters can also be used to give accurate exposures for areas to be burned-in or held back.

In addition, you can use a spot meter to determine which is the correct grade of paper for your negative, by comparing the densities of negative shadows and highlights. In this way you can obtain prints of acceptable density and contrast from all but the worst negatives.

Because the light sensitive cell of a spot meter has to be smaller than that of an integrating meter, spot meters tend to be more expensive. The extra sensitivity of these meters is provided by a built-in amplifier.

Your needs will determine whether you choose the more versatile spot meter or the simpler, but less adaptable integrating type. You can, however, easily convert a spot meter into an integrating meter by holding a diffuser under the enlarger lens—a piece of draughtsman's frosted acetate is ideal.

Combined timer-meters

Some manufacturers produce meters which incorporate a built-in electronic enlarger timer. This works rather like automatic exposure in a camera, because setting the meter sets the timer ready for the enlarger exposure. Although these units are convenient, they can be expensive. Avoid the type which does not have provision for manual override because these limit the exposure range with a given negative.

Simple enlarging meters help you find exposure settings for prints of a given density quickly and simply. This one has LED indicators

Integrating meters The Paterson meter (below right) gives a spot reading, so for average exposures the diffuser must be used. The more sophisticated Hauck MSA 100 is a combined timer–meter. As a timer, it can store up to nine exposure times. As a meter, it is used to measure the density of a number of points of the image on the baseboard. Up to nine measurements can be made, and the values stored. It can then compute the average figure automatically.
Both the Hauck and the Paterson can also be used simply as spot meters

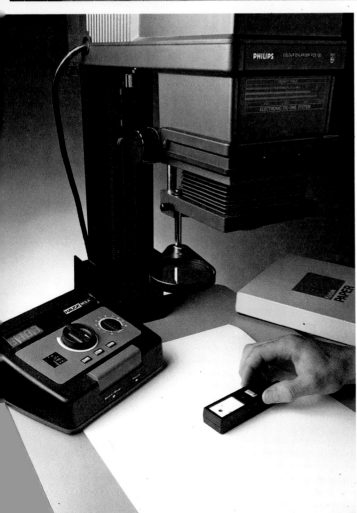

WASHERS AND DRYERS

Print washing and drying processes are among the dullest and most time consuming of darkroom chores. And yet these tasks, which simply involve either holding prints under a running tap or fanning them in the air, are of vital importance to the final quality of the images you produce. However, much of the tedium and the time spent can be considerably reduced if you buy washing and drying equipment to do these jobs for you.

The range of products available for washing and drying prints is extensive, and your choice of equipment will depend on how much printing you do, the facilities in your darkroom and the size of your budget. If you print only the odd frame or two at infrequent intervals, then even the smallest outlay might seem an unnecessary expense. But if you frequently print 20 or 36 frames at a time washing and drying equipment will soon pay for itself—but it must be chosen carefully if it is to be put to best use and be economical.

Few amateurs have a darkroom with running water, where a washer can be set up permanently. And unless you have a spacious bathroom or kitchen where you can do this, you will have to choose equipment that can be set up and dismantled easily and quickly. Space is less of a problem for print dryers. A corner in any room with a power point will suffice, but it should not be too far from the darkroom or you will probably end up spilling chemicals while moving between rooms. In any case, it is worth laying a trail of polythene sheeting.

One other factor that will affect your choice of equipment is the type of paper you usually use. Many photographic papers—both colour and black and white—are made with a resin-coated base, which is covered on both sides by a thin layer of polythene to prevent it absorbing water and chemicals. Resin-coated papers can, therefore, be processed, washed and dried much quicker than traditional papers in which the paper base soaks up the solutions. But it is not sufficient just to leave resin-coated papers immersed with a minimum of stirring: rapid water flow or stirring in chemical-free water is essential for rapid washing, whereas with traditional papers it is the length of time that the paper spends in the water that is more important for proper washing.

Overflow devices, *placed in the plug hole of a sink or bath, are the simplest and cheapest means of washing prints on any type of paper but it is important to ensure they don't become clogged*

Overflows and syphons

For fibre-based paper, which requires little stirring, the simplest and least expensive print washing device consists of an overflow tube placed in the water outlet or plug hole of a sink or bath so that it protrudes upwards. It maintains a constant head of water into which the prints to be washed are immersed while the tap flows.

Such a device has a flow rate limited by the size of the outlet. It is also possible for a print or small test strip to wrap itself round the outlet, covering the holes and risking an overflow.

One variation on the overflow principle consists of a tube within a tube, both being jointed at the lower ends. Water from the tap enters the inner tube and jets through holes at the base into the sink or bath. The jets of water cause turbulence, which stirs the water and washes the prints effectively.

High speed washers, *intended for resin-coated papers, provide a rapid flow of water over both surfaces of the prints, and are compact but they can only take a few prints at once*

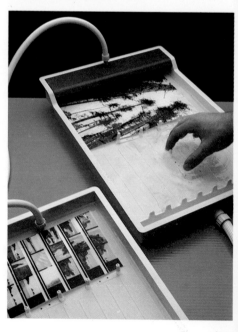

A constant water level can also be maintained with a simple syphon. This is a U-shaped tube that clips on to the side of a print dish or other container. The short curved end dips in the water and the straight end hangs outside and over the water outlet. Such a syphon is simple and inexpensive, but it has the disadvantage of changing the water in the sink or container at a slow rate.

A much more sophisticated device is the autosyphon. It costs about the same as a roll of Kodachrome and functions either as a simple overflow or as a syphon. Overflow action is achieved by removing the outer dome of the device, leaving an inner pipe which maintains a constant level. With the dome fitted, water rises to the height of the device and the syphon action drains the water to a lower level. The level rises again and the process is repeated. In this way the water is changed constantly.

Only a small number of prints can be washed conveniently in a sink without having them overlapping and adhering to each other. And the sink cannot be used for any other purpose while the prints are being washed. So although overflow devices are least expensive, they might not be suitable for amateurs working in small, improvised darkrooms or kitchens. Under such conditions, an automatic print washer could be better.

Auto washers

A basic auto print washer costs less than 200 sheets of black and white A4 paper. It has a large capacity yet can be placed on a draining board or in the sink itself with plenty of room to spare.

Essentially, the auto washer is a tank fitted with an inlet and an overflow. Each print is placed vertically in separate compartments of a cradle, which slots inside the tank. Automation is achieved by a thrust mechanism driven by the force of inflowing water. This rocks the cradle so that water flows freely over both surfaces of each print. The rocking action can be stopped to insert or remove prints, and the cradle can be

lifted clear of the water by a handle at each end.

The water flow is so efficient that the washer is suitable for resin-coated paper, although it is designed primarily for fibre-based paper. But its main advantage is that a standard model can hold 12 prints up to 24 × 30 cm or 24 prints measuring 13 × 18 cm or smaller. Larger models hold similar numbers of larger prints, and have a built-in syphon to empty the tank after use. Cheaper units are available which lack the rocking device, but which may take larger paper sizes.

The main differences between the various makes of similar washers are the volume of the tank, and the size and number of prints they can take. Near the top of the range, Kindermann make a couple of wash tanks that are suitable for the professional darkroom or the larger-budget amateur workshop. The smaller model measures 40 × 40 cm and costs about the same as a budget SLR. The larger model costs twice as much and measures 50 × 50 cm.

High speed washers

To utilize the rapid processing property of resin-coated paper, manufacturers have designed a range of high speed washers. In order to wash in a short time it is essential that chemical-free water flows rapidly over both surfaces of the prints. A typical high speed washer consists essentially of a tray with an inlet hose connected to the tap. The base of the tray is ridged so that water can flow over the under surface as well as the upper surface of the print and out through a drain hose at the other end of the tray. The prints are separated by pegs, which can be inserted into various holes in the base of the tray. These can be arranged for prints of two different sizes, or removed altogether to accommodate a single large print.

The capacity of the tray is four, two or one—depending on the size of print. This might seem small but, in fact, it is adequate for most amateurs when you

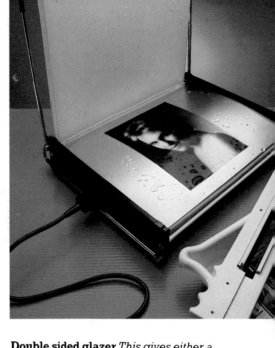

Double sided glazer *This gives either a glazed or a matt finish to prints on fibre-based paper, and ensures they dry without wrinkles or curled-up edges*

consider that the device washes resin-coated paper in just two to four minutes, compared with five minutes for the auto washer and 30 minutes for fibre-based paper in an ordinary washer.

Drying the prints

As with the washing process, the arrangement for drying prints can vary enormously. It is not unusual to remove excess water from prints and lay them flat in a dust-free atmosphere to dry. They dry even quicker if placed on blotting paper. Left like this, a print on resin-coated paper dries in about ten minutes, but fibre-based paper takes much longer—usually more than an hour. Many amateurs dry both types of paper even quicker by playing warm air from a hair dryer over the surfaces.

Besides its quick-drying property,

An auto washer *(left) has a rocking action, which causes water to pass rapidly over both surfaces of prints stacked vertically in a plastic cradle. Water flow causes the rocking*

Rotary glazer *This employs a rotary metal cylinder and a motorized canvas loop to give high throughput of prints on fibre-based paper up to about 50 cm wide*

Drying fibre-based paper

One of the major drawbacks with fibre based paper is that it must be kept fla during drying. The most common way to do this is to hold the print against a flat o slightly curved surface using an absorbent blanket: heat is applied through the metal surface.

The most elementary dryers for fibre based papers are of the flat-bed variety These have a double sided metal bec containing heating elements, over which

resin-coated paper has another important advantage—it dries without curling, unlike fibre-based paper. So prints can be placed vertically to aid drying. An ideal piece of equipment for such prints is a drying rack. One model has five compartments, with separators that have small pips to ensure minimum contact with the prints. The design is compact, requiring little room. And two or more racks can be combined to increase capacity. Costing about the same as three rolls of Kodachrome each, this type of purpose-built rack would be worthwhile if you print large numbers of frames at once.

A print *squeegee* is a useful aid for drying resin-coated paper naturally. This is a tweezer-like device with soft, rubber blades that squeezes excess water evenly from both sides of the print. The design ensures that you cannot damage the prints by applying too much force to the blades. Without the use of a squeegee, resin-coated paper would take much longer to dry.

The squeegee is incorporated in print drying machines that can produce completely dry prints in a matter of seconds. But instead of a pair of blades, these employ a pair of rollers. Usually, one roller is made of rubber, and the other is made of an absorbent material. A wet print straight from the wash tank can be fed between the rollers to be squeezed evenly before being dried.

Heat assisted dryers

Lower-priced dryers for resin-coated paper are operated manually by turning a handle, which deposits the damp print into the drying compartment. You can choose between a warm air or an infrared type of dryer. The range is extensive and the amount you pay depends on the facilities provided, as well as the size and speed of the dryers. Whatever the

system, excess water must be wiped from the print before being dried, but this operation may be done separately. A completely automatic system with motorized conveyer, thermostat and speed control, drip tray, print tray and heating element can cost more than a good SLR. But professional studio dryers can cost about as much as a typical top-range camera such as a Leica. The drying rate depends on the power rating of the heater element and motor speed.

Warm air dryers consist basically of an electrical heating element over which air is blown by an electric fan. The heat is controlled thermostatically, and the warm air is channelled over the surfaces of the prints in a drying compartment. Once in the compartment, a timer is set to stop the process after the drying time has elapsed. Some automatic machines have speed and temperature controls. The speed control varies the time taken for the prints to pass through the drying chamber. Using both controls, almost any type of material can be dried either in a few seconds or over any extended period. Infrared dryers are similarly arranged but they heat the prints directly by a radiating element.

All these dryers are designed for use with resin-coated papers. They will work with fibre-based paper, but the results are likely to be less satisfactory, producing prints with crinkled edges.

the absorbent blankets are stretched. The more expensive units have thermostats. Prints are dried in these units within 10 minutes particularly if they are squeegeed first.

It is important to place the print with its emulsion facing the blanket—otherwise it will probably stick to the hot metal. If the prints are to be glazed, however, they must be held with the emulsion towards a highly polished metal plate, which is an optional extra.

Most amateurs will be content with a flat-bed dryer, but they do have the disadvantage of a slow drying rate. You can only dry two A4 sheets per side on the smaller sizes, which means that you can dry 24 prints in an hour. If you produce large numbers of prints you may need to use a rotary glazer, which consists of a large glazed drum in contact with a continuous blanket loop. The drum rotates at a variable rate and is usually equipped with a thermostat. Throughput can be as high as several hundred prints per hour. Typically, a rotary glazer capable of drying 40 × 50 mm prints is large and weighs more than 40 kg.

All dryers for fibre-based papers have some disadvantages: both blanket and glazing sheets can become stained, and must be used with care; they are not suitable for drying resin-coated papers, unless the working temperature can be reduced to 90°C, or less.

PRINT MOUNTING AIDS

Prints can be mounted with little or no special apparatus, but with hot mounting equipment, it is easy to avoid the normal pitfalls of print mounting—air bubbles, lumps and creases—and achieve a good finish virtually every time. It can also be remarkably quick and clean and provides the scope to apply a variety of special finishes. Unfortunately the necessary equipment is very expensive—even the cheapest hot mounting press can cost more than a basic SLR.

The basic equipment for hot dry mounting is a flat heat source, and a tissue impregnated with shellac or a similar substance which is dry at ordinary room temperatures but melts when heated. The tissue is placed between the print and the mount and, when heated, the shellac melts and sticks the print firmly to the mount.

Although you can hot mount with an ordinary domestic iron, it is difficult to achieve good results. The temperature of an iron is rarely even over the whole surface and it may fluctuate from time to time because the thermostat is insufficiently sensitive. This means that it is impossible to perform many special hot

mounting techniques, such as adding surface texture to the mounted print, because this needs accurate temperature control. Nevertheless, if you cannot afford a special mounting press, it is certainly worth experimenting with an ordinary iron.

Similarly, you can use an ordinary domestic iron to tack the tissue to the print and mount to keep them in position while under the press. Proper tacking irons are much better, however. They give you greater control over heat output and are thus less likely to damage your prints.

Mounting presses

A purpose-built mounting press has a flat base on to which the mounting material, tissue and print are placed, and a heated platen which is either hinged or screwed down during mounting.

There are two types of mounting presses: *soft bed* and *hard bed*. The soft bed type has a compressible material, usually a kind of firm sponge, as the base of the press, and a flat, metal platen above. The hard bed type has a completely flat metal base. Either is equally

effective for hot dry mounting, although the hard bed type is suitable for 'cold' mounting as well—soft bed presses cannot usually provide sufficient pressure for cold mounting.

One of the first things to consider when choosing a press is its size. Presses vary in size between portable desk top types about 30 × 25 cm to large and expensive free standing ones up to 50 × 60 cm. Choose a press size to suit the size of prints that you want to mount. Although it is possible to mount a large print on a small press by feeding it through in sections, this is time consuming and can produce uneven and unsatisfactory results. A larger press does the job much better. If you can only afford a smaller press, look for one that is open on three sides, or which has space all around it to allow larger prints to be mounted in sections. A small 25 × 30 cm press which is open on three sides can be used for mounting prints up to 60 cm wide and of any length.

If you want to buy a large press, it is worth making sure that the power source in your darkroom is sufficient—the largest presses often have a heating

Mounting press *The most useful item of equipment for top quality print mounting is the mounting press (above left). Most models have thermostatic controls (above) which allow the temperature of the press to be altered for different types of paper. Another useful feature is a light which tells you when the press has reached the required temperature*

element of several thousand watts and may require a 30 amp power supply.

The heating control system is another important feature to consider when selecting a dry mounting press. The system should be capable of reaching and maintaining a temperature sufficient to melt the adhesive without damaging the print materials. This is normally around 80°C.

Some presses have a built-in thermometer or coloured lights which indicate when the press is warming up and when it has reached the correct temperature. Some have an adjustable thermostat as well—others have only an adjustable thermostat marked either with temperature settings or index marks. Index marks can be a nuisance because you have to make tests to find the best settings for different types of print material. Double weight fibre-based papers, for example, can normally be safely given a little extra heat to speed up the mounting process while resin coated papers must be treated more carefully—the polythene coating of the base tends to melt if too much heat is applied.

It is also worth considering how long the press takes to heat up. Small presses are usually quicker to warm up than larger ones and if you share the press with other people, this time saving may be important. Presses which take a long time to heat up also use more electricity and are consequently more expensive to run. When buying, make sure that any specifications given for warming up time refer to the time taken to heat the whole platen since the centre always tends to warm up more quickly than the edges.

If you want to mount your prints on a variety of materials of different thicknesses, you may need a press with a variable pressure facility. The pressure exerted by a mounting press is not to increase adhesion but to ensure that the mount and print are kept perfectly flat during the mounting process.

Tissues and tacking irons

Mounting tissues for hot mounting can be bought in sheet or in roll form. The sheets range in size from about 9 × 12 cm to about 60 × 75 cm. Rolls come in widths of between about 520 mm and 1 m and contain lengths of between 25 and 250 m of tissue. Since it is easier to cut tissue down to size rather than add pieces together, it is usually better to buy larger rolls or sheets—though the largest are very expensive. Nevertheless you can mount larger prints using several small sheets—although any overlapping of tissues may create unsightly bumps on the finished print.

Tacking irons are electrically heated devices rather like soldering irons. They are used to attach a small area of the centre of the tissue to the print and the corners of the tissue to the mount. This allows you to trim prints, tissues and mounts together and ensures that the print cannot move during mounting.

The cheapest tacking irons have a small head—around 1.5 cm square. Better results can be obtained using irons with a larger head and with a built-in thermostat that gives control over the temperature of the head—if the tacking head gets too hot it could damage the print, particularly with RC paper.

Rather more expensive are Teflon

The technique of dry mounting

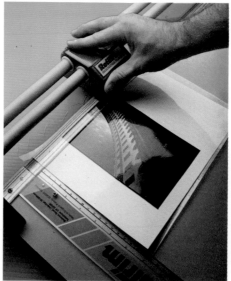

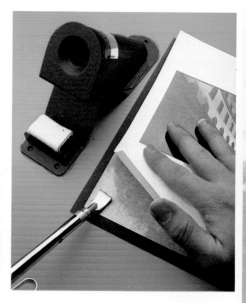

1 *Attach a piece of mounting tissue, the same size or slightly larger than the picture, to the back of the print by tacking it in the centre.*
2 *Next, trim the print to the required size so that the print and tissues are exactly the same size.*
3 *The print is attached to the mounting board by lifting the corners and tacking the tissues to the board. This prevents the print from moving when it is placed in the press. So if a prepared mount is used, it is vital that you place the print accurately.*
4 *Place the print in the press. It is a good idea to cover the print with a layer of paper, such as the paper which comes with the mounting tissue, to protect the surface from any dirt which may have got into the press.*
5 *The mounted print*

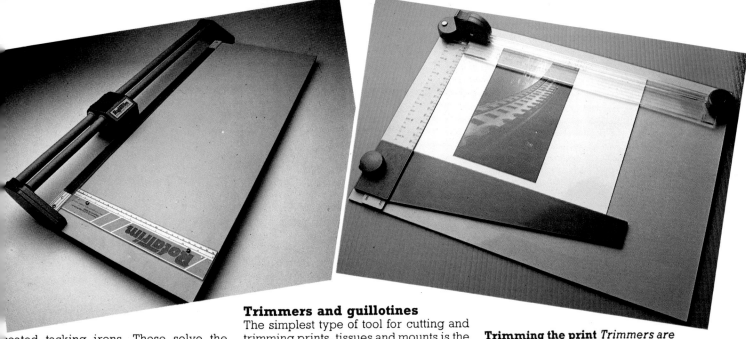

Trimmers and guillotines

The simplest type of tool for cutting and trimming prints, tissues and mounts is the guillotine. It is rather like an ordinary paper guillotine, consisting of a long blade, hinged at one end on to a board. If you want to mount your prints on to very thick card, you will almost certainly need the extra strength of a guillotine.

coated tacking irons. These solve the problem of hot shellac sticking to the iron head. But while this is useful the extra cost is rarely justified since the shellac which builds up on ordinary tacking irons can be removed simply by rubbing the head with sandpaper.

Trimming the print Trimmers are useful for both mounting and darkroom work. The rotary trimmer (left) is the best general purpose type, but for cutting prints only, chaaper models which use fixed blades (right) are perfectly adequate

Another type of cutter, usually called a *desk trimmer*, has two long blades that act in a sort of scissors motion. Desk trimmers are fine for cutting through prints, tissues and thin mounting card but they may be defeated by thicker types of board.

Although both guillotines and desk trimmers can be fitted with guards to prevent accidents, the safest type of cutters for operation in the darkroom are *rotary* trimmers. These have a circular blade that runs along a long straight blade to cut the print. Most rotary trimmers can cut material a little thicker than a postcard and so are perfect for prints and tissues, cutting cleanly and giving good, straight edges and corners. Blades on rotary trimmers range in size between 25 cm and 130 cm. For most amateurs, a 40 cm blade is quite sufficient since prints are rarely likely to be much bigger than this.

When choosing any type of guillotine or trimmer it is worth looking for one which actually grips the material being cut. It can be infuriating if mounting card or valuable prints slip and are slashed by the cutting blade.

Mounting materials

Prints can be mounted on card of any type, but it is better to use card at least 0.5 mm thick—very thin card or paper tends to buckle under the heat from the press and may become bent and dog-eared if handled excessively. If you can afford it, the most convenient card to use is special mounting board which can be bought in most art and craft shops and in good stationers. It comes in a wide variety of colours and thicknesses. But any good quality card will do.

Tissue types Mounting tissue can be bought in sheet and roll form and is available in a range of sizes

Chapter 10
COLOUR DARKROOM
COLOUR PROCESSING EQUIPMENT

Processing colour prints at home used to be considered too difficult for all but the most dedicated amateurs. Modern equipment, together with less temperamental chemical processes, has now made colour processing almost as easy as black and white. Indeed, in some respects, making colour prints can be even easier than black and white—provided you choose the most suitable equipment.

While black and white prints can be processed in simple open dishes, more elaborate equipment is generally required for colour printing for a number of reasons. First of all, because there is no good safelight for colour paper, processing has to be performed in almost complete darkness—moving a print from dish to dish would be awkward and messy. Second, colour printing needs a degree of precision in temper-

Roll your own
There are different sizes of drum. Some are revolved by turning a handle. Other, smaller drums, are rolled by hand

Loading the drum *Curve the print slightly and push it, emulsion inwards, into the drum. Print dividers allow you to load two prints. You must load the drum in total darkness*

ature control that would be difficult to achieve with open dishes. Third, colour print processing chemicals will oxidize rapidly in open dishes, releasing unpleasant fumes into the confined atmosphere of the darkroom and making it difficult to maintain the chemicals at the precise concentrations needed.

The simplest and most popular solution to these problems is to use a special print processing drum, though there are other more expensive and elaborate alternatives.

Processing drums

Like film developing tanks, colour print processing drums are light-tight cylinders, usually made from plastic, with a

Dismantled drum *It is important to be able to take a processing drum apart easily so it can be thoroughly cleaned and dried between sessions*

special opening at one end that allows chemicals to be poured in and out without light reaching the print. Once the print is rolled up and laid around the inside of the drum and the lid screwed on, the whole process can be performed in normal room lighting using just enough chemicals to cover the print. Until the moment the solutions are used, they can be kept covered in containers in a water bath, minimizing oxidation and making precise temperature control much easier.

There are two main types of drum available. One type is filled with chemicals while in a horizontal position. This type of drum usually rests on short legs while the chemicals are poured in. The print inside the drum is fitted around the inner wall in such a way that the chemicals form a small pool between the ends of the sheet of paper while the drum is resting on its legs. Processing begins when the drum is rolled across the workbench, allowing the chemicals to flow

over the surface of the print.

The second type is loaded vertically and has a cup under the lid of the drum that holds chemicals. When the drum is tipped into a horizontal position it allows the chemicals to flow out of the cup and over the print.

Both horizontally and vertically loaded drums use relatively small amounts of chemicals, which are thrown away after each print is processed. This ensures that the concentrations of the solutions are consistent. Prints are agitated and kept immersed in the processing solutions either by rolling the drum manually back and forth along the work bench, or by using a motorized drum roller. This constant agitation usually gives very even results.

Generally, however, the vertical drums are slightly easier to use because they can be filled with water for prewarming the drum. With horizontal drums, water may slop out of their narrow filling spouts as they are being filled.

Some drums have ribbed inner walls. This is an advantage because it prevents chemicals from being trapped behind the print, which may cause staining and contaminate subsequent solutions in smooth walled drums. The best drums are those which can be completely dismantled for cleaning after use.

Most drums can hold more than one print at a time, and have movable dividers that slot into the drum walls to prevent prints from sliding over each

other. This is a considerable advantage, since it means that two or more prints can be processed as quickly as one. It is usually best to buy as large a drum as you can afford, although it can be expensive to process only one print in a drum designed to take chemicals sufficient for four prints.

Extra equipment

Although processing drums are simple to use with little additional equipment, there are various accessories which can make print processing much easier, particularly when making large numbers of prints.

One of the most useful extras is a *motorized drum roller*. After the initial excitement of making your own colour prints has worn off, you may find that manually agitating a processing drum is extremely tedious—dull enough to pose a threat to the consistency of your processing. Motorized drum rollers remove this tedium.

They are available in several different types. The simplest is the plain roller base that spins the drum on its horizontal axis. Some of these turn the drum in only one direction; others have eccentric rollers that rock the drum slightly while it turns, giving better agitation. Perhaps the best are those that incorporate a reversing motor that automatically turns the drum first in one direction, then in the other.

To save warming the drum before

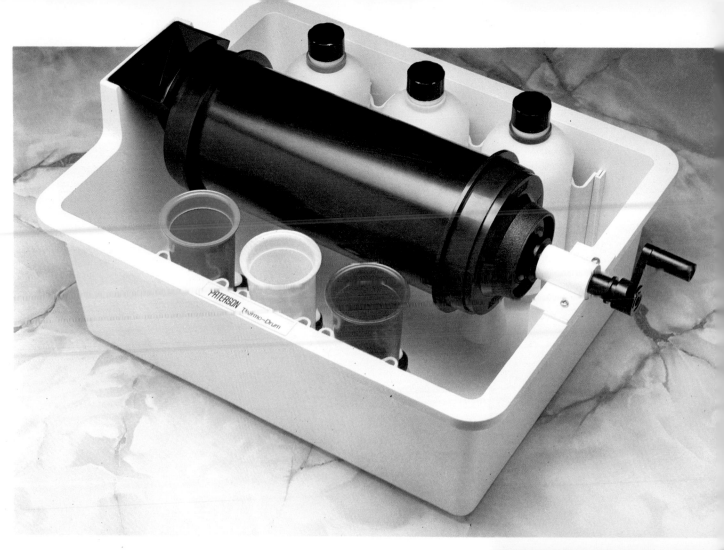

Colour processor *This has its own tempering bath which you fill with hot water to keep the solutions warm while turning the drum with a handle*

Motorized drum *This processor can also be fitted with a battery-powered motor which saves you the trouble of turning the drum manually*

each print is processed and to ensure accurate temperature control throughout the process, you can also use special drum rollers that incorporate a thermostatically controlled water bath. The drum is rotated in the machine while partially immersed in the water bath. There is usually a section of the bath into which chemical storage bottles can be placed to ensure that they too are at the correct processing temperature. These machines are expensive, but give excellent results. Separate temperature control units solely for chemicals are also available. These units are usually known as *tempering boxes*. Most use water baths, but one unit heats the chemicals with a hot air fan. Tempering boxes are not strictly necessary, but some printers find them very useful.

One device you can use to make colour processing much easier is a programmable timer. These are usually simple clockwork minute timers with dials into which small plastic markers can be slipped. As each marker reaches an index mark, a bell is rung reminding you to pour out one solution and move to the next processing step. More expensive electronic timers are also available, some of which can be connected to a drum roller so that processing is automatically halted at the correct time.

Other approaches

While drums are ideal for amateurs who work on a small scale, they have a number of drawbacks for processing large numbers of prints or single large prints. If you need to process a large number of prints quickly, for instance, it is a chore to have to clean and dry a drum thoroughly after each set of prints is processed. The dividers that hold prints apart in drums may also cause very slight unevenness in processing at the edges of prints, and this can only be trimmed off after the print has dried. Extracting wet prints from a drum at the end of the processing sequence can cause damage to the delicate wet print emulsion, particularly if you are in a great hurry.

One solution to the problem of limited drum size is simply to use a larger drum. Drums intended for the small scale user usually start at print sizes of 20 × 25 cm and go up to about 40 × 50 cm. Very large drums up to 60 × 80 cm are available, but these are moving away from the simple drum principle. They take a large number of smaller size prints, are mechanically driven, have thermostatic control of solutions, temperatures, and even include automatic chemical emptying.

For semi-professional printers, the

simplest alternative is a *deep tank* processor. In principle, these are very similar to dishes, but without some of the disadvantages. Deep tanks of solution are held at a constant temperature by a thermostatic heater. Exposed sheets of paper are loaded on to hangers and placed in the tanks. Oxidation is reduced by the small surface area of the chemicals exposed to air.

These units need to be used in total darkness, but since they are compact and easily manipulated, this is not too great a problem. They are particularly suitable for use with Cibachrome, since normal room lighting can be turned on halfway through the second processing step (the bleach) without noticeably affecting the results. Chemical concentrations are maintained by replenishment—adding a small quantity of fresh solution to each tank after each processing run. Floating tank lids prevent chemicals oxidizing when the unit is not in use.

Roller processors are a more sophisticated method of print processing usually only found in professional darkrooms, though there are a few small roller processors suitable for home use. They consist of a motorized unit incorporating temperature control and usually some means of automatic chemical replenishment that transports exposed printing paper through a series of rollers and into chemical baths. Exposed prints are simply fed into a slot at one end of the machine and removed fully processed from the other end a few minutes

Built-in motor *Some sophisticated processors have a built-in motor and thermostatically controlled water bath to keep the temperature steady*

later. A continuous stream of prints can be produced with little effort, once the machine has been set up. Their main disadvantage is their complexity and they have to be carefully taken apart and cleaned after each printing session. Roller processors that handle prints from negatives cannot usually be adapted to making prints from slides and vice versa. The main drawback for the amateur, however, is that even the smallest roller processor is very expensive.

Other approaches to colour print processing have been tried in the past, such as laminar flow processors, which run a thin film of processing solution over the surface of the print, and the 'Colour Canoe', which was an intermediate stage between dishes and drums.

Alternative methods that may one day rival the supremacy of the drum in the small darkroom are the special Agfachrome Speed and Kodak Ektaflex print making systems which use instant picture technology to make prints from slides or negatives with only one processing machine. However, at present, the Kodak system only works with Kodak products and is relatively expensive. For the present, the colour processing drum is still the simplest and most economical way of making prints from your colour slides and negatives.

ENLARGERS FOR COLOUR

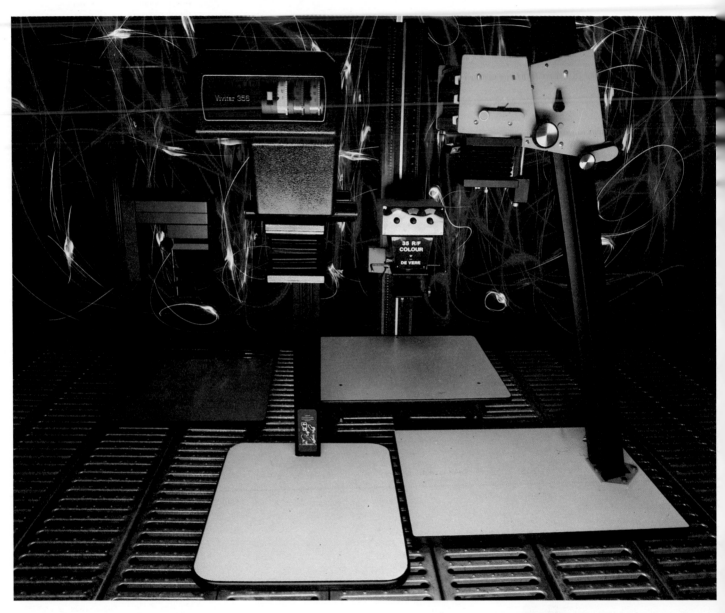

If you want to make colour prints regularly, you must have some means of controlling the colour of the light passing through the negative. This allows you to not only compensate for differences between types of film or paper, but also to adjust the colour balance of a print. You can either convert your black and white enlarger for this purpose, or you can buy a special colour enlarger.

All but the simplest or oldest black and white enlargers have a filter drawer, which can take different combinations of coloured filters. This is the simplest and cheapest way of controlling the colour of light. If the lamp house or *head* of the include filters of different strengths, and in printing a *filter pack* is made up to

enlarger is interchangeable, you can convert a black and white enlarger by fitting a *colour head*, which has a built in facility for colour filtration, Alternatively, you can buy a complete colour enlarger with a colour head already fitted.

Using filters

The filter drawers of black and white enlargers usually accept filters 75 mm or 100 mm square. These can be bought as coloured sheets in sets comprising the three subtractive primary colours— yellow, magenta and cyan. The sets produce a given colour correction. The disadvantage of this method is that you cannot have a continuous variation of strength. and are limited to the steps

Coloured light. *Some enlargers colour light additively; most work subtractively*

available from your set of filters.

On most enlargers, the filter drawer fits between the lamp house and the film carrier. Where the design of the enlarger does not permit this, you can still introduce filtration by fitting a filter holder below the enlarging lens. This is not the ideal situation, though, because filters in this position can affect the sharpness of the projected image. Another possibility is to put filters on top of the condenser lens—though this is only feasible if the lamp house is easily removable to allow filter changes.

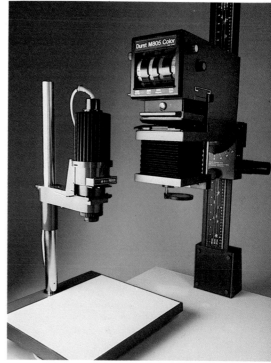

Filter details *Most colour heads use dials to control the amount of cyan, yellow and magenta light transmitted*

Head and drawer *The cheaper model on the left has a filter drawer, giving a simpler and more compact design*

The major advantages of this system are cheapness and simplicity—filters cost no more than a couple of rolls of film and you do not need to worry about converting the enlarger.

Colour heads

Some colour heads, known as filter bank heads, have a set of built in filters, mounted already to slide into position. Only magenta and yellow are incorporated usually, because they are used most frequently when printing negatives. On those occasions when a cyan filter is needed, it can be inserted in a separate filter drawer, as can extra filters needed for printing certain negative films. If you usually print only negatives, rather than transparencies, which require cyan filtration, this type of head may be adequate. The Paterson Color 35 enlarger has this type of head.

Another type, called variable filtration heads, do not use separate filter sheets, but have three very pure, deep coloured filters which are gradually introduced into the light path to change the intensity of a given colour. This is controlled by means of dials marked in units, one dial for each colour. A diffusing or mixing chamber incorporated in the head mixes the different colours of the light thoroughly and avoids patchy illumination.

Most heads of this type—also known as dial-in heads—use *dichroic* glass filters, which do not fade and give very pure colours. Some cheaper models use dyed glass or plastic—the Durst C35, for example, has only two plastic filters, yellow and magenta.

A third method of controlling the colour of light is to have three coloured light sources in the colour head—red, green and blue. These primaries give the required colour when mixed in the right proportions. This system is convenient because brightness is electronically controlled, and remains constant irrespective of the colours used in the combination. This means that you do not need to make any exposure compensations when using this system. The Philips Tri-One enlarger is an example of this type of head.

Most colour heads incorporate built in ultraviolet and heat resistant filters, but some of the cheaper ones do not. If they are not supplied with the enlarger, they can be bought separately and inserted in the filter drawer.

Converting for colour

If you already own a good quality black and white enlarger, you can convert it for colour use by exchanging the existing head for a colour one. A great choice is available, but which you buy depends to a great extent on which heads fit the black and white model you already own.

'Dedicated' colour heads or conversion kits usually fit only one model—the C35 conversion for the Durst B35 black and white enlarger, and the colour module for the Leitz Focomat V are examples. Multi-mode heads, on the other hand, usually fit the range of only one maker, but several models in that range. One of the Durst colour heads fits all the 6 × 6 cm models, another all the 6 × 9 cm ones, and a third all the 5 × 4 inch ones. Some types fit the whole range by a given make—the Meochrom head for the Czechoslovakian Meopta enlargers, for example.

There are also some independent colour heads available which fit a number of different makes. The best known of these is the German Wallner colour

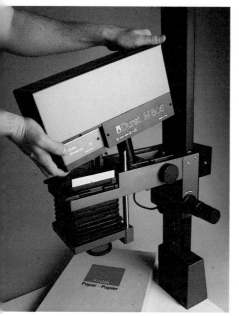

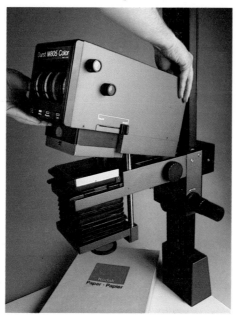

Changing heads *With many black and white enlargers it is possible to remove the lamp housing (far left) and replace it with a colour head. This contains both the lamp and the colour filter system*

head, which can be bought with adapters for Leitz, Dunco, IFF and a number of other makes, including some enlargers meant for black and white work only.

If you do not already own a black and white enlarger or only possess a cheap one which cannot be adapted for colour printing, you might want to buy a colour enlarger. These have built in colour heads—the cheaper ones usually have a fixed head, while some of the more expensive ones have interchangeable heads. Whether you buy an enlarger or a colour head, the same considerations apply with regard to light sources and colour controls.

Light sources

The type of lamp used in an enlarger or colour head determines the brightness of the projected image and the filtration required. Simple filter drawer enlargers may use ordinary mains voltage, 75 to 150 watt enlarger bulbs—the Durst C35, for example, uses a 75 watt bulb with a built in silvered reflector.

However, since small voltage fluctuations can affect the colour of the light from the bulb, this is not the ideal source for colour work. A better light source is a low voltage lamp running from a transformer which gives a stabilized output. Tungsten halogen lamps, which often have built in reflectors, have a high light output and run on low voltages, usually 12 or 24 volts, so they must be used with a transformer. Typical power outputs are 50, 75 or 100 watts. Bulb life is anything from 50 to several hundred hours, maybe longer if the lamp has a fan-cooled head.

Halogen lamps need more filtration than ordinary tungsten bulbs because the colour temperature is higher, but

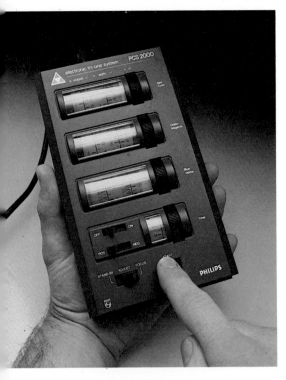

Remote control *Some enlargers feature separate control panels which are very convenient in operation*

Legible head *To avoid mistakes it is important that the scales on the filter dials are very easy to read*

they are much brighter. Maximum output is obtained if you overrun the lamp, but this reduces lamp life. Underrunning the lamp produces a warmer, dimmer light, and lengthens lamp life. Colour negatives can fade with repeated exposure to bright light, and underrunning reduces this, but unfortunately you can rarely tell whether a lamp will be overrun or underrun when choosing enlargers.

It is important that the lamp house of an enlarger or colour head should be properly cooled if you are to obtain the best service from your bulbs. Overheating shortens lamp life and changes colour temperature, so you may need to make adjustments when you change a bulb if your head is not cooled properly.

Diffused and direct light

The majority of enlargers and colour heads use a diffuser box to mix the coloured light. Diffuser boxes take various forms—they may be shaped chambers, frosted mirrors, or sheets of opal perspex. The more thoroughly the

light is mixed, the more light is lost—cheap models may give a slight colour shift from the centre of the edges, to avoid a dim image, while the more expensive models give the highest light output compatible with proper mixing.

Diffused light is the most common in colour printing, because it gives low contrast and does not emphasize grain and marks on the negative. However, some colour heads, such as the Philips Tri-One, use a condenser lens, which gives the direct light more often used in black and white work. Condensers mix the light just as well as diffusers, but are much brighter. The resulting prints have saturated colours and good contrast, but every blemish on the negative is shown up, so processing and negative storage must be perfect. Some enlargers have a diffuser plus optional condenser illumination—this makes them very suitable for both colour and monochrome.

Colour controls

Most enlargers and heads have three dials for controlling the colour settings, usually on the head itself. On a small enlarger, this can cause vibration if you adjust the controls just before making an exposure. Other models have the con-

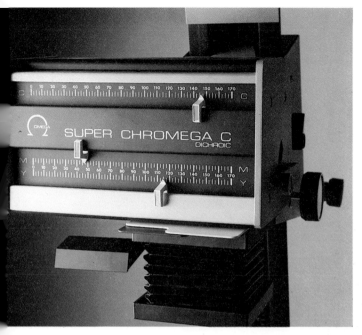

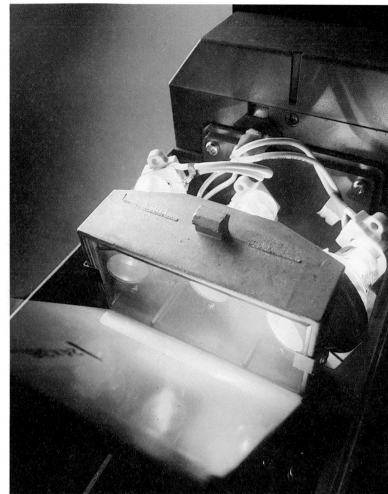

trols at bench height, while one, the Philips, has an electronic benchtop console. Both these arrangements avoid vibration of the enlarger head, and make it easier to use the controls when it is at maximum column height.

Cheap enlargers and heads may have non-linear filter scales, which means that the distance between 0 and 5 on the control may be the same as between 75 and 100. This makes accurate settings difficult at high filtration values. More sophisticated models have a linear scale, where the distance between all values is the same. These are accurate to within five units, some of them even to within one. For occasional negative printing, or working from transparencies, accuracy within five to 10 units is acceptable, but for fine control in negative printing you need to be accurate within one or two units.

Another useful feature in an enlarger or colour head is illuminated scales, with large clear markings which are easy to read in the dark. A white light control is also convenient—this removes all filtration instantly, allowing you to focus in bright light, and then replace the filtration at the preset values, ready for the exposure.

Many enlargers and heads have the controls combined with a timer—the Philips colour console is of this type. Though designs vary, they all work on the principle that having determined exposure and filtration, you set filtration and timing on the colour controls. The unit then gives consistent exposure times at the set filtration.

Some more sophisticated units also have built in colour analyzers, which determine the colour balance of a negative. From the data they provide, you can work out the correct filtration for a given negative. Some of these even have an electronic memory which stores filter and exposure data—the Vivitar Darkroom Computer is an example, intended for use with Vivitar colour enlargers. Although not part of the colour head,

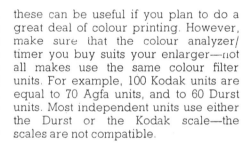

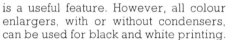

Colour control
A few enlargers feature sliding scales which are easy to check at a glance
Colour source
Some enlargers use three lamps rather than one lamp and three filters

these can be useful if you plan to do a great deal of colour printing. However, make sure that the colour analyzer/timer you buy suits your enlarger—not all makes use the same colour filter units. For example, 100 Kodak units are equal to 70 Agfa units, and to 60 Durst units. Most independent units use either the Durst or the Kodak scale—the scales are not compatible.

What to buy
What you buy depends on how much printing you want to do. If you want to make prints from transparencies, or only print from negatives occasionally, then it may not be worth your while buying a head or a complete enlarger. A set of filters that fit into your colour drawer should be sufficient for your purposes as reversal printing requires comparatively few filter changes.

If you want to do serious colour work, you should buy a good quality colour enlarger, or, if you already have a good convertible black and white enlarger, a compatible colour head. It does not make any difference whether you convert a black and white enlarger or use a colour one—print quality is equally good, provided you use dichroic filters. Make sure, too, that your enlarger or head has a diffuser as opposed to a condenser, unless you are prepared to work to the standards demanded by condenser illumination in colour printing. If you want to use your enlarger for black and white work, optional condenser illumination

is a useful feature. However, all colour enlargers, with or without condensers, can be used for black and white printing.

Many of the cheaper colour heads and enlargers have plastic housings—these tend to attract dust, however, and retain heat. Metal housings are preferable, and are less prone to static electricity than plastic ones.

Lighting, too, is an important consideration. Low voltage lighting run off a transformer is a very useful feature in colour work. If you buy an enlarger with this type of light source, one with a built in transformer saves space in the darkroom. Another useful feature on enlargers is a column marked in centimetres, or in magnification values for the lens in use—this allows easy calculations of any changes in exposure you may need to make when you adjust the degree of enlargement. If there are no markings on the column, details of the necessary exposure adjustments should be in the instruction book.

If you decide to buy an enlarger, a fast enlarging lens—say f/2.8—is an advantage, as exposures in colour work can be quite long. The lens should be fully colour corrected. Other useful points to look out for are a reversible column and a 90° head tilt, which allow you to project the image on the floor or wall for very big enlargements. When you buy your enlarger, remember that a model sold with all negative carriers and accessories complete may mean a considerable saving.

TECHNICAL GUIDE
INSIDE THE SLR

The most popular type of camera available for the enthusiast is undoubtedly the 35 mm *single lens reflex*. This rather long and complex name describes what is essentially a straightforward optical system which makes focusing and viewing simple. *reflex*, because the light from the lens bounces off a mirror before reaching the photographer's eye, and *single lens,* because there is only one lens which serves both for viewing and for taking the picture. (Some reflex cameras—twin lens reflexes, or TLRs—have two lenses, one for viewing and a separate one for taking the picture.)

The reflex system is simple and usually very reliable. It has three main elements: a hinged mirror, a matt focusing screen, and a five-sided glass prism called a *pentaprism*. The mirror normally rests at an angle of 45° below the focusing screen, behind the lens, and projects the image formed by the lens upwards onto the screen. The pentaprism reflects this

image so that it can be seen through the eyepiece—in effect, a simple magnifying glass—at the back of the camera, behind the prism.

The mirror and screen
The reflex mirror is a thin sheet of glass, coated on the front with aluminium—coating on the back would result in double images. It is hinged at the top. When the shutter release is pressed, it swings up out of the way, so that

Cycle race *SLRs are essential for accurate composition with long telephoto lenses*

light can reach the film. It also seals off the viewfinder so that light entering the eyepiece cannot reach the film. After the exposure, the mirror swings back down again, so that the image is once more visible in the viewfinder. For most exposures, the image vanishes for a very short period, less than

the blink of an eye.

The focusing screen is generally made of plastic (despite the fact that it is usually called 'matt glass', or 'ground glass') and the image formed on the lens, which is reflected by the mirror, is seen on this screen. Since the film and screen are the same distance from the lens, the image formed on each is the same. When one is in focus, the other one will also be sharp. Turning the lens barrel brings the image into focus, so the photographer can see the effect on the screen. This is probably the greatest advantage of the SLR: what you see on the screen is precisely what you get on the negative or slide.

The screen has a number of aids to focusing. These are called microprisms and split image rangefinders, and are described in detail in the box on page 209. They make it easier to see the exact point of sharp focus, though in normal light this should not be difficult.

If an ordinary matt screen were used, it would be bright in the centre, and dark at the corners. To avoid this, all SLRs have a type of lens below the screen to gather the light, making the image appear equally bright all over. This is a *fresnel lens*— it is thin and flat, and not convex like a normal lens.

The focusing screen in most cameras shows only a certain amount of the image— usually about 90 per cent. The cut off at the edges of the frame gives a small margin for error in the composition of the photograph.

The prism and eyepiece
The pentaprism reflects the image of the screen three times before it reaches the eyepiece. These reflections ensure that, when the photographer looks through the

Camera construction *Most 35 mm SLRs have the same general arrangement*

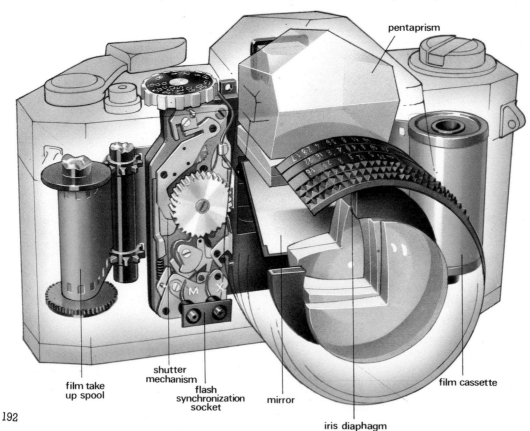

film take up spool

shutter mechanism

flash synchronization socket

mirror

iris diaphagm

film cassette

Elapsed time

ms

Viewing *Before the shutter is released the lens diaphragm is at full aperture to aid focusing*

Button pressed *The mirror rises and the diaphragm closes to working aperture within 6 milliseconds*

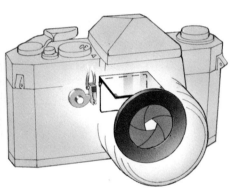

Shutter open *When the shutter is fully open, the flash contacts are closed to trigger the flash*

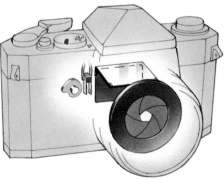

Shutter closes *As soon as the set time has elapsed, the shutter snaps shut, covering the film*

Mirror falls *Finally the mirror falls, and the aperture opens up again for viewing*

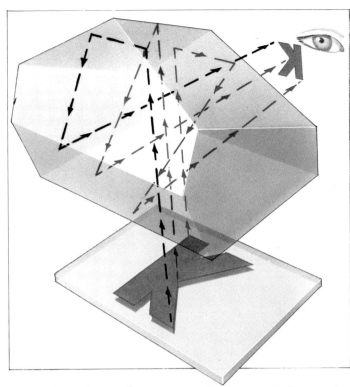

Pentaprism *Three reflections reverse the image on the focusing screen*

viewfinder, the image is seen the right way round, and not inverted. The image on the film is both inverted and reversed, which makes composition difficult. The correcting action of the prism remedies this.

The eyepiece of most SLRs is adjusted for people of normal eyesight. Short- and longsighted photographers need corrective eyepieces if they are to use the camera without their spectacles.

The lens

All 35 mm SLRs accept interchangeable lenses, which are usually fixed to the camera body by some kind of bayonet fitting. Focusing the lens is carried out by a screw thread whcih runs round the inside of the lens tube. This is called a *helicoid*. When the lens barrel is turned, the lens moves closer or further away from the film, and distant or nearby objects are thus made sharp.

All the lenses contain an *iris diaphragm*, which is described more fully on page 212. On most SLRs this is kept at full aperture for focusing and composing, and is stopped down at the moment of exposure to the working aperture, which is

SLR sequence *At 1/30 sec shutter speed, the sequence takes 3/4 sec to complete*

set by a control ring on the lens. This means that the image on the focusing screen is bright and easy to see through the viewfinder, but is the correct brightness when it reaches the film.

Exposure meter

Most SLRs have some sort of an exposure meter, which usually reads through the lens (often abbreviated to TTL). This measures the light falling on the focusing screen, and on an automatic camera adjusts the aperture or the shutter speed to give the correct exposure.

On manual models, the meter causes a display in the viewfinder to indicate correct exposure. The photographer then has to set the camera controls to give the right exposure.

Besides the exposure meter readout, which often takes the form of light emitting diodes—LEDs—or a meter needle, many cameras display either the shutter speed set, or the aperture in use, sometimes both.

The shutter

Virtually every 35 mm SLR has a *focal plane shutter* (see page 12). These simplify the construction of the camera, and make it easier to use interchangeable lenses. The shutter, the aperture and the mirror all work together in a precise sequence, repeated each time a picture is taken. This is controlled by gears and cams in the camera body.

THE CAMERA COMPUTER

In recent years, there has been an explosion in the application of computer and electronic technology to SLR camera operation. Indeed, in cameras such as the Minolta 7000 and the Canon T80, the majority of camera functions depend completely on programs preset in an electronic memory.

Electronic technology was first exploited to time the shutter and simplify and automate exposure control, and there are now very few SLRs which do not incorporate some electronic technology in these areas. Now, however, electronic technology is being exploited to automate focusing, provide viewfinder and other functions. And the sophistication of automatic exposure control has increased dramatically.

Shutter control

The most common use of electronics is in the timing of the camera shutter, with the actual movement of the shutter blinds or leaves remaining mechanically operated In electronic cameras, the mechanical timing has been replaced by a standard form of electronic timing circuit, consisting of a battery which charges a *capacitor*—a device for temporarily storing current—to a set level. When this level is achieved, a two-transistor electronic trigger actuates an electromagnet called a *solenoid*. When actuated, the solenoid closed the shutter.

The charging process is started the moment the shutter opens. This means that the time the capacitor takes to reach the correct charge level corresponds to the time the shutter is open—the shutter speed. The time it takes for the capacitor to charge up, and so the shutter speed, is altered by varying the resistance in the circuit. This system is accurate and usually-reliable.

Electronic cameras at first used a set of resistors of different values. In manual operation of the shutter speed, moving the dial still simply selects the appropriate resistor. But it was soon realized that the cameras already contained a variable resistor—the photocell.

Automatic exposure

The resistance of the *CdS* cells which many cameras use as light meters, varies according to the intensity of light falling on them. By using these cells in the control circuit, the shutter is automatically controlled by the

Aperture control *The curved electric contact registers the selected aperture*

The microcomputer *A large range of features is made possible by the small size of the electronic components*

metering system. In this way, the shutter speed varies with the light level, giving *aperture priority* automation (see pages: 6-9). Using the photocell has the further advantage of giving a continuous rather than stepped range of shutter speeds, since the resistance of the cell is continuously variable.

The necessary control circuit for this kind of operation is very simple. The principle requirement is a pair of *potentiometers* which are devices for varying voltage. One represents film speed, and the other represents the chosen aperture.

This basic circuit has been added to considerably as cameras have become more sophisticated. A rearrangement of circuit elements allows shutter priority operation by precise control of the iris (using a solenoid). The CdS cell has, in many cases, been replaced by the *silicon photodiode* (SPD) which needs an additional amplifier to boost its weak signals to useful levels but works much more quickly. The fast acting SPD allows off-the-film metering for both ordinary and flash operations —which need extra circuits.

More electronics
There are many other features for which electronic control circuits are used. The battery power may need a voltage control, for instance, and, as with many of the circuits, this usually includes a microchip. Accurate timing for time exposures is often achieved by counting the pulses of a quartz crystal oscillator, but this calls for extra control and counting circuits. Programmed exposure (see page 9-10) is also electronically controlled. So is the operation of many motor drives, which must synchronize with the given shutter speed.

The traditional viewfinder display of needle and pointer has largely been replaced by Light Emitting Diodes (LEDs) and Liquid Crystal Displays (LCDs), or illuminated letters and numbers. All this needs additional control circuitry.

All this information would be useless if it was represented as levels of electrical resistance or voltage — *analogue data*—and must be translated to a more understandable form. In sophisticated cameras this is converted, by microchips, to *digital* data. Digital processing, which uses a microcomputer, employs a special coding method, and can cope with vast amounts of information. It requires a special preset *program*—a basic set of instructions—to work through, and a timing circuit to control the place of each step in the overall sequence.

If a large number of circuits is used in a camera, an extra control is needed to keep order. This task is carried out by a *Central Processing Unit* (CPU). This receives input information in digital form about the shutter speed, film speed, aperture settings and meter reading. Use of the motor drive, dedicated flash, self timer and stop down control all register directly with the CPU. After calculations, the output is converted from digital form into a form suitable for control of the shutter and iris. The information in the viewfinder is also supplied by the CPU. The full sequence, involving several hundred calculations needed to synchronize all operations, takes only a fraction of a second.

Silicon chips *The top shot shows microprocessor memory systems using silicon chips. The leader line (lower) points to part of a chip the thickness of a human hair*

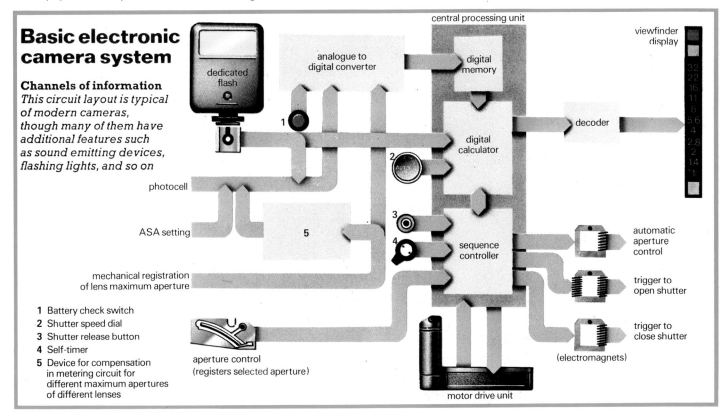

Basic electronic camera system

Channels of information
This circuit layout is typical of modern cameras, though many of them have additional features such as sound emitting devices, flashing lights, and so on

central processing unit

dedicated flash

analogue to digital converter

digital memory

digital calculator

decoder

viewfinder display

32 22 16 11 8 5.6 4 2.8 2 1.4 1

photocell

ASA setting

5

AUTO

sequence controller

automatic aperture control

trigger to open shutter

trigger to close shutter

(electromagnets)

mechanical registration of lens maximum aperture

1 Battery check switch
2 Shutter speed dial
3 Shutter release button
4 Self-timer
5 Device for compensation in metering circuit for different maximum apertures of different lenses

aperture control (registers selected aperture)

motor drive unit

HOW LIGHT METERS WORK

For good results, accurate exposure is essential; both aperture and shutter speed must be set precisely according to the amount of light available. Yet how do you know how much light there is in order to set the exposure correctly?

In the early days of photography, there was no means of measuring light and photographers had to guess on the basis of experience. This worked reasonably well for the simple, outdoor shots common at the time, and many experienced photographers still rely on their own judgement when using black and white film because black and white gives enough exposure latitude to allow small errors. But, in unfamilar situations or when using colour film, most photographers need an exposure meter to measure the light accurately.

All exposure meters, whether they are separate hand-held meters or built into the camera body, rely on the fact that the properties of certain substances including compounds of gallium, selenium, cadmium and silicon are altered by exposure to light.

When light falls on selenium, for instance, a weak electrical current is generated and the current is proportional to the intensity of the light—the more light that falls on the selenium compound, the more current is generated. By measuring the electricity generated, it is possible to estimate the intensity of light.

With other compounds, light changes electrical resistance. By passing a current through cells made from these compounds the amount of light can be measured simply by metering the change in resistance.

Even though they need no battery to power them, selenium cells are used less than other types because they need to have a large surface area, and are relatively insensitive to low light levels.

Spotlit gymnast *Spotmeters measure the light reflected from a small part of the scene—ideal for spotlit subjects*

Many hand-held meters do still have selenium cells because a large surface area is not such a disadvantage, but, for built-in meters, they are generally only used on cheap snapshot cameras.

The other types of cell are more useful to designers of more sophisticated cameras. They are sensitive to very low light levels and can be made very small in size, so that they are easily incorporated into the body of a single lens reflex camera.

Modern meter *The most sophisticated meters now contain microcomputers that indicate the exposure on a digital display*

Built-in meters

With early built-in units, the meter recorded the light coming through an aperture on the front of the camera. The photographer read off from the meter and adjusted the camera controls to suit the lighting conditions.

All modern built-in meters are linked directly to the aperture and shutter controls, and read light levels not from the subject itself but from the image of the subject formed on the film, or the focusing screen. This method has the advantage of measuring the light through the camera lens, and so if the angle of view of the lens is narrow, so too is the angle of view of the meter.

The very first through-the-lens (TTL) meters took an average reading for brightness over the whole focusing screen. But the more sophisticated cameras that are now on sale use an increasing variety of clever metering patterns designed to increase the reliability of exposure metering, including: measuring small areas of the frame only (*spot metering*); giving emphasis to the centre (*centre-weighted*); averaging a selection of points across the frame (*multi-pattern*) and many more. Some cameras now even offer the photographer a choice of metering pattern. The Olympus OM3 and OM4's highly sophisticated computer-based metering system, for instance, allows the photographer to select particular points in the picture to provide the basis for the exposure or, alternatively, analyzes the entire picture and sets the correct exposure entirely automatically. Indeed, built-in exposure metering has progressed so far that a photographer who trusts the programmed exposure (see page 9-10) completely will get accurate exposures nearly all the time.

Built-in meters used to be fooled by a wide variety of 'unusual' subjects, such as backlit subjects, or

xceptionally dark or light oloured subjects. With the nore sophisticated cameras, nis is now rarely true. Jevertheless, many photo-raphers still prefer the xtra control possible with and-held meters, which nake it much easier to take eadings close to the subject nd open the way to *incident ight* readings.

pot meters

3y using a small light-sensi-ive cell, and an arrangement of lenses, it is possible to :onstruct a light meter that neasures the brightness of only a small part of the sub-ect. Such meters are called *pot meters,* and have a neasuring angle of only one or two degrees. The photo-grapher lines up the meter on he subject through a view-inder that usually shows the neasured area as a small :ircle within a larger frame.

Since these meters read he light reflected from a small area, they are ideal for circumstances where the im-portant part of the subject is very brightly lit, or very distant. For example, the correct exposure for a figure standing on a stage under a bright spotlight could be measured with a spot meter from the stalls of a theatre.

Incident light meters

Built-in meters can often give incorrect exposure because they are only capable of mea-

White wall *A reflected light meter would wrongly compensate for light subjects like this and give less exposure than necessary*

suring light reflected from the subject. They can be fooled, therefore, by different toned subjects. A TTL meter works well when the subject is grey, for example, but if it is black, the meter will give extra ex-posure so that the black sub-ject appears grey in the final photograph. Conversely, a

white subject will be under-exposed because the meter again assumes that it is being pointed at something grey in colour and compensates ac-cordingly. Under many cir-cumstances, most particularly where colour transparency film is being used, a more accurate exposure reading is obtained by measuring the light that falls on the subject, not the light that is reflected back from it.

This is the principle that is used in incident light meters.

These have a white plastic dome covering the light sen-sitive cell, and, instead of holding the meter next to the camera and pointing it at the subject, you stand near the subject and point it at the camera. Incident light meters therefore give the same re-sults whatever the tone of the subject. Though most useful when colour slide film is in the camera, incident light meters are also invaluable when measuring light for copying.

Reflected and incident light meters

Reflected light *Built-in meters, and many hand-held ones, measure the light reflected from the subject. This method works well with the average subject but is less successful when there are many dark or light tones in the picture*

Incident light *Fitting a white plastic panel to the meter converts it so that it measures the light actually falling on the subject. This technique gives good results particularly when using colour transparency film*

AUTO-EXPOSURE

Advances in basic camera technology over the years have meant that, nowadays, nearly every 'snapshot' camera is automatic. The photographer no longer has to estimate the light and make a complex series of adjustments to the camera controls. or be content with shooting in a very limited range of situations. He simply points the camera and shoots, and the camera mechanism adjusts the shutter speed or aperture, or both, to give the correct exposure.

Exposure automation

The best way to understand how exposure automation works is to look at a simple practical example. Many 35 mm compact cameras use a system known as *trapped needle*, and the following example is based on the system used in the Olympus Trip camera. The explanation has been slightly simplified for the sake of clarity.

The first stage in setting the exposure is performed by a selenium photocell which produces a current when light falls on it. As the cell must be fairly large (see page 196), it is usually in the form of a ring surrounding the camera lens.

To keep the angle of 'view' or acceptance of the photocell to roughly the same as the angle of view of the lens, the cell is covered with a clear plastic panel, moulded with a series of crude lenses. Light falling on the camera from outside the angle of view is refracted out again, and never reaches the light sensitive cell. The transparent panel also serves to protect the cell.

The current generated in the photocell by the light falling on it is measured by a sensitive galvanometer. The needle of this meter is visible in the viewfinder on some models, where it moves

Snapshooter *Auto-exposure cameras, such as the Olympus Trip, use the pressure on the shutter release to set the aperture*

Exposure mechanism *The ti. stepped bar on the lower right engages with the meter needle to set the aperture*

across a scale of aperture values to indicate the exposure being given to the film. The more light that falls on the photocell, the more current flows, and the further the needle is deflected.

Gentle pressure on the shutter release causes a metal plate to move upwards until it engages on the galvanometer needle.

This metal plate controls the lens aperture—the further up the plate moves, the wider the lens aperture becomes. How far the metal plate moves before trapping the meter needle and coming to rest, is dictated by the position of the needle itself. The top of the plate is shaped like the teeth of a saw, and when the needle on the meter has moved a long way to the left, the metal plate moves up only a short distance and a small aperture is set. This happens in bright light. In dim light, the needle is deflected only a little, the plate moves a long way before trapping it, and a wide aperture is set.

If there is insufficient light to take a picture, the needle hardly moves at all, and a shutter lock is engaged which prevents a picture from being

taken. A red flag is simultaneously raised in the viewfinder to indicate that flash should be used.

If there is sufficient light, full pressure on the shutter

release button opens the shutter for a fixed time. The type usually used is a leaf shutter (see page 36) which means that the whole of the exposure setting mechanism

Trapped needle cameras

Simple auto-exposure cameras use a system called trapped needle to set the correct exposure. This schematic diagram shows the method of operation of a typical compact camera

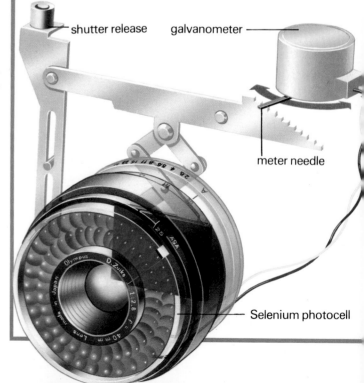

shutter release   galvanometer

meter needle

Selenium photocell

an be incorporated in a ~~hood~~ od around the lens, and the ~~body~~ ody of the camera is just a ~~shell~~ hell that houses the film.

This description is very ~~general~~ general, and a lot of trapped ~~needle~~ needle cameras, including ~~the~~ he Olympus Trip, have an ~~auxiliary~~ uxiliary trapped needle ~~device~~ device which sets the shutter ~~speed~~ peed in the same way as ~~the~~ he aperture. This results in ~~an~~ n exposure program which ~~starts~~ tarts in very dim light with ~~an~~ n aperture of $f/2.8$ and a ~~shutter~~ hutter speed of 1/40 sec, ~~and~~ nd gradually closes the lens ~~aperture~~ perture to $f/11$ as the light ~~gets~~ ets brighter. At this point, ~~a~~ change-over takes place ~~and~~ nd the camera opens the ~~lens~~ ens aperture again to $f/5.6$. ~~Simultaneously~~ imultaneously the shutter ~~speed~~ peed changes to 1/200 sec. ~~As~~ As the light gets brighter ~~still~~ till, the aperture is then ~~gradually~~ gradually closed to $f/22$.

These cameras can be ~~used~~ used with film that ranges ~~from~~ rom 25 to 400 (ISO) ASA, ~~allowing~~ allowing you to work with ~~slow~~ low colour slide film on the ~~one~~ one hand, and the fastest ~~black~~ black and white and colour ~~films~~ films on the other. Setting ~~the~~ the speed of your chosen ~~film~~ film usually involves turning ~~a~~ ring that controls a mask ~~operating~~ operating in front of the ~~photocell~~ photocell. For fast film, the ~~whole~~ whole of the cell area is ~~exposed~~ exposed to the light and ~~needle~~ needle deflection is great.

For slow films much of it is covered, so the needle moves less far across the scale.

Perfect exposure?
Quite apart from convenience, there are obvious advantages in having an automatic exposure system. For example, not having to transfer any meter readings to camera settings means that errors are reduced. Small format films such as 35 mm demand precision in this respect if the sharpness and grain characteristics of a film are to be used properly. Even so, automatics are not perfect.

The simple automatic compact camera with a selenium cell encircling the lens tends to be influenced by bright areas outside the field of view of the lens, unlike through-the-lens metering systems. In particular, a large expanse of very light sky can so affect the meter that underexposure results.

Developments
The mechanical control of shutter speeds is gradually being superseded by electronic shutter systems, and although many snapshot cameras are still mechanically operated, it seems likely that electronic automatic cameras will become the rule rather than the exception in the next few years.

Tree view *Simple automatic cameras give poor results when a dark or light tone dominates the whole picture*

In bright light, the galvanometer needle swings a long way across, and pressure on the shutter release quickly traps the needle against a stepped metal bar. This is linked to a simple twin blade iris diaphragm, which opens only a little way

When the light level is low, the meter needle moves less far, and the stepped bar can move a long way before trapping it. The increased travel of the bar allows the iris diaphragm to move farther, and so a wider aperture is set

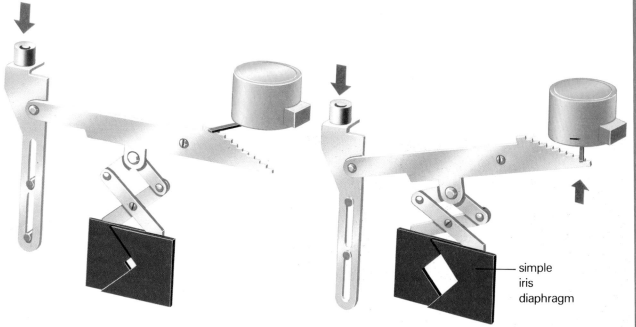

simple iris diaphragm

AUTOFOCUS

Only a few years ago, many photographs taken with simple cameras displayed two common faults—poor focus and incorrect exposure. But while exposure problems have largely been overcome, even on cheaper cameras, by way of automatic exposure control, problems arising from incorrect focusing have remained until the advent of automatic focusing.

Automatic focusing on cameras is achieved in a variety of ways depending on the system used to measure the camera-to-subject distance. Such systems are described as *active* or *passive*.

Active systems

Active systems work by sending out a pulse of sound or light—this distinguishes them from passive systems, which emit no such signal.

The simplest of the active autofocus systems is that used by Polaroid on their Sonar cameras. These have a small module above the lens which contains, among other things, a gold-plated disc mounted behind a perforated plate. This disc is actually an *ultrasonic transducer*. To activate the automatic focusing system, the shutter release is partially depressed causing the transducer to emit a 'chirp' of ultrasound. This is a very high pitched squeak, too high to be heard by the human ear and is much like the sound 'radar' that bats use to detect objects in their flightpath. At the same mo-

ment, a quartz clock is started and the camera begins to measure how long the echo of its ultrasonic chirp takes to return from the subject.

If the subject of the picture is a long distance from the camera, like a landscape for example, the echo will take a long time to return or else there will be no echo at all. In such cases, the lens of the camera remains at rest, focused on infinity.

If the echo returns quickly, though, the timing circuit in the camera measures the delay and, from the reference point of the speed of sound, calculates the distance of the subject. A tiny electric motor then winds the lens out, away from the film. Once the lens has been wound out far enough to focus the image, the camera's computer 'brain' stops the motor, and the camera is ready to take a picture. Further pressure on the shutter release opens the shutter, and makes the exposure.

This system has the advantage that it can be used in total darkness, and the lens can be focused and refocused as many times as necessary before the photographer takes the picture, in much the same way as an ordinary camera. On the other hand, the system is not foolproof.

Centre the subject *A few autofocus cameras demand a central subject. They would be 'fooled' by this scene*

Automatic focus *Cameras use different systems to focus the picture—ultrasound, infrared and subject contrast*

A subject on the far side of a window, for example, will cause problems for the camera. The sound echo will bounce back from the glass rather than from the subject behind it and, therefore, focus will be incorrect.

Another active system, which is used on Canon cameras, uses a beam of infrared light to measure the distance to the subject. Similar to an ordinary optical rangefinder (see page 202), this system has two small windows which scan the subject. Behind one window is an infrared light source, and behind the other, a photocell which responds only to infrared light.

The infrared light source is pivoted and mechanically linked to the lens. The system is set up ready for operation by first winding on the film. As this is done, the lens is racked out from the camera, so that it is focused on very close objects. The infrared lamp initially points inwards. Then the

camera is aimed and the shutter release pressed, but the exposure is not made instantaneously. Instead, the lens begins to move in towards the camera under spring pressure. Because it is linked to the lens, the pivoting infrared source also moves, emitting light in the process as it begins to swing out to scan the subject.

At some point in the arc through which the light source swings, the beam of infrared light hits the subject. The photocell detects the reflected light, causing the electrical current flowing from it to reach a peak. The 'pulse' of electricity stops the movement of the lens and releases the shutter.

If the subject is close to the camera, the infrared beam will not have to swing very far before coming to rest, but if the subject is at infinity, the beam will swing right out before the exposure is made. At this point, the lens will have moved a long way back towards the film before stopping and so the camera is focused on infinity.

Because it is an active system, the infrared focusing method shares some of the

advantages of the Sonar method. It can be used in total darkness, and is not confused by low contrast or plain subjects. It does have problems with sources of infrared light, though, and if the sun is just behind the subject of the picture, incorrect focusing may result.

This system can also be fooled by highly reflective surfaces. For example, an infrared light beam will bounce off a wet car bonnet at an angle instead of reflecting directly back to the camera.

Since this system employs a spring to move the lens and the spring is set by winding on the film, there is only one opportunity for focusing. If you get it wrong, there is no second chance, and the shutter is released anyway.

Passive systems

Passive focusing systems do not work on the principle of sound or light emission, instead they scan the subject optically. The basis of passive systems is the Honeywell Visatronic system, and this is used by a number of different camera manufacturers.

The system uses two rangefinder windows, just like a conventional rangefinder camera. A single swinging mirror scans across the subject, and throws an image into one of the rangefinder windows. The other window 'sees' a fixed image of the subject. The two image reflections are projected on to light sensitive cells within the rangefinder module, and this tries to match them up. When the image from each window is identical, the system registers a peak in electrical current—the outputs from the two light sensitive cells reinforce each other.

A circuit in the camera detects this peak, and moves the lens to a point that results in the sharpest focus.

The electronic circuitry recognizes when the images are perfectly superimposed by recognizing the increase in contrast and this sytem of automatic focusing is called *contrast recognition*. This works because when the two images are slightly apart, contrast is low since shadows and highlights overlap, reducing their intensity. They only acheive their full value when they coincide.

Like other systems, contrast recognition has its limitations. It will not work in low light conditions, and can easily be misled by high contrast objects in front of the subject. For example, an animal in a cage might be incorrectly focused if the bars of the cage are quite close together. The animal presents the camera with a low contrast target, whereas the cage bars are quite high in contrast, so the camera focuses on the bars rather than the animal. This system will, however, focus through a window.

Other systems

At present there is no commercially available system for automatic through the lens focusing, though there is at least one prototype.

This is operated by using two photoelectric cells, one fitted slightly below the focusing screen, and one above it. These measure the light intensity of the image coming through the lens. When the image is in focus, the light falling on each of the cells is equal, but when the image is out of focus, one photocell is more brightly illuminated than the other. By comparing the current from each photocell, the point of sharp focus can be recognised. This is actually a variation of the contrast recognition system.

How autofocus works

Infrared focusing *Canon's system (right) uses a beam of infrared light which scans as the lens moves. When it strikes the subject, a signal returns to the IR detector and the lens is focused by triangulation*

Ultrasound *By measuring the time lag between the emission of an ultrasonic chirp and its echo returning, Polaroid's Sonar camera calculates subject distance and sets the*

lens accordingly (centre)
Image matching *When a lens-linked moving mirror and a*

fixed lens both project the same image on to a Visatronic module, the lens is focused and the shutter released

RANGEFINDERS

For pin sharp pictures you must focus perfectly on the subject. With SLRs, focusing is visual and you simply adjust the lens until the subject appears sharp in the viewfinder. With other cameras you estimate the distance of the subject and rely on good depth of field to cover any errors. But there are some cameras that show you when perfect focus has been achieved.

These cameras, known as *rangefinder* cameras, actually measure the distance from the camera to the subject with an optical device linked to the lens.

Triangulation
Rangefinders work on the same principle that surveyors use to measure distance, the principle of *triangulation*. Triangulation is a simple geometric technique based on the premise that if you know the length of one side of a triangle—the *base line*—and two angles, then you can work out the length of the other two sides. So, by looking at a distant object from two points of known dist-

ance apart, you can calculate how far away the object is. This is done by measuring the angle between the baseline—that is, the line between the two observation points—and the distant object, from each of the two observation points.

When we use our eyes to judge distance, we are unconsciously making use of triangulation. We are familiar with the distance between our eyes, and this makes up one side of the triangle. We use the muscles around our eyes to make them converge on the object we are looking at. When they have completely converged, we see one image instead of two—the angle of each eye then gives an idea of how far away the object is. This process is completely automatic, but it enables us to make rapid judgements of distance.

Camera rangefinders
The rangefinder on a camera uses two different viewpoints, just like our eyes. These take the form of two windows on the front of the camera, each of which sees a slightly dif-

Compact or classic ? Both cameras use rangefinders for focusing. The little Olympus uses a base length of about half that of the rugged Leica

ferent view of the subject. One window sees the subject directly, but is fixed behind a semi-transparent mirror set at 45°. The mirror not only allows the first window to see the subject directly, but also reflects an identical image of the subject to the second window. Behind the second, smaller rangefinder window is a swinging mirror or prism which is coupled to the movement of the lens.

Though this seems rather complicated, the effect it has is simple—when you look through the viewfinder of the camera, you see a double image of any object in the centre of the screen. One of the two images is often slightly coloured. Only by focusing the camera can the two images be united to form a single one, because turning the focusing ring moves the pivoting prism, and this in turn moves the secondary image in the viewfinder.

Rangefinder accuracy
The distance between the two windows of a rangefinder is known as the *base length*. The longer the base length the more accurate the rangefinder is likely to be. Specialized rangefinders like those used for military purposes have a base length of a metre or so, but on cameras the base length is much shorter. The Leica, for instance, has a base length of about 48 mm and on some compacts the base length is as short as 18 mm.

Interchangeable lenses
Adapting a rangefinder to work with various lenses can be very complicated, but a number of rangefinder cameras will accept interchangeable lenses. Such lenses are fitted with a special coupling mechanism. This consists of a cam at the rear end of the lens which abuts a small roller at the end of the arm. This arm moves the rotating prism of the rangefinder. As the focusing ring is turned, the cam moves the arm in and out to rotate the prism.

There is a limit to the focal length of lenses with which a rangefinder will work, and this is set by the base length of the rangefinder. Cameras with a long base length, such as the Leica, can be used with lenses as long as 135 mm—the accuracy of focusing increases with shorter focal length lenses. The short base lengths on compact cameras are usually sufficiently accurate to focus the short focal length lenses with which they are fitted—wide-angle lenses have great depth of field.

Since the photographer does not look through the lens of the camera but through a separate window, most rangefinder cameras have bright white lines in the viewfinder to indicate the frame. Some cameras that can accept interchangeable lenses have a device that shows a different brightline frame for each lens that is used. When a long focal

length lens is fitted, the lines in the viewfinder mark out a smaller frame in the middle of the viewfinder. With wide angle lenses, a bigger area is shown.

Parallax error
Because the view of the subject that you see in the viewfinder is slightly different to that of the lens, rangefinder cameras, like all non-reflex cameras, can suffer from parallax error (see page 21) particularly when focusing on nearby subjects. To counteract this,

Double image *The centre of the viewfinder shows a double image of out-of-focus parts of the subject. Correct focus involves bringing the images together to form a single one*

the bright-line frames in the viewfinder move down and across the viewfinder as the camera is focused on closer subjects. This is called *automatic parallax compensation*, and brings the framing in the viewfinder into line with the framing on the film.

Rangefinder or SLR ?
At first glance, it may seem that focusing a camera by rangefinder, rather than by

eye, is unnecessarily complex but it does have a number of advantages.

The most important of these is that the point of sharp focus is very easy to detect. SLR cameras are often difficult to focus, particularly in bad light or with wide angle lenses. Indeed, with a lens as wide as 21 mm, an SLR may be no more accurate when focused by eye than if the photographer guessed the

distance and set it on the lens. Rangefinder cameras are actually more accurate when used with shorter lenses.

Because single lens reflex cameras have a mirror system to direct light up to the viewfinder, they are noisy and bulky, and the image disappears at the moment of exposure. Rangefinder cameras can be made smaller, and are quieter in operation. The loud 'snap' sound of the mirror rising is eliminated and there is less delay between shutter release and exposure.

How the rangefinder works

Twin windows on a rangefinder form a double image in the viewfinder. When the lens is turned to focus, a prism is turned, and lines of sight from the two windows converge

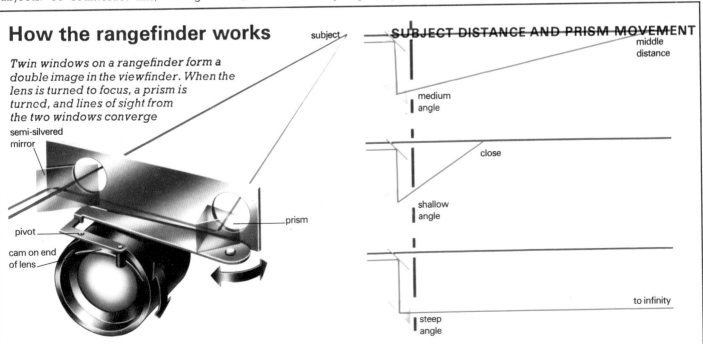

semi-silvered mirror

subject

pivot

cam on end of lens

prism

SUBJECT DISTANCE AND PRISM MOVEMENT

middle distance

medium angle

close

shallow angle

to infinity

steep angle

FOCUSING SCREENS

The focusing screen of the modern reflex camera seems to be a very simple component, but it has a vital role to play—without it, the camera could not be focused. And aids to focusing and the need for a bright, clear images mean that the focusing screen in an SLR can actually be quite complex.

In reflex cameras, focusing depends upon seeing the image formed by the camera lens clearly, and it is this image that the focusing screen shows. Although you can see through the lens clearly, it is not usually possible to see the image unless a surface is placed at the point of focus. Without such a surface, the image is a barely visible *aerial image*. If you concentrate, you can sometimes just see this image through the open back of the camera (with the shutter held open) around the edge of a knife held at the film plane. But it is almost impossible to focus. It is also impossible to see all the picture format at once.

Basic screen

It would be possible, in theory, to focus the image on an opaque screen like a projection screen, but this would be totally impractical in a camera. Camera construction is much easier if you can see 'through' the screen. A clear glass screen would not register the image, so one

side of the glass is finely ground to make it translucent. The grinding is done using fine abrasives which form millions of small irregular prisms on the surface. These have the effect of diffusing the light through the screen.

A very finely ground surface gives a dim image but allows critical focusing of fine

SLR focusing screens
incorporate tiny prisms

detail. A coarse surface gives a brighter image but loss of fine detail. Newer screens use laser treated surfaces to produce smoother prism surfaces and brighter images.

The ground side of the screen is accurately posi-

tioned either in the actual focal plane of the camera (as on large format types) or at an *equivalent focal plane* (with reflex types) where the distance from the lens to the screen via the mirror is the same as the distance from the lens to the film.

This basic screen is still sometimes used on large format cameras, though it has a number of drawbacks. The scattering of light means that the image is very dim, especially when compared with the aerial image. In addition, the edges are darker than the centre, giving a pronounced *hotspot*.

This happens because light near the edge of the frame is hitting the screen at an angle; so much of the emerging light is directed away from the eye. This is noticeable with wide angle lenses.

A simple cure is to have the ground surface as the flat side of a plano-convex shaped lens with the surface facing the viewer. This has the effect of bending the light rays coming from the screen inwards towards the eye, giving a more even appearance.

While such lenses are still used in some 35 mm SLRs, the necessary size and weight for large format cameras make this system inconvenient. Fortunately there is an almost flat equivalent in the form of the *Fresnel* lens which is often made of moulded transparent plastic. This consists of concentric circular ridges which act like lenses to bend the light inwards. The depth of all the ridges is the same, though the curvature changes so that the ridges near the edge of the frame bend the light more than those in the centre. The rings are so small that they are hard to detect.

Fresnel *With a normal screen (left) light is lost at the edge, but with a Fresnel (right), edges bend the light and keep the image even*

How a Fresnel screen works

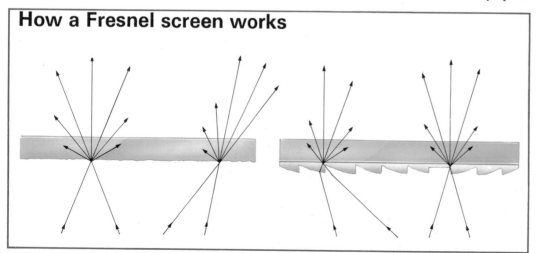

Focusing aids

As a further assistance to focusing, many screens incorporate aids in the form of *split image rangefinders* and *microprism* arrays. These are 'passive' devices in that they have no moving parts and rely for their effect on the deviation of light by small thin prisms.

The basic split image rangefinder consists of two wedge-shaped prisms placed together but sloping in opposite directions. These are set into the focusing surface of the screen. When the image is in focus the apex of the cone of light coming from the lens coincides with the focusing surface. This light passes undeviated through the prisms. When the image is out of focus the apex of the cone falls behind or in front of the screen. The section of the cone falling on the prisms is split and displaced in opposite directions thereby splitting the image. These displacements need not be very large to be detected by the eye. The human visual system is very sensitive to even minute displacements— a property called *vernier accuracy*—and so such devices are very effective.

Microprisms are a logical extension of this split image principle and consist of a very large number of very small pyramid shaped prisms. The pyramids are usually three or four sided and have base lengths anywhere between 0.01 mm (for movie cameras) and 0.1 mm. They cannot be resolved by the eye due to their size, but when the image is out of focus the effect is one of a 'shimmering' image. This is caused by multiple splitting of the image. When the image is focused the microprism clears and gives an undistorted view.

As these parts of the screen do not have any ground surfaces the image seen through them is an aerial one. The result is that the image is bright and nearly always in focus. This makes them useful for focusing wide angle lenses which are difficult to focus normally due to their large depth of field. The bright image also makes them useful in low light.

The accuracy of split image rangefinders and microprisms depends greatly on the aperture in use, so large aperture lenses give greater accuracy. With apertures of around *f*/5.6 or smaller the exit pupil of the lens and viewfinder system is very small. So if the eye is not located in just the right place the light from one of

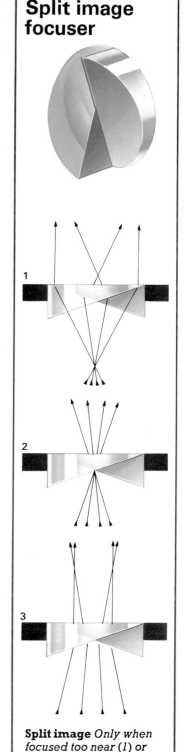

Split image *Only when focused too near (1) or too far (3), does the prism split the image*

the rangefinder halves, or from parts of the microprism, may not reach the eye and so half of the rangefinder appears black. With very small apertures it can be impossible to place the eye in such a way as to see all the images from the prisms.

To help overcome this, cameras with interchangeable screens often have special microprism screens available suitable for lenses such as wide angles or telephotos.

Normal screen *Fine ground screens, sacrifice brightness for detail*

Acute matte *Although coarser, these regular prisms are clear and bright*

Split image focuser

205

LENS AND APERTURE

To the newcomer, photography seems to be a world of numbers. There are focal lengths, f-numbers, focusing distances, film speeds, shutter speeds . . . not to mention the often intricate designations for camera models.

These days, auto-exposure cameras make it possible to disregard the technicalities and still get good pictures. But the numbers remain, and to get the most from your camera it pays to be able to understand what they mean.

The f-numbers seem the most arbitrary set of all: they run 2, 2.8, 4, 5.6, 8, 11, 16 . . . around the barrel of a lens. There seems no logic to them at first—they are not an obvious series, since they contain such oddities as 2.8 and 5.6. There is a good reason for their choice, but the most important thing is that they are a distinctive set

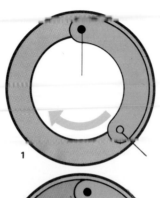

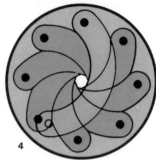

Diaphragm blades *An iris diaphragm has many blades, each of which moves across the lens opening. One end of each is fixed, the other is attached to a short slot in a ring. Turning this ring moves the blades*

of numbers. Any photographer picking up a new camera or lens can recognize them for what they are, so there is little risk that they will be confused with, for example, the focusing scale.

What the numbers mean
The f-numbers describe the aperture of the lens—that is the diameter of the lens opening. Most lenses used in photography have a variable aperture, controlled by means of the iris diaphragm, which has become a symbol for photography. The numbers refer to the aperture of the lens at various iris settings.

It is easy to appreciate that the larger the aperture, the more light is let on to the film. So why not simply describe apertures in, say, millimetres? Then a small aperture would be 2 mm and

Using aperture to control exposure

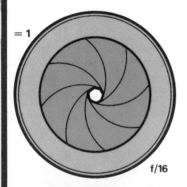

= 1

f/16

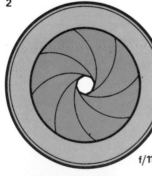

2

f/11

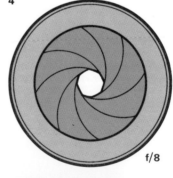

4

f/8

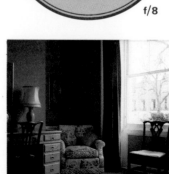

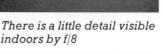

8

f/5·6

At f/16, the whole image is much too dark

The view outside is correctly exposed at f/11

There is a little detail visible indoors by f/8

The best picture is produced by using an aperture of f/5.6

a large one perhaps 25 mm—a scale which gets larger as the aperture does, compared with the *f*-number scale which, confusingly, runs the opposite way.

The problem is that we are not so much concerned with the amount of light passing through the lens as the actual brightness of the image. This depends not only on the size of the aperture through which the light passes, but also on the *focal length* of the lens you are using.

The focal length of a lens—broadly speaking, the distance from the lens to the film—gives an indication to the photographer of the size that the image of the subject is going to appear on the film. A lens with a long focal length—often called a telephoto lens—produces an image which is bigger than that formed by a standard lens. Conversely, a short focal length lens, that is to say, a wide angle lens, gives an image that is actually reduced in size.

The focal length of the lens, measured in millimetres, is engraved on the front of the barrel. It tells you how far the glass elements of the lens must be placed from the film in order to form an image of distant objects. This is why

Stopping down *The job of the iris diaphragm is to reduce the effective aperture of a lens. The upper diagram shows the lens at a wide aperture, about f/2.8. Reducing the aperture narrows the 'cone' of light, and when the lens is at f/16 it forms a very dim image*

telephoto lenses are physically longer than standard lenses: the lens elements have to be moved farther from the film.

Since the image formed by a long focus lens is larger than that formed by a standard lens, light from one part of the subject is spread over a larger area when the long focus lens is in use, and is therefore much dimmer. This means that if both lenses have an aperture that is equally wide, the long focus lens will form an image that is larger but less bright.

Calculating the numbers

This is why photographers use the scale of *f*-numbers. These take the focal length into account so that the image brightness for a given subject is always the same at any particular *f*-number—at least in theory.

An *f*-number of a lens is

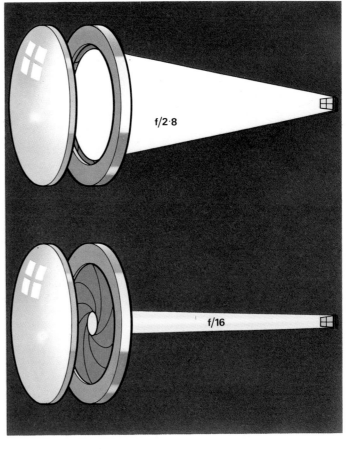

simply its focal length divided by its aperture. For instance, a lens of 50 mm focal length with an aperture of 25 mm has an *f*-number of 2, written *f*/2. Move the iris so as to reduce the aperture to

12.5 mm and it is working at *f*/4. Stop it down still further to 3 mm and it is approximately *f*/16.

When using a lens, the most helpful scale is one that shows changes by a factor of two—that is, with the image brightness doubling or halving. This means that the clear area of the lens doubles or halves. Since area changes with the square of the diameter of the lens, the *f*-numbers are actually the square roots of the numbers in the two-times table. Take the numbers 1, 2, 4, 8, 16, 32, 64 . . . and work out their square roots. You get 1.000, 1.414, 2, 2.828, 4, 5.657, 8, 11.314, 16 . . . These numbers are rounded off to give the familiar series, except that strictly speaking 5.657 is closer to 5.7 than 5.6. So there is logic in the series —each setting is a halving in area of the previous one. It is unfortunate that the series runs the 'wrong' way, and that the numbers seem a little arbitrary. But they are universal and distinctive, and mean a lot.

Exposure control *Opening the diaphragm by one stop doubles the area of the aperture, and lets twice as much light reach the film. These pictures show the effect this has on exposure*

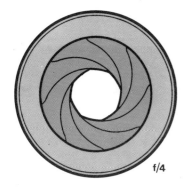

f/4

f/2·8

f/2

Even at f/4 the picture is just about acceptable

At f/2.8 the image is quite clearly overexposed

At full aperture, the picture is totally useless

HYPERFOCAL DISTANCE

Of all the technical qualities of a photograph, one of the most prized is sharpness. In a good photograph, the parts of the picture that the photographer wants to be in focus are perfectly sharp: the rest are blurred. Yet there is only one means of controlling what can be made sharp and what can not and this is by exploiting the camera's depth of field. Consequently, depth of field calculations have an important part to play in photography.

When focusing on your subject, you normally focus on one point only, yet because the lens has depth of field, points both nearer and further away from the camera than the focusing point are sharp. When photographing landscapes or other distant subjects photographers often choose infinity as their focus point, believing that this will ensure everything is in focus. Yet, if the lens is focused on infinity, a good deal of potential depth of field is wasted, because it extends beyond infinity.

Maximum depth of field is achieved by focusing on the *hyperfocal distance*—a point nearer to the camera than infinity—so that the depth of field extends just to infinity but includes points much nearer to the camera than if the camera were focused at the infinity setting.

The hyperfocal point is, in fact, located at the nearest point that is in focus with the camera focused on infinity. The distance from this point to the camera lens is known as the hyperfocal distance.

When the lens is focused on the hyperfocal point, the depth of field is extended so that every part of the subject from half the hyperfocal distance to infinity is rendered acceptably sharp in the image.

With a wide angle lens, which has a large depth of field anyway, setting the lens

Maximum depth *Sharp focus extends from near objects to infinity with the lens focused on the hyperfocal distance*

in this way can avoid the need to focus for snapshot pictures. The lenses of simple cameras, both stills and movie, are often fixed to focus on the hyperfocal distance. But this distance partly depends on the aperture in use—as the aperture in use changes, so does the hyperfocal distance. Some movie cameras shift the point of focus automatically to allow for this.

However, the distance depends, not only on the aperture, but also on the focal length of the lens, and on what is defined as being 'acceptably sharp'.

Standards of sharpness

When discussing the image formed by a lens, it is usual to have a point as the subject. The image of this point is actually a very small disc of light. In theory, this disc is infinitely small and is a true point. But this can never be achieved in practice:

These discs, known as *circles of confusion* technically, are smallest at the point of focus. So if the focus point for a particular object does not coincide with the film plane (the object is out of focus), but falls in front or behind it, the image disc

recorded by the film will be larger. An overall image made up of large discs of light looks unsharp, and the larger the discs, the more unsharp the image looks.

If the discs are below a certain diameter, however, the image will look perfectly sharp to the unaided eyes, even if the focusing is not absolutely precise. This is because the eyes are not able to resolve details below this size. Looking at the image with a magnifier reveals its lack of critical sharpness. It is generally accepted that circles of confusion up to 0.033 mm in diameter are indistinguishable from true points, even with good eyesight. This is regarded as a reasonable standard of sharpness in images that will be viewed without magnification. However, for images that are to be greatly enlarged from a small negative, a slightly finer circle of confusion, usually 0.025 mm, might be required to give an acceptably sharp image. It must be remembered, though, that the concept of a circle of confusion is essentially theoretical and, in practice, the quality and resolution of the image is affected by many other factors, such as variations in brightness across the image circle and the fact that a halo looks sharper than a disc.

In simple terms, the disc of light at the point of focus can be seen as the pinnacle of a cone of light. The base of the cone is the aperture. If the size of the aperture is reduced (stopped down) the cone becomes narrower. A cross section of the cone, at any point along its length, represents a circle of confusion. But at one particular point is the circle or disc which has the maximum permissible diameter for sharpness. If the cone becomes narrower, this point effectively moves farther towards the

Lens at infinity *With the aperture set at f/8, the depth of field index mark for this value indicates the hyperfocal distance—in this case, 10 m*

Lens at hyperfocal distance *Still at f/8, the infinity mark is moved to the index for this stop, so giving maximum depth of field for this aperture*

Stopped down *Changes in aperture alter the hyperfocal distance, which, at the smallest stop, gives the maximum possible depth of field for the lens*

ens. In this way, the depth of focus is increased, and this corresponds to an increase in depth of field.

It should be noted that most negatives are printed by enlargement, and most transparencies are projected or reproduced larger than the original. The standard of sharpness must therefore be great enough to permit the required degree of enlargement without the final image looking unsharp.

For 35 mm pictures, a maximum diameter for the circle of confusion is taken to be 1/30 mm. A 35 mm negative or transparency reaching this standard can be enlarged $7\frac{1}{2}$ times without loss of sharpness. Bigger enlargements are generally looked at from proportionately greater distances, and so a lower standard of sharpness is acceptable.

Calculating the distance

Hyperfocal distance forms the basis for depth of field calculations. But the distance can itself be worked out using a standard formula. This involves values for the focal length of the lens, the selected aperture, and the size of the maximum permissible circle of confusion.

For a 50 mm lens at f/2, the hyperfocal distance works out to be 37.5 metres. If the f-number is doubled to f/4, the hyperfocal distance is halved to 18.75 m. At f/8, the distance is halved again to 9.375 m, and so on. At f/11, the hyperfocal distance is around 6.8 m. If the lens is focused at this distance, the depth of field extends from

3.4 m to infinity, sufficient for most distant and some semi-distant scenes.

Fortunately it is not usually necessary to calculate the hyperfocal distance or depth of field. Most lenses are sold with printed tables which show the depth of field for each aperture, for a range of focused distances. So, these tables can be used to accurately set the lens for the maximum sharpness range.

Separate tables, published in books and guides, can be used for lenses which do not

have tables provided. But some of these tables are misleading. Many were compiled when lenses of particular focal lengths were meant for particular film formats. The maximum circle of confusion, upon which the tables are based, is calculated according to this format. But now there is no strict relationship between focal length and format. A range of tables may be needed for a single focal length, calculated according to the different formats for which it can be used.

A less accurate way of judging depth of field, and so hyperfocal distance, is by using the scale printed on the barrels of most lenses. With the lens focused at infinity, and the aperture set at, say, f/8, the index mark for this aperture gives the hyperfocal distance. Alternatively, with the infinity mark set at the f/8 index, the focusing mark shows the hyperfocal distance. This is how the lens is set for maximum depth of field to allow snapshot photography without focusing.

Criteria for sharpness *The image of a point appears to be sharp if the circle of confusion it forms is below a certain size. In the lower diagram the lens is focused closer than infinity. But a point at infinity is sharp when the lens is stopped down*

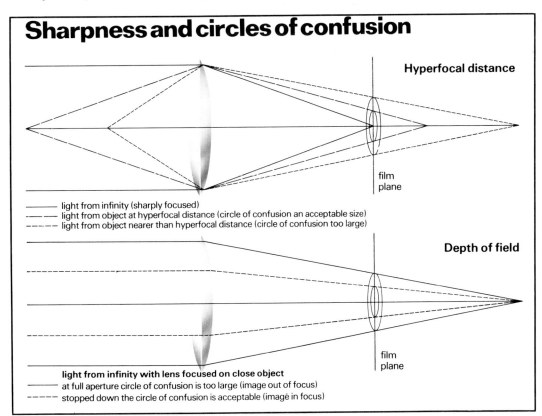

Sharpness and circles of confusion

Hyperfocal distance

film plane

——— light from infinity (sharply focused)
– – – light from object at hyperfocal distance (circle of confusion an acceptable size)
- - - light from object nearer than hyperfocal distance (circle of confusion too large)

Depth of field

film plane

light from infinity with lens focused on close object
——— at full aperture circle of confusion is too large (image out of focus)
– – – stopped down the circle of confusion is acceptable (image in focus)

DEPTH OF FOCUS

A high quality lens projects a sharp image but it will not give sharp pictures if this sharp image does not coincide with the film—if the image is formed either well in front or well behind the film the picture will be blurred. Fortunately, it is not always necessary for the sharp image to fall exactly on the film plane because of a phenomenon called *depth of focus.*

The term depth of focus is often wrongly used in place of depth of field. Depth of field refers essentially to the subject, and the distance within the subject that is focused sharply by the lens. Depth of focus, on the other hand, refers to the image behind the lens: it is the extent of the sharp image projected by the lens.

Unlike depth of field, which is generally large and measured in metres, depth of focus is very small and measured in millimetres, or even fractions of a millimetre. It allows some tolerance in focusing, and, perhaps more important, in the positioning of the film, though the latitude is not very large.

As the lens is stopped

down, depth of focus increases. Large format cameras tend to be used with small apertures, and the larger film size allows for a larger circle of confusion (see page 214). So the depth of focus with these cameras is usually quite large, and this allows the film plane to be moved in order to alter the depth of field and control perspective.

The depth of focus increases when the lens is focused on close objects. This is because the lens is moved away from the film to focus on subjects closer than infinity. As a result, the position of the maximum permissible circle of confusion also moves further from the film plane. This is different from depth of field which is smaller for close-ups.

Sharp centre *Depth of focus ensures that, even if the film is not quite flat, the centre of the picture will still be sharp (left) Nevertheless, pressure plates in the camera to ensure the film is held as flat as possible reduce the depth of focus needed*

Star trails *During long time exposures, the film surface may bend slightly, giving defocused star trails*

Practical value

The fact that depth of focus is greatest at close distances and small apertures can be very useful. For example, when making big enlargements with the lens well stopped down, the masking frame can be tilted to give some correction for converging verticals while still giving a sharp overall image.

When the lens is at full aperture, depth of focus is very small. Although this makes it harder to achieve perfect focus, it can also be useful for the technique of *rear focusing,* for example.

Rear focusing is valuable with large format cameras, or other cameras attached to bellows units. Normal focusing is achieved by moving the lens and this changes not only the lens to film distance but also the lens to subject distance. The result is that magnification is altered as well, and this can be quite noticeable in macro work. Rear focusing works by moving the film plane, and so changing only the lens to film distance. Changes in sharpness are quite abrupt, and so focusing is easier. This technique is most successful with shorter focal length lenses since depth of focus increases with longer focal lengths.

A basic formula allows depth of focus to be calculated. This shows that for a 50 mm lens, focused on infinity, with an aperture of f/16 and a maximum circle of confusion of 0.03 mm, the depth of focus is 0.96 mm. When the aperture is increased to f/1.4, depth of focus is reduced to only 0.084 mm. This has great practical significance. It means that the distance from the lens to the film must be kept accurate to this amount if large aperture lenses are used. The cost of precision cameras is, in part, due to the care and accuracy used in their mechanical assembly and tolerance testing. Perhaps the most important aspect is keeping the film in position. It is also important that interchangeable lenses are accurately aligned every time they are fitted to the camera.

Film flatness

Photographic film has an unfortunate tendency to curl. This can be due to either natural curvature caused by the layer structure, or to the way some film is stored, tightly coiled in a cassette, just prior to exposure. If the film is curved during exposure, parts of the picture will be unsharp, as not all of the film is in the focal plane. Depth of focus helps to overcome this problem by extending the areas of sharp focus. But it is also important to keep the film relatively flat.

This is usually achieved by providing a shallow channel in which the film lies, and a pressure plate to hold it in this channel. However, the channel, formed by the use of guide rails, is often around 0.2 mm deep. And as the thickness of film base is typically 0.13 to 0.15 mm, the film may still be slightly bowed against the pressure plate. Fortunately, most lenses give an image that is slightly concave, and this may correspond approximately to the shape of the film.

The larger the film area, the more difficult it is to keep flat. An oversprung pressure plate may cause marks or scratches on the film surface as it is advanced over rollers in the camera.

Film cartridges of the 126 and 110 type do not allow the camera to have a pressure plate since they are self-contained. For this reason the film in such cartridges is not very flat and so large aperture lenses are seldom used. Limits of f/5.6 and f/11 are common for 110 and 126 cameras respectively so as to give good depth of focus and ensure sharp pictures.

Large format cameras using dark slides have similar problems. Fortunately the depth of focus is correspondingly greater. For instance a standard 150 mm f/5.6 lens for a 5 × 4 inch camera has a depth of focus of 1.12 mm at this aperture assuming a maximum circle of confusion of 0.1 mm which is normal for this format.

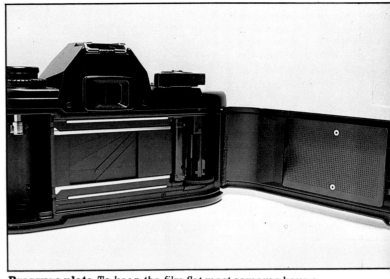

Pressure plate *To keep the film flat most cameras have a sprung pressure plate incorporated in the camera back*

Practical applications of depth of focus

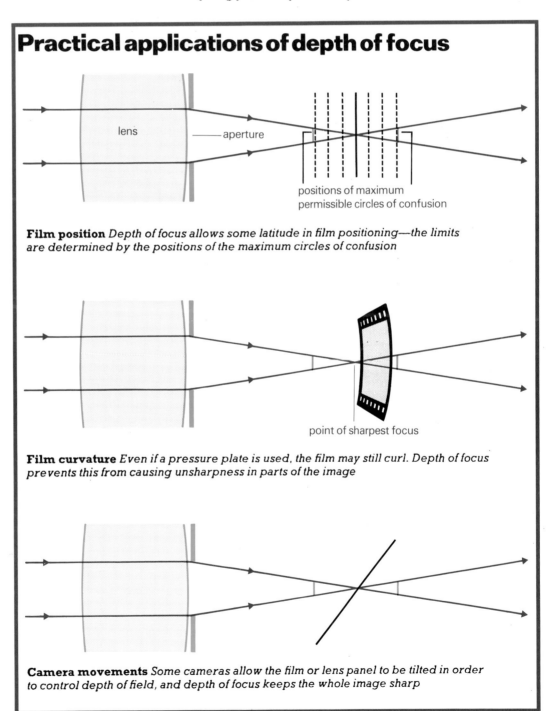

Film position *Depth of focus allows some latitude in film positioning—the limits are determined by the positions of the maximum circles of confusion*

Film curvature *Even if a pressure plate is used, the film may still curl. Depth of focus prevents this from causing unsharpness in parts of the image*

Camera movements *Some cameras allow the film or lens panel to be tilted in order to control depth of field, and depth of focus keeps the whole image sharp*

BASIC LENS OPTICS

Most photographers know how to use lenses without actually knowing how they work. This is hardly surprising considering how complex modern photographic lenses are. However, although modern lenses often seem dauntingly complex, all lenses conform to a few basic laws. It is useful to know the principles on which these laws are based in order to understand just how lenses are designed.

Lenses work by bending, or refracting, the light rays passing through them together. In fact, all transparent materials refract light, but lenses do it in a more controlled and precise way. The most important factors in this respect are the refractive index of the material from which the lens is made—that is, the amount it bends light—and the shape of the lens.

Most lenses have curved surfaces. These either curve outward, and are called *convex*, or inward, and are called *concave*. Lenses also vary in the degree to which they curve. By combining surfaces of different types and curvatures, a wide variety of lenses can be produced, each with its own characteristics. But for the sake of simplicity, they can be divided into two main types—*positive* and *negative*.

Positive lenses are important to photography because

Simple positive lenses

double   plano-   convergent
convex   convex   meniscus

Focal length *The lenses above have different focal lengths so the light is focused at different distances*

only they produce *real* images—ones that can be focused on to a screen such as film. Lenses of this type are used as the main elements in photographic lenses. They can have two convex surfaces (*double* convex), one flat and one convex surface (*plano* convex), or a mixture of both where the edges of the lens are thinner than the middle (*convergent meniscus*).

Negative lenses, on the other hand, give *virtual* images which cannot be focused on to a surface, but can be viewed by the eye. Instead of the light converging to a point—as it does with positive lenses—it diverges after passing through the lens. They thus have exactly the opposite effect to positive lenses. Combine a positive lens with a corresponding negative lens, therefore, and they cancel each other out—negative lenses are often used in conjunction with positive elements in

camera lenses, to control focal length and aberrations. Negative lenses are also used for camera viewfinders, and as spectacle lenses for people who are short sighted. In a similar way to positive lenses, negative lenses can be divided into double concave, plano concave and *divergent* meniscus types. In each case the centre of the lens is thinner than the edges.

Every lens, both positive and negative, has a particular focal length. With a positive lens, when rays of light, which are parallel both to each other, and to the *optical axis*—a line passing through the very centre of the lens, known as the optical centre—are refracted by the lens, they converge on a particular point. This is the *rear principal focus*, and the distance from this to the lens is the focal length of the lens.

Other light rays, which are not parallel to the optical axis, are brought to separate focus points. But these are all

in the focal plane which is at right angles to, and passes through, the principal focus. With a negative lens, the rays do not converge, and the focus of a negative lens is simply a theoretical point found by tracing the divergent rays back to their apparent origin. This article, though is mainly concerned with positive lenses.

The focal length of a particular lens is usually found by the process of ray tracing (see page 932). This involves mathematical calculations for which it is necessary to know the refractive index of the glass. The various types of optical glass have refractive indices from about 1.4 to 1.9. The former is of the *crown* type, commonly used as window glass. The latter is a typical value for glasses of the *flint* or *dense flint* types, which are heavy and commonly used for cut crystal glasses. Some lens manufacturers—such as Leitz—have special glasses made with specific refractive indices, to conform with their lens design.

The focal length is found by establishing the shortest distance from the lens at which an image can be formed. While light rays from infinity converge on the principle focus of the lens, rays from objects closer than infinity are brought to a focus farther away from the lens.

Simple negative lenses

double   plano-   divergent
concave   concave   meniscus

If the image needs to be focused on a fixed surface such as the film in a camera, therefore, it is necessary to move the lens away from this surface in order to focus on closer objects. This is why extension tubes and bellows are used for macrophotography. They simply increase the lens to film distance.

As light can pass both ways through a lens, there are in fact, two main focus points. In the case of a lens which is symmetrical, the *front principal focus* is the same distance from the lens as the rear principal focus, though on the opposite side to it. With lenses which have two different surfaces, the respective distances will also be different.

Once the focal length of a lens has been found, this information can be used to determine other aspects of

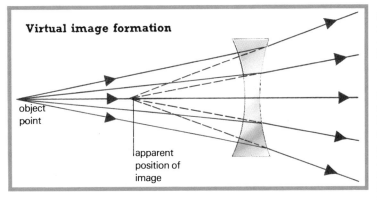

Virtual image formation

object point

apparent position of image

Negative lenses *The image formed by a negative lens is virtual, and so the focal point is only theoretical*

the image, such as its position and magnification. The technique used is based on *geometrical optics* and, although similar to ray tracing, uses graphical methods rather than mathematical calculations.

The process involves the use of scale drawings, and

allows the image to be measured, and compared with the subject. It can also be repeated for subjects at various distances from the lens. But to avoid having to repeat the process dozens of times, a formula derived from the geometry of image formation can be used

instead. And from this basic formula, known as the *lens equation*, other equations can be produced, relating to image magnification.

Most of these equations and ray tracing methods are mainly used for positive lenses. This is because although negative elements are used in photographic lenses, the final effect of a complete lens system must be positive in order to form an image. But the calculations can equally be applied to negative lenses if a negative value is given to the appropriate figures (the lens to image distance will be negative).

In addition, although the above examples have been applied to a *simple* lens (one element only), the principles are equally applicable to a photographic lens which has several elements.

How focusing affects image size

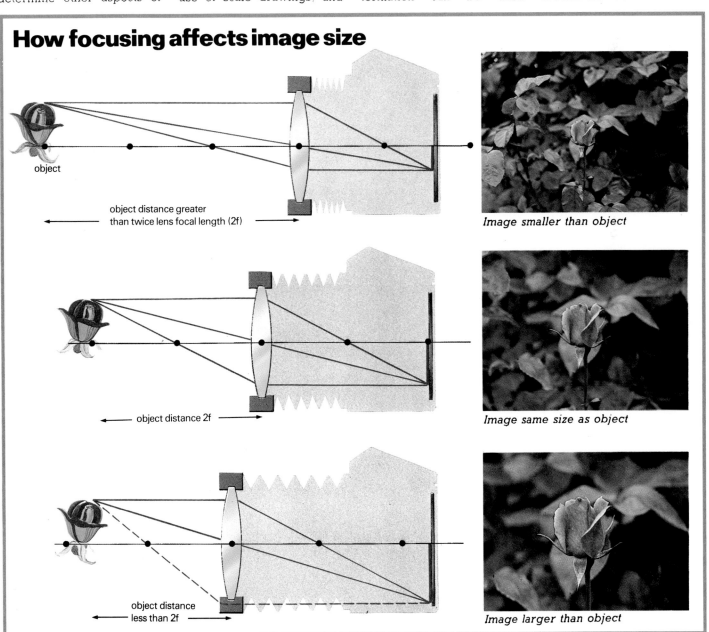

object

object distance greater than twice lens focal length (2f)

Image smaller than object

object distance 2f

Image same size as object

object distance less than 2f

Image larger than object

BASIC LENS DESIGN

High quality photographic lenses such as those for most SLRs can produce images of startling clarity and sharpness. But designing a lens of this standard, where aberrations are at a minimum and resolution is at a maximum, involves many complex calculations and development procedures.

The theory that goes into lens design is generally straightforward. The most important fact that the designer must know is the *refractive index* of the glasses that are to be used for the lens. The refractive index of a glass is a measure of its light bending power—usually measured to several decimal places for each type of glass.

Once the refractive index is known, the lens designer can calculate what happens to any light that falls on the lens and so determine whether the design is a good design before it is actually made. But the calculations are long and complicated, particularly with multi-element lenses such as zooms, and, not surprisingly, computers are now becoming an increasingly important part of the design process. Computers can perform tedious and complex calculations in a fraction of the time taken by previous methods.

A basic starting point is still needed, and this is provided by a design team headed by an optical designer. Their experience and knowledge help to avoid designs which, in the end, are unlikely to produce satisfactory lenses.

Predesign

The first step in any design process is to identify what the lens needs to do. It may be required to fill a gap in the manufacturer's range, or to replace an old design with a lens that is more compact or has a larger maximum aperture. A *specification* is produced, listing the required focal length, aperture range,

field of view, resolving power, closest focusing distance, overall size, and other features.

Most importantly, however, the designers must ensure that the final cost of the lens is geared to the market it is aimed at—a high quality lens is useless if no one can afford to buy it. In addition, there may be special considerations, such as the use of special glass — types of optical glass can vary in cost by a factor of 300 or more.

Designers achieve the required specification by varying the number of glass elements, their shapes—the

way the surfaces curve, their diameter and thickness — their spacings and the type of glass, plus the position of the iris diaphragm. All these features interact and must be combined to meet the specification with the minimum of aberrations. For example, the number of elements needed is related to the maximum usable aperture and the angle of view required. A 50 mm *f*/2 lens may need six elements where one of *f*/1.4 needs seven. A 24 mm wide angle lens may need ten elements, but a 200 mm long focus lens can perform well with only four.

With general purpose lenses, the final design is often a compromise. With lenses designed for more specialized purposes, one aspect of the design may be given greater importance. For example, a lens intended for copying work is usually corrected for aberrations at the expense of speed and has a relatively small maximum aperture.

Once a possible configuration is decided upon, from experience or a past design, a *thin lens* predesign calculation is made. This is a quick 'try-out', using a pro-

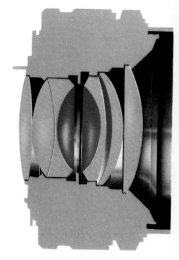

50 mm standard lens

grammable calculator or minicomputer to calculate the effects of the design. The lenses are treated as having negligible thickness, allowing greatly simplified formulae to be used. In this way, the designers can get an idea of the best layout of the elements. These calculations include allowances for different types of glass as well.

The basic routine is one of repeated *ray tracing*—calculating the path of each ray of light as it is refracted by the elements. This is achieved by applying a formula given by *Snell's Law* which makes it possible to calculate the refraction of a light ray at every air–glass surface or glass–glass interface, according to

First improvements

Meniscus lens (Wollaston 'landscape' lens)

Rapid rectilinear

Early designs
The top diagram shows one of the first designs to use a stop. The symmetrical layout of the lower design is the basis for many lens fault corrections

he angle at which it arrives, and the refractive index of the glass. Aberrations can also be allowed for in the calculations.

To improve the lens, one of the variables is altered, such as the curvature of one of the lens surfaces or the position of an element, and more ray traces are done to see the effects. Some aberrations are very sensitive to small changes in such variables, others are not. The pre-design is for light of a single wavelength. Later the lens can be colour corrected, by applying a similar process.

Design optimization
The result of the predesign efforts, often an excellent result, is then further refined by a design optimization pro-gram in a computer. This is another ray tracing process which assesses how the finished lens will behave, particularly in regard to re-sidual aberrations (see page

Three standards
The three 50 mm lenses above all have maximum apertures of f/1.8. But they differ in design and size. There is no single answer to the basic design specification
Design variation
Different focal lengths require very different designs, with variations in the number and type of elements

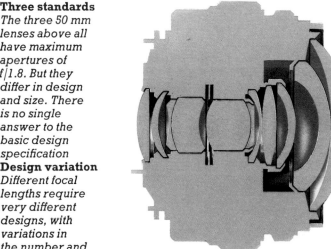

18 mm wide angle lens

226). The computer can then present a final design.

Thousands of calculations are performed to rework the lens to give the required performance. The result is then passed on to the optical engineer, who can make judgements as to its suit-ability for manufacture. An element may be too thin or too steeply curved for easy manufacture. It may be pos-sible, with a curvature which is nearly flat, to actually make it flat by slightly altering other elements, so reducing manufacturing costs.

There must be some toler-ance in the design to very slight variations in manu-facture and assembly, setting limits on thickness, the re-

fractive index of each ele-ment in the mount, and other variables. A design with a high rejection rate in manu-facture is a costly lens. The design is then reworked until an acceptable compromise is reached, and a barrel and focusing mount designed for it as a separate mechanical design job.

Variety of designs
That there is no perfect solu-tion to a lens design is shown by the variety of lenses with the same specifications — there are, for example, many 50 mm f/1.8 lenses—differing in the arrangement of ele-

ments and glasses as well as performance.

Lenses also have more subtle characteristics put in by the designer. A lens may be corrected to give a high contrast image at the expense of resolving power, or the converse. It may give a very sharp central image with poorer corners, or a more even overall performance of lesser sharpness. More am-bitious designs can now be tackled, such as wide angle zoom lenses, as better con-figurations are learnt from design progress. A lens may be made in many different configurations.

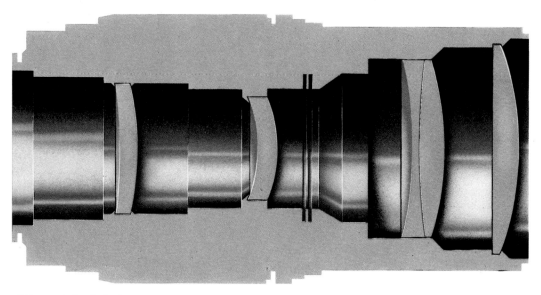

200 mm telephoto lens

PROGRESS IN LENS DESIGN

Early photographic lenses were very simple compared to their modern equivalents, but by the end of the last century, many improvements had been made which improved the quality of the images produced.

In particular, lens designers had realized that an effective way of reducing aberrations while still maintaining a reasonable aperture was to combine positive and negative elements symmetrically —so the negative element helped to cancel out the defects in the positive. The development of anastigmatic lenses—that is, lenses free from astigmatism—was one of the first major steps on the road to fast, high quality lenses, but there was still a long way to go.

One of the most significant advances was the *double anastigmatic* lens. Like basic symmetrical lenses, this used one element to cancel out the defects in another and so improve the performance. But the double anastigmat, rather than combining single elements, combined two complete anastigmatic lens units. One popular double anastigmat lens, for instance, combined a pair of Zeiss Amatar anastigmatic lenses back to back, either side of the aperture. The Zeiss Amatar lenses were triplets— that is, they had three elements cemented together— and the combination gave really excellent correction for distortion and some aberrations, though a small stop was still needed to reduce spherical aberration.

One particular advantage of the double anastigmat was that with some designs the two components could be used separately. This gave a choice of three focal lengths from the one *convertible* lens. The classic example was the *Dagor* which was produced by Goerz.

To give even better correction, double anastigmats were further developed by the process of *splitting* elements —that is, by replacing one element with two or more separate ones. But this led to lenses with up to ten elements. Such lenses were heavy and expensive.

A much simpler but more effective lens was devised by H. D. Taylor, an optical designer, in the late 1890s. He took as his basis the achromatic doublet design which was developed to give an achromatic triplet. This was split into its positive and negative elements, and then the positive part was further split into two elements which were placed either side of the negative element. The three elements were not cemented, but instead were air spaced. This allowed the elements to be placed very precisely, relative to each other, for maximum benefit.

This arrangement was called the *Cooke Triplet*, and was a fundamental advance in design because although it was simple, cheap and easy to make, it performed much better than the previously popular Rapid Rectilinear. The maximum aperture was initially only *f*/6.3, but later improvements allowed apertures as wide as *f*/2.8. The design is still used, in modified form, in some telephoto lenses as it gives

Softer shot *The image given by a simple early lens (right) is much softer than that taken with a more complex modern design*

good quality over a small field of view.

The basic three element configuration has been developed to give a huge family of derivations. The simplest of these was achieved by *compounding* the rear element. This is the technique of replacing one element with two or more cemented elements. As with splitting, compounding elements produces better correction by allowing a variety of different lens and glass types to be used together. The classic example is the Tessar, credited to Rudolph in 1902, and still widely used for budget standard lenses up to $f/2.8$.

Other derivatives allowed even wider apertures due to their improved performances. The notable example is the Zeiss Sonnar design which appeared in a number of variants. The early versions had a split front and compound centre elements producing a characteristic thick middle group. Some variants on this design were sufficiently free of spherical aberration to allow apertures of up to $f/1.5$. The quality and speed of these lenses were important in the acceptance of the 35 mm format, especially for available light photography. An important feature of the Sonnar design was that even before the availability of antireflection coatings, it was relatively free from flare, due to the small number of air–glass surfaces. And because it was compact and used large elements, it was remarkably free from vignetting at large apertures.

The Double Gauss design

At the same time that achromatic triplets were being developed, another lens type was also being used. This was the *Double Gauss* design, based on a lens devised by the mathematician Gauss in the early 1800s. This had two air spaced mensicus lenses, both concave to the front. As such it was not widely used. But two lens designers, Rodenstock and Busch, found that two of these Gauss lenses mounted symmetrically front to front, with a central stop, gave excellent correction even using the old glass types. As with other symmetrical lenses, the rear lens group cancelled many of the faults of the front group. In

Lens progress Lenses became increasingly complex as more and more elements were added to improve performance

particular, this design gave a flatter field than other lenses of the 1880s.

To further improve the optical quality this basic Double Gauss design was frequently modified to produce a large number of Double Gauss Derivatives. The first was the famous Zeiss Planar, designed in 1896, which involved the use of new glasses and replaced the inner meniscus lenses with cemented doublets. As the name suggests, it gave a very flat field. But spherical aberration was not sufficiently corrected to allow large apertures.

The design lay dormant for some time as it was expensive to make compared with the triplet lens. But it was revived in the 1920s when Hollywood needed high definition, large aperture lenses to allow filming by tungsten lighting when sound movies made the noisy carbon arc lamps obsolete. Movie cameras use lenses which cover a narrower field. By using only the centre of the lens's field, apertures of up to $f/2$ were made possible—a good example of this type of lens was the Speed Panchro.

The introduction of the Leica camera in 1925 boosted development of the large aperture anastigmats. The Zeiss Biotar $f/1.4$ and the Leitz Summar at $f/1.5$ were further derivatives with additional elements. The Double Gauss design has now been highly developed and is very widely used today, having benefited from the introduction of new types of very high refractive index glass which has low colour dispersion. This allows fewer elements to be used, though six elements are still needed for a well corrected $f/2$ lens and seven for $f/1.4$.

Before the invention of antireflection coatings on lenses, Double Gauss designs suffered more from flare than contemporary triplets such as the Sonnar, as they had more elements. This led to lower image contrast. But when coatings were introduced in 1935, they gave the Double Gauss design an equal status.

Gauss and double Gauss designs

The Gauss telescope lens

The basic Double Gauss design

Double Gauss derivative— the Zeiss Planar (1896)

Triplet lenses

The Cooke triplet (1893)

Sonnar type derivative (e.g. 50 mm $f/2$ Nikkor)

The double anastigmat

Dagor convertible lens (1900)

TELEPHOTO AND RETROFOCUS

The focal length of a lens is one of its most important features. Changing the focal length allows the photographer to control how much of a scene is included in the picture as focal length determines the size of the image. As focal length increases—to give a long focus lens—so does the image size, and this can be used to allow the photographer to fill the frame with the subject without having to get too close to it.

Unfortunately, as the focal length increases so does the physical length of the lens. Although the classical optical designs of achromatic doublet, triplet, symmetrical, Petzval or Double Gauss (see pages 216 to 217) can all be used, these designs produce lenses whose actual lengths are the same or longer than their focal lengths—a 300 mm lens would be over 300 mm long. Such long lenses are unwieldy and their extreme length leads to mechanical complications, particularly when it comes to providing a focusing mechanism.

The telephoto lens

To overcome this problem, the *telephoto* design was invented. Many people use the term telephoto to describe any lens longer than the standard, but that is technically inaccurate. A telephoto lens is one which has a positive front element and a negative rear element.

To understand how a telephoto works, it is essential to appreciate just why a long focal length gives a larger image. A slide projector provides a simple analogy. As you move the screen further away from the projector, the image spreads out more and more and becomes larger. In the same way, light passing through a lens with a long focal length converges more gradually and the image is focused further away from the lens. At the point where the image is focused, therefore, the image is spread out more and so is larger. So the further away from the lens that the image is brought to focus, the larger it is.

The advantage of the tele-

Curved ruins *Fisheye lenses with their very short focal lengths are extreme examples of the retrofocus design*

photo design is that it brings an equally large image to focus in a much shorter distance. This is achieved by placing a negative group of lenses between· the normal positive group and the film plane. Because this negative rear group reduces the convergence produced by the positive front group, the combination gives the same gradual convergence of a lens placed much further from the film plane. So the telephoto gives a similar amount of image spreading and so an equally large image to a single lens group with a long focal length, but the front element is much closer to the film plane.

Indeed, a telephoto could give an image as big as that given by a 300 mm basic lens, even though the front element was only 200 mm away from the film plane. When a telephoto lens is described as having a focal length of 300

mm, therefore, it does not really mean that the lens is 300 mm from the film plane it simply means, in practical terms, that the lens gives an image the same size as given by a non-telephoto 300 mm lens.

Another effect of telephotos is that, because the light from the front element is already converging when it reaches the rear element, the rear element can be smaller than with other designs. This makes the design and construction of the lens housing simpler as well as keeping to a minimum the diameter of the lens mounting.

The end result is that the lens is smaller than would be possible with other designs. This compression can be expressed as the *telephoto power*, which is the ratio of the focal length to the distance from the front element to the film, at infinity focus.

A negative lens was first used to give a telephoto effect by the astronomer Barlow as long ago as 1834. Barlow lenses are still widely sold in the form of teleconverters, which increase the focal length of normal lenses in the same way that the rear element of a telephoto lens acts on the front element or group.

Whereas the Barlow lens used a negative element with an existing lens, a lens invented by Dallmeyer in 1891 was self-contained and so was the first true telephoto. Other early designs used variable separation of the two elements to give variable focal length as a form of primitive zoom, though image quality was very poor.

One frequent drawback of the telephoto design is that, because it is not symmetrical, it tends to suffer from distortion, particularly pincushion. When the telephoto power is high—that is in physically short long focal length lenses—this distortion can be especially severe. Fortunately, this has been overcome to a large extent

ing the size, weight and cost of the lens compared to an equivalent symmetrical design, has other advantages apart from the large BFD. For example, one effect of having a negative front element is to reduce the angle at which light from the edges of the field of view passes through the lens. This helps to reduce vignetting and so gives more even illumination at the edges of the frame (see page 231). The negative group also reduces field curvature.

Due to the asymmetric design, early retrofocus len-

ses tended to suffer from barrel distortion. In most modern lenses improved optical glasses have reduced this to an almost unnoticeable level. Field angles up to 90 degrees or more are commonly available. Beyond about 110 degrees (as given by a 15 mm lens on the 35 mm format) correction of distortion becomes very difficult. If this is abandoned and severe barrel distortion permitted, then fisheye lenses with focal lengths down to 6 mm and field angles of up to 220 degrees are possible.

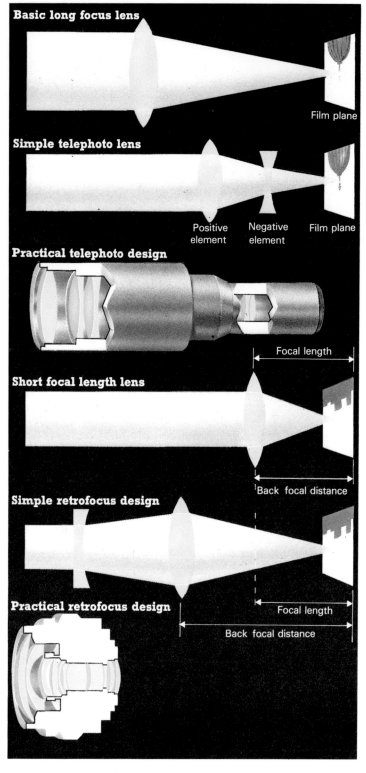

in modern lenses by the use of extra correction elements. But in less powerful telephotos—in the order of one and a half to two—quite simple triplet and Double Gauss designs (see page 224) are adequate, and these are frequently used in derived form with a negative rear group.

As always with refracting lenses of long focal length, the limit to performance is set by chromatic aberration. But the use of extra low dispersion (ED) glass gives better results and so allows larger apertures to be used while maintaining quality.

The retrofocus lens
The telephoto principle is also used in a slightly different form to produce wide angle lenses. With conventional designs, such as symmetrical lenses, the short focal length necessary to give the required angle of view can cause problems. This is because the *back focal distance* (BFD) —the distance from the rear element to the film—is very short.

With direct vision cameras and large format monorail cameras this small clearance is usually no problem. But when an optical device, such as a reflex mirror or a beam

Curved lines *Telephotos tend to be non-symmetrical and so suffer from distortion*

splitter, is to be situated between the lens and film, the optical design of the lens must be changed to give a long BFD but keep the focal length short. In the case of a modern SLR camera, a BFD of about 45 to 50 mm is needed to allow for the mirror, though lenses with focal lengths of 20 mm and less are available.

This is the reverse of the needs of a telephoto lens, and the required effect is given by the *retrofocus* (also known as *reversed* or *inverted telephoto*) design.

The basic design consists of a negative front group of large diameter followed by a positive rear group of small diameter. The negative group forms a close virtual image of the subject which is then focused on to the film by the rear group. This design, while considerably increas-

Lens layouts *Telephoto and retrofocus designs use extra elements to spread the light in various ways. In actual lenses the situation is complicated by the presence of more elements which are used to correct aberrations*

ZOOM LENSES

Composing photographs is undoubtedly made much easier if you can choose the focal length of the lens to give exactly the framing you require. Unfortunately, with fixed focal length lenses, this means not only time wasting and inconvenient lens changing, but also that you may not be able to get precisely the framing you want because it falls between two focal length steps. The zoom lens solves both these problems for still photographers, and, for movie makers, it has the added advantage of allowing the cameraman to change the focal length while shooting.

The basic principle behind zoom lenses is quite simple, relying essentially on two moving elements to vary the focal length. But in practice they are actually fairly complex and include a large number of extra correction elements. Zoom lenses should not be confused with the far simpler *varifocal* design which also gives the facility for changing focal length but

will not hold the subject in focus as the focal length is changed.

The range of focal lengths of a zoom lens is given by the *zoom ratio*. This is the ratio of the longest to the shortest focal lengths, so that an 80–200 mm zoom lens has a zoom ratio of 2.5:1. For 35 mm still photography zoom ratios of 2:1 to 6:1 are common. For movie photography and video cameras, zoom ratios of 10:1 to 20:1 or even more are used. This is because the small formats of movie and video cameras use only the sharp centre of the image produced by the lens so less correction is needed, allowing more ambitious designs.

A basic variable focal length lens can be made from just two elements. Each element has its own focal length, with either negative or positive properties (see page 218). The focal length of the two combined, often called the *equivalent focal length,* is given by a complex formula involving not only

the individual focal lengths of the elements but also the distances between them along the optical axis—the *separations.*

If an element is moved along the optical axis, the separation changes, and so does the equivalent focal length. The simplest arrangement would be a positive front element and a negative rear element. As they are moved nearer to each other focal length increases because the rear element progressively spreads the light coming from the front element. This means that the image is formed further away from the lens.

Unfortunately, such a lens would suffer from two major defects: the lens would have to be refocused after every movement—that is, it would be varifocal—and it would suffer severely from aberrations. To correct these faults, a large number of extra elements are needed, and zoom lenses may have between 8 and 20.

Changing size *The advantage of a zoom lies in being able to choose the best focal length without the trouble of changing lenses*

Focus compensation
Extra elements are used, moving in conjunction with the zoom element, to keep the image in focus. This form of correction is called *compensation* and there are two types—*optical* and *mechanical*—commonly used in modern zoom lenses.

Optical compensation means the zoom and correction elements are coupled together so that they move the same distance. The correction is achieved by careful choice of the correcting element or group, in terms of glass and lens types, so that it interacts with the other elements in the right way at every setting.

With mechanical compensation, the zoom and correction elements are separate, moving at different rates and sometimes in different direc-ons, so compensation is achieved by variation of the lens separations.

Optical compensation was originally preferred, as the lens unit and internal mechanisms were easier to manufacture. But now that complex control cams can be cut using computer controlled lathes, mechanical compensation is more popular since it allows higher levels of correction.

If you look into the front of a modern zoom while turning the zoom ring, you can often see the lens groups moving. Quite often the groups follow non-linear paths—that is, as the zoom control is turned through its range the elements advance, then recede, then advance again. Even some optically corrected zooms also use some degree of mechanical compensation in order to obtain the best possible results.

The classic zoom lens design has four groups of elements. The zoom and correcting groups are located between a front group which moves to focus the image, and a fixed rear group which contains the iris diaphragm. This rear group is positive and focuses the image formed by the other groups on to the film.

The fact that the rear group is fixed also helps to keep the aperture constant as the focal length is changed. This is because the effective f-number depends on the exit pupil. This is the image of the iris diaphragm as seen through the rear of the lens, and its size depends on the size of the aperture and the optical design of the lens. As the rear group remains fixed the exit pupil also remains fixed for each aperture setting, no matter which focal length setting is used.

One drawback with this type of design is that the closest focusing distance is far from the lens. Sometimes the closest distance is one or even two metres. This has been overcome to some

Moving elements *To keep the image in focus as the focal length is changed, zoom lenses use compensating elements or groups linked to the zoom elements. In the case of optical compensation the two elements are linked together, but with mechanical compensation they move independently*

Variable focus *In order to simplify the design this lens is a varifocal and the distance scale marked on the lens barrel changes with the focal length*

extent in recent designs which move all the elements when focusing. Unfortunately, this means that the f-number also changes when the lens is zoomed giving a loss of a half to one stop from minimum to maximum setting.

This problem can be avoided by using a separate focusing mechanism for close distances, and many zoom lenses have a 'macro-zoom' control. With the focal length set at a particular point (usually at one end of the scale) operating a switch allows the zoom ring to be used as a focus control. Focusing is achieved by moving one or more of the groups to give a form of *internal focusing* over a limited close-up range.

The performance with this type of system is often mediocre with the image suffering badly from field curvature and barrel distortion (see page 906). In fact distortion is a common problem with zoom lenses because of the asymmetrical layout which they use. The longer focal length setting tends to give pincushion distortion, and some lenses give barrel distortion at the shorter setting. However, modern computer designs and improved optical glasses mean that performance is usually good enough and may approach that of a fixed focal length lens. The main exceptions are wide-to-telephoto zooms, such as a 35-70 mm, which may give one type of distortion as a wide angle and another as a telephoto.

Focus compensation

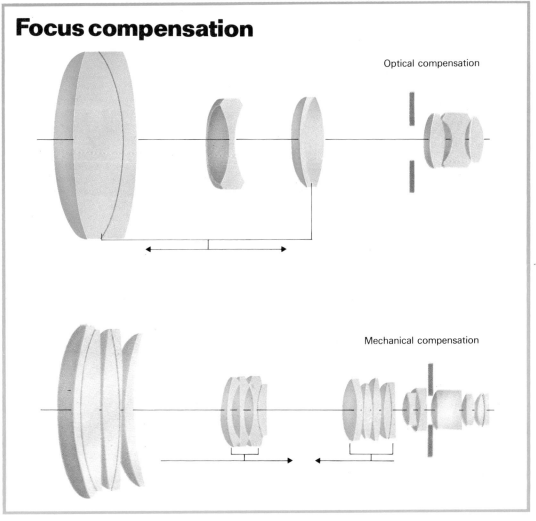

Optical compensation

Mechanical compensation

MIRROR LENSES

Mirror lenses are becoming increasingly popular with both amateur and professional photographers because they are much more compact than conventional lenses of similar focal lengths. By using mirrors to focus the light, some of the problems encountered with long focal length lenses—such as chromatic aberration—are avoided or reduced. The optical principles of mirror lenses are quite straightforward, although their layout does create special problems both for the designer and user.

The mirror lens design is often regarded as a recent innovation, but its origins actually predate conventional achromatic lenses. In the late 1600s, Isaac Newton discovered that the coloured fringes which degraded the images from the primitive telescopes of that time were due to *dispersion*. This is the way glass, or any other substance, splits light which is refracted through it into separate colours, and is the cause of chromatic aberration.

Unable to devise a cure, Newton abandoned *dioptric* lenses (those using refracting elements) and used curved mirrors instead. These do not disperse light as no refraction is involved.

The mirrors were surface silvered to avoid double reflections, and made concave. In this way they acted just like optical elements in that they focused light to form real images. The main problem was that the image was formed in front of the mirror. But this was solved by putting a secondary flat mirror part way up the telescope tube to reflect the rays through 90° to form an image outside the tube. This two-mirror design is called a Newtonian telescope and is an example of a *catoptric* lens—that is, one using mirrors only.

This basic layout has been extensively developed. One of the most important im-

Ghosted flowers *The depth of field with a mirror lens is very small and cannot be improved by stopping down, as usual. Defocused images may have a ghostly appearance*

provements was the *Cassegrainian* telescope where the secondary mirror 'folds' the light path back down the tube through an aperture in the main mirror, rather than out through the side. This means that the viewer (or camera) is directly behind the lens, which is more convenient. So it is this design which provides the basic for photographic mirror lenses. The folding of the light in this way also gives a lens which is about one third the length of a conventional lens.

Catadioptric lenses

Another improvement was made in the 1930s when Bernhard Schmidt showed that a specially ground aspheric lens, mounted in the front of the mirror lens greatly improved performance by reducing spherical aberration. Although the cost of such a design effectively rules it out for photographic use, the principle of using both mirrors and lenses—that is, a *catadioptric* lens—has since been widely adopted; all modern photographic mirror lenses are catadioptric.

Although Schmidt's idea was itself impractical, ten years later two designers working independently of each other—Bouwers and Maksutov—made the dis-

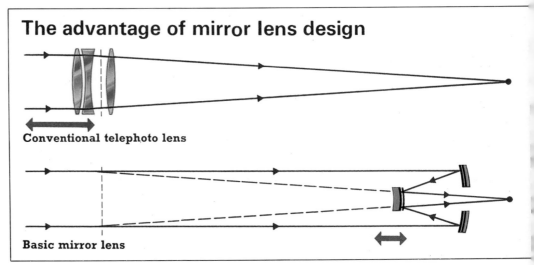

The advantage of mirror lens design

Conventional telephoto lens

Basic mirror lens

Mirror lens types

Newtonian telescope

Cassegrainian catoptric telescope

Bouwers-Maksutov catadioptric lens

Catadioptric lens with Mangin mirrors

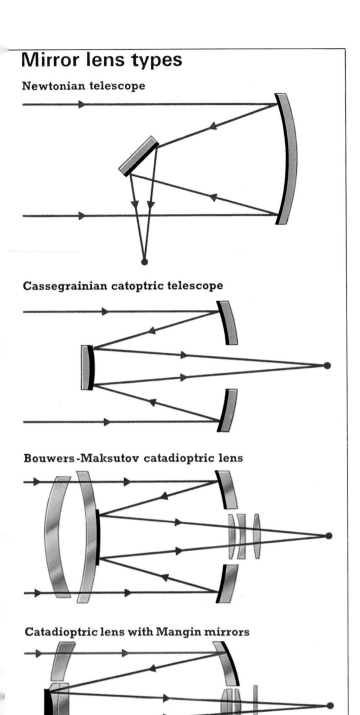

Newton's telescope *The first mirror lens was made to reduce the problems of chromatic aberration*

Mirror lenses *have come far since the original Newtonian design—from the mirror hole in the Cassegrainian allowing the viewer to see forward, through the first practical design to include lenses— the Bouwers-Maksutov—to the rear silvered spherical elements of the Mangin mirror*

Mirror advantage *By folding light rays, mirror lenses can be focused right behind the rear element, giving a short lens even with a long focal length—a conventional lens of similar focal length may be three times as long*

covery that made catadioptric lenses a much more practical solution to the problem of spherical aberration. They discovered that simple spherical mirrors give adequate results if a large meniscus lens, also with spherical surfaces, is placed at the front of the tube. The spherical aberration of one is effectively cancelled out by the other. This *corrector* lens is also useful for positioning the secondary mirror.

Many catadioptric lenses— particularly 500 mm *f*/8 models—are of the Bouwers– Maksutov Cassegrainian type,

though they are usually slightly more complex. Additional elements are normally used to flatten the image field and correct colour aberrations, and common designs use five to eight elements in all.

An alternative approach is to use a *Mangin mirror*. This is where, instead of using surface silvering, the silvering is applied to the rear of spherical lenses, so giving greater protection. The lenses also give the necessary corrections, allowing apertures of up to *f*/5.6. Combining elements and mirrors in this way allows very compact lenses to be made, and close focusing is possible with only a few millimetres extension of the secondary mirror.

The fact that small movements of the mirrors can have a great effect on focusing is also a problem. It is essential that the elements remain correctly aligned. Small knocks which would have a negligible effect on a refracting lens can cause serious problems with mirror lenses. And changes in temperature, which cause expansion or contraction of the lens materials, can create a focus shift. This is why mirror lenses always focus past infinity.

Another problem can arise with filters. The very large diameter of the front element makes front mounted filters impractical, both from the point of view of cost and

optical quality. So with most mirrors lenses the filters are rear mounted, often in the form of a built in 'turret'. So these filters behave as additional optical elements and the lens is designed to take them into account. So when a coloured filter is not in place, a clear glass (UV) filter must be used. Without a filter, the optical performance of the lens is impaired.

Mirror lens speed

Mirror lenses rarely have diaphragms for varying the aperture—partly as such a device would have to be very large. But it is also concerned with the problems of retaining a perfect *annulus* (doughnut shape) over such a large area. Any distortion of this annulus results in degrading of the image.

With no diaphragm, the aperture of a mirror lens cannot be varied so the correct exposure is achieved by altering the shutter speed or placing neutral density filters over the lens. The *f*-number for any particular lens is calculated with normal optics geometry by dividing the focal length by the aperture, which in this case is represented by the main mirror.

This calculation gives the quoted speed—say *f*/8—but the secondary mirror blocks some of this aperture. So in terms of actual light transmission the aperture may be reduced by as much as a stop, giving *f*/11 in practice.

WIDE-ANGLE DISTORTION

There is nothing inherently different about the pictures taken through lenses of different focal length. The only real difference is in the proportion of the scene they take in—that is, the angle of view. Look closely at a pair of photographs of the same scene shot through different lenses and you will see that the picture shot on the longer lens can be seen within the picture shot on the shorter lens.

Nevertheless, the different size of the 'window on the world' provided by each focal length means that each focal length gives a picture with a distinctive look. With wide-angle lenses, this look is particularly distinctive, and the construction of wide-angle lens involves particular problems which can sometime add genuine distortion to this distinctive look.

Image distortion

Wide angle lenses are often said to produce distortion. Four different kinds can be identified although, strictly speaking, only one of them is really distortion caused by the lens itself. This is a type of curvilinear distortion called *barrel distortion*. This causes straight lines near the edges of a picture to bend outwards in the middle, giving the bulging shape of a barrel.

An extreme example of barrel distortion is that shown by a fisheye lens, where rectilinear projection is sacrificed to achieve an angle of view of 180° or more.

You may come across slight curvilinear distortion with some less expensive wide angle lenses and certainly the shorter the focal length the greater the likelihood of the fault. Even with a high quality lens of say 24 mm focal length, some bending of straight lines may occur but

Big feet *Filling the frame by getting close to the subject often leads to exaggerated perspective. Close viewpoints cause this, not lenses*

you would not normally notice it unless there are some strong straight lines near the edge of the picture.

Converging verticals

When you are using a wide angle lens to photograph the whole of a building from fairly close to, tilting the camera slightly upwards to include the roof will produce violently converging verticals in the picture—that is, the building will narrow unnaturally towards the top. Tilting the camera slightly downwards in photographing a room interior will give the same effect but this time the vertical lines converge so that a door looks much nar-

rower at the bottom than at the top of the frame.

These effects have nothing to do with the lens at all but are examples of the steep perspective caused by close viewpoint. A pinhole camera will give exactly the same results from the same view-

points. If you stand fairly close to a tall building and look up at it you will see the converging verticals in the same way as a camera, but your brain interprets the messages sent to it by the eyes and because it knows that a building has vertical walls the convergence passes unnoticed.

Similar examples of abrupt perspective occur when a portrait is taken from fairly close to the model. Parts of the face nearer to the camera than the rest, such as the nose and chin, look unnaturally big and a more distant ear may look too small. A short focus lens encourages such close viewpoints because of the smallness of the images it gives from further away. It is important to remember that the perspective that will be seen in a photograph is exactly the same as that which will be seen if the eye is placed at the position of the camera lens when the picture is taken.

Romany family *Wide angle lenses distort objects at the edges and corners of the frame. The camera records three dimensions on to a piece of flat film, so some parts of the picture are squashed out of shape, as shown in the diagram at right.*

Distortion of shapes

In a wide angle photograph, objects such as human heads and spherical light globes in the corners of the field of view, will be stretched into elongated shapes that can look quite grotesque. Again, a pinhole will give exactly the same result which arises because the image of the subject in the camera is projected onto a flat surface. Despite the wide angle of view of the eyes, we do not see such distortions because our retinas are strongly curved. Some cameras designed expressly for taking very wide angle pictures of landscapes or large groups of people hold the film in a curve to avoid such distortions of shape.

Avoiding distortion

The barrel distortion given by a fisheye lens cannot be avoided, so do not use one if bending straight lines is unacceptable. If a cheap wide angle lens shows uncorrected curvilinear distortion, take care to avoid having straight lines in the subject falling at

Boxing ring *A lot of wide angle lenses have barrel distortion. The fish eye lens is an extreme example*

Tall buildings *Tilting the camera up gets everything in, but leads to dramatically converging vertical lines*

the edges of your pictures. It is only away from the lens axis that bending occurs. It is also good sense to buy the best wide angle lens you can afford, especially if you are interested in architectural photography.

Converging verticals can be avoided by making sure that the film plane is always kept vertical. In photographing buildings this is sometimes difficult and for some 35 mm cameras there are perspective control or 'shift' lenses which give the equivalent of the rising and shifting

front found on a technical camera. With such a lens it may still be possible to include the top of a building without having to tilt the camera.

You can prevent the stretching out of faces at the corners of wide angle shots only by keeping people more or less in the middle of the picture. Watch also for other shapes that will look strange if distorted in this way and keep them away from the edges of the frame as far as possible.

For portraits, unless you are trying to caricature your sitters, never take a close-up with a wide angle lens. For more or less formal head and shoulder portraits with a 35 mm camera, a 90 mm lens enables the camera to be kept at about 2 metres from the subject, which is far enough away to give natural looking perspective. Using a wide angle lens at such a distance gives a very small image and a print of reasonable size would involve such a large magnification that objectionable graininess and serious loss of sharpness would be almost inevitable.

Print viewing distance

There is no such thing as 'distorted' perspective. It can look wrong, however, through looking at a print or a picture on a screen from the wrong distance. The right distance for natural looking perspective is the focal length of the camera lens multiplied by the magnification used in making the print or projecting the slide. Thus a negative made with a 24 mm lens and enlarged 7 diameters to make a print 250 mm long should, ideally, be viewed from a distance of about 18 mm—much closer than the eyes can focus. The same picture as a slide enlarged 40 diameters on a screen should be viewed from a distance of a little more than 1000 mm—much too close for comfort. In reality, of course, we see all prints from the same distance, regardless of what is 'right'.

When using a camera fitted with the standard lens of about 50 mm focal length, viewing the finished picture from the right distance for natural perspective may not be so difficult. It is this fact that gives rise to the idea, mistaken as it is, that wide angle lenses distort the perspective of a photograph.

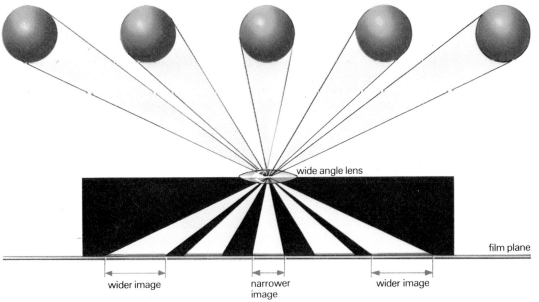

wide angle lens

film plane

wider image   narrower image   wider image

225

LENS FAULTS

Modern camera lenses give remarkably high quality results; yet even the best lens cannot give an image that is completely sharp—every lens suffers from a number of defects known as aberrations, giving less than perfect focus.

Lens aberrations take a number of different forms, but their effects are often indistinguishable. Ideally, all the light from any point in the subject would be focused by the lens on a corresponding point on the film. Unfortunately, lens aberrations mean that not all the light is focused at quite the same point and so the image is slightly blurred. Some types of aberrations affect the entire picture, even the very centre, along the axis of the lens. This type of aberration is referred to as direct or axial. Others do not affect the centre of the image at all but grow steadily worse towards the edges—this is oblique or off-axis aberration. With careful lens design involving multi-element lenses, these aberrations can be reduced to a minimum but there are always some residual effects.

Lens shape

Photographic lenses depend upon their shape to work properly. They work by refracting (bending) light rays so that all light from a particular direction—from a particular point in the scene—is brought to focus on the film.

Unfortunately, the lens shape that would produce minimum aberration is not the easiest to manufacture and the majority of photographic lenses have spherical surfaces—that is, the surface of each side of the lens is shaped like part of a sphere. Surfaces this shape are easy to grind, but it gives various types of aberration.

In particular it gives a form of direct aberration, spherical aberration, affecting the whole image. With a spherical lens surface, light rays refracted by different parts of the lens come to focus at slightly different distances. Thus, light rays passing through the outer regions of the lens are focused closer to the lens than those passing through the centre. The result is a generally soft focus over the whole picture.

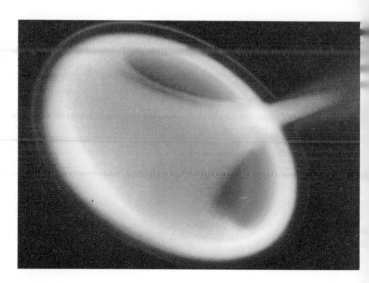

Point of light *Both coma and chromatic aberration affect this image*

While some portrait lenses exploit controlled spherical aberration to give special soft focus effects, it is usually undesirable. The simplest way to reduce spherical aberration is to stop down the aperture so that only the central portion of the lens is used. Of course, since light refracted by the centre of the lens focuses slightly further back than that refracted by the edge, stopping down has the effect of shifting the focus a little further away from the lens. While the focus shift may be negligible for most shots, the lens must always be refocused after stopping down for very close shots with a camera or for quality work in the darkroom.

Unfortunately, it is not always possible to stop down sufficiently far to reduce spherical aberration and alternatives must be included in the lens design. One approach is to use a weak diverging (concave) lens element in conjunction with the main element. The diverging lens also produces spherical aberration but in exactly the opposite direction to that produced by the main lens and so, used in conjunction, they cancel each other out.

Close-up lenses often use a floating element which moves along the axis of the lens according to the focusing distance. An expensive alter-

native is to avoid a spherical surface altogether and produce a specially shaped aspheric lens element.

The spherical lens shape also produces aberrations to light rays falling obliquely on the lens surface and the image of a point is fanned out around the point like the tail of a comet—this aberration is therefore known as coma. Like direct spherical aberration, coma can be reduced by stopping down and adding correcting elements to the lens.

There are two other significant types of oblique aberration: distortion and astigmatism. Distortion occurs because the aperture stop prevents oblique light passing through the centre of the lens. This means that magnification of the image varies from centre to edge. The image of a rectangular subject either bows in, to give pincushion distortion, or out, to give barrel distortion.

This form of distortion occurs whenever the lens elements are not arranged symmetrically around the aperture stop, unless the stop is very carefully located. Stopping down has no effect on distortion, as the problem is image shape and not sharpness.

Sharp centre *Only the centre of the picture is sharp due to shallow depth of field and slight field curvature*

Telephoto lenses tend to suffer from distortion as they are usually very asymmetrical. A zoom lens can vary from one type of distortion to the other as the focal length is changed. A symmetrical design, such as the rapid rectilinear, avoids distortion. It does this by combining a front lens group, which has pincushion distortion, with a rear group which has barrel distortion.

When a lens suffers from astigmatism it is impossible to focus a point in the scene into anything but one of two straight lines at right angles to each other. This is because rays of light converging vertically come to focus a different distance from the lens to rays converging horizontally. So when vertical rays of light are focused, horizontal rays are still a little spread out—or have spread out again beyond their focus—and this spread of horizontal rays registers as a horizontal straight line. If, on the other hand, the lens is focused at the point where horizontal rays converge, the vertical rays are spread out and register as a vertical straight line. The best compromise is to focus midway between the vertical and horizontal foci so that a point in the scene registers as a small circular patch.

One other important aberration is caused by the fact that a curved lens is used to project an image on to a flat film surface. The image of a flat subject, formed by a simple lens, is saucer shaped. This effect is known as *Petzval curvature.* If no correction were made, the centre of the image would be sharp, while the outer edges would be out of focus—or vice versa. Correction is made by using a mixture of negative and positive elements to force this natural curvature into a flat surface, or flat field.

All aberrations caused by the shape of the lens can occur with light of a single colour and wavelength but normal 'white' light consists of many different colours and wavelengths, and the different ways in which different colours of lights are refracted also produces aberrations.

Chromatic aberration
When white light passes through a simple lens, short blue wavelengths are refracted slightly more than long red wavelengths and the light is dispersed into a spectrum. This produces chromatic or colour aberration.

Axial chromatic aberration occurs because blue light comes to focus nearer to the lens than red light—green light is focused midway between. The lens, therefore, has a different focal length for each colour and it is impossible to focus one without the others being out of focus and giving colour fringes.

The aberration can be reduced by stopping down to give a greater depth of field, but the best correction is made by combining the main lens with a diverging element which cancels the effect. This diverging element must be made from a different type of glass, so that the aberration is corrected but the combination remains convergent. Unfortunately, a different element is needed for each colour.

An achromatic lens has two types of glass and is corrected so that green and blue—two colours—usually focus at the same point, with the other colours slightly out. An apochromatic lens includes at least three different glasses and is corrected for three wavelengths—red, green and blue. With both these lenses, a separate focusing index is needed for infrared, though a superachromat is corrected for this as well.

Even if axial chromatic aberration is corrected by using mutually cancelling lens elements, the different focal length for each colour may still cause transverse chromatic aberration of light falling obliquely on the lens. Because each colour has a different focal length, the size of the image projected by each colour is slightly different. In a lens suffering from transverse chromatic aberration the red part of the image of a white subject is therefore slightly larger than the blue image. The effect is to produce pronounced colour fringes towards the edge of the picture area.

Transverse chromatic aberration can often be very obvious and it sets a limit to the performance of long focus lenses although low dispersion (ED) glass or fluorite elements can significantly reduce its effects.

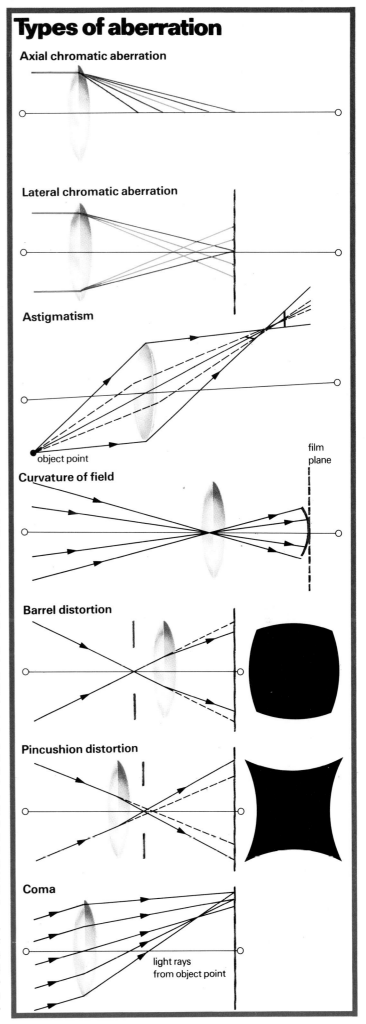

Types of aberration

Axial chromatic aberration

Lateral chromatic aberration

Astigmatism

object point

film plane

Curvature of field

Barrel distortion

Pincushion distortion

Coma

light rays from object point

227

LENS FLARE

Flare patches *Perhaps the most common type of flare appears as one or more coloured patches. These often take the form of a distorted image of the aperture*

When a film is exposed in a camera, ideally only light directly reflected from the subject would affect the film and the contrast of the image reaching the film would be exactly the same as that of the subject itself. Unfortunately, in every camera, unwanted light or flare can reach the film from various sources and cut down contrast, sometimes severely. And with colour film in the camera, flare can produce washed out colours.

In the right circumstances, you can actually see flare in the viewfinder of an SLR camera. If you look through the viewfinder with the sun behind you and then turn around to face the sun, you will notice that image contrast drops dramatically and the shadows become grey.

The most important source of flare, known as lens flare, comes from multiple reflec-

tions from the surfaces of the glass lens elements— wherever there is a glass/air surface, a small proportion of the light passing through the lens is scattered. If the lens has a large number of elements with many glass/air surfaces, then the amount of light scattered could be quite significant.

Although some of this scattered light is reflected back out of the lens, a great deal can reach the film. Because there are so many reflections and re-reflections from the various glass surfaces, the scattered light reaches the film more or less at random. It falls on the film as a fairly even flood of light almost as if, inside the camera, there is a small light source which is switched on

every time the shutter opens. Under some circumstances some of the flare light can appear as out of focus ghost images of light sources in or just outside the field of view.

Additional flare may come from reflections from iris diaphragm leaves, the interior of the lens mount, or from the imperfectly blackened ground edges of lens elements. Even light reflected from the film surface on to the blackened interiors of some cameras can add to the general flare level, particularly when bright sunlight strikes the front surface of a lens obliquely. Bellows cameras are far less prone to this form of flare than modern rigid-bodied cameras because the corrugated cloth bellows can be almost com-

pletely non-reflecting.

Although flare reduces contrast in general, it affects the shadow areas in particular With colour slide film it reduces colour saturation and may give unwanted colour casts because the flare is tinted by a large strongly coloured area in the subject. Ghost images of the iris diaphragm of the lens or light sources just outside the field of view are also common.

Flare tends to increase with scene contrast and a scene with bright highlights and deep shadows often creates a great deal of flare. This can actually be useful since the flare will serve to cut down excessive contrast.

It is usual to state flare as a factor by which scene contrast is reduced in the image projected on the film. If a subject with a luminance range of 100 to 1 forms an

image with a range of only 50 to 1, the flare factor is 2. Flare factors can vary from about two to as high as ten under adverse conditions but values depend on subject conditions as much as on the lens and camera. Shoot into the sun and the flare factor rises sharply.

Lens manufacturers can establish roughly how much flare there is in a darkroom. They set up an illuminated panel, such as a light box, in front of the camera and switch off the room lights. They then open up the back of the camera so that the image of the panel is projected on to a screen held close behind the camera. Any light falling on the screen outside the image of the panel is flare. With the right equipment, this flare can be measured.

However, in everyday photography and in studying tone reproduction, flare has to be evaluated by comparing the characteristic curve of a film (see page 131) plotted for no-flare and flare conditions.

Obviously lens designers go to considerable trouble to cut down flare. Their most important technique is lens coating and this is covered in a subsequent article.

Shooting into the sun *With some lenses, this will produce concentric rings of light, if the sun, or any other strong light source, is centred in the shot (left)*

Veiling effect *Instead of patches or rings, flare can show up as an overall lowering of contrast. This gives a shots a softness which can be attractive (right)*

Sources of lens flare

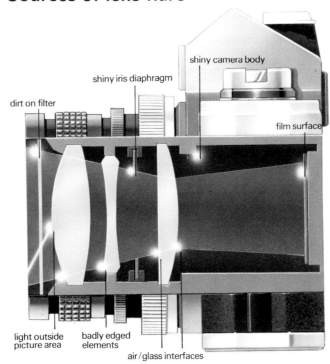

Camera and lens *Both contain many potential sources of flare. Blackening of interior surfaces reduces or eliminates the effects produced by some of them*

Good blackening of the interior of the lens, also helps to keep flare to a minimum. Unfortunately no finish has yet been devised that is totally non-reflective and telephoto lenses in particular may suffer from a marked lack of contrast.

A good lens hood can make a substantial difference but it must cut out all light from outside the picture area but not cut off any light from the picture itself. Again, this ideal is hard to fulfil.

Surprisingly, perhaps, one of the biggest contributors to flare is dirt. Lens surfaces should always be protected from dust and especially from greasy fingermarks. A single fingerprint on the front surface of a lens can make images so lacking in contrast that they are useless. If a lens is badly marked it should be cleaned gently with well-crumpled lens cleaning tissue. But a lens which is polished repeatedly with even the softest material accumulates many tiny scratches and the surface is dulled. The result is a permanently increased flare level. So to keep flare to a minimum and retain the full contrast range in your shots, make sure your fingers never touch the lens!

LIGHT THROUGH THE LENS

For correct exposure, it is vital to know exactly how much light is coming through the lens. While TTL meters can measure the light directly it is useful to know just what controls the amount of light transmitted through the lens.

The main limitation on light transmission is the aperture of the lens (see page 212). Indeed, on the vast majority of camera lenses the aperture can be varied to control light intensity. The amount of light actually reaching the film is also affected by the distance it has to travel from the lens. So the system used to represent the aperture—*f*-numbers—is related to the focal length of the lens. In fact, the *f* stands for focal length, and this is divided to give the aperture size. So for a 100 mm lens, *f*/4 means an aperture of 25 mm.

The *f*-number for each size of aperture is calculated for a lens set at infinity. When the lens is moved away from the film, to focus on closer objects, the light has to travel further. The consequent spreading out of the light as it travels further and further means that less light reaches the film. This decrease in light intensity can be calculated. Tables are available for close-up work, where the effect is most noticeable, to show how much extra exposure is needed to compensate. But even when all the theoretical calculations have been made, the result may still not give a precise indication of the light transmitted by the lens for a number of reasons.

Light losses

The glass used for photographic lenses is highly polished and so is highly reflective. This means that some of the light falling on a lens element is reflected by it. This becomes apparent when you look at the front element of a lens. Clear reflections of light can be seen, repeated at each glass surface.

Fall off *Vignetting causes light loss at the corners*

For an uncoated surface, reflection losses are four per cent of the arriving—incident—light, increasing with the refractive index of the glass. When the light passes through the next surface, four per cent of the light transmitted by the first surface is lost. A four-element lens has eight surfaces, and the resulting light loss may be over 25 per cent. An uncoated lens with 15 elements, such as a zoom, transmits only 30 per cent of the incident light.

Fortunately, a single anti-reflection coating on a lens surface increases transmission to about 98 per cent, and multi-layer coatings to better than 99 per cent. In the case of the 15 element zoom, this increases transmission from 30 to 74 per cent.

But even with the aid of coatings, there are still some transmission losses, partly due to absorption of light by the glass, and partly to residual reflections. A great deal depends on the precise construction of the lens. As the number of elements affects the reflections, so the thicknesses of the elements affect the degree of absorption.

A side effect is that different types of glass absorb differently over the spectrum. This *differential absorption* causes slight differences in colour balance or rendition from lens to lens. Some lenses

Complex lens *Light loss can occur as each element reflects some of the light*

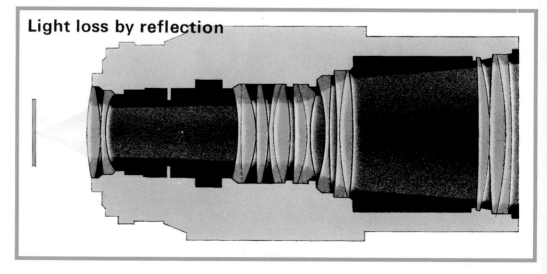

Light loss by reflection

230

Sunset *Unlike a mirror lens, a conventional lens does not have a central obstruction, and gives this result at f/5.6*

Mirror shot *A shot taken with a mirror lens is darker, even though it has a nominal aperture of f/5.6*

may seem to be marginally 'warmer' or 'colder' than others. Manufacturers often take care to make a series of lenses consistent in terms of colour, so that photographers can change lenses without worrying about the colour changing. This is achieved by variations in lens coatings.

Dark corners

A more selective type of light loss is *vignetting*. This is characterized by darkening of the corners of the image, and is worse at large apertures. Vignetting occurs simply because, like any long tube, the barrel of the lens cuts out some light. A beam of light travelling parallel to the axis of the lens is unaffected. But light at an angle to the axis may strike the sides of the barrel and is lost to the picture. Wide angle lenses, because of their wide view—so that light from a very steep angle is included in the view—are more prone to vignetting than longer lenses. However, wide aperture lenses which emphasize the difference between the central beam and the off-axis beams, also suffer.

The result of all these losses is that the light actually transmitted by the lens does not correspond exactly with the marked aperture. The f-numbers are calculated by geometrical methods and take no account of these losses. For example, two different lenses, such as a 12 element wide angle and a five element telephoto, both set at the same f-stop, will actually transmit different amounts of light.

Solving the problem

Through-the-lens metering allows for light losses. But when separate meters are being used, and especially in critical applications such as cinematography and television work, the lens aperture may be determined *photometrically*, that is, by actual measurement of the light transmitted. In this case, the f-stop scale is replaced by a T-stop scale (T stands for transmission). An aperture which would be given a geometric value of, say, f/2, may be reduced in extreme cases to T/2.8.

A good example of the difference between T-stops and f-stops is the case of mirror lenses. The f stops given with such lenses are calculated geometrically using the diameter of the main mirror. But, due to the obstruction caused by the secondary mirror set in to the front, the T-stop may be as much as one stop slower. A hand-held meter can therefor give an incorrect reading.

Vignetting *The barrel of the lens cuts out some of the light arriving at an angle*

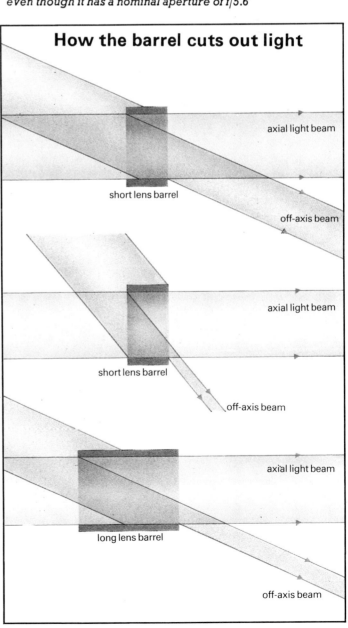

How the barrel cuts out light

axial light beam

off-axis beam

short lens barrel

axial light beam

short lens barrel

off-axis beam

axial light beam

long lens barrel

off-axis beam

LENS PERFORMANCE

can resolve. For this reason the test charts contain lines of various separations. The film used when making lens tests should have a performance which is better than that of the lens itself, or the results will not be meaningful.

At the limit of a lens's performance, some deterioration in quality is inevitable. Oddly enough, the various criteria of performance do not go hand in hand. A lens with good resolving power will not necessarily give an image that looks critically sharp. Even a picture which shows excellent reproduction of fine details may not have the 'crisp' appearance nor-

Soft focus *Some lenses are deliberately made 'soft' in order to produce special pictorial effects*

Pincushion distortion *Even a sharp lens may suffer from distortion, which makes it unsuitable for some subjects*

Photographers often talk about a particular lens as being 'good' or 'poor'. But defining exactly what these terms mean is not easy. Opinions about a specific item often differ. So it is useful to make objective tests of *sharpness*, *resolution* and *definition*.

Lens performance

Early astronomers tested new telescope lenses by looking at known double stars to see if both were visible as separate points—that is, if they were *resolved*. A lens with good resolving power, then, is one which is capable of showing fine details clearly. Many people regard good resolving power as being the primary requirement of a lens. And indeed some photographers test their lenses for resolving power by using a special test chart and slow film. The chart consists of groups of black lines on a white ground, spaces and lines being equal in width.

A lens is judged by how many lines per millimetre it

Television image *This is a case of the image looking 'sharp' but having poor resolution of detail*

mally associated with sharpness. It is equally possible for a photograph to appear very sharp when the reproduction of detail is actually very coarse. A good example of the latter is a correctly adjusted television set showing a studio transmission. The image may look crisply sharp, but its resolving power is very poor.

There is a problem in that the term 'sharpness' does not have a fixed meaning. Different people use it in different ways. But there is one aspect, concerned with contrast, which is largely responsible for producing sharp looking images.

It is possible to use a lens test chart to illustrate this aspect of sharpness. A lens with good resolving power shows the lines of the chart as separate lines in the image. But the edges of the lines may not be particularly clear. Instead of a distinct border between the black line and the white space, the image consists of an area where one fades into the other.

With an image which is 'sharp', however, the contrast between the lines and spaces is more abrupt—the edges of the lines are more clearly defined. However, some lines merge into others, giving lower resolution.

Sharpness is largely subjective. But it can be represented in terms of *acutance*. Measuring this involves plotting a graph showing density against distance for a 'knife-edge', which is reproduced on the film. This is a highly technical procedure. But a good indication of sharpness can be gained by applying a

similar principle to the image of a line from a test chart.

Values are plotted for the black line, the white space, and points in between. The resulting graph will include a slope showing the gradual fall-off in density at the edge of the line. This slope can be represented by its gradient, which is known as the *edge gradient*. The steeper the gradient, the sharper the image appears. This result shows the sharpness of the lens–film combination. To study the sharpness of the lens alone it is necessary to examine the actual image projected by it. This is not usually done because the results would not be particularly informative. As with other aspects of lens quality, it is how the lens performs under normal conditions of use which is important. The type of film and method of development contribute significantly to the impression of sharpness since they can affect the contrast of the resulting photograph.

Definition

Another term, often used instead of sharpness, is *definition*. To be more precise, this usually means the combination of sharpness and resolution. A lens which can resolve reasonably fine detail and give good edge sharpness is said to have good definition.

With most lenses, sharpness and good resolving power go together. But the lens designer may decide to favour one of them. In addition, some lenses give better resolution with low contrast subjects, and some with high contrast ones. So these aspects of lens performance help to give a lens its individual characteristics.

The limits to resolving power and sharpness are often set by the residual aberrations of the lens (see page 226), so that stopping down can give better results. Lenses are classed as *aberration limited* or, if they are almost free of aberrations, *diffraction limited*.

With a diffraction limited lens, the best definition is at full aperture, when the effects of diffraction (which produces progressively unsharp images as the lens is stopped down) are at a minimum. But with an aberration limited lens, definition is better with the lens stopped down slightly, to reduce spherical and chromatic aberrations. Furthermore the resolution tends to deteriorate towards the edges of the field. Stopping down helps in this respect.

If the lens is stopped down too far, so that the light passes through a rather small

aperture, diffraction cancels out the benefit gained by having less spherical and chromatic aberrations. There is an optimum aperture which produces the best compromise. But this may not be the same for the edges of the field as for the centre. So for the best overall result, the lens is stopped down slightly further—say another half stop—to improve the detail at the edge of the frame.

Even if the lens is free from those aberrations which affect definition, it may suffer from distortion. Such a lens can produce images which are very sharp and full of fine detail. But its use is restricted because it tends to distort straight lines.

At the other extreme, some portrait lenses deliberately sacrifice definition in order to produce a soft focus effect. They do this by not correcting for some of the spherical aberration produced by the basic lens design. Both these examples show that sharpness and resolution are not necessarily the only criteria for judging a lens. The quality or value of a lens can only be determined by looking at what it is needed for, **and how it is likely to be used.**

Sharpness and resolution *Fine detail (represented by lines on a test chart) can be affected in different ways by a lens. It can have clearly visible edges—good edge sharpness—without the separate details being resolved. Or, all the details may be resolved without the image looking very sharp*

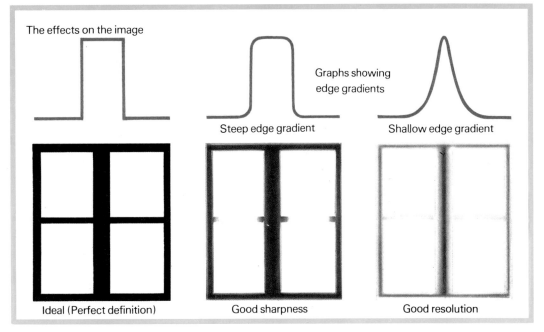

The effects on the image

Graphs showing edge gradients

Steep edge gradient

Shallow edge gradient

Ideal (Perfect definition)

Good sharpness

Good resolution

LENS TESTING

Great store is put by lens performance and lens tests are an important part of lens manufacture.

The function of a camera lens is to reproduce, as accurately as possible, an image of the original subject. The perfect image is unattainable, however, as lens aberrations cannot be fully corrected. This means that the image quality inevitably varies from centre to edge, and at different apertures. And even an otherwise perfect lens suffers from the effects of diffraction.

In addition, the complexity of a lens and the fact that each element is ground and polished individually, rather than being cast from a mould, means that individual variations and the accuracy of assembly will give variations in performance from sample to sample of the same design. To achieve quality control, and as a final check by the purchaser, various lens tests have been devised most of which determine the resolving power. All of them are useful, but no single test can give a full picture of performance.

Lens testing charts

The assumption is that the complete assembled lens is to be tested, and not the individual elements. A prime criterion of performance is the resolving power (see page 232) of the lens. This is its ability to distinguish between closely adjacent points in the subject, as limited by residual aberrations and diffraction.

To test for resolution, and obtain a numerical value for it, a *test chart* (sometimes called a *bar* or *target chart*) is used. Instead of point sources, this has short parallel lines printed on paper. Many patterns have been devised, but most use black bars or lines with a length to width ratio of 5:1, printed on a white background. These are often

grouped in two sets of three, with each set at right angles to the other, to test for astigmatism (see page 906).

One bar or line with its adjacent space is called a line-pair. Resolving power is expressed in terms of *spatial frequency*—that is, the frequency with which the lines appear on the image—and this is measured in line-pairs per millimetre or lpm—also sometimes known as cycles per mm. The bars are in groups of decreasing spatial frequency and distributed over a large area—often more than a metre square— to cover the whole field of view of the lens. If a bar has a width of 0.1 mm, the line pair is 0.2 mm wide, and gives a spatial frequency of 5 lpm.

This is the fineness of detail which the average human eye can perceive in a 6 ×8 inch (153×203 mm) print at a distance of 250 mm. This frequency is often quoted as a minimum standard for

resolution in prints. But although the spatial frequency which must be resolved in the print is only 5 lpm, for a 35 mm shot to produce this result the image on the negative must resolve 30 lpm, as it needs a ×6 enlargement to reach the required print size. Most lenses will give far better resolution than this, even at full aperture, so greater enlargements are possible.

When a test chart is photographed, it is very unusual for the image size to be the same as the object size (1:1 reproduction). The size is reduced in the image. A 5 lpm pattern which is reduced 20 times will produce a spatial frequency of 100 lpm on the film.

Tests for resolving power also depend on the *Target Optical Contrast* (TOC). A high contrast helps to distinguish between the lines and spaces and gives a higher value for resolving power.

Fall off *With every lens, definition deteriorates towards the edge of the frame—here exaggerated*

Photographing the chart

The actual image of the test chart formed by a lens can be examined using a microscope. This prevents the results being affected by the film and processing. But for most people it is necessary to record the image on film and examine the negative.

It is important that the chart is evenly illuminated and photographed with the camera solidly supported, with the film plane parallel to the chart. The position of the film in the camera is normally marked by a film plane symbol, a circle with a line through it. The distance from the lens to the chart is 26 times the focal length of the lens, which gives a 25:1 reduction from chart to image. By using this set up, the chart fills the frame, and the spatial frequencies of the bars in the image correspond to the values on the chart.

The chart is photographed using a slow, fine grain film in order to record as much detail as possible. The film is exposed and processed carefully, as too much or too little exposure or development can affect the results. Even when perfectly exposed and developed, film cannot record all the detail given by a top quality lens. So the information about performance given by these tests is for the lens plus film combination.

A line or bar is resolved if it can just be distinguished from the background. Practice is needed to judge this, and a powerful magnifier or microscope is required to examine the negative. This technique does not allow the absolute performance of the lens to be measured. But standardizing the film and development allows different lenses to be compared. Furthermore, the same lens can be compared at different apertures, and across the field of view. The accuracy of the focusing system or scale can be checked by repeating exposures at various settings of the focusing ring. Any darkening of the image towards the edges shows that the lens suffers from vignetting. And distortion—barrel and pincushion—is revealed by bending of the straight edges of the chart.

A typical resolving power for a good lens is 100 lpm at the centre of its field, dropping to 35 lpm at the edge at its best aperture.

Infinity tests
By their nature, test charts must be photographed in-

Infinity test *The collimator set-up effectively produces a subject at infinity, and can reveal lens aberrations*

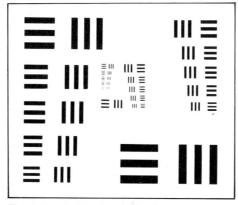

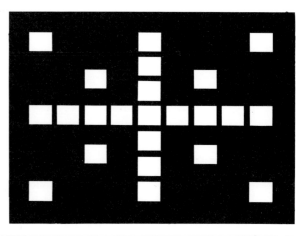

Test charts *The basic design (left) is repeated over a large area (above right). Another chart design is shown on the right. These illustrations cannot be used to make your own tests*

doors at comparatively close distances. This can be unsatisfactory for a number of reasons, the most important of which is that most lenses are designed to perform best with distant subjects.

One way to simulate an infinitely distant subject is to use a *collimator.* This is a well corrected lens used to form a tiny point of light, which then becomes the object for the lens under test. This is called a *star test*, and a number of aberrations, such as coma, can be detected by it. If such aberrations are present, the point is distorted. However, this is a laboratory method which, once again, uses a microscope to examine the actual image formed by the lens, rather than using film.

MTF tests
Testing using bar charts only gives an indication of resolution. The slightly more subjective aspects of sharpness and definition are not accounted for. A more sophisticated test method, using the *Modulation Transfer Function* (MTF) can allow for contrast (which affects sharpness) and is dealt with in the following section.

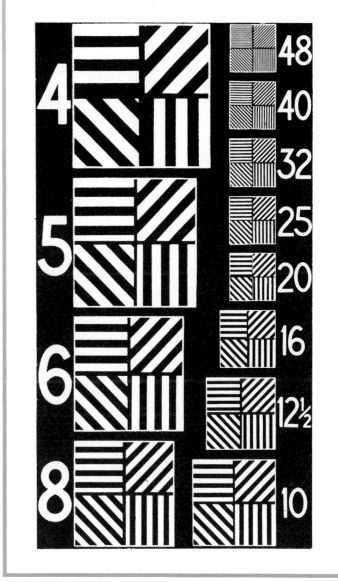

Star testing using a collimator

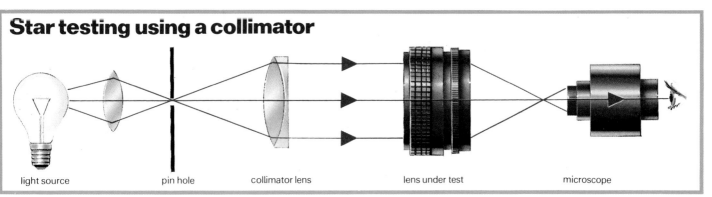

light source | pin hole | collimator lens | lens under test | microscope

MTF CURVES

Photographers often used to be beguiled by advertisements which lauded the remarkable resolving power of a particular lens. It seemed that the lens which could resolve the most lines per millimetre must inevitably give the sharpest image. But there is more to sharpness than resolution alone and, for a complete picture of the qualities of a lens, designers plot its *Modulation Transfer Function* or MTF.

The most important feature of MTF is that it involves the measurement of contrast—without good contrast in the areas of fine detail, definition appears poor, no matter how many lines per millimetre are resolved. In fact, *modulation* is simply another word for contrast, although it is only appropriate in the context of MTF. Modulation is basically the difference in intensity between the darkest and lightest parts of the image.

The MTF system works by comparing modulation in the image projected by the lens with that in the original subject. Inevitably, modulation is slightly less in the projected image than in the subject—that is, some of the original subject contrast is lost as it is *transferred* through the lens. The ratio between the modulation in the original subject and the modulation in the projected image is known as the *modulation transfer factor* and forms the basis of MTF calculations.

With a perfect lens, none of the original subject contrast would be lost and modulation in the projected image and the original subject would be identical. The modulation transfer factor would therefore be one and this is the maximum possible value. Unfortunately, no lens can reach the ideal, and all values for the modulation transfer factor are less than one.

For every lens, though, there is not just a single factor but a whole range—factors can be calculated for different subjects, different apertures, for the centre of the image and for the edge, and for many other conditions. For the MTF, it is the variation of the modulation transfer factor with the fineness of detail that is important. Indeed, the MTF is simply a graph on which the modulation transfer factor is plotted against a measure of fineness of subject detail.

Spatial frequencies

As with resolution tests, the fineness of subject detail for MTF tests is shown by the spatial frequency of line pairs (see page 1074). However, the lines on the test

Sharpness *A contrasty shot can look sharp even when resolution is poor (left). A low contrast shot, on the other hand, looks unsharp despite the fine detail shown, as you can see by examining the insets closely*

chart are not solid black bars separated by white spaces. Instead, the dark lines are faded very gradually into the lighter spaces in between. The fading is very even and carefully controlled so that if the intensity of shading is measured at various points across the pattern of lines and plotted on a graph, the graph shows a sequence of symmetrical waves, referred to as *sine waves*.

Consequently, scientific wave terminology is used to describe the characteristics of the pattern. Fineness of detail is therefore described in terms of the *frequency* of dark lines on the chart. A line-pair—a single wave on the graph—is a *cycle* and so spatial frequencies are given in terms of the number of waves in a given space—

that is, in cycles per millimetre. With coarse detail, there are few waves—few cycles—per millimetre: with fine detail, there are many waves—cycles—per mm.

MTF curves

Modulation transfer factors— the loss of contrast in the projected image—can be worked out for various spatial frequencies and plotted on a graph. This graph is the MTF of the lens under test, and it is specific to that lens.

Nevertheless, it is noticeable that as the fineness of detail increases, so does the loss of contrast—as frequency increases, so modulation falls. Eventually a point is reached where the contrast is so low that detail is lost. This, therefore, is the limit of resolving power of the lens. This limit is often taken to be the point where the modulation transfer factor has a value of 0.1 (sometimes stated as ten per cent).

Measuring MTF

Measuring MTF and producing MTF data requires equipment which is beyond the reach of most due to complexity and cost. A typical set-up uses a target at the focus of a collimator lens (see page 1075). This lens makes rays of light from any point in the subject parallel, so that the target is effectively at infinity. The target itself is not usually like a simple bar chart, but often consists of rotating optical gratings which generate all the spatial frequencies needed.

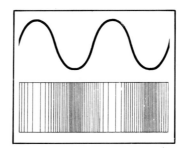

Sinusoidal target *MTF tests use a target with a gradual change from black to white. The target is oscillated to blur the black lines into a continuous tone*

After passing through the collimator lens, the light is focused by the lens under test, and examined with an image analyzer. This is a sensitive photocell which scans and measures the image intensities at each frequency.

Modulation is measured identically in both subject and image so that the modulation factor for each frequency can be found. With modern test apparatus the MTF curve is plotted automatically by a machine linked to the image analyzer.

Unfortunately, a single curve is inadequate, so a set is needed to give a fuller picture of behaviour. Curves are produced for on and off axis positions, with various wavelengths of light, and at different target orientations for each aperture setting of the lens.

A very useful property of MTF curves is that they can be combined or *cascaded* together, to produce a single

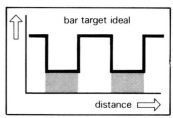
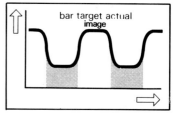
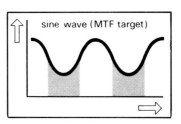

Graphs *showing the change in tone across various test targets. The middle graph shows how the lens softens the edges of the bars in the projected image*

curve. This is done by simply multiplying together the transfer factor values of each part of the system at each frequency to give the resultant MTF of the system.

MTF curves can be produced for other parts of the photographic system, such as the film and the enlarger. The resulting curves can then be cascaded to give an MTF for the whole system, showing the performance from subject to final image.

Typical MTF curves *Lens A gives high contrast with coarse detail but cannot resolve fine detail. Lens B gives generally lower contrast except at high spatial frequencies, where it is better than lens A*

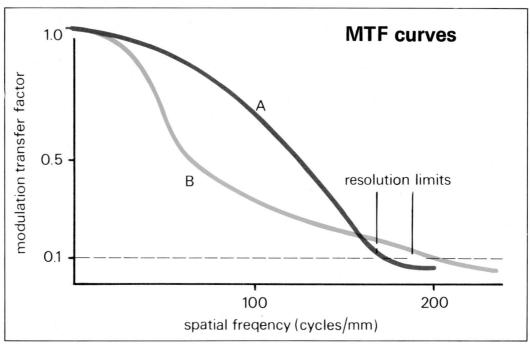

COLOUR TEMPERATURE

The most noticeable difference between the light from the sun, and the light from a 40 watt light bulb is that of quantity—the sunlight is obviously much brighter. There is, however, another difference which is of great importance to almost all photographers: light from the sun is of quite a different colour from that of the light bulb.

This difference in colour passes unnoticed most of the time, because the human eye is very accommodating. But if you see someone sitting by a window with their face lit by daylight on one side, and by a light bulb on the other, it is easy to see the difference. The daylight is much bluer than the light from indoors, which is tinged with yellow or orange.

Although our eyes can overlook minor colour shifts like this, colour film cannot. It is manufactured to very rigid specifications as to the colour of light under which it should be used. Most colour transparency film is balanced so that it will give correct results under noon daylight—that is, on a sunny day with blue sky. If photographs

Mixed light *The firelight is too yellow for daylight film and the people's faces have a yellow colour cast*

are to be taken in light which is not the same colour as daylight, then a filter must be used, either over the source of light, or over the camera lens. If this precaution is not taken, the pictures that result will have an overall colour cast—they will be tinged throughout with a particular colour. If you have ever taken colour pictures indoors by available light, you will be familiar with this problem, because the pictures will all have a yellow or orange colour cast.

In order to be able to correct for the colour cast, a guidance system known as *colour temperature* has been developed (see box). Every film is balanced to reproduce colours accurately in certain lighting conditions. The colour temperature system allows the photographer to

Blue landscape *In overcast weather, pictures will be too blue in colour unless correct filtration is used*

Colour and kelvins

Candles and sunlight *This chart shows, in kelvins, the colour of the most common sources of light for photography*

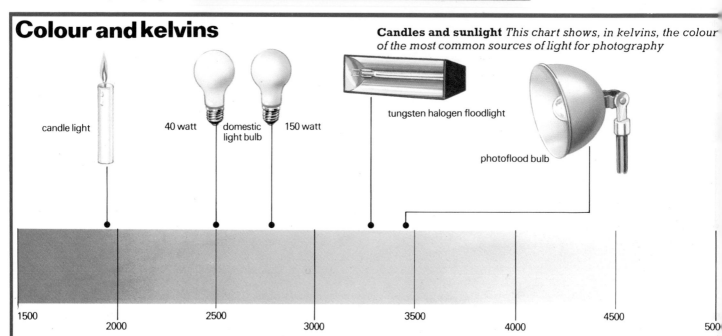

candle light

40 watt

domestic light bulb

150 watt

tungsten halogen floodlight

photoflood bulb

1500   2000   2500   3000   3500   4000   4500   500

correct the colour cast produced by any lighting system.

Ordinary 'daylight type' colour transparency film is balanced for light with a colour temperature of around 5500K, and if it is to be used indoors under ordinary light bulbs, a blue filter must be used over the lens of the camera. Conversely, if the subject of the pictures is lit only by light from a blue sky—in the shade under a tree, for example—a yellow filter would have to be used.

Which filter ?

The colour temperature system seems complicated at first glance, because there are so many possible colours of light. Fortunately, though, the number of different light sources that are used for photography is small, and manufacturers produce glass and gelatine filters which compensate for most types of lighting.

To take a practical example on an overcast day, the colour of light from the sky lies between 6500K and 7500K, and unless corrected, will produce a blue cast on colour transparency film. This can be compensated for by using a series 81 filter—an 81A, 81B or 81C. The 81A is the palest of the three, and is used in slightly overcast weather, whereas the deepest, the 81C, would be used only on a very dull day. The 81B is the best compromise, and can be used for correction on most overcast days.

Light from the sun is much

Evening light *Around dawn and dusk the colour temperature drops, and sunlight looks much redder in colour*

redder in colour in the morning and evening, and here the correction that is needed lies towards the blue end of the spectrum. An 82A filter produces the correct colour balance within two hours of dawn and dusk.

Tungsten balanced film

Since it is sometimes necessary to take pictures in tungsten lighting in the studio, a few film manufacturers make a slide film that is balanced for use in this light. This is called 'type B' film, or just 'tungsten film'. Most professional lighting gives off a light which has a colour temperature of 3200K, so this is the colour temperature for which tungsten film is balanced.

If you have daylight film in your camera, and you want to take a few pictures under tungsten light, there is a deep blue filter available which can compensate for this—an 80B —but the results may not be perfect. This solution should only really be used as a stop gap measure.

Colour negative film users have fewer problems than photographers who take colour slides, because much of the colour cast which results from incorrect matching of light and film can be compensated for in printing.

Light sources and colour

Photographers use a system called 'colour temperature' to specify the colour of any particular source of light. This system is based on the idea that hot objects glow and give off a particular colour of light at a particular temperature. A hot iron bar, for example, will glow red at fairly low temperatures, and as it is heated further will change colour to orange, through yellow, to white.

By specifying the temperature at which the heated object— actually a theoretical object called a 'perfect black bodied radiator'—gives off light of a certain colour, it is possible to refer to the colour of any light source.

Since this system was devised for scientific use, colour temperature is measured in the units most commonly used in science, which are called kelvins or K. These are the same heat intervals as degrees centigrade, but start at absolute zero—minus 273 degrees centigrade. Consequently, water boils at 373K and freezes at 273K.

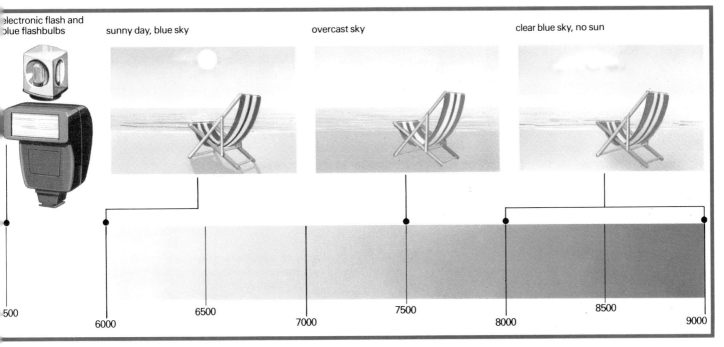

electronic flash and blue flashbulbs   sunny day, blue sky   overcast sky   clear blue sky, no sun

5500   6000   6500   7000   7500   8000   8500   9000

FILTER GUIDE

Many problems in photography can be overcome by the use of suitable coloured filters. And even simple filters can be used creatively to turn an ordinary shot into something worthwhile. As well as special effects filters, there are the straightforward gelatin filters, which are less often mentioned in catalogues. It is useful to know what types there are.

These pages provide a list of most of the filters available in gelatin form, which is the most versatile and wide ranging type. The numbers in the main list refer to the Kodak Wratten number, though the same numbers are used by most other manufacturers too. The filters in each section are listed in order of their density. The additional tables suggest ways of using some of these filters to correct for artificial lighting, and the final one shows exposure increases for a range of colour compensating filters, which are used to 'fine tune' colour temperature.

Pink

1A Pale pink These filters, often called *skylight* filters, are used to absorb excess UV radiation. For general photography they are of comparatively little use. However, they do have some effect in reducing the blueness caused by haze at high altitudes. They are also occasionally useful when there is a great deal of UV, such as a snow covered landscape under a blue sky, though an 81A is often better. The glass in modern lens elements usually filters out a sufficient amount of UV, though some photographers use glass versions of this filter as protection for their lenses, in place of the more usual UV types.

Yellows

Yellow filters also absorb ultraviolet radiation. They are sometimes used to filter for haze, particularly in black and white work, and are popular for aerial photography. They are also used to darken blue skies, and increase contrast with black and white film. The darker yellow filters are used with colour infrared (false colour) film to prevent the result being too blue.

2A Pale yellow Absorbs UV below 405 nm. Used to reduce haze at high altitudes

2B Pale yellow Absorbs UV below 390 nm. Better than 2A at reducing haze

2E Pale yellow Absorbs UV below 415 nm. Like the 2B but has more effect on UV

3 Light yellow Often used in aerial photography to correct for excess blue

8 Yellow Gives correct rendition of sky and foliage on black and white film

9 Deep yellow Similar to No. 8, but gives a stronger, more dramatic effect

11 Yellow–green Gives correct rendering in tungsten light on monochrome film

12 Deep yellow Used for haze penetration in aerial photography and for monochrome infrared materials

15 Deep yellow This produces even more dramatic effects than No. 8 or No. 9. It is used for black and white copying of documents on yellowed paper. It is also used for infrared and fluorescence photography

Oranges and reds

These filters are designed to absorb ultraviolet and blue, and also varying amounts of green. With black and white film they are used to increase contrast—for example, to darken blue skies, bring out the grain in wood, or pick out the detail in brick. Red filters are also used for technical work, such as colour separation, colour printing and two-colour photography. The last is a method of producing colour pictures by breaking down the image into two colour components.

16 Yellow–orange filters are mostly used for emphasizing detail in wood and brick, and also widely used for darkening blue skies, in both cases using black and white materials

21 Orange is the most popular orange filter, used to give greater contrast on black and white film

22 Deep orange Commonly used in photomicrography with blue preparations, this filter has greater green absorption than the other orange types

23A Light red Used in colour separation work and also for increased contrast with black and white film

24 Red is used mostly for two-colour photography in conjunction with a 57 (green) filter

25 Red One of the most useful red filters, the 25 reduces haze in black and white aerial shots and filters out excess blue light for monochrome infrared work. It is also used for colour separation and tricolour printing

29 Deep red Principally used for colour separation and tricolour printing

Magentas and violets

These filters principally absorb green, and are mostly used for technical applications, such as reproduction processes and photomicrography. Other magenta filters (CC filters) are used to correct for fluorescent light.

30 Light magenta Used in photomicrography to give increased contrast particularly with green subjects
32 Magenta Used to subtract green
33 Magenta absorbs green strongly and is used in colour reproduction processes to produce masks
34 Deep violet Contrast filter
35 Purple The main use for this filter is to provide contrast in photomicrography. It provides total green absorption and also absorbs some blue and red

Greens

These are mostly used for black and white photography as contrast filters (to lighten foliage for example) and in technical processes such as colour reproduction and colour printing.

54 Deep green This contrast filter absorbs nearly all red and blue light, and a little green light
57 Green Used for two-colour photography with a red (24) filter
58 Green Used as a contrast filter in photomicrography and also for colour separation and tricolour printing
61 Deep green Used for colour separation and tricolour printing work with red (29) and blue (47) filters

Blues and blue—greens

These filters are designed mainly for colour separation work, tricolour printing, contrast effects in photomicrography, and to heighten contrast in black and white work. Blue conversion and light balancing filters are dealt with in a separate section. On black and white film blue filters darken reds. By emphasizing blue tones they can be used to exaggerate mist or fog.

38 Light blue is useful in tungsten lighting with black and white film to prevent red tones from reproducing too light
38A Blue absorbs a large amount of red light, plus a certain amount of ultraviolet and green
44 Light blue—green filters out red and ultraviolet
44A Light blue—green substracts red
45 Blue—green Mostly used in photomicrography, this contrast filter is designed to absorb ultraviolet and red
47 Blue is the filter used to give contrast effects with monochrome film. Also used for colour separation
47B Deep blue This filter is intended mainly for use in colour separation and tricolour printing
50 Deep blue is a monochromat filter (see *narrow band* filters) which transmits the mercury line at 436 nm, and lines at 398, 405 and 408 nm

Narrow band

These are *monochromat* filters which transmit very small parts of the spectrum (see pages 2022 to 2023). As a result, they are very dense and are only used for technical purposes. The most common use for narrow-band, or *narrow cut* filters is in colour separation work, particularly when the separation negatives are being made from transparencies or negatives.

70 Dark red This is used in colour separation work to produce separation positives from colour negatives. It is also used when making colour prints with the tricolour printing method
72B Dark orange—yellow
74 Dark green This transmits only 10 per cent of green light and filters out practically all yellow light from mercury-vapour lamps. This gives monochromatic green light which is useful in experimental optical work as the principal focus, in lenses corrected for one colour, is computed for green light
75 Dark blue—green

Filtering for effect *The windmill shot was taken on colour infrared film. If no filtration is used this film tends to give results which are very blue. You can use a variety of filters to cut down the amount of blue light, including yellow, orange, red and opaque types. In this case an orange filter was used. The black and white shot was taken on normal film, but a red filter was used to darken the sky and generally increase contrast, producing this dramatic effect*

Conversion

These filters are used to convert daylight to tungsten, or vice versa. They are most commonly used on the camera lens, but they can be used over lights. For example, some photographers use the blue (80) filter over tungsten lights so that they can use them with daylight and daylight film (see picture on page 2598). Use of these filters is dealt with separately.

80 series, blue These are used with daylight film in tungsten lighting. The complete range is: 80A, 80B, 80C

85 series, amber These are used with tungsten film in daylight. The complete range is: 85, 85B, 85BN6, 86C, 85N3, 85N6, 85N9 (includes 0.9 neutral density)

Light balancing

These are paler versions of the conversion filters, and are designed to modify colour temperature for minor corrections. They are nearly always placed over the camera lens. You can use them with conversion filters to give full correction for light sources such as domestic bulbs (see separate table) or to give slight overcorrection for creative effect.

81 series, pale amber These slightly lower the colour temperature. The range is: 81, 81A, 81B, 81C, 81D, 81EF

82 series, pale blue These slightly raise the effective colour temperature. The range is: 82, 82A, 82B, 82C

Balancing colour

If the colour temperature of a light source is 3200K or 3400K then you can use an 80 series filter with daylight film or, in the case of the latter figure, tungsten film. But it is rare that the light is exactly the right colour, so the table below shows you what extra filtration is needed to bring the colour to the above figures.

3200K from	3400K from	Filter	Exposure increase in stops
2490K	2610K	82C + 82C	1⅓
2570K	2700K	82C + 82B	1⅓
2650K	2780K	82C + 82A	1
2720K	2870K	82C + 82	1
2800K	2950K	82C	⅔
2900K	3060K	82B	⅔
3000K	3180K	82A	⅓
3100K	3290K	82	⅓
3300K	3510K	81	⅓
3400K	3630K	81A	⅓
3500K	3740K	81B	⅓
3600K	3850K	81C	⅔
3850K	4140K	81EF	⅔

Miscellaneous

These are filters which do not fit into any of the other categories. They are all intended for various technical applications but are worth knowing about in case you ever come across them.

87 Visually opaque There are two versions of this filter—87 and 87C. Their main use is for infrared work as they absorb all visible light but transmit infrared radiation. This means that the exposure is achieved solely with infrared which is useful for analytical work. And for creative photography it means that the strange effects casued by infrared are even more dramatic

88A Visually opaque Similar to the 87

89B Visually opaque This is also used for infrared photography, particularly aerial work. It transmits radiation of wavelengths between 700 and 800 nm

90 Dark greyish amber This filter is meant for visual use, not for taking pictures with. Looking through the filter, the view is monochromatic and this gives you an idea of how the tones and colours will reproduce on black and white film

92 Red This is used, with 93 and 94, to take densitometer readings of colour films and papers

93 Green Used, with 92 and 94, to take densitometer readings of colour films and papers

94 Blue Used, with 92 and 93, to take densitometer readings from colour films and papers

96 Neutral density See separate table

98 Blue Equivalent to a 47B plus a 2B. Used in colour separation work and tricolour printing

99 Green Equivalent to a 61 plus a 16. Used in colour separation work and tricolour printing

Warm tones *When using flash, the skin tones tend to reproduce slightly too cold. You can produce a much warmer and healthier effect by using an 81A (below)*

Light balance *If you want to have the controllability of tungsten lights but prefer to use daylight film you will have to use an 80 series filter (right)*

Fluorescent conversion

This table shows the filtration and exposure increase necessary to get acceptable results with different types of fluorescent tube. It is based on Kodak films, but with a little experimentation you can adapt it for other makes. In any case, the figures are only intended as a guide, and for critical results you should always make tests.

Type of tube	Daylight films Neg. films, Ektachrome 200 and Kodachrome 25	Ektachrome 64 and 400, Kodachrome 64	Tungsten films
Daylight	40M + 40Y + 1 stop	50M + 50Y + 1⅓ stops	85B + 40M + 30Y + 1²/₃ stops
White	20C + 30M + 1 stop	40M + ²/₃ stop	60M + 40Y + 1²/₃ stops
Warm white	40C + 40M + 1⅓ stops	20C + 40M + 1 stop	50M + 40Y + 1 stop
Warm white deluxe	60C + 30M + 2 stops	60C + 30M + 2 stops	10M + 10Y + ²/₃ stop
Cool white	30M + ²/₃ stop	40M + 10Y + 1 stop	10R + 50M + 50Y + 1²/₃ stops
Cool white deluxe	20C + 10M + ²/₃ stop	20C + 10M + ²/₃ stop	20M + 40Y ²/₃ stop
Unknown	10B + 10M + ²/₃ stop	30M + ²/₃ stop	50R 1 stop

Neutral density

Neutral density (ND) filters have no effect on colour, but simply cut down the amount of light entering the lens, allowing you to use a larger stop, longer exposures or to take pictures of objects which are otherwise far too bright (such as the sun). The values listed are the strengths available using single filters, though other strengths can be obtained using combinations. The precise effects of these filters will vary depending on the conditions of use, as there will be reciprocity effects with long exposure times, so you should experiment.

Filter	Filter factor	Transmission (%)	Exposure increase in stops
0.1	1¼	80	¹/₃
0.2	1½	63	²/₃
0.3	2	50	1
0.4	2½	40	1¹/₃
0.5	3	32	1²/₃
0.6	4	25	2
0.7	5	20	2¹/₃
0.8	6	16	2²/₃
0.9	8	13	3
1.0	10	10	3¹/₃
2.0	100	1	6²/₃
3.0	1000	0.1	10
4.0	10,000	0.01	13¹/₃

Colour compensating (CC)

These filters are very useful for making slight modifications to colour temperature so that you can get the exact colour that you want. They can also be used to give slight colour casts for creative effect. And used in filter packs they can correct for unusual lighting, such as fluorescent (see separate table). When mentioned in tables or articles they are often written without the CC prefix. But in technical information and on the packets they come in, they carry the prefix shown in the table.

Cyan	CC05C	CC10C	CC20C	CC30C	CC40C	CC50C
exposure increase	¹/₃ stop	¹/₃ stop	¹/₃ stop	²/₃ stop	²/₃ stop	1 stop
Magenta	CC05M	CC10M	CC20M	CC30M	CC40M	CC50M
exposure increase	¹/₃ stop	¹/₃ stop	¹/₃ stop	²/₃ stop	²/₃ stop	²/₃ stop
Yellow	CC05Y	CC10Y	CC20Y	CC30Y	CC40Y	CC50Y
exposure increase		¹/₃ stop	¹/₃ stop	¹/₃ stop	¹/₃ stop	²/₃ stop
Red	CC05R	CC10R	CC20R	CC30R	CC40R	CC50R
exposure increase	¹/₃ stop	¹/₃ stop	¹/₃ stop	²/₃ stop	²/₃ stop	1 stop
Green	CC05G	CC10G	CC20G	CC30G	CC40G	CC50G
exposure increase	¹/₃ stop	¹/₃ stop	¹/₃ stop	²/₃ stop	²/₃ stop	1 stop
Blue	CC05B	CC10B	CC20B	CC30B	CC40B	CC50B
exposure increase	¹/₃ stop	¹/₃ stop	²/₃ stop	²/₃ stop	1 stop	1¹/₃ stop

INDEX

Numbers in italics refer to illustrations

wide-view equipment 56-9
wildlife photography, lenses for 12
Wratten filters 120, 122

Y
Yashicamat cameras 47

Z
Zeiss: Amatar lenses 216; Biotar lenses 217;
   Ikon beamsplitter *54;* Planar lens 217;
   Sonnar lens 223
Zenith 47; E 63; Horizont 59